Sound Pedagogy

MUSIC IN AMERICAN LIFE

The Music in American Life series documents and celebrates the dynamic and multifaceted relationship between music and American culture. From its first publication in 1972 through its half-century mark and beyond, the series has embraced a wide variety of methodologies, from biography and memoir to history and musical analysis, and spans the full range of musical forms, from classical through all types of vernacular music. The series showcases the wealth of musical practice and expression that characterizes American music, as well as the rich diversity of its stylistic, regional, racial, ethnic, and gendered contexts. Characterized by a firm grounding in material culture, whether archival or ethnographic, and by work that honors the musical activities of ordinary people and their communities, Music in American Life continually redefines and expands the very definition of what constitutes music in American culture, whose voices are heard, and how music and musical practices are understood and valued.

For a list of books in the series, please see our website at www.press.uillinois.edu.

Sound Pedagogy

Radical Care in Music

Edited by
COLLEEN RENIHAN, JOHN SPILKER,
AND TRUDI WRIGHT

Foreword by
WILLIAM CHENG

UNIVERSITY OF
ILLINOIS PRESS
Urbana, Chicago, and Springfield

Publication was supported by a grant from the Howard D. and Marjorie L. Brooks Fund for Progressive Thought and the General Fund of the American Musicological Society. Publication was also supported in part by the National Endowment for the Humanities, the Andrew W. Mellon Foundation, and Queen's University's Queens Scholarly Publishing Fund.

1 2 3 4 5 C P 5 4 3 2 1
♾ This book is printed on acid-free paper.

Library of Congress Cataloging-in-Publication Data
Names: Renihan, Colleen, editor. | Spilker, John D., editor. | Wright, Trudi, editor. | Cheng, William, 1985– writer of foreword.
Title: Sound pedagogy : radical care in music / edited by Colleen Renihan, John Spilker, and Trudi Wright ; foreword by William Cheng.
Description: Urbana : University of Illinois Press, 2023. | Series: Music in American life | Includes bibliographical references and index.
Identifiers: LCCN 2023025343 (print) | LCCN 2023025344 (ebook) | ISBN 9780252045592 (hardback) | ISBN 9780252087707 (paperback) | ISBN 9780252055256 (ebook)
Subjects: LCSH: Music—Instruction and study—Social aspects. | Music—Instruction and study—Psychological aspects. | Music—Instruction and study—Moral and ethical aspects. | Music—Instruction and study—Political aspects. | Music—Instruction and study—Philosophy. | Education, Higher—Philosophy.
Classification: LCC MT1 .S618 2023 (print) | LCC MT1 (ebook) | DDC 780.71—dc23/eng/20230614
LC record available at https://lccn.loc.gov/2023025343
LC ebook record available at https://lccn.loc.gov/2023025344

To my students, with whom I learn. And
to my father, whose care-full approach to
teaching I work to channel every day.
—Colleen Renihan

To Elijah and Niko, "My Love, My Life" (ABBA).
And to Anna Mary, Johnny, Tiny, and all the ancestors,
for whom I certainly must be their wildest dreams.
—John Spilker

To Caleb, Samson, Jim, and Joyce—
my constant, beloved teachers.
—Trudi Wright

Contents

FOREWORD

Everything Is Song (If We Care to Listen Otherwise)

What is song? For many students in my college classes, song is a catch-all word for any discrete work of music. "Bohemian Rhapsody" is a song. But so might be a film score or a video game soundtrack, a Chopin piano étude or a Mozart string quartet, a pop anthem or a bloopy ringtone. Everything is said to be song until someone says otherwise.

I have been that someone. As their dutiful instructor, I've explained to students, "No, no, this violin sonata isn't really a song. It's a piece of music. Songs are sung and typically feature voices and lyrics (or voice-like and lyrical qualities). All songs are pieces of music, but not every piece of music is technically a song."

On the surface, this is a matter of precise vocabulary and taxonomy. Students should find it useful to distinguish songs among musics writ large, just as they learn to distinguish mammals among animals, or haikus among poems. Yet my lexical corrections must also lead students to realize they've been misusing a basic four-letter word their entire lives. Song, once so familiar and capacious, now defamiliarized and wreathed with rules anew.

Aside from professional music scholars and performers, do most people recognize (much less insist on) semantic disambiguations between pieces of music that are songs and pieces of music that are not songs? To what extent are people today relying on flattened nomenclatures adopted by commercial streaming services such as Apple Music (whereby a Machaut motet and a Yebba ballad alike are labeled as songs or, when part of an album or playlist, as tracks)? What am I doing when I cross out erroneous instances of ~~song~~ on a student essay and scrawl alternatives in the margins?

None of these questions would have occurred to me had I not received, a while back, a sneak peek of *Sound Pedagogy*. Every chapter here pulses with accessible, actionable wisdoms into not just how we teach music but also why we still teach this thing called music at all, what with our world on literal fire and our species at neverending war. Why care, why now? If we choose to care, then how? The authors have answers for us. I am profoundly grateful to these colleagues for even daring to dream up affirmative, radical, topsy-turvy configurations of the music classroom and its normative hierarchies.

For some students, a correction around song will register as fact-forward epiphany, and so they will resolve to readjust, perhaps with diminishing slip-ups as they retrain their tongue. For other students, the unlearning might not stick. They will perhaps continue to call all music songs during the school term and for the rest of their lives.

When teaching a music course spanning an array of vocal and instrumental musics, I tell students early on the importance of accurate and precise terminology. Words matter. If, on an exam or paper for a course in nineteenth-century European art music, a student calls Beethoven's Fifth Symphony "a song," and labels a Schubert Lied "a string sextet," then this student and I have not achieved some key learning and teaching outcomes. Same goes for an Introduction to World Music course. If a student exclusively uses the word "song" to name all examples of instrumental and vocal musics across all cultures, then we have more work to do.

But instructors can do two things at once: we can teach students vocabulary while maintaining some humility as to why people coalesce around apparent misuses of certain words in the first place.

While drafting this foreword, I browsed some online listicles of words that don't mean what a lot of people think they mean. "30 Common Words You're Using All Wrong," "75 Incorrectly Used Words That Can Make You Look Dumb," "11 Commonly Misused Phrases That Instantly Reveal People's Ignorance": the clickbait headings tap into our human insecurities about sounding bad and wrong in front of other people. "Nip it in the bud, not nip it in the butt," one article begins, "imply[ing] you cut a new bud (off a plant), not bite someone in the backside." Helpful glossaries aside, what these articles don't explain is why some words are so frequently misused, nor how the apparent ubiquity of quotidian verbal errors maps onto the conventions and stakes of dialogue, persuasion, and knowledge creation in different societies. So whereas the lists taught me that I have, to date, been misusing words such as "factoid," "travesty," "enormity," and "plethora" in my writing and conversations, I couldn't help feeling stuck on whether our shared legible misnomers in daily life can tell us something about, at the very least, what we're *trying* to say, and how we navigate the vast spaces between linguistic utterance and significance.

In an effort to bring this spirit of curiosity into the music classroom, I've recently pondered why many students call all music songs, and what it means that they do so. My first hunch was simply that maybe students call all music songs because, these days, they're predominantly listening to pop songs in particular and vocal music more generally; much of the music they're encountering indeed contains singing and lyrics. Yet think of all the instrumental music sans voices (including but not limited to classical European art musics) saturating our advertising industries, entertainment media, and public soundscapes. With regular exposure to vocal and nonvocal music alike, people presumably recognize that there exists music with singing voices, and music without.

Maybe my ruminations are still missing the mark. Maybe rather than dwelling on what semantic mistakes tell us about the students who utter them, we can tune our ears beyond the mere frequencies of error . . . and listen to what else these students might already be saying, consciously or not, when they say *song*. Here, then, are five things I hear (or imagine hearing) when I hear my students calling all music songs.

> One. At root, the students have vital access to a longstanding, reliable, and widely shared word with which to name the materials, phenomena, and foci of varied musical encounters. The word is *song*.
>
> Two. Their incorrect word choice nonetheless correctly underscores the considerable challenges of determining and articulating the fuzzy distinctions between something not sung and something sung. (And students may possess an implicit understanding of this nuance without having ever read Roland Barthes, Adriana Cavarero, Fred Moten, and texts from voice studies, sound studies, deconstruction, phenomenology, metaphysics, and musicology.)
>
> Three. They grasp, furthermore, that a human body at rest and a human body at song are not mutually exclusive states. Especially if we account for subvocalizations (things we quietly or silently say and sing to ourselves) and imagined sounds, then our sonorous fleshy bodies are, in one sense, often potentialized toward songfulness.
>
> Four. Even when these potential energies are not converted into audible singing, they constitute a real reservoir of creative vitality that speaks to music's capacity to be lyricized, hummed, whistled, rapped, sung, or otherwise envoiced and vocally engageable.
>
> Five. Saying *song* can be, in the end, a tacit reminder that they—we—have voice (audible or not, ablenormative or not) qua consequential agencies (for better or worse); and that everyday swirls of musical recognition, remembrance, and enchantment may be songful insofar as the sympathetic vibrations of our auditing bodies are always already at play and at song with the sounds around, among, and within us.

Does this merry train of thought pull into my mind every time I hear the word *song*? Certainly not. These are just ideas I toy with sometimes while I weave through my identities, responsibilities, and aspirations as a writer, teacher, and musician.

Let's learn from our mistakes, we tell students. One application of this principle would instruct a student to learn from their misuse of *song* on an assignment and to find apter words going forward. That's just a start, however. For there are more things *song* might be saying. What *song* says is things are singable. What *song* says is there will be song, and a need for song, at some point in the future. What *song* says is there will be a future. And that can be music to our ears.

William Cheng

Acknowledgments

Our work could not have sprouted, been sustained, or been carried to fruition without our soulful seminars in collaboration and the careful guidance of the midwives. Therefore, we collectively thank the individuals in each of our journeys who have brought us to the place where we might conceive of a volume like this one. Our teachers, mentors, students, friends, colleagues, and families have all contributed to this volume in a multitude of ways.

We offer profound gratitude to our contributors. We knew these individuals had powerful contributions to make to this conversation, but we didn't expect the joy of collaborating with them over this long journey together. We are honored to include their chapters in this book, and in the years to come look forward to ongoing conversations with all of them about care-based work.

We knew we had found our dream editor in Laurie Matheson the first time we met with her. She has cared for our work and for our project with such expertise and kindness, and we remain very grateful for her and the entire team at the University of Illinois Press.

Our teachers and mentors noticed and nurtured the spark of possibilities within us. They introduced new ways of thinking, seeing, and knowing. They led us, walked with us, encouraged us, carried us, and carved out space for our work. Together, we honor: Christian Asplund, Kaitlin Beck, Marsha Bowman, Michael Buchler, Richard Burleson, Stephen Dupree, Robin Elliott, Kirstie Engel, Sheila Heidgerken Gerwing, Elissa Guralnick, Gerise Herndon, Carol Hess, Michael Hicks, Chris Holobek, Steven Johnson, Annettra Jones, Steven Kaup, Sherry Lee, Steve Lindeman, Sandra McBride, T. J. McDowell, Leta Miller, Judy Muyskens, Mary Natvig, David Nicholls, David Patterson, Anne-Marie Reynolds, Tom Riis, Deborah Roshto, Karri Sanderson, Douglass

Seaton, Matthew Shaftel, Everette Smith, Scott Swagger, Judith Tick, Denise Von Glahn, Robyn Williams, and Susan Wortmann.

In addition to the Teaching Music History Conference, where the three of us first met and conversed about our shared interest in this topic, several communities have been formative for us over the years. Profound thanks for the Society for American Music, College Music Society, EnLITE (Educational Leadership in Teaching Excellence) program, colleagues at the Office of Teaching and Learning at the University of Guelph, the Centre for Teaching and Learning at Queen's University, colleagues and mentors at the Purdy Crawford Teaching Centre at Mount Allison University, members of the Regis University Manresa Experience for Faculty, Integrative Teaching Workshops, the Reboot Institute, and members of the Regis College Faculty Development Committee who granted us funds for the index, colleagues and mentoring cohorts in the Gender Studies Program and Archway Curriculum at Nebraska Wesleyan University, and the cojourners at the Whidbey Institute's "Powers of Leadership" program.

All of our colleagues and students, both nationwide and within our home institutions, labored with us, supported us, and tested and challenged our teaching and research work. In short, they made room for our growth. We thank in particular the ongoing support and community provided by the AMS Pedagogy Study Group. Together, we offer a special debt of gratitude to Kara Cavel, William Cheng, Mark Clague, Sara Cohen, Rick Cypert, Mark Davenport, Andrew Dell'Antonio, Louis Epstein, Jessie Fillerup, Molly Fitzke, Craig Fleck, Mary Francis, Kyra Gaunt, Sandra Graham, Andrew Granade, Sara Haefeli, Eileen Hayes, Jana Holzmeier, Candice Howell, Chris Johnson, Mark Katz, Tammy Kernodle, Kari Kloos, Alyse Knorr, Rita Lester, Lisa Lynde, Christie Lynk, Sandra Mathews, Judith Mitchell, Kay Norton, Loretta Notareschi, Laura Moore Pruett, Allen Scott, Jason Taylor, Becky Vartabedian, and Kathy Wolfe.

Our beloveds see us, know us, and hold our stories. They are confidants when it all falls apart and coconspirators as we work to put it back together again to make art. They stand with us at the edge of our mystery. Together, we renew our love and gratitude for Sarah and TJ a'Becket, Elijah Beed and Niko Spilker, Mary Lou and Matt Cohen, Shannon Corey and Zed Zavaletta, Jeannine Baumgart d'Estries, Kirstie and Stephen Engel, Joanne Hartmann, Geoff, Fintan, and Ronan Hendry, Peggy and Scott Mengel, Joan and Pat Renihan, Scott Smith and Taylor Daigrepont, John Michael and Josephine Spilker, Donna Spilker, Anthony Spilker, Jim and Joyce Vorp, Michael Vorp, Scott Walker and Caleb Parker, Jean Weaver, Neil Whitaker, Shanna Lesniak Whitney, Carol and Gordon Wright, and Caleb and Samson Wright.

In the words of adrienne maree brown, "Meaningful collaboration both relies on and deepens relationship—the stronger the bond between the people or groups in collaboration, the more possibility you can hold. In beginning this work, notice who you feel drawn to, and where you find ease. And notice who challenges you, who makes the edges of your ideas grow or fortify. I find that my best work has happened during the most challenging collaborations, because there are actual differences that are converging and creating more space, ways forward that serve more than one worldview."[1] This collaboration has grown and deepened over the course of some very difficult years both in terms of teaching and in our personal lives—those of 2018 through 2022. Through conversation, debate, struggle, laughter, and tears, we worked our way through many powerful realizations as we wrote this book together. We learned about our work, our pasts, our students, and ourselves. We also learned how to collaborate *care*fully. We therefore, finally, dedicate this project to one another and to the gift it has been for all three of us.

Notes

1. adrienne maree brown, *Emergent Strategy: Shaping Change, Changing Worlds* (Chico, CA: AK Press, 2017), 159.

Sound Pedagogy

Introduction

Radical Care

COLLEEN RENIHAN, JOHN SPILKER,
AND TRUDI WRIGHT

Caring, Now

A reckoning and a certain disillusionment must occur in order to reimagine our discipline in a way that is responsive and accountable to the communities in which our lives and work remain nested. Music in higher education needs repair through radical care. To define a shift as "radical" connotes, for some, introducing drastic, extreme, or deviant change. It may even call to mind the specter of bringing politics into an arena that has not welcomed the political. Radical shifts are often viewed negatively, and described as change thrust upon a group of people not ready for it. But despite the fact that our discipline may not be ready, deeply entrenched as it is in white, Eurocentric practices and values, and beholden to definitions of "rigor" and "discipline" justified by tradition and aesthetic autonomy—or, rather, *because of this*—our students and many faculty members have been ready. And those who cannot even imagine themselves part of our academic communities as they presently exist are certainly ready. Based on sustained calls for racial justice, our communities have been ready for a longer time than white folks have cared to learn about. Radical changes need to occur in order to teach music from a place of honesty and intersectional equity, in ways that foster self-actualization and self-determination, with a commitment to engaging in the reparative work for which our local and global communities cry out. We need care.

As scholar Dylan Robinson writes in his open letter to "heads of music departments, directors and deans of music schools, and all those including faculty and staff who work in music programs, departments and schools," "As the continuation of anti-Black and anti-Indigenous violence for the past months, years, and lifetimes has made evident, the time has ended for further working groups and 'Equity, Diversity, and Inclusion' (EDI) recommendation committees on how we as educators across all scholarly disciplines must work toward systemic forms of change that are decolonial and anti-racist. We no longer have the luxury of proceeding with small steps, and snail's-pace increments."[1] The time, readers, is now. In fact, by the release date of this collection, this work will be *overdue*. Indeed, we recognize the shifting and growing nature of these questions, of these calls, and indeed of our ecosystems in music, and recognize that what is called for will need to be repositioned within a variety of new circumstances and considerations.

Functioning under the umbrella of social justice, care pedagogy remains vital to higher education, because our students continue to experience crisis.[2] According to the American College Health Association "National College Health Assessment" (2016), and the UCLA Cooperative Institutional Research Program's *American Freshman: National Norms Fall 2016*, students arrive over-programmed, stressed, depressed, and uninspired. First-year students reported feeling overwhelmed (87%), very lonely (62%), and hopeless (53%), and were dealing with trauma (52%).[3] The World Health Organization reports the global prevalence of anxiety and depression increased by a massive 25% in 2020.[4] Certainly the speed, production, consumption, isolation, and extraction born of unfettered capitalism takes a toll on everyone's mental health. This is deeply felt in contemporary expectations of students and faculty. Furthermore, intersectional systemic oppression exponentially exacerbates financial and emotional pressures that inevitably impact teaching and learning. The crisis extends to faculty, with 70% of the workforce at American universities adjunct or otherwise contingent, and many instructors also suffering from anxiety, depression, burnout, hunger, and homelessness.[5] How can we focus on disciplinary questions and concerns when the people in our academic communities are struggling so much? Given the inextricable connections between the well-being and success of faculty and students, we direly need a humane pedagogy along with administrative policies and practices that value care at their core, or root.[6]

The premise of this book is, ultimately, that care-based approaches to pedagogy can facilitate the systemic change and transformation that remains possible and necessary for our discipline. We believe, inherently, that an approach rooted in care and kindness for people coexists alongside the dismantling of systems that no longer serve us and our best goals in music. We invoke "radical," a term deriving from the late Middle English *radicalis* (*radix, radic-* meaning "root"), to underscore a return to the roots or essence of a sound pedagogy. Indeed, while introducing care in our teaching may feel radical (political, bold), it deeply grounds us in ways of being in community and knowledge-sharing essential to the heart of informed teaching.[7] Thus, care pedagogy equips students and faculty to honestly reckon with the inequities at the foundation of our discipline, and to participate in larger truth-telling conversations about the devastation wrought by intersecting oppressions—systems that function silently and surreptitiously in our music communities.

In 2014, the College Music Society issued the report of the Task Force on the Undergraduate Music Major.[8] The document, "Transforming Music Study from Its Foundations," identifies three core deficiencies, the second of which is ethnocentrism. The authors report that many music students do not experience musical cultures beyond the European classical repertory and do not engage with their local multicultural communities through immersion, outreach, or invited community artists. This lack of student experience with musics and musicians outside the Western tradition is juxtaposed with administrative rhetoric, which "articulates their universities' commitments to diversity, and equality of opportunity." The report rightly "views the culturally narrow horizons of music study as nothing short of a social justice crisis." This crisis has been articulated since 2014 in many discussions about decolonization and music curricula, amplified in Canada following the Truth and Reconciliation Commission's 2015 investigation into the nation's history with residential schools for First Nations children.[9] In her 2018 article "The Musicological Elite," Tamara Levitz critiqued musicology's desire to escape its exclusionary Eurocentric, heteronormative, settler colonial legacies in its attempts at curricular reform.[10] Some institutions have tried to remedy this by revamping their curricula to reflect the necessities of our contemporary world.[11] But unfortunately, though this work is timely and needed, it is not easily done.

Discussions of potential ways forward have taken place at conferences, in publications, and in online platforms. However, the radical, ideological, and *human* changes required by these curricular transformations have not been sufficiently unpacked and charted, much less accepted. Most music history curricula in the United States and Canada do not reflect the urgent plea of the College Music Society.[12] In fact, many faculty continue to express entrenchment and pushback, thus furthering music departments' investment in patriarchy, white supremacy, and capitalism—and thus, disinvestment in care.

Practices in music departments are cemented in a revered form of "tradition," as it were. And, as many scholars working on antiracist and decolonization projects have demonstrated in recent years, our discipline remains a bastion of whiteness, and our socialization into the culture of higher-education music programs cements our performance and guardianship of whiteness.[13] Unless disrupted, the pervading white racial frame remains invisible for most white people, and is often rationalized through concepts of rigor, purity, authenticity, tradition, aesthetic autonomy, and history.[14] One example includes the "race-neutral" language of music, noted by Loren Kajikawa in "The Possessive Investment in Classical Music," which is most often seen in discussions of music's so-called universality.[15] Informed by a conservatory model of study, our disciplinary norms, values, and practices silently uphold white supremacy. Some include our most celebrated gatekeeping practices—rigid valuations of success and competence, screening and audition processes required for acceptance and advancement, the repertoire deemed suitable for study and achievement, and the narrowly-defined and prescriptive modes of listening, playing, and sounding that are valued and rewarded. Most, if not all, of these measures favor those who have studied western art music prior to college, especially those who have taken private lessons through a conservatory-style program.[16] Furthermore, access and success demand the privileges of socioeconomic status, ability, race, and gender. Many of these values, priorities, and structures remain uncontested because they are so *deeply* embedded in our curricula and practices. Thus, Tema Okun's articulation of "white supremacy culture," which identifies perfectionism, concentration of power, individualism, and progress as central features, sits heavily on our students and colleagues, weighing down any possibility of movement or shift, so desperately called for right now in our world.[17] Given the often invisible pull of the "imperialist white-supremacist capitalist patriarchy," our discipline needs creative interventions of care.[18] Values that we espouse and support in higher-education music call for perfectionism and a metric of workaholism. We assign worth based on one's pedigree of who one has studied with; we value and reward driving oneself to emotional and physical overload (a type of violence to the body and spirit) in devotion to music; we value note-perfect reproduction of music from the past; we value and prize particular canons of music over others, particular sounds over others, particular pronunciations of language, and so forth. Musicianship (ear *training*) classes teach and value Western modes of listening and definitions of music. Even the parsing of the disciplines of musicology, music education, music theory, and ethnomusicology are symptomatic of a white supremacy culture, all of which do damage to many individuals who engage with them. Who belongs and who does not? Who receives care through our work and who does not? We must consider presence and absence, power, and the many hidden ways our pedagogical practices in music contribute to problems and solutions. We urgently need conversations about how care can intervene as we interrupt the ways that music, as it functions in higher education, can be a profoundly *un*caring place.

"Tradition," as it it known, pervades, even haunts, our discipline. It excuses the recalcitrance of music schools and colleagues in refusing to engage in substantive reparative transformation. The silent hegemony of "art music" and the "conservatory model" over higher-education music curricula keeps music departments suspended in the past, their growth stunted by structural inequities, as argued in "Transforming Music Study from Its Foundations," and the work of Kajikawa, who unpacks the oppressive nature of the Western European art-music tradition and "explores how U.S. music schools share a 'possessive investment' in classical music that perpetuates, or is at least complicit with, white supremacy."[19] He writes, "Accepted as normal by most instructors and students, this status quo permeates daily routines and habits of thought—so much so that most college brochures and websites simply advertise that prospective students can major in 'music.'" This resonates with Brandon Keith Brown's experience of racism at a Chicago Lyric Opera gala in early 2020. His chilling reality names the trauma of concert attendance and calls out the world of classical music performance as "sonic refuge[s] of Whiteness," laying bare uncomfortable truths about the art we teach, perform, and love; things we need to examine and eradicate.[20] We affirm that in matters of racism, "time's up."[21] Just as Western European art music is understood to define or signify "music" in music programs across the United States and Canada, so are white, able-bodied, cisgender, straight students taken as the "norm." Without a pedagogy of care situated in social justice, students and faculty continue to be ignored, erased, and continually harmed.[22]

Care, Defined

As we explore throughout the book, the change that is so urgently needed in post-secondary music can be achieved through transforming our pedagogical approaches to music. In fact, we believe that through pedagogical interventions inspired by a philosophy of care in music, music curricula and structures in higher education can in turn and in time organically transform into more equitable and care-full spaces. Inspired by the work of William Cheng, we advance a definition of care pedagogy in music with a broad scope—informed by interdisciplinary scholarship of teaching and learning—that is also inextricably linked to intersectional equity work. Furthermore, *Sound Pedagogy* advances musicology (broadly writ as music and culture both past and present) as a pedagogical practice that can inform teaching in other subdisciplines of music and beyond our discipline. Indeed, we would suggest that in order to fully invest in care in this discipline, music history instructors need to invest in interdisciplinarity.

As the authors in this collection suggest through their work, care pedagogy is complicated and multifaceted. But in short, care pedagogy for us is teaching that prioritizes the *individuals* we are teaching—whole, complicated people with specific life stories and divergent definitions of and connections with music—above the traditions, history, and priorities of the *discipline*(s) in which we work. It is that simple, and also that complicated. It is radical because of the significant shifts this implies for the discipline more broadly—shifts, as the contributors of this volume suggest, in curriculum, in philosophical orientation, and in pedagogy. Care involves acknowledging the people who constitute our musical communities and systems, and working to more fully understand and then confront the ways they are not given equitable space to fully flourish. It also means recognizing who remains absent from these spaces—who feels unwelcome, unnecessary, ignored. It means acknowledging the ways that work in music *does* and *should* have so-called "real-world" accountability to, and impact in, our local and global communities. When we care for and with people, when we understand the deep implications, reach, and possibilities of our work, we need to reconcile and repair the ways that people (including ourselves) have wielded music—its systems, institutions, traditions, priorities, values—for good *and* bad. The work of care pedagogy in music comes from a particular *approach* to teaching—not only through content shifts, but through learning facilitation *practices* that enhance student agency, care for our world, and contend *carefully* with the problematic, utopian, and simplistic belief that music performances bring good to the world.

The roots of care pedagogy can be located in the foundational work of philosopher and educator Nel Noddings. Her first major publication, *Caring: A Feminine Approach to Ethics and Moral Education* (1984), builds on psychologist Carol Gilligan's *In A Different Voice* (1982). Noddings develops Gilligan's thesis, "that women develop their moral reasoning along a separate, but not inferior path compared to the male model offered by [psychologist Lawrence] Kohlberg and adds that lessons of caring in education should be based on the care of a specific person (a student, for example) rather than on an abstract moral principle."[23] The historically gendered distinctions of care have been criticized by many, but as we outline below, care has also been assumed and transformed by feminist scholars of care ethics, who argue that it can be a powerful subversive tool in one's pedagogical toolbox. Of primary importance to this volume, the moral education ideas of Noddings assert that students should gain a life-long ethical ideal and an understanding of caring, rather than focusing on purely academic goals. Although some would argue that lessons in morality remain the sole domain of home and church, Noddings believes that the act of caring and teaching students to care is actually the responsibility of all: parents, community members, and educators. Because schools (including higher-education music programs) have traditionally taught abstraction, objectivity, and detachment, educators have not been given the time or training for teaching students how to dialogue about their feelings or create affective relationships or priorities in the classrooms. More than ever, North American culture needs this one-on-one empathy to be infused into our classrooms, homes, and communities, as Nodding argues throughout her publications.[24]

Recognizing the rich history of care-based work in humanizing pedagogy, critical pedagogy, black studies, queer and gender studies, feminist care ethics, and disability studies, we propose an understanding of care pedagogy in music as the cocreation, with our students, of just, equitable, and reparative communities and spaces that empower all participants, including faculty. We argue that a focus on care and kindness in teaching spaces in music represents a reach to the core or roots of teaching rather than a move in a new direction. This begins by cofacilitating an environment of trust and community in which identities are earnestly acknowledged, valued, and lived out loud (see Langfitt, Natvig, Peterbark, Pruett, Soto, Spilker, Wright, and Wissner in this volume). Care pedagogy helps us learn how to lean into and live across difference. It invites participants from the dominant social group to see, hear, and value those who have been silenced and oppressed by social systems. Positioning care at the center of the process of decolonization and antioppression illuminates ways that music and musicking are inevitably social, political, ideological, and personal.

Care pedagogy eschews a cheap customer-service orientation to education. By design, industrialized capitalist economies dismantle self-care and communal care at almost every turn, insisting on administratively controlled, continuous, predictable, quantifiable work time and products. This comes at the expense of sustainable human living and working, which requires rest, play, spontaneity, collaboration, and time for ideas to germinate and bear fruit. Thus, there is a need to interrogate the neoliberal university, with its emphasis on integrating market logic into its organizational structure and strategic plans, prioritizing competition over collaboration, collecting performance data, and so forth, and the often harmful misrepresentation that is involved in the work of what Rebecca Lund calls the performance of being the "ideal academic."[25]

A few significant exceptions signal a hopeful turn toward situating higher-education music-learning spaces within the broader discussion about care and social justice. Inspired by this work, music-education scholars have illuminated the ethics of care in classroom music teaching and community musicking. The scholarship of Marissa Silverman, Elizabeth Cassidy Parker, Janelize Morelli, and Merlin Thompson, among others, represents a dedicated concern for care ethics in the work of music educators.[26] Silverman's extensive work on care ethics, relationality, and empathy, for example, focuses on how relationality and an ethics of care impact work in music education. In "Virtue Ethics, Care Ethics, and 'The Good Life of Teaching,'" she argues that "we need a concept of care ethics that places major emphasis on the relational nature and the inseparability of self and other," an idea that Renihan explores in her chapter "Empathy in Opera" in this volume.[27] In musicology, Bonnie Gordon's essay "Why We

Matter," addresses the value of music pedagogy in light of continued acts of violence against women, arguing for the ways that an education in music can prepare students for relationality in the world outside the classroom.[28] Travis Stimeling and Kayla Tokar's 2020 article "Narratives of Musical Resilience and the Perpetuation of Whiteness in the Music History Classroom" signals the crisis of particular narratives of resilience that we often include in narratives of music history in good faith but perpetuate systemic oppression and racism and continue to center whiteness, a concern that Eric Hung extends in his contribution in this volume.[29] And in *Compassionate Music Teaching*, Karin Hendricks explores strategies for colleagues working with traditional ensembles and in studio settings. Her methods center trust, empathy, patience, inclusion, community, and authentic connection.[30] With these contributions, the seeds of this work have been firmly planted in music. We now need to quickly and seriously reckon with the serious implications for this work if we are indeed hoping to create inclusive and equitable spaces in our classrooms.

Begun in 2017, the editors' collective work on care pedagogy in music builds most recently and firmly on the foundation laid by William Cheng's *Just Vibrations*.[31] Along with the imperative to uphold exceptional performance as the pinnacle of personal and departmental success, music's highly insular culture remains positioned by many as exempt from conversations and waves of change in other departments or in the world around us. *Just Vibrations* allows musicians and music scholars to acknowledge the lack of awareness of and often resistance to learn about the experiences of minoritized groups and the problems this causes for the mental and physical well-being and academic success of our students and colleagues. To illustrate the adversarial orientations that persist in musical learning spaces, Cheng draws on Eve Kosofsky Sedgwick's work on paranoid (so-called critical readings, marked by "hatred, envy, and anxiety") and reparative (additive, nurturing) readings.[32] He suggests that more effective and compassionate ways of teaching and learning can be created from Sedgwick's reparative readings and micro-repairs, drawn from Michael Shapiro's concept of "micro-politics of justice."[33] The call to action for music faculty reverberates from *Just Vibrations*: first, acknowledge how the concept of aesthetic autonomy keeps us from seeing outside the art of music to embrace the realities of the world in which humans and music exist; second, cultivate a transdisciplinary approach to learn about care and empathy and create possibilities for educational reparations in music learning spaces.[34] More specifically, Cheng's application of critical race theory, queer theory, and disability studies provides new possibilities for music faculty members to learn how and why they should care. Thus, care asks us to learn about, notice, and dismantle oppressive ideologies and practices in our learning spaces.

Through an illustration of ways of speaking, Cheng compellingly calls attention to systemic and surreptitious maneuvers of power, representation, equity, and the impact of ideologies of domination in the discipline. Cheng speaks about a privileging of aesthetic autonomy over empathy when he asserts, "Literate societies put huge stock in rhetorical ability—yet for reasons of alterity, disability, or disenfranchisement, some people do not speak well (by societal conventions), some are admonished for speaking too much (oversharing and making noise), some do not speak frequently (due to, say, shyness), some speak unusually (slowly, or with a stutter, or via conspicuous technological assistance), some do not speak at all (from injury or trauma), and some speak but nevertheless go unheard."[35]

Cheng's questions point to a mutually reinforcing relationship between the development of music skills and empathic capacities, or "currencies of care": "Do musical skills ever enable or prime us to listen better to people and to take up love's labors more broadly? . . . Is it possible that people who work with music for a living can lead by example in agendas of interpersonal care and communication? Could we go beyond modest empathy as a resonant form of musicality? . . . If some people seem to lack rational faculties and rhetorical virtuosity, where do their voices fit in the chorus of just debate?"[36]

Several chapters in the volume extend Cheng's ideas, including those of Galloway, Katz, and Renihan, which consider ways teaching students how to listen differently to music can be a form of care-full engagement with music.

Care as Social Justice: Call to Action

With gratitude for previous, current, and future scholarship in music, we seek in *Sound Pedagogy* to position higher-education music classrooms, broadly conceived, as offering particular and powerful opportunities for the work of care. We see care and kindness as forms of resistance to traditional, linear, exclusive ideas of how to lead, coach, and teach students, and even ideas of who our students are and endeavor to become. Resistance against pervasive neoliberal values of competition, individualism, and productivity. Resistance against increasingly limited conceptions of teaching and learning in higher education writ large, and music more specifically. Resistance against the pervasive frame of whiteness that undergirds the discipline, our work, and our understandings.

Care pedagogy, at its root, invites faculty to unpack and interrogate our tendency to erase or ignore the humanity and difference in our students, colleagues, and even ourselves. Brené Brown connects her work on vulnerability and shame to rehumanizing education and work through "disruptive engagement."[37] When invoking the need for humanity in education, we honor that human experiences remain fraught with systemic inequities enforced by institutions and ideologies.[38] Thus, care pedagogy practitioners need "social justice education," which, according to Lee Anne Bell, "includes both an interdisciplinary conceptual framework for analyzing multiple forms of oppression and their intersections, as well as *a set of interactive, experiential pedagogical principles and methods/practices*."[39] Bell advocates for "fair and equitable *distribution of resources* with the imperative to address those who are least advantaged . . . [and] the importance of fair and equitable *social processes*, including recognition and respect for marginalized or subjugated cultures and groups."[40] Care undergirds the goal, process, and vision in Bell's definition of social justice.[41] Faculty must care about the oppressed experiences endured by individuals in minoritized identity groups in order to see, hear, and value them. Furthermore, we must care enough to learn about the ways our work and lives suffer from the exclusion of minoritized voices, experiences, and contributions. Care asks us to learn how to facilitate and enact the goal of "full and equitable participation of people from all social identity groups in a society that is mutually shaped to meet their needs."[42] Finally, Bell's vision of social justice names the impact of care when she writes, "all members are physically and psychologically safe and secure, recognized, and treated with respect."[43]

Care ethics in pedagogy has historically been theorized by feminist scholars and writers, and *Sound Pedagogy* extends many of these theoretical threads. In professional culture, kindness is a suspicious concept due to its rejection of "divide-and-conquer models of labor, an emphasis on 'audit culture,' and an intensification of competition."[44] Kindness in pedagogy fosters collaborative, flexible learning spaces that serve as alliances—principles core to disability theory and universal design for learning (UDL). bell hooks advocates for closeness and connection in education in many of her publications. In *Teaching Community*, she writes, "Emotional connections tend to be suspect in a world where the mind is valued above all else, where the idea that one should and can be objective is paramount."[45] Furthermore, by withholding connection and closeness, we reinforce values of domination, sexism, and white supremacy.[46] This is particularly fraught and present in higher-education music programs, which prize an apprenticeship, disciple, or protégé model used by musicians for centuries; extending hooks's line of thinking, an educational model rife with favoritism and individualism and one that promotes a general feeling of lack among students. By contrast, hooks advocates for a "learning environment that values wholeness over division, disassociation, splitting," in which "the democratic educator works to create closeness."[47] Intersectional feminism offers microtechniques of resistance, which are productive in framing and understanding care pedagogy.[48]

From a feminist perspective, Carol Gilligan and Sarah Ruddick argue that normative approaches to education and policy are too narrow and exclusive. Premised on values of individualism and autonomy, they remain tied to traditional conceptions of masculine gender identity.[49] Feminist understandings of care have been articulated in powerfully political and social terms by Virginia

Held and Joan Tronto and in the intersectional work of black feminists and critical race scholars like Kimberlé Crenshaw.[50] Lorelle Meadows and colleagues assert, "The absence of discussion [about difference and bias] more often effectively treats everyone as a white male, erasing differences rather than achieving intentional equality," a statement that echoes the ways that "music" in "schools/departments/faculties of music" treats everyone as an aspiring Western classical performer.[51]

We promote Shoshana Magnet, Corinne Mason, and Kathryn Trevenen's idea of care as a "technology of social transformation" and a powerful tool in one's "toolbox of resistance."[52] bell hooks argues that educators often reinforce values of domination, sexism, and white supremacy through a deliberate attempt to destroy "connection and closeness when in the academy."[53] Movements for justice have marginalized race in the past. Thus, we center issues of race as being tightly bound with mitigating and repairing the impact of capitalism and patriarchy in our pedagogical spaces. Modeling and teaching antiracist behaviors may seem more complex than traditional understandings of care will accommodate. However, we affirm the foundational connections between care pedagogy and antiracism. Indeed, BIPOC scholars writing about intersectional antiracist equity in education have theorized and enacted many core principles of care pedagogy.[54] The theme of care in higher education infuses *Race, Equity, and the Learning Environment* and *Difficult Subjects*.[55] bell hooks's concept of "education as the practice of freedom" centers awareness of our students' selves, experiences, and struggles. As she explains,

> There can be no better place than the classroom, that setting where we invite students to open their minds and think beyond all boundaries to challenge, confront, and change the hidden trauma of shame. We do this by enacting a politics of affirmation where difference is accorded respect and all voices deemed worthy. As teachers, we can make the classroom a place where we help students come out of shame. We can allow them to experience their vulnerability among a community of learners who will dare to hold them up should they falter or fail when triggered by past scenarios of shame—a community that will constantly give recognition and respect.[56]

A Complicated Care: The Tensions We Hold

Some colleagues suspicious of care-based approaches share an understandable concern that we lack training to do particular kinds of care work. In fact, Geoff Pfeifer and Elisabeth Stoddard note that faculty members are often reticent to address equity or any topic outside the purview of their highly specialized postgraduate training.[57] Music colleagues should not be doing the specialized work of mental health professionals, and the work in this volume does not ask colleagues to do that. And yet, we unabashedly affirm that many aspects of our teaching, professional development, and service must attend to, or for a start acknowledge, the mental health and well-being of our students and colleagues. Sound pedagogy centers student and faculty well-being rather than ignores it. Surely concern for mental health can only transform our work for the betterment of all students and colleagues. Particularities to music teaching and learning activities across our heavily siloed subdisciplines infringe on identity politics, affect, emotion, and selfhood in ways that differ markedly from work in other disciplines. We want to acknowledge that, problematize it, and prompt conversations that continue beyond *Sound Pedagogy*. Given our commitment to intellectual development through lifelong learning, it's worth noting that Pfeifer and Stoddard ultimately conclude that faculty do indeed have the capacity to develop proficiencies around intersectional equity and teaching through research and practice.[58] We hope this book serves as part of that development.

Of course, care is complicated, complex, and contingent. It is not universal, but rather is performed and received differently depending on who gives and receives it. As we've been reminded during the COVID-19 pandemic, the value of care, together with flexibility and adaptability, has been questioned historically, but may finally be receiving increasing recognition as crucial work in university music communities. The gendered nature of care calls attention to such complexities. For a female-identifying professor, for example, care and kindness remain complicated tools. Viewed as a maternal project, care is imbricated unavoidably in the history of the gendered and thus near-invisible nature of this work. While awareness surrounding the impact of emotional labor has increased in recent years, little has changed in the workplace, and it nevertheless remains true that women, and especially women of color, continue to be expected to perform unrecognized and uncompensated emotional labor more frequently than men.[59] Often misunderstood as simply doing work that involves emotions, the term *emotional labor* has a significant resonance, one that suggests that "consumers (and employers) expect employees to fulfill certain social roles that carry with them emotional obligations. This is a required but unpaid part of their work."[60] The number of female-identifying contributors to this volume, for example, is tellingly nearly double that of male-identifying authors. The term *kindness* finds its roots in the idea of kin or kinship—it builds alliances and relationships across barriers. But it has also been mobilized historically as an emotion associated with the domestic sphere, a realm contrasted with masculine toil.[61]

In other contexts, care brings with it moral superiority bred out of bourgeois subjectivity, historically situating European colonizers as the bestowers of kindness and charity upon the "Other" in need of civilization.[62] Furthermore, care can be performed to detrimental ends, a charity model of kindness through which the "Other" is to be pitied, further entrenching the us-they binary. And of course, as Kimberlé Crenshaw reminds us, these violences against female-identifying people of color remain more complex still.[63] We hold all of these historical and associative ideas about care and kindness in tension, struggling in particular with the misuse and misunderstanding of kindness as a form of pedagogical and professional labor expected from women in place of anger, and expected by administrators of the neoliberal academy as performative customer service.

Some colleagues remain indifferent, disagree, or openly register dissent to care-based approaches. But now is the time to show up differently and more boldly about care and intersectional equity than we have in the past.[64] For many, this work is new, nonlinear, and heavy. And yet, in doing it, we acknowledge the importance of Brené Brown's research about recognizing and working through shame in order to be more effective advocates for equity, "because you cannot talk about race without talking about privilege. And when people start talking about privilege, they get paralyzed by shame."[65] Robin DiAngelo unpacks the "Good/Bad Binary," by which white people distance ourselves from unpacking our unwanted socialization into dominance.[66] No one wants to be called sexist, racist, or ableist. We view "those people" as bad and thus reduce those terms to individualized actions against someone from a minoritized group, rather than systems of privilege and oppression that formed our institutions and ideologies and operate throughout. Given the many recent community movements toward intersectional equity, and the misunderstandings and misgivings about such important steps toward equity, educators must come to grips with the fact that we have been socialized into oppressive ways of being and knowing, and now must decide how to reckon with that knowledge and work toward repair. We have been conditioned to value our good *intentions*, rather than listening to understand and own the hurtful *impacts* of our actions. Thus, our learning process requires a care for self *and* communities.

Brown tells students, "If you're comfortable, I'm not teaching and you're not learning. It's going to get uncomfortable in here and that's okay. It's normal and it's part of the process."[67] In this spirit, we encourage you to show up as your student-self, open to disquieting feelings, so that learning can occur. As scholars and teachers, our academic socialization to function as experts may understandably leave us feeling defensive, especially when learning outside our hyperspecialized areas in music. To assist our journey, social justice education scholars Brian Arao, Kristi Clemens, and Jasmine Harris provide helpful frameworks to facilitate transformative uncomfortable learning.[68] And DiAngelo reminds us, "Authentic antiracism is rarely comfortable. Discomfort is key to my growth and thus desirable. White comfort maintains the racial status quo, so discomfort is necessary and important. I must not confuse comfort with safety; as a white person I am safe in discussions of racism."[69] This discomfort happens in the body as well as the mind. We believe that care pedagogy entails paying attention to the physical reactions connected to this work and the signals they provide.

While reading this book you may feel challenged or troubled, like we are, by fraught words and phrases with definitions that have been misrepresented and complicated by history, politics, and the media; these include *white supremacy*, *racism*, *patriarchy*, *capitalism*, *sexism*, *ableism*, and *oppression*. For example, for many, the term *white supremacy* has been reduced to signaling violent hate groups such as the Ku Klux Klan rather than a system of control that establishes white ways of being as the norm and better than other cultural ways of being. Due to centuries of racialized trauma, Resmaa Menakem invites readers of *My Grandmother's Hands* to "watch your body closely and notice what sensations, impulses, and emotions arise. . . . If you have a white body, there will be times when it will reflexively constrict in order to protect you from some of the truths you'll encounter."[70] Simply reading specific words may cause a physical reaction due to their power within white culture. By acknowledging and understanding our reactions, however, and working through them, we can think and act in ways that promote our values of equity and thus become stronger care pedagogues.[71]

With these tensions woven into the fabric of our work, we uphold care as a core tenet of a sound pedagogy for music faculty. Recognizing the paradoxes and contradictions of care, along with the challenges care poses to traditional ways of knowing and being in music departments, we argue that music faculty remain perhaps more ideally situated than we may think to address and enliven debates about social justice. This kind of sound pedagogy has the potential to animate students with a caring, conscious, equitable approach to surviving and thriving in the twenty-first century. Indeed, now is the time to share ideas about how we might transform music-learning environments into spaces of care—even reparation and healing.

Roots of Care and Critical Pedagogy

Transformative learning, engaged pedagogy, humanist pedagogy, critical pedagogy, and antioppression pedagogy remain well-established in higher education, offering respected concepts and tools of value to care orientations in pedagogy. The pedagogies of Paulo Freire, bell hooks, and Parker Palmer call on teachers to facilitate care-filled environments attuned to wholeness and integration.[72] Their individual approaches to critical pedagogy and their student-centered focus are central to our understanding of care pedagogy in music.

In *Race, Equity, and the Learning Environment*, Liza Ann Bolitzer, Milagros Castillo-Montoya, and Leslie Williams offer a framework for intersectionality that "draw[s] attention to the ways that multiple aspects of identity may interact and provide a framework for countering the social, political, and institutional structures that marginalize individuals and groups."[73] Central to challenging music's practices requires, of course, understanding the ways music is connected with a long history of oppressive policies, values, and practices, which at their core have always been racist, sexist, and ableist in nature. Heeding calls to confront legacies of white supremacy in music schools and departments in the United States and Canada, we thus position pedagogical care as central to opportunities for all forms of intersectional equity work.

The challenges of this work are not insignificant. Still, our experience, along with that of the other contributors, demonstrates that care pedagogy provides a productive and positive way forward for everyone working and learning in the discipline of music. This position, however, requires a more nuanced discussion that accounts for holding tensions—and the often grey, murky, slippery territory that these topics inhabit—a discussion we hope to encourage through *Sound Pedagogy*. For example, while we are not advocating for a lazy or uncommitted approach to musicking, or for lowering standards, we ask: how can we examine the ways in which those oft stated defensive accusations in fact reflect problematic postures and therefore fruitful frontiers for professional development? We draw inspiration from Susan Cain's *Quiet*, and from Maggie Berg and Barbara Seeber's *The Slow Professor*, in their assertion of different value systems and the price we pay in a culture that values more, better, louder, faster.[74] Precarious employment circumstances and positions restrict many colleagues from embracing slowness and other curricular disruptions that care pedagogy requires. Thus, we argue that the approaches explored throughout the volume can and should be used and promoted by those who occupy positions of privilege to bolster and support colleagues in marginalized and exploitative working arrangements.

Disability activism invites different understandings and complications of care. In *Care Work*, Leah Lakshmi Piepzna-Samarasinha writes that disabled and sick people have been forced to rely on state support or biological family support, often with abuse or lack of control.[75] By naming this forced reliance on others, she reminds us of the need to re-create and reinscribe care in our pedagogical spaces as a community way-of-being that doesn't overburden or unnecessarily encumber only a few. Piepzna-Samarasinha speaks of care webs that have existed through time, such as the STAR House, which was started by Black and brown trans femme sex worker revolutionaries Marsha P. Johnson and Sylbia Rivera. This and other successful peer-to-peer programs that enact a web-of-caring philosophy hold powerful examples of care work in *action*.

Imagine the revolutionary work that care-webs could enact in our classrooms if students were guided to care for each other? Do ensembles engage in care work that could be bolstered by care-web praxis? How can our students be taught and supported to create more inclusive, expansive care-webs, perhaps ones that hold communities close and secure in times of need? Imagine the remarkable pedagogical transformations that might be possible if teaching music overlapped with teaching community care grounded by Piepzna-Samarasinha's research, and extending community-care ideals from transformative justice.

Particularly prescient for us, Freire's work focuses on understanding pedagogical structures and spaces as vehicles for the reparative work of caring and community-building. His critique of the traditional banking model of education—a Freireian concept wherein the instructor deposits learning, ideas, and capital into students (i.e., the empty vessels in the classroom)—carries pointed relevance in music, focused as it often is on a hierarchical pedagogical structure.[76] Mired as our discipline is in tradition, faculty often use classrooms and rehearsal and performance venues as spaces of oppression and exclusion.[77] Freire summons Beethoven specifically when describing the oppressors' comfortable lives when he writes, "Conditioned by the position of oppressing others, any situation other than their former seems to them like oppression. Formerly, they could eat, dress, wear shoes, be educated, travel, and hear Beethoven; while millions did not eat, had no clothes or shoes, neither studied nor traveled, much less listened to Beethoven."[78] Freire associates Beethoven with oppression and hierarchy, which begs a careful consideration of the associations of class, status, and power that Western classical music has wielded throughout history.

Freire also focuses on cooperation and empowering students as cocreators of knowledge. As music pedagogues, these ground our work in a respect for possibilities students bring to collaborative learning ventures, and in a belief in their potential to do good work in the world right now, not after nor exclusively because of our "training" them. Freire's insistence that teachers focus on current and local concerns, struggles, and circumstances resonates with our understanding of the social, political, and personal work of caring in pedagogical contexts, not to mention a widening of music studies to embrace local communities, concerns, struggles, and circumstances.[79] Central to empowerment, Freire advocates for students to learn how to critically engage with their education and their lived contexts, and to acknowledge their positionality and subjectivities, as these impact and influence their learning and even the content itself.

Difficult and messy work, critical pedagogy lives in the liminal, interstitial spaces between the professional and the personal, and between theory and practice, the praxis for which Freire so passionately advocates. Thus, it upsets the carefully guarded status quo of music programs' traditional disciplinary and institutional borders and invites the personal and individual into the spaces of learning. We acknowledge the precarity of infusing lived experience into the learning environment. And still, we affirm that the desperate need outweighs the risks, particularly in the context of music pedagogy, which often remains focused on the historical legacy of a narrow, privileged population.[80] Freire invites us to explore the shortcomings of music departments in light of the discipline's "racialized legacy," as Loren Kajikawa describes it—a legacy that "impedes our collective ability to imagine a more just and equitable future."[81]

In *An Urgency of Teachers*, Sean Michael Morris and Jesse Stommel build on Freireian pedagogy when they write, "Critical Pedagogy suggests a specific kind of anti-capitalist, liberatory praxis. This is deeply personal and political work, through which pedagogues cannot and do not remain objective. Rather, pedagogy, and particularly Critical Pedagogy, is work to which we must bring our full selves, and work to which every learner must come with full agency."[82] By introducing democratic learning, the celebration of closeness and connection, and the empowerment of our students, we create more equitable learning environments for everyone, but especially those who have traditionally been excluded from learning spaces in higher education. We also resist the often silent expectations and discourses of "rigor for rigor's sake," the hard-nosed white-supremacist myth of objectivism, and suffering for the integrity of the art, all of which remain prevalent in our discipline.[83] Note that "art" music remains unnamed as the focus of work in music departments, and that other genres (and culturally appropriate knowledge about them) are merely tokenized, not deeply integrated in our work.

Central to Freire's democratic learning and the empowerment of students is trusting our students and believing in the possibilities inherent in their self-determination. Care pedagogy must be recognized as an unfamiliar approach—it values things other than the ways of assessing, teaching, and relating that have been ingrained in our higher-education learning and teaching socialization. William Cheng aptly identifies "a hermeneutics of suspicion" celebrated in most academic research contexts. Indeed, this can be seen in the ways we often configure the work of teaching in higher education.[84] An equally strong, if not more potent, hermeneutics of suspicion exists in our learning environments. Institutional and disciplinary methods and traditions socialize faculty to be suspicious of, critical of, and distanced from our students. Beckie Supanio points out that faculty distrust of students lies within the most basic practices of the learning process: assignments and grading.[85] Similarly, Robin Wharton suggests that educators take a hard look at how their policies and practices around student plagiarism may foster an environment in which students are disenfranchised and relegated to the status of mere consumers in the education process.[86] A hermeneutics of suspicion manifests itself in other pedagogical forms: the dismissal and misunderstanding of students,' colleagues,' and our own struggles and crises along with their impact on our work in the academy, the growing suspicion over millennials and Gen Zers/Gen Zeds (derisively labeled "snowflakes"), the simultaneous proclaiming and shaming of a loss of "rigor" in higher education, and the furious critique of colleagues' work that examines contemporary political and economic realities. *Sound Pedagogy* contributes to an ongoing conversation throughout the United States and Canada, in which colleagues begin to confront these suspicions in order to reconstruct and repair our higher-education music communities with care as the thesis.

Kevin Gannon calls for a pedagogical orientation that eschews blame and judgment toward students who arrive with different academic experience or ways of knowing. Higher education socializes faculty to view students' struggles as deficiency, low effort, or lack of dedication. Instead of lamenting what we view as a lack of preparedness and placing blame on the student, he introduces a pedagogy of radical hope.[87] Centered in Freireian thought, Gannon's teaching framework is "life-affirming, inclusive, and centers student agency and praxis."[88] He builds on the scholarship of Amy Collier and Jen Ross, who celebrate the "not-yetness" or nascent skills students possess, a concept desperately needed for care pedagogy in music.[89] Consider, for example, how often we shame and penalize students for not learning something we believe they were supposed to in a previous course. Gannon states, "Not-yetness urges us to encounter students as people in process, not as fixed and insurmountable deficits."[90] "Students can't [sight read, hear chordal progressions, or use software to notate music]? Well, not yet. But they will. Can't [imagine the ways that music upholds systemic oppression]? Not yet, at least. But our job is to help them find the ways to get closer to yet."[91] Together with Gannon, we believe care pedagogy can transform our learning spaces to serve as sites of potential and becoming.

A sound pedagogy of radical, or rooted, care in music moves beyond foundational work in critical pedagogy, and centers care for students' mental health in innovative ways. In recent decades, scholars have been investigating the intersection of mindfulness practices and higher education.[92] Daniel Barbezat and Mirabai Bush advance practical applications of contemplative practices across the disciplines in order to foster students' development of human connection, empathy, and critical thinking.[93] In *Integrating Mindfulness into Anti-Oppression Pedagogy*, women's studies scholar Beth Berila explores ways to "interrupt oppression at its roots in our bodies, our hearts, and our minds" and, in turn, create more-compassionate learning environments where students learn to recognize and transform oppression in the classroom and the world beyond.[94] In *Sentipensante (Sensing/Thinking) Pedagogy*, Laura Rendón applies contemplative practices and multiculturalism to create a liberatory, relationship-centered pedagogy. She confronts several entrenched agreements in education that obstruct the cultivation of wholeness. Transcending limiting views about themselves, students become poised to enact social justice in their communities.[95] In *The Book of Awakening*, Mark Nepo develops a definition of "transformational education," a process of educating by "actualizing individual and global awakening, and by participating in compassionate communities."[96] In *Teaching with Tenderness*, Becky Thompson draws on multiracial feminist pedagogy, trauma theory, and activism. Acknowledging the consequences of shifting power dynamics in classrooms and communities, she advocates for embodied teaching that leverages contemplative practices to help students reckon with interlocking systems of oppression.[97]

Our understanding of the vital role of care in a pedagogical context resonates with priorities in the growing subfield of trauma-informed pedagogy, which represents necessary next steps to deepen the practices of which we speak here. Trauma-informed pedagogy is based on the conviction that students' past and present selves and experiences influence their ability to learn because of the long-term impact of these experiences on their well-being. By foregrounding care in our pedagogies, we recognize these student realities as legitimate and allow them to inform the pedagogical choices we make on a number of levels. Trauma theory informs the work of music educator Karin Hendricks, who connects students' safety with our abilities to foster spaces of trust, both incredibly necessary in the context of a trauma-informed pedagogy.[98] A trauma-informed pedagogical lens is of course even more necessary considering all the uncertainty, grief, and trauma that we navigated during the COVID-19 pandemic and beyond.[99]

Indeed, if we build connections with students based on their personal and individual relationships with music, we cease to ignore what they bring to the learning environment as learners and what we bring as individual teachers. As Parker Palmer writes, "Good teachers join self and subject and students in the fabric of life. Good teachers possess a capacity for connectedness. They are able to weave a complex web of connections among themselves, their subjects, and their students so that students can learn to weave a world for themselves."[100] In this, Palmer, like Freire, emphasizes the vital intersection of connection, community, and good teaching.

Traditional approaches to education prize intellectual prowess and eschew personal development. By contrast, Palmer introduces the concept of well-being as a curricular issue positioned alongside content and learning processes. Simply put, we cannot teach well without investing in the complexities of care. Furthermore, well-being assumes an especially powerful role, along with fraught meanings, when social justice topics arise as a result of the subject matter. What cultural forces define wellness? Who is allowed to be well and what resources are they provided to pursue well-being? These care pedagogy topics need continual consideration in music learning spaces.

Who Cares?

Thinking about fruitful opportunities for care and reparation inherent in studying music, we want to open the discussion more broadly to structural aspects of higher-education music study that position it as a difficult and problematic site for caring and kindness. We ask: what special opportunities do music classes offer to care for students and to care for ourselves as music educators? What can recent work in pedagogy, disability studies, queer studies, and so on teach us about how to better care in music pedagogy? How can we conceive of music classrooms as places of opportunity where fresh and crucial ideas in caring approaches to pedagogy can be advanced? How can voices traditionally relegated to the periphery resonate more powerfully in music courses?

In light of the #metoo movement, and the legacy of systemic abuses of power in the music industry, we want to apply pressure on the disciplinary skills and values that remain silently and surreptitiously embedded in our ways of knowing about and making music. We wonder how traditional music study, particularly the master-student conservatory model of private music study, shapes our thinking about what musical instruction and education can and should be. What does it mean to be a trained musician? Are we better listeners because we are trained musicians?[101] And conversely, do we listen to and follow instruction of a conductor or master teacher perhaps too well or too easily? Do our honed listening skills allow us to listen to or for other messages? Does our musical training allow us to collaborate with people around us ("ensembles") to create more equitable models of music pedagogy? For this to occur, to whom do we need to listen? Could we then understand listening as a mode of caring? Does knowing how to listen help us to care? How and why should we care?

Our contributors bring a wide range of perspectives to these crucial questions, raising productive dissonances that challenge traditional, and perhaps disciplinary or disciplined, perceptions of the purpose of higher-education music study. They address issues such as radical kindness through universal design in the music classroom, listening with care to nonhuman musicality, public musicology as a forum for social justice discourse, teaching first-generation college students in music, and brave approaches to teaching about race through music. Authors draw from teaching and advising experiences with course topics ranging from the music history survey to operatic spectatorship and environmental humanities. Of course, this collection is not and could not be exhaustive. Our work remains limited by our cultural white-supremacist socialization, which is reinforced within our discipline. We hope to forge a music discipline that centers teaching and learning with care and kindness, as fraught and tension-filled as these concepts remain.

We write collectively as workers for academic institutions in the United States and Canada. *Sound Pedagogy* represents a first step of music scholars, teachers, administrators, and counselors, taking action toward care and recognizing that care initiates and continually undergirds a sustained journey of social justice.[102] We position ourselves working alongside our colleagues who fight tirelessly and constantly to combat the deeply seated racism and inequalities in the current economic, social, and political systems in which and through which we educate music students in higher education. Invoking Bettina Love's research on abolitionist teaching, we seek to become coconspirators in dismantling systems of oppression, since allyship from dominant-group members often occurs passively from a safe distance.[103] Many authors, including Hung, Natvig, Pruett, Soto, Spilker, Wissner, and Wright, bring perspectives to care pedagogy through their experiences that diverge from socially constructed mythical norms, including race, gender, age, size, ability, mental health status, socioeconomic status, and educational background. Bianca Williams's vital work on "radical honesty" reminds us that every person teaches, researches, and writes through their lived experience.[104] Self-reflexive critical exploration remains an ongoing process of care.

This book explores what care pedagogy might look like, and indeed has looked like, from various perspectives in and configurations of music classrooms—it outlines and theorizes about practical examples of care work in music teaching in higher education. Most authors are musicologists, but all contributors have reinterpreted their positionality and work in novel ways that support care pedagogy in its varied, messy iterations. Authors present theoretical and/or practical discussions of their work, thus offering a variety of contributions to the complex discussions and applications of care pedagogy in music. We hope our experiences incite a rich and vibrant continuous dialogue inside the discipline and beyond its carefully guarded borders in order to foster further work on this crucial and timely topic.

Sound Pedagogy presents a set of deliberations and practices in higher-education music pedagogy, and chapters should be viewed as being in dialogue with one another. The book's organization mirrors a broader arc that teaching and learning might follow: notably, starting inside the classroom, moving outward to redefine and transgress boundaries, and moving inward, caring together for students and colleagues. The chapters cover notably diverse topics and approaches to care, evidencing the diverse points of active entry into this work in the post-secondary music classroom. No two chapters approach care in the same way, but all center the care of students' well-being. Many discuss the difficult work of repositioning the discipline's most fraught hallmark features—rigor, white supremacy, patriarchy, and ableism—in an effort to steer work in music in a radically different direction moving forward, one that acknowledges care of self and others as central to the discipline. We see the divergence of definitions of care and approaches to care as a benefit here—our hope is that readers see themselves and their students in some or many of these case studies, and can thus imagine one or several ways forward.

The first section of the book, "The Heart of Curricular Interventions," begins with Sara Haefeli's possibilities for reenchanting the music history classroom. Returning to love and transcendence as historical ways of engaging with music might teach us and our students, anew, how to be better citizens. Molly Breckling uses the racist backlash from practitioners of classical music to Kendrick Lamar's 2018 Pulitzer Prize to approach fraught classroom discussions about a local white supremacist rally, outlining the courage it took to center care and community context as music content. Renihan explores the potential for operatic spectatorship and performance to provide students with hands-on experiences of empathy, positing operatic engagement as a surprising antidote to the empathy deficit, while acknowledging the challenges of doing so at a predominantly white institution in Canada. John Spilker integrates well-being and social justice scholarship throughout restructured coursework in music history and culture. In an open, coconstructed, humane learning community, his teaching approach positions emotional self-awareness and resilience alongside discipline-specific learning outcomes. From the perspective of a music school admissions administrator, Frederick Peterbark, a music school dean, uses a bioecological model that considers students' music and academic skills along with their lived experiences and helps him qualify and quantify the music program's impact on students in the areas of diversity, equity, community engagement, admission practices, and student retention. Stephanie Jensen-Moulton theorizes radical kindness as universal design. She writes, "In highly competitive fields such as music performance, where students must compete with their peers on a daily basis, both kindness and universal design prepare students to enter the twenty-first-century workforce with the crucial [and highly desired] skill of collegiality."

The book's second section, "Unmeasured Pedagogical Horizons," explores the pressing need to expand our work into the community and in engagement with audiences beyond our usual fans. Mark Katz outlines two projects in which students learn collaboration, empathy, and self-care while dialoguing with their communities through DJing. His applications of care pedagogy engage students in social justice work around race, queer identities, and rape culture, among other pressing topics. Eric Hung explores teaching that benefits and minimizes harm to communities; this requires the exploration of contrasting epistemologies, a focus on the agency and resistance of marginalized populations, and an understanding that some topics and repertoires should only be taught under rare circumstances. He offers readers a sample eight-week module that demonstrates a "community intervention" approach to teaching music. William Everett and Matteo Magarotto discuss public musicology as an opportunity for disrupting traditional narratives and for care. They offer practical ideas for considering the role of the arts in fostering opportunities for community dialogue. Kate Galloway extends reparative musicology and categories of musical difference to the nonhuman environment along with its sounding and musicking citizens. By extending our consideration of music, she invites us to learn how to listen differently and across sound cultures and consider new possibilities that exist beyond the porous boundaries of care pedagogy.

Reinforcing that self-care remains a vital first step that must radiate outward to communal care, the final section of the book, "Self-Care, The Root of Teaching," returns to the heart, urgently focusing on crucial, often life-and-death, and frequently silenced issues of mental health and personal connection. Essays center the instructor as an essential subject in care pedagogy. Authors do not shy away from discussing and indeed foregrounding their own experiences and struggles—keeping Brené Brown's ideas about shame, vulnerability, and resilience at the core of care pedagogy approaches.[105] Nathan Langfitt lays bare the emotional and mental stressors of music study, along with opportunities for radical care from his valuable perspective being employed by a music department as a therapist for music students. Rooted in her lived experience as a contingent faculty worker at multiple institutions simultaneously, Reba Wissner leveraged her experiences as a first-generation music student to create teaching approaches to better understand and mitigate the obstacles first-generation college students face in the music history classroom. Amanda Soto explores the difficulties of engaging global learning initiatives in higher-education music programs. She centers her challenges of being a Tejana music faculty member at a school of music in Texas. Drawing from teaching and personal experiences, Soto asks vital questions about transforming the undergraduate curriculum despite resistance to change, and negotiating historical and cultural aspects of the place in which and constituency that we teach. Laura Moore Pruett discusses difficult negotiations with temporary injuries that drastically impacted her cognitive abilities and physical mobility, and their impact on her lifelong battle to understand and live productively through depression. Her work with care pedagogy helped her reconsider teaching, connecting with, and better understanding the experiences of her students. Mary Natvig shares her experiences confronting rising numbers of students with mental health concerns and bravely examines the possibilities of a pedagogy of disclosure, sharing timely best practices for this crucial work. Finally, Trudi Wright considers the root ways that a philosophy of self-care might be modeled in and beyond the classroom to effect broader change within ourselves, the university, the field of musicology, and beyond.

Considering, designing, and enacting care pedagogy in higher-education music remains challenging, urgent, and absolutely attainable work. It meets us where we are, with whatever and whomever we are teaching, researching, or serving. Care pedagogy needs to connect with and grow from our individual ways of thinking and doing, informed by care-based content that resonates with how we each feel called to work in the world. In short, care pedagogy builds on each person's strengths. To help, chapters include perspectives from teachers, administrators, counselors, and students, with the idea that each necessarily affects and involves the other. Throughout *Sound Pedagogy*, we hold in tension curricular interventions that understandably lie along a spectrum of understandings about privilege, social justice, and equity, and the inextricable connections between one's teaching and the self.

Insisting on care pedagogy in higher-education music transforms the learning environments in which we work, along with our students and colleagues. Viewing the examples in this volume as igniting conversation and action toward change, how else could we each envision enacting care pedagogy in our (virtual and face-to-face) classrooms, meeting spaces, rehearsal halls, and daily work lives? We know that further research and praxis by our readers will reveal new and exciting ways to do this work. Embracing care as *radical*, as both the root of and rooted in equitable teaching and learning, enables a sound pedagogy.

Notes

1. See Dylan Robinson, "To All Who Should Be Concerned," *Intersections* 39, no. 1 (2019): 137.

2. Two of the many issues students face are food insecurity and homelessness, which have previously gone unnoticed. See #collegehunger and #collegehomelessness on Twitter. In one study, over thirty percent of students interviewed felt food insecure at college. See resources in United States Government Accountability Office, "Food Insecurity: Better Information Could Help Eligible College Students Access Federal Food Assistance Benefits" (published December 21, 2018, publicly released January 9, 2019), https://www.gao.gov/products/GAO-19-95. A CBS news story on college homelessness points listeners to programs around the country offering resources for students in need. See "Homelessness on Campus," CBS News, January 20, 2019, www.cbsnews.com.

3. American College Health Association, "National College Health Assessment II, Spring 2016 Reference Group Executive Summary," https://www.acha.org/documents/ncha/NCHA-II%20SPRING%202016%20US%20REFERENCE%20GROUP%20EXECUTIVE%20SUMMARY.pdf; Kevin Eagan, Ellen Bara Stolzenberg, Hilary B. Zimmerman, Melissa C. Aragon, Hannah Whang Sayson, and Cecilia Rios-Aguilar, *The American Freshman: National Norms Fall 2016* (Los Angeles: Higher Education Research

Institute, 2017), https://www.heri.ucla.edu/monographs/TheAmericanFreshman2016 .pdf.

4. See https://www.who.int/news/item/02-03-2022-covid-19-pandemic-triggers -25-increase-in-prevalence-of-anxiety-and-depression-worldwide.

5. Rebecca Pope-Ruark, *Unraveling Faculty Burnout: Pathways to Reckoning and Renewal* (Baltimore: Johns Hopkins University Press, 2022). In addition to the higher education profession, burnout has become such a hallmark in music training and the profession that Amelia Nagoski, a collegiate choral conductor, coauthored with her sister Emily Nagoski, *Burnout: The Secret to Unlocking the Stress Cycle* (New York: Random House, 2020). Regarding the financial precarity of adjunct faculty, see Florida Public Service Union, "Life on the Edge of the Blackboard: Florida Adjunct Faculty Survey 2017," https://seiufacultyforward.org/wp-content/uploads/2017/11/Life-on-the-Edge.pdf; Herb Childress, "This Is How You Kill a Profession: How Did We Decide That Professors Don't Deserve Job Security or a Decent Salary?," *Chronicle of Higher Education*, March 27, 2019, https://www.chronicle.com/interactives/2019-03-27-childress; Carolyn Foster Segal, "Academic Hunger Games," *Inside Higher Ed*, October 18, 2012, https://www .insidehighered.com/views/2012/10/18/new-academic-underclass-adjunct-committee -member-essay.

6. Victoria Honeybourne, *The Neurodiverse Classroom: A Teacher's Guide to Individual Learning Needs and How to Meet Them* (London: Jessica Kingsley Publishers, 2018), 146; Beckie Supiano, "Student Success Requires Faculty Well-Being," *Chronicle of Higher Education*, May 26, 2022, https://www.chronicle.com/newsletter/teaching/2022-05-26; Marcelle Hayashida, "A Broader Way of Thinking about Well-Being," *Inside Higher Ed*, December 4, 2022, https://www.insidehighered.com/views/2022/12/05/broader-way-thinking-about-well-being-opinion; Ashley Mowreader, "Wellness Tip: Teach Professors Mindfulness," *Inside Higher Ed*, March 22, 2023, https://www.insidehighered.com/news/2023/03/23/faculty-mental-health-program-supports-students.

7. Our favorite definition of *radical* is "Of a quality, attribute, or feature, inherent in the nature or essence of a person or thing; fundamental. Now ***rare***" (boldface added). See *Oxford English Dictionary*, accessed June 18, 2020, www.oed.com.

8. Ed Sarath et al., "Transforming Music Study from Its Foundations: A Manifesto for Progressive Change in the Undergraduate Preparation of Music Majors," College Music Society, November 2014, edited January 2016, https://www.music.org/pdf/pubs/tfumm/TFUMM.pdf.

9. For reports and a summary of the Truth and Reconciliation Commission's work, see http://www.trc.ca/, accessed May 19, 2020. See also Margaret Walker, "Towards a Decolonized Music History Curriculum," *Journal of Music History Pedagogy* 10, no. 1 (2020): 1–19.

10. Tamara Levitz, "The Musicological Elite," *Current Musicology* 102 (spring 2018): 9–80.

11. See William Robin, "What Controversial Changes at Harvard Mean for Music in the University," *National Sawdust*, April 25, 2017, https://www.nationalsawdust.org/thelog/2017-04-25-what-controversial-changes-at-harvard-means-for-music-in-the -university. For information on DePauw's Twenty-First Century Musician Initiative, see https://www.depauw.edu/music/21cm/, accessed February 2, 2023.

12. See Deborah Bradley, "Decentering the European Music Canon," in *College Music Curricula for a New Century*, ed. Robin Moore (New York: Oxford University Press, 2017), 211–12; David Chavennes and Maria Ryan, "Decolonizing the Music Survey: A Manifesto for Action," June 15, 2018, http://www.dchavannes.com/read/; Tamara Levitz, "Decolonizing the Society for American Music," *The Bulletin of the Society of American Music* 43, no. 3 (2017): 1–13; Reinhard Strohm, ed., *The Music Road: Coherence and Diversity in Music from the Mediterranean to India* (New York: Oxford University Press, 2019); Walker, "Decolonized Curriculum."

13. Part of this is built directly into the ableist nature of the term "Higher Education," which Jay Dolmage has explained by noting the ways that disability has been constructed historically as the inverse or opposite of higher education, institutionally and even architecturally. See Jay Dolmage, *Academic Ableism: Disability and Higher Education* (Ann Arbor: University of Michigan Press, 2017).

14. See Joe Feagin, *The White Racial Frame: Centuries of Racial Framing and Counter-Framing* (New York: Routledge, 2020).

15. Loren Kajikawa, "The Possessive Investment in Classical Music: Confronting Legacies of White Supremacy in U.S. Schools and Departments of Music," in *Seeing Race Again: Countering Colorblindness across the Disciplines*, ed. Kimberlé Williams Crenshaw, Luke Charles Harris, Daniel Martinez HoSang, and George Lipsitz (Berkeley: University of California Press, 2019), 155–74.

16. In Canada, the Royal Conservatory of Music system governs most formal, private music lessons across the country, and examiners from Toronto visit rural areas annually to examine students' skills and knowledge of the classical canon. Although in recent years the Royal Conservatory of Music has expanded their repertoire to include more popular selections, the colonialist legacy of the organization continues to be felt in many of its structures and practices.

17. Tema Okun describes the ways that white supremacy culture occurs in the workplace in "White Supremacy Culture," accessed July 8, 2020, https://www.dismantlingracism.org/uploads/4/3/5/7/43579015/okun_-_white_sup_culture.pdf. The Centre for Community Organizations' recent publication *White Supremacy Culture in Organizations* features sections on Perfectionist Culture, Concentration of Power, Worship of the Written Word, and Individualism, among others—all of which reflect powerfully the culture of music in higher education. The table of contents, in fact, reads as a values list of classical music culture. See Emily Yee Clare, Emil Briones, Kira Page, and Philippe Angers-Trottier, adapting Tema Okun, *White Supremacy Culture in Organizations* (Montreal: Centre des Organismes Communautaires, 2019), https://ccednet-rcdec.ca/sites/ccednet-rcdec.ca/wp-content/uploads/2022/09/white_supremacy_culture_in_organizations_0.pdf.

18. This terminology for interlocking systems of oppression is discussed in bell hooks, *Understanding Patriarchy* (Louisville Anarchist Federation Federation and No Borders: Louisville's Radical Lending Library), accessed May 20, 2020, https://imaginenoborders.org/pdf/zines/UnderstandingPatriarchy.pdf.

19. Sarath et al., "Transforming Music Study"; Kajikawa, "Possessive Investment," 156.

20. Brandon Keith Brown, "When Black Conductors Aren't Comfortable at Con-

certs, Classical Music Has a Real Problem," *Level*, February 1, 2020, https://level.medium.com/black-concert-trauma-5fa0459e5b3. See also Danielle Brown, "An Open Letter on Racism in Music Studies: Especially Ethnomusicology and Music Education," June 12, 2020, https://www.mypeopletellstories.com/blog/open-letter.

21. See https://timesupnow.org/about/; Alix Langone, "#MeToo and Time's Up Founders Explain the Difference between the 2 Movements—And How They're Alike," *Time*, March 8, 2018, https://time.com/5189945/whats-the-difference-between-the-metoo-and-times-up-movements/.

22. As *Sound Pedagogy* heads to press, we celebrate the publication of Phillip Ewell, *On Music Theory, and Making Music More Welcoming for Everyone* (Ann Arbor: University of Michigan Press, 2023) and Horace Maxile Jr. and Kristen Turner, *Race and Gender in the Western Music History Survey: A Teacher's Guide* (New York: Routledge, 2022). We look forward to the publication of Laura Moore Pruett and Olivia Lucas, eds., *Teaching and Learning Difficult Topics in the Music Classroom* (Ann Arbor: University of Michigan Press, forthcoming).

23. Joy Rice, review of *Caring: A Feminine Approach to Ethics and Moral Education*, by Nel Noddings, *Sex Roles* 14, no. 3–4 (1986): 230.

24. See Nel Noddings, *Educating Moral People: A Caring Alternative to Character Education* (New York: Teachers College Press, 2002); *The Maternal Factor: Two Paths to Morality* (Berkeley: University of California Press, 2010); *Education and Democracy in the 21st Century* (New York: Teachers College Press, 2013); and, with Laurie Brooks, *Teaching Controversial Issues: The Case for Critical Thinking and Moral Commitment in the Classroom* (New York: Teachers College Press, 2017).

25. See Alex Usher, "What People Mean When They Talk about Neoliberal Universities: Part I," Higher Education Strategy Associates, November 20, 2017, https://higheredstrategy.com/publications/. See also Rebecca Lund, "The Social Organization of Boasting in the Neoliberal University," *Gender and Education* 32/4 (2020): 466–85.

26. See Elizabeth Parker, "A Grounded Theory of Adolescent High School Women's Choir Singers' Process of Social Identity Development," *Journal of Research in Music Education* 65, no. 4 (2018): 439–60; Marissa Silverman, "Virtue Ethics, Care Ethics, and 'The Good Life of Teaching,'" *Action, Criticism, and Theory for Music Education* 11, no. 2 (2012): 100; Rechallda Mouton and Janelize Morelli, "A Conceptual Framework of the Relationship between Musicking and Personal and Social Well-Being for Intermediate Phase Learners in the South African Context," *The Journal for Transdisciplinary Research in Southern Africa* 17, no. 1 (2021): 8; Liesl van der Merwe, Ewie Erasmus, Janelize Morelli, H. Potgieter, J. Modise, Etienne Viviers, et al., "Stories of the Role Musicking Plays in Coping with the COVID-19 Pandemic in South Africa," *Psychology of Music* (2021), https://doi.org/10.1177/03057356211026959; Merlin Thompson, "Teaching the Student," in *Fundamentals of Piano Pedagogy: Fueling Authentic Student Musicians from the Beginning* (SpringerBriefs in Education, 2018), 61–74; Janelize Van der Merwe, "Student-Teachers' Lived Experiences in the Naledi Community Music Program through the Lens of (Un)Caring" (PhD diss., New York University, 2019). Karin Hendricks's *Oxford Handbook of Care in Music Education* (New York: Oxford, 2023) will compliment and dialogue with the chapters in this book.

27. Silverman, "Virtue Ethics," 100.

28. Bonnie Gordon, "Why We Matter," *Women and Music: A Journal of Gender and Culture* 19 (2015): 116–24.

29. Travis Stimeling and Kayla Tokar, "Narratives of Musical Resilience and the Perpetuation of Whiteness in the Music History Classroom," *Journal of Music History Pedagogy* 10, no. 1 (2020): 20–38.

30. Karin Hendricks, *Compassionate Music Teaching: A Framework for Motivation and Engagement in the 21st Century* (Lanham, MD: Rowman and Littlefield, 2018).

31. William Cheng, *Just Vibrations: The Purpose of Sounding Good* (Ann Arbor: University of Michigan Press, 2016). John Spilker's review of Cheng's book aptly illustrates how our work on care pedagogy builds on the foundation of Cheng's work. See *Journal of the Society for American Music* 13, no. 1 (2019): 110–13.

32. Cheng, *Just Vibrations.* Paranoid and reparative readings are first discussed on page 3, then referred to throughout. Eve Kosofsky Sedgwick, "Paranoid Reading and Reparative Reading, or, You're So Paranoid, You Probably Think This Essay Is about You," in *Touching Feeling: Affect, Pedagogy, Performativity* (Durham, NC: Duke University Press, 2003), 123–51, especially 128. See also Ellis Hanson, "The Future's Eve: Reparative Reading after Sedgwick," *South Atlantic Quarterly* 110, no. 1 (2011): 101–19.

33. Cheng, *Just Vibrations,* 88; See also Michael J. Shapiro, *Studies in Trans-Disciplinary Method: After the Aesthetic Turn* (New York: Routledge, 2013), 100–116.

34. Definitions of *multidisciplinary*, *interdisciplinary*, and *transdisciplinary* approaches are found in Kristin Boudreau and Derren Rosbach, "The Value of a Transdisciplinary Approach," in *Project-Based Learning in the First Year: Beyond All Expectations,* ed. Kristin Wobbe and Elisabeth Stoddard (Sterling, VA: Stylus Publishing, 2019), 35.

35. Cheng, *Just Vibrations,* 8–9.

36. Cheng, 10.

37. Brené Brown, *Daring Greatly: How the Courage to Be Vulnerable Changes the Way We Live, Love, Parent, and Lead* (New York: Gotham Books, 2012), 184–213.

38. See Sean Michael Morris and Jesse Stommel, *An Urgency of Teachers: The Work of Critical Digital Pedagogy,* September 12, 2018, https://criticaldigitalpedagogy.pressbooks.com/, introduction; Dorina Carter Andrews and Bernadette Castillo, "Humanizing Pedagogy for Examinations of Race and Culture in Teacher Education," in *Race, Equity, and the Learning Environment: The Global Relevance of Critical and Inclusive Pedagogies in Higher Education,* ed. Frank Tuitt, Chayla Haynes, and Saran Stewart (Sterling, VA: Stylus Publishing, 2016), 112–28. The concept of "humanizing pedagogy" addresses connections between equity, care, and teaching and learning.

39. Lee Anne Bell, "Theoretical Foundations for Social Justice Education," in *Teaching for Diversity and Social Justice,* 3rd ed., ed. Maurianne Adams, Lee Anne Bell, and Pat Griffin (New York: Routledge, 2016), 4 (italics in original). Bell notes, "we use the term 'oppression' rather than discrimination, bias, prejudice, or bigotry to emphasize the pervasive nature of social inequality that is woven throughout social institutions as well as embedded within individual consciousness."

40. Bell, 3 (italics in original).

41. Bell, 3.

42. Bell, 3.

43. A common dynamic of white dominance involves shutting down BIPOC voices by invoking white definitions of respect or niceness. This occurs as the result of white people experiencing discomfort from modes of expression that challenge white supremacy. See Kathy Obear, *But I'm Not Racist: Tools for Well-Meaning Whites* (McLean, VA: Difference Press, 2017); Robin DiAngelo, *White Fragility: Why It's So Hard for White People to Talk about Racism* (Boston: Beacon Press, 2018); Robin DiAngelo, *Nice Racism: How Progressive White People Perpetuate Racial Harm* (Boston: Beacon Press, 2021).

44. Shoshana Magnet, Corinne Lysandra Mason, and Kathryn Trevenen, "Feminism, Pedagogy, and the Politics of Kindness," *Feminist Teacher* 25, no. 1 (2014): 3, quoting Stephen Rowland, "Kindness," *London Review of Education* 7, no. 3 (2009): 207–10.

45. bell hooks, *Teaching Community: A Pedagogy of Hope* (New York: Routledge, 2004), 127.

46. hooks, xv.

47. hooks, 49.

48. Becky Thompson, *Teaching with Tenderness: Toward an Embodied Practice* (Urbana: University of Illinois Press, 2017).

49. Carol Gilligan, *In a Different Voice: Psychological Theory and Women's Development* (Cambridge, MA: Harvard University Press, 2016); Sarah Ruddick, *Maternal Thinking: Towards a Politics of Peace* (Boston: Beacon Press, 1995).

50. See Kimberlé Crenshaw, "Demarginalizing the Intersection of Race and Sex: A Black Feminist Critique of Antidiscrimination Doctrine, Feminist Theory and Antiracist Politics," *The University of Chicago Legal Forum* 140 (1989): 139–67; Kimberlé Crenshaw, "Mapping the Margins: Intersectionality, Identity Politics, and Violence against Women of Color," *Stanford Law Review* 43, no. 6 (1991): 1241–99; Virginia Held, *Feminist Morality: Transforming Culture, Society, and Politics* (Chicago: University of Chicago Press, 1993); Virginia Held, ed., *Justice and Care: Essential Readings in Feminist Ethics* (Boulder, CO: Westview Press, 1995); Virginia Held, *The Ethics of Care: Personal, Political, and Global* (New York: Oxford University Press, 2006); Joan Tronto, "Care as a Basis for Radical Political Judgments," *Hypatia* 10, no. 2 (1995): 141–49; Joan Tronto, "Care as the Work of Citizens: A Modest Proposal," in *Women and Citizenship*, ed. Marily Friedman (New York: Oxford University Press, 2005), 130–45.

51. Lorelle Meadows, Denise Sekaquaptewa, Marie C. Paretti, Alice L. Pawley, Shawn S. Jordan, Debbie Chachra Olin, and Adrienne Minerick, "Interactive Panel: Improving the Experiences of Marginalized Students on Engineering Design Teams (Paper ID 11803)," American Society for Engineering Education Annual Conference, 2015, https://peer.asee.org/interactive-panel-improving-the-experiences-of-marginalized-students-on-engineering-design-teams.

52. Magnet, Mason, and Trevenen, "Feminism," 1–22.

53. hooks, *Teaching Community*, xv.

54. See Gloria Ladson-Billings, *The Dreamkeepers: Successful Teachers of African American Children, 2nd ed.* (San Francisco: Jossey-Bass, 2009); Gloria Ladson-Billings, *Crossing Over to Canaan: The Journey of New Teachers in Diverse Classrooms* (San Francisco: Jossey-Bass, 2001); Gloria Ladson-Billings, *Beyond the Big House: African

American Educators on Teacher Education (New York: Teachers College Press, 2005); Beverly Daniel Tatum, *Why Are All the Black Kids Sitting Together in the Cafeteria? And Other Conversations about Race*, 2nd ed. (New York: Basic Books, 2017); Beverly Daniel Tatum, *Can We Talk about Race? And Other Conversations in an Era of School Resegregation* (Boston: Beacon Press, 2008); bell hooks, *Teaching to Transgress: Education as the Practice of Freedom* (New York: Routledge, 1994); hooks, *Teaching Community*; bell hooks, *Teaching Critical Thinking: Practical Wisdom* (New York: Routledge, 2010).

55. Frank Tuitt, Chayla Haynes, and Saran Stewart, eds., *Race, Equity, and the Learning Environment* (Sterling, VA: Stylus Publishing, 2016); Badia Ahad-Legardy and OiYan A. Poon, eds., *Difficult Subjects: Insights and Strategies for Teaching about Race, Sexuality, and Gender* (Sterling, VA: Stylus Publishing, 2018).

56. hooks, *Teaching Community*, 103.

57. Geoff Pfeifer and Elisabeth Stoddard, "Equitable and Effective Student Teams: Creating and Managing Team Dynamics for Equitable Learning Outcomes," in *Project-Based Learning in the First Year*, ed. Kristin Wobbe and Elisabeth Stoddard (Sterling, VA: Stylus Publishing, 2019), 238–39.

58. Pfeifer and Stoddard, "Student Teams," 238–39.

59. The term "emotional labor" was coined in Arlie Hochschild's *The Managed Heart: Commercialization of Human Feeling* (Berkeley: University of California Press, 1983). See also Arlie Hochschild and Barbara Ehrenreich, *Global Women: Nannies, Maids, and Sex Workers in the New Economy* (New York: Metropolitan Owl Books, 2004).

60. Susan Wortmann and Jie Gao, "Emotional Labor," in *Encyclopedia of Consumer Culture*, ed. Dale Southerton (Thousand Oaks, CA: Sage Publications, 2011).

61. Magnet, Mason, and Trevenen, "Feminism," 2.

62. Magnet, Mason, and Trevenen, 3.

63. Crenshaw, "Demarginalizing."

64. See Cheng, *Just Vibrations*.

65. Brené Brown, "Listening to Shame," 2012 TED Conference, https://www.ted.com/talks/brene_brown_listening_to_shame/transcript. Referring to Bryan Stevenson's talk, "We Need to Talk about an Injustice," presented earlier at the conference, Brown asserts, "We heard the most compelling call ever to have a conversation in this country, and I think globally, around race, right? We cannot have that conversation without shame." For Brown's research on shame and learning see *Daring Greatly*. She discusses learning and privilege in *Rising Strong: The Reckoning, the Rumble, the Revolution* (New York: Spiegel and Grau, 2015). For Bryan Stevenson's research on racial inequity see *Just Mercy: A Story of Justice and Redemption* (Spiegel and Grau, 2015) and the Equal Justice Initiative, https://eji.org/.

66. DiAngelo, *White Fragility*.

67. Brown, *Daring Greatly*, 199.

68. Jasmine Harris, "Uncomfortable Learning," in *Difficult Subjects*, 248–65; Brian Arao and Kristi Clemens, "From Safe Spaces to Brave Spaces," in *The Art of Effective Facilitation: Reflections from Social Justice Educators*, ed. Lisa Landreman (Sterling, VA: Stylus Publishing, 2013), 135–50.

69. DiAngelo, *White Fragility*, 143.

70. Resmaa Menakem, *My Grandmother's Hands: Racialized Trauma and the Pathway to Mending Our Hearts and Bodies* (Las Vegas: Central Recovery Press, 2017), xiii.

71. See Brené Brown, "Brené on Shame and Accountability," July 1, 2020, in *Unlocking Us*, podcast, https://brenebrown.com/podcast-show/unlocking-us/; Brené Brown, "Brené on Words, Actions, Dehumanization, and Accountability," January 13, 2021, in *Unlocking Us*, podcast, https://brenebrown.com/podcast-show/unlocking-us/.

72. Paulo Freire, *Pedagogy of the Oppressed* (New York: Penguin Books, 1970); Paulo Freire, *Education for Critical Consciousness* (New York: Seabury Press, 1973); Paulo Freire, *Pedagogy in Process: The Letters to Guinea-Bissau* (New York: Bloomsbury Publishing, 2016); Paulo Freire, *Pedagogy of Hope: Reliving Pedagogy of the Oppressed* (New York: Bloomsbury Academic, 2014); Paulo Freire, *Pedagogy of the Heart* (New York: Bloomsbury Academic, 2016); hooks, *Teaching to Transgress*; hooks, *Teaching Community*; hooks, *Teaching Critical Thinking*; Parker Palmer, *The Courage to Teach* (San Francisco: Jossey-Bass, 1997); Parker Palmer, *The Heart of Higher Education: A Call to Renewal* (San Francisco: Jossey-Bass, 2010); Parker Palmer, *A Hidden Wholeness: The Journey toward an Undivided Life* (San Francisco: Jossey-Bass, 2004); Parker Palmer, *Let Your Life Speak: Listening for the Voice of Vocation* (San Francisco: Jossey-Bass, 1999).

73. Liza Ann Bolitzer, Milagros Castillo-Montoya, and Leslie A. Williams, "Pursuing Equity through Diversity: Perspectives and Propositions for Teaching and Learning in Higher Education," in *Race, Equity, and the Learning Environment*, 27.

74. Maggie Berg and Barbara Seeber, *The Slow Professor: Challenging the Culture of Speed in the Academy* (Toronto: University of Toronto Press, 2016); Susan Cain, *Quiet: The Power of Introverts in a World That Can't Stop Talking* (New York: Random House, 2012).

75. Leah Lakshmi Piepzna-Samarasinha, *Care Work: Dreaming Disability Justice* (Vancouver: Arsenal Pulp Press, 2018), 43.

76. Freire, *Pedagogy of the Oppressed*, 71–86.

77. The exclusionary nature of educational spaces in music is discussed in Bryan Powell, Gareth Smith, and Abigail D'Amore, "Challenging Symbolic Violence and Hegemony in Music Education through Contemporary Pedagogical Approaches," *Education 3–13: International Journal of Primary, Elementary and Early Years Education* 45, no. 6 (2017): 734–43; Ruth Wright, "Democracy, Social Exclusion and Music Education: Possibilities for Change," in *Sociology and Music Education*, ed. Ruth Wright (New York: Routledge, 2010), 263–82; Kajikawa, "Possessive Investment."

78. Freire, *Pedagogy of the Oppressed*, 57.

79. Freire, 95–96.

80. See Kajikawa, "Possessive Investment."

81. Kajikawa, 157.

82. Morris and Stommel, *An Urgency of Teachers*.

83. See SUNY Cortland, "A Democratic Learning Environment," accessed May 29, 2020, https://www2.cortland.edu/centers/character/wheel/democratic-classroom.dot.

84. Cheng discusses the idea throughout *Just Vibrations*.

85. Certainly students feel this distrust. They express fear about being honest with faculty because of the power we hold over their grades. They worry that if we don't like a

student, we can find hidden ways to grade them lower, even if we use seemingly objective rubrics. Could our orientation of distrusting student motivations to learn and work fuel their fear, and thus deepen the chasm between faculty and student? See Beckie Supiano, "Forget Grades and Turnitin. Start Trusting Students," *Chronicle of Higher Education*, October 27, 2019, https://www.chronicle.com/article/forget-grades-and-turnitin-start-trusting-students/.

86. Robin Wharton, "Re-Thinking Plagiarism as Unfair Competition: Presented at CCCC, Chicago, IL, March 24, 2006," https://robinwharton.net/uncategorized/re-thinking-plagiarism-as-unfair-competition-presented-at-cccc-chicago-il-24-march-2006/.

87. Kevin Gannon, *Radical Hope: A Teaching Manifesto* (Morgantown: West Virginia University Press, 2020).

88. Gannon, 24–26.

89. "Not-yetness" appears in Amy Collier and Jen Ross, "For Whom, and For What? Not-Yetness and Thinking beyond Open Content," *Open Praxis* 9, no. 1 (2017): 7–16; Amy Collier and Jen Ross, "Complexity, Mess, and Not-yetness: Teaching Online with Emerging Technologies," in *Emergence and Innovation in Digital Learning: Foundations and Applications*, ed. George Veletsianos (Edmonton, AB: Athabasca University Press, 2016), 17–33.

90. Gannon, *Radical Hope*, 25.

91. Gannon, 25.

92. See Shauna Shapiro, Kirk Warren Brown, and John Astin, "Toward the Integration of Meditation into Higher Education: A Review of Research," Center for Contemplative Mind in Society, October 2008, https://www.contemplativemind.org/files/MedandHigherEd.pdf.

93. Daniel Barbezat and Mirabai Bush, *Contemplative Practices in Higher Education: Powerful Methods to Transform Teaching and Learning* (San Francisco: Jossey-Bass, 2014).

94. Beth Berila, *Integrating Mindfulness into Anti-Oppression Pedagogy: Social Justice in Higher Education* (New York: Routledge, 2015).

95. Laura Rendón, *Sentipensante (Sensing/Thinking) Pedagogy: Educating for Wholeness, Social Justice, and Liberation* (Sterling, VA: Stylus Publishing, 2014).

96. Mark Nepo, *The Book of Awakening: Having the Life You Want by Being Present to the Life You Have* (San Francisco: Conari Press, 2000), vii.

97. Thompson, *Teaching with Tenderness.*

98. "Compassionate Music Teaching with Karin Hendricks Part 1/3," February 22, 2021, in *Music and Peacebuilding Podcast*, season 2, episode 2, https://www.musicpeacebuilding.com/compassionatemusic.

99. Virginia Strand and Jo Ann Coe Regan, steering committee chairs, *Specialized Practice Curricular Guide for Trauma-Informed Social Work Practice* (Alexandria, VA: Council on Social Work Education, 2018), https://www.cswe.org/getattachment/Education-Resources/2015-Curricular-Guides/2015EPAS_TraumaInformedSW_Final-WEB.pdf; Janice Carello and Phyllis Thompson, *Lessons from the Pandemic: Trauma-Informed Approaches to College, Crisis, and Change* (New York: Palgrave Macmillan, 2021); Phyllis Thompson and Janice Carello, eds. *Trauma-Informed Pedagogies: A Guide for Responding*

to Crisis and Inequality in Higher Education (New York: Palgrave Macmillan, 2022); Cia Verschelden, *Bandwidth Recovery: Helping Students Reclaim Cognitive Resources Lost to Poverty, Racism, and Social Marginalization* (Sterling, VA: Stylus Publishing, 2017); Oprah Winfrey and Bruce D. Perry, *What Happened to You?: Conversations on Trauma, Resilience, and Healing* (New York: Flatiron Books, 2021). The musicological community gathered in February 2021 for a conference on Music, Sound, and Trauma: Interdisciplinary Perspectives. The call for proposals anticipates a forthcoming special issue on Trauma-Informed Pedagogy in the *Journal of Music History Pedagogy*. See https://musicsoundtraumaconf2021.com/call-for-papers/. The conference named a growing interest in the context of the pandemic and other crises of 2020 (such as the murder of George Floyd) in the ramifications of trauma studies for teaching and learning. The Teaching Music History Conference in 2022 also featured a panel on "Violence, Trauma, and Music Education: Towards an Ethics of Music History Pedagogy in the 21st Century," featuring work by Erin Brooks, Erin Johnson-Williams, Michelle Meinhart, and Jillian Rogers.

100. Palmer, *Courage to Teach*, 52.

101. There is a rich, growing literature on the structural inequities in the ways we teach musical listening. See Rose Rosengard Subotnik, *Deconstructive Variations: Music and Reason in Western Society* (Minneapolis: University of Minnesota Press, 1995); Andrew Dell'Antonio, "Structural Listening," *Avid Listener*, October 20, 2014, https://www.theavidlistener.com/2014/10/structural-listening.html. Jessica Holmes, "Expert Listening beyond the Limits of Hearing: Music and Deafness," *Journal of the American Musicological Society* 70, no. 1 (2017): 171–220.

102. Freire's *Pedagogy of the Oppressed* begins with this epigraph: "To the oppressed, and to those who suffer with them and fight at their side." Like Freire, we view the work of active, invested allyship as central to care and equity in the classroom. We continue learning about how scholars, ourselves included, have been socialized to naturalize oppressive norms, whiteness in particular. We hope our lifelong commitment to care and equity in teaching and learning contributes to social justice and invites music colleagues to join us.

103. See Bettina Love, *We Want to Do More Than Survive: Abolitionist Teaching and the Pursuit of Educational Freedom* (Boston: Beacon Press, 2019).

104. Bianca Williams, "Radical Honesty: Truth-Telling as Pedagogy for Working through Shame in Academic Spaces," in *Race, Equity, and the Learning Environment*, 71–82.

105. Brené Brown, *Gifts of Imperfection: Let Go of Who You Think You're Supposed to Be and Embrace Who You Are* (Center City, MN: Hazelden Publishing, 2010); Brown, *Daring Greatly*; Brown, *Rising Strong*; Brené Brown, *Braving the Wilderness: The Quest for True Belonging and the Courage to Stand Alone* (New York: Random House, 2017); Brené Brown, *Dare to Lead: Brave Work. Tough Conversations. Whole Hearts.* (New York: Random House, 2018); Turana Burke and Brené Brown, eds., *You Are Your Best Thing: Vulnerability, Shame Resilience, and the Black Experience* (New York: Random House, 2021); Brené Brown, *Atlas of the Heart: Mapping Meaningful Connection and the Language of Human Experience* (New York: Random House, 2021).

PART I

The Heart of Curricular Interventions

CHAPTER 1

Reenchanting Music History

SARA HAEFELI

Where is the wisdom we have lost in knowledge?
Where is the knowledge we have lost in information?
—T. S. Eliot

I start this chapter with three stories of disenchantment. First, during Black Lives Matter protests on my campus in 2015,[1] a student from my first semester survey course asked if we could discuss the protests in class. My immediate reaction was defensive, likely inspired by the value that I placed at the time on curricular content and high academic standards. Losing a single day of instruction sometimes meant losing an entire genre of music. I paused before saying "no" and realized that the student didn't want to take class time to talk about unrelated political events on campus, but that the protest on campus was connected to our classroom. What the students said during this discussion about the music history and theory curricula was not surprising: despite (or perhaps indeed *because of*) the fact that we were a majority white institution, they wanted far greater representation in what they studied, and that while they loved much of the repertoire, they didn't see how it connected to their lives. They worked hard to prepare for tests, and yet they felt unprepared to go out into the broader, working world of music and musicians, and they felt especially unprepared as future educators to teach a diverse student body. In short, they felt disenchanted by the white, male, Eurocentric content of the music history curriculum.

My second story comes from the third semester of our music history survey. After I introduced the Morton Feldman graphic notation piece *Projections I* a student provocatively asked, "Why are we studying *this* piece, when surely there were other similar examples—perhaps one by a woman or a composer of color?" In essence, she was asking, why this esoteric piece in an esoteric style by yet another dead white male composer? I began to explain that it was a groundbreaking work—one of the first graphic notation pieces—and Feldman is a great composer. I found myself caught in a trap created by my training in a teleological history of "great" music and tried to pedal back from the great man narrative. "But why *this* piece?" the student insisted. "I mean, what is the standard of 'greatness' when there aren't any rules?" The student had clearly seen through what I was offering as a parade of "greatness" in the survey course and wanted more.

The third story comes from my own experience as a graduate student studying Pierre Bourdieu's concept of cultural capital—the idea that the arts, perhaps especially high-art musical practices, are used to define class differences and divide people.[2] Studying Bourdieu made me struggle with the notion that if I devoted my life to the study of classical music I would be a tool of oppression. It opened my eyes to the moral complexities of teaching "good" music to students in order to make them "good" thinkers or "good" people. If knowledge of high-art music was used as a key to high society and a moneyed caste, I was perpetuating a system that continued to exclude and oppress people for whom a musical education was out of reach. I tried to ameliorate my discomfort by attempting to balance musicological research with arts advocacy, but never came to a satisfactory conclusion about my work vis-à-vis Bourdieu's concept of cultural capital.

My stories illustrate experiences of disenchantment, which are likely common among *both* faculty and students in music in higher education today. Although we currently lack survey data, anecdotal evidence suggests that many of our students lose their passion for music during their studies with us. Some are turned off by the competitive performance environment, often encouraged by studio professors and conductors trying to create the next virtuoso. Others find the sheer amount of work oppressive. But let's be frank, too many are disenchanted by their music history and theory classes that seem disconnected from their identities, or their "real" interest, which is making music—of all kinds, not just the kind taught from notation in our narrow curricula. And yet, they stand in conflict with some of their professors and peers who believe that they *need* the kind of exclusive, white, colonialist content represented in the vast majority of music history surveys in order to "make it" as elite performers or educators. This may be because, as they transition from adolescence to young adulthood and start to think deeply about the world around them and life beyond college, some experience a crisis, wondering why they are "wasting their time" on this esoteric art practice when there are *real* problems in the *real* world like political and economic injustice, inequality, and climate change.[3]

I have had to come to terms with the fact that while I was urging students to think more broadly and critically about music in its historical contexts, I was simultaneously reinforcing curriculum shaped by a white supremacist history[4] and standards of professionalism that "are heavily defined by white supremacy culture—or the systemic, institutionalized centering of whiteness."[5] As Paulo Freire would describe it, I had internalized the oppression that I had experienced as a student and had become the oppressor.[6]

My use of the word *disenchanted* in reference to my three case studies is designed to resonate with its use in the field of philosophy to describe our modern, secular, scientistic, and bureaucratic Western world.[7] To become reenchanted, then, is not to be deprived of agency—as one is when under a magical spell—but to be open to the numinous, the mystical, and the magical.[8] Perhaps ironically, this "reenchantment" can be found by bringing music back into its lived contexts, "on the ground," so to speak, through a process I refer to as "loving-as-knowing."[9]

This chapter is a preliminary attempt to change the oppressive dynamics of the music history curriculum by decentering the composer and the composition and placing musical practices into lived contexts. I hope to initiate a discussion about how to reenchant a study of music history by connecting the music to the students' real-world lives and identities, not just as musicians but as human beings situated in communities of practice. In what follows I first discuss fundamental problems with music history curricula based on flawed curricular design philosophies and the exclusionary history of our discipline. Second, I offer some philosophical solutions that might help us value multiple modes of knowing and being in the classroom, including a middle stance between objective cognition and subjective experience. I hope to encourage in my students an embodied cognition called *loving-as-knowing*. I assert that the solution to the disenchanting, scientistic studies of musical artifacts is to connect the musical artifact to the embodied communities that created or participated in the musical practice. Third, I offer a case study that demonstrates a more embodied and contextualized study that might inspire loving-as-knowing. Finally, I close with a proposal to consider what kind of human beings we want to support through our curricula, rather than simply what kind of content we hope to teach.

* * *

Schools of music are struggling to design curricula to address issues of diversity and inclusion[10] and to create pedagogical experiences that feel authentic, that are culturally and socially responsive, and that require active engagement. Our students come to us with a love of music and we want to deepen and enrich that love. When we shape curriculum around content, we assume that the curriculum is a structure within which the student has limited agency. Typically, the professor controls the course content and how students are to interact with the content, despite the fact that the goal is ostensibly for the student to develop independent, critical thought and autonomy.

I propose something different. Instead of thinking about the *structures* in which we interact with identity and difference, I propose focusing on the *agents*. Let me clarify: instead of asking simply, what do students need to *know*, I ask, what kinds of selves do we need to *be*? This existentialist turn prompts questions such as, How should students think about identity? How does one interact with difference in respectful, productive, creative ways? And what is the role of the instructor in these radically transformative educational experiences? These questions shift the focus from content acquisition to skill development, especially the skills of critical inquiry, social bonding, and engaging with ambiguity. I want to move beyond thinking about *what* we teach in order to foster the radical transformation called for by critical pedagogy scholars and demanded by our students.[11]

* * *

Despite the fact that current musicological research often engages questions of power and privilege, many of us teachers are still using the same materials and positivistic methods as those from the mid-twentieth century. We are most often concerned with fact-based narratives of basic concepts, major players, styles, genres, and forms. If we do veer from that curricular ideology and address larger issues of patronage, social change, identity, gender, and race, we do so merely through explication, not inquiry. We are quite good at teaching positivistic content and enculturating students in our own critical points of view, but we aren't as good at addressing the subjectivity of the musical experience. When we fail to explore the power of music to create identity, group bonding, and social status, we depoliticize, disembody, and disempower it.

The twentieth-century split of the field into ethnomusicology, music theory, and historical musicology has deprived us of tools to evaluate and articulate the value of all music as a shared, communal practice. We know that the historical repertoires we teach mean something (at least to someone, if not to us), but we have trouble articulating *how* and *to whom*. We have a hard time justifying time spent in this area of inquiry because we continue to value "coverage" of content and because its subjectivity makes it difficult to assess.[12]

When we focus on individual composers and masterworks in a more-or-less canonic narrative of music history, we tend to ignore the larger social contexts in which music is made and consumed. As a result, we reinforce the notion that music is disembodied and apolitical—an unfortunate bias that many of our students already have before entering our classrooms. Perhaps our pedagogical difficulties stem from the odd separation of the arts from the sciences we've inherited from the Enlightenment. Theologian N. T. Wright writes:

> I was brought up in a world where the arts constituted, as it were, the pretty border around the edge of reality rather than a window on reality. It was nice

to have good music, great art, fine architecture, even perhaps brilliant dancing . . . but within the modernism of my youth it didn't seem to integrate with real life in the world. The arts were recreation and relaxation for those who liked that kind of thing, but . . . we didn't expect them to impinge on how we organized the world, how we ran the country, how we did our work, or indeed how we understood and expressed our faith.[13]

Despite the postmodern turn, the modernist perception that the arts are largely decorative remains. Music, most especially art music, is separated from the "real world," and even though we suspect that it's essential to our well-being we can't quite articulate why or how.[14] Meaning has simply become a performative assertion and authenticity is suspect.[15]

In order to fight the suspicion that the study of music is not serious, intellectual work, we've developed scientistic methodologies and pedagogical habits that have by design relegated the appreciation of music to the subfield of aesthetics.[16] Thus our students come to us in a disenchanted crisis. Their love of music is not valued as an important outcome of their studies and therefore their studies seem disconnected or disembodied from their identity as musicians.

* * *

Both modernist and postmodernist approaches to the field focus on cognition-based approaches to music as text and both have shunted the sheer physical, embodied enjoyment of music to the side.[17] The philosopher of cognitive science Hanne De Jaegher proposes a solution to this problem by making a distinction between *cognition* and *knowing*. Cognition is abstract, computational, logical, individual, hegemonic, and based on a false idea of universals. We see cognition at work most clearly "when we see it dividing and conquering." While cognition may be part of knowing, there is a "realm of sophisticated knowing that has remained out of cognitive science's purview." Yet this kind of knowing guides "how we most often deal with the world, ourselves, and each other." De Jaegher suggests that this kind of knowing is at play when we know "what is going on with someone from seeing the way they lift their gaze," when we "make maple syrup," or when we "make ideas felt in poetry, music, or dancing." She argues that our "most sophisticated knowing is full of uncertainty, inconsistencies, ambiguity, [and] contradictions," and that truth is neither objective nor subjective, but relational.[18]

Building on De Jaegher's insights that knowledge is complex and truth is relational, I suggest we embrace the notion of *intersubjectivity*; that is, a kind of knowledge that is neither an objective truth (cognition) nor simply a subjective experience, but knowledge that can be verified because it is shared between and among individuals. Intersubjective knowledge is not fixed, but is always changing and developing as both the object and the subject develop and change. This kind of knowing goes beyond the subject of study as an object—an isolated entity to be analyzed and dismembered—to seeing the subject as part of a much larger system of interlocking social connections.[19] This kind of knowing is engaged, embodied, concrete, particular, participatory, and risky. Moreover, because it has to do with how we engage with others, it is inherently ethical.

Intersubjectivity can assist us in a return to the appreciation of music as De Jaegher sees "an existential overlap between loving and knowing."[20] She describes what I call *loving-as-knowing* as a dialectic between subject and object that is continually shaped and reshaped by changes in both. It requires "participatory sense-making" that moves us toward an explanation of "human knowing, with its dialectical approach to how people make sense together in moving, breathing, and living together."[21] Indeed, what T. S. Eliot calls "wisdom" in the epigraph is the kind of knowing that we develop when we learn a piece of music, especially in ensemble with others. Love inspires deep curiosity and a desire for discovery. Loving-as-knowing transcends the mind/body dichotomy and manifests as an embodied social interaction.[22] Indeed, to love music means to recognize that it is not an autonomous object but a deeply meaningful, shared, embodied, social experience.

What does it mean to teach music history by way of loving-as-knowing? How can the appeal to love as a valued form of knowledge be taught or applied in the classroom? The following are some preliminary suggestions for such an approach:

1. Reevaluate curricula and their purported *rigor* and *importance*. For all repertoires, I suggest we ask, What is its purpose? Why are we teaching it? Is it our job to teach repertoire? Chronology? Style recognition? Should we perhaps be teaching methodology and inquiry? We may each come to a different conclusion based on the needs of our students, our physical locations and resources, and our own sense of vocation and personal teaching philosophy.[23] We need to ask, Is the content of my course designed with intentionality, or is it shaped by tradition or a textbook?
2. Pair analysis with synthesis. As music historians, we've been good at taking things apart to teach our students how they work (either through objective musical analysis or through subjective deconstruction), but we have largely failed to put them back together to explore what they might mean. Too many students have left our classrooms hating the analysis of music because it has "ruined" pieces for them. Analysis becomes dissection or dismemberment when the artifact is taken from its lived, social context. Synthesis, however, makes connections between analysis and the sounded, embodied, contextual experience of the piece.
3. Draw from the numerous subfields that speak to multiple ways of knowing and demonstrating knowledge; not just ethnomusicology, but se-

miotics, gender studies, critical race studies, and disability studies that honor a variety of ways of seeing, hearing, knowing, and being.[24]

4. Teach creative inquiry.[25] Questions should be at the center of the student experience; indeed Paulo Freire asserts that inquiry and problem-based learning are the key to revealing inequities and injustices and to developing student agency.[26]
5. Consider how notation is a limiting frame that excludes diverse musical styles, especially those from marginalized communities. We should grieve the fact that students have musical "guilty pleasures" and are hesitant to admit them in the music history classroom. This hesitance to see all music as worthy of study and analysis is a sign of dis-integration and evidence of the mind-body dichotomy reinforced in higher education.[27]
6. Allow for the transcendent to enter in. We have separated God, Mystery, the Sacred, and Spirituality from the public (and academic) realm, which is, ironically, antithetical to the vast majority of repertoires we teach. Many of our students decided to seriously train in music because of transcendent experiences. Can we not affirm that desire in the classroom? After all, the words *inspire*, *enthuse*, and *enchant* all stem from references to the divine.[28]

* * *

I turn now to how I teach early Christian chant as an example of how I have attempted to reenchant the music history survey class by connecting the course content to embodied communities of practice and by bridging the gap between the students' world and the historical world of this repertoire.

I am uncomfortable with the traditional historical focus on chant for two reasons. First, I wonder why we spend so much time on "Gregorian" chant when there are endless chant repertoires including, just to name a few, the Muslim call to prayer, Tibetan chant, and Indigenous sacred song. The focus at the very beginning of the traditional music history survey on early Christian chant seems artificial given the diversity of other chant repertoires. I discuss this ideological problem with the students after listening to a variety of chants from all over the world. Many of my students from diverse faith backgrounds discuss how frustrating it is to be left out of the traditional music-historical narrative and feel affirmed that they are not alone in their discomfort.

My second issue is that the way we teach the repertoire has very little to do with how this body of melodies *functioned* in the early church and in the life of its practitioners. Indeed, other than how the chant was positioned within the liturgy, most studies of chant are not interested in *function*. Rather, the questions of the chant scholars of the early twentieth century were more about the creation, notation, and organization of the melodies. One exception is the chant scholar James McKinnon, who does indeed address the context of the earliest chant melodies. In his book *The Advent Project* McKinnon offers a fantastic description of a group of desert hermits, including a large number of both monks and nuns. According to McKinnon, "The central idea of the first desert monks was to put into literal practice the Pauline maxim 'to pray without ceasing' (1 Thes 5:17)." They achieved this with "an entirely new practice—psalmody 'in course,' or continuous psalmody, the saying at one time of extended portions of the Psalter in numerical order." The desert monks chanted the entire Book of Psalms from memory, not "as a splendid display of choral praise . . . but rather a mantra-like inducement to meditation."[29]

This captivating image of hundreds of desert monastics singing in order to achieve an altered state of consciousness excites the imagination. What might this have sounded like? How did they survive in the desert? Where would they have slept? Would they have moved or danced while chanting? Everything about this way of life—including their profound dedication—is almost wholly foreign to us. And yet we have heard, and maybe experienced, chant designed to induce a meditative or trance-like state, or participated in festivals in the desert, such as Burning Man or Electric Daisy Carnival, or in all-night raves. The image of the desert monastics "praying ceaselessly" contrasts sharply with descriptions of more aesthetic, musical praise practices that were part of the early Christian agape feast inside the church, highlighting the differences between repetitive psalm tones and the more musical antiphons.

I stress to the students here that pre-Humanist people did not conceive of themselves as individuals; instead, one defined oneself by one's family or clan. In a collectivist society, one is conditioned to express the opinions of the group (not of one's self) and conformity is of extreme importance.[30] I remind my students that when we think of chant as "expressive" or "sublime" we are employing an individualistic mindset and applying a Romantic conception of the role of the composer.

Instead of simply stressing the music-theoretical qualities of the chant repertoire, my students and I proceed to explore its function after it moves from the desert into the physical church. Yes, it is heightened prayer (as with the desert monastics), but it is also a way to project text throughout a large space (such as a Romanesque cathedral). We sing the chant together and discover what it feels like. My goal with this unit is to spark an historical imagination and ignite curiosity about the time period, about faith and devotion, about the connection between the voice and prayer, about music-induced altered states of consciousness, and about the nature of the individual within a collectivist society. They don't need to memorize the modes and the parts of the mass proper and ordinary because they have those facts at their fingertips.

In this example, the students have gone beyond an introduction to a repertoire or style to connect the music to the human beings involved in its production and reproduction. In other words, they are able to connect the *what* and the *how* to the *who*. They explore how the music is meaningful intersubjectively, and because I am not assessing cognition-based facts, they are free to explore loving-as-knowing. When students feel that they can bring their whole, authentic selves to the study of music—even music as esoteric as ancient chant—they feel cared for. And when students feel cared for and are emotionally engaged, they are more likely to learn.[31] If indeed they are inspired, enthused, or enchanted it is because they can see themselves reflected in the selves present in the historical record and they are able to actively participate in the exploration of the music's embodied, social, religious, and political implications.

* * *

Edward Said suggests that "inside the academy we should be able to discover and travel among other selves, other identities, other varieties of the human adventure."[32] Indeed, Said asserts that "we should regard knowledge as something for which to *risk* identity, and we should think of academic freedom as an invitation to give up on identity in the hope of understanding."[33] My students have challenged me to teach music as more than just a source of entertainment and status for the elite and instead as a way to inspire critical inquiry and social activism. We can do this by decentering authority wherever we find it. That shift is impossible if the curriculum only engages a body of *works* and not bodies of sounding *communities*.

If the metaphor of the migrant traveler is one that allows for agency and for a diversity of outcomes, then we can begin to give up control and recognize that learning is not something that instructors do for students but is what students do for themselves. We can, however, design learning outcomes and assessment practices that reflect what we want the students to experience in the classroom and beyond. Advocates of Freire's critical pedagogy understand that knowledge is power (or at least is not neutral vis-à-vis power structures), that teaching is a political act, and that teaching and learning are social justice in action. But love is a greater power, and it is love that lights the magical spark that inspires deep learning, which in turn leads to wisdom both within and beyond our classrooms.

Notes

Epigraph: T. S. Eliot, "Choruses from *The Rock*" (1934), *Collected Poems 1909–1962* (New York: Harcourt Brace and Company, 1968), 147.

1. See for example Mariana Fang, "Ithaca College Students Demand School's President Step Down in Mizzou-Inspired Protest," *Huffington Post*, November 11, 2015, https://www.huffpost.com; and Brandon Griggs, "The Next Missouri? Ithaca College Students Stage Walkout," *CNN*, November 11, 2015, https://www.cnn.com/.

2. Pierre Bourdieu, "The Forms of Capital," in *Handbook of Theory and Research for the Sociology of Education*, ed. J. Richardson (New York: Greenword Press, 1986), 241–58.

3. Research shows that in young adults the ability to think critically about complex or ambiguous ethical issues is one of the last developmental stages. See Richard Bonnie, Claire Stroud, Heather Breiner, eds., *Investing in the Health and Well-Being of Young Adults* (Washington, DC: National Academies Press, 2015), https://www.ncbi.nlm.nih.gov/books/NBK284782/.

4. See Loren Kajikawa, "The Possessive Investment in Classical Music," in *Seeing Race Again: Countering Colorblindness across the Curriculum*, ed. Kimberlé Crenshaw, Luke Charles Harris, Daniel Martinez HoSang, and George Lipsitz (Berkeley: University of California Press, 2019), 155–74; and Philip Ewell, "Music Theory and the White Racial Frame," *Music Theory Online* 26, no. 2 (September 2020), https://www.mtosmt.org/.

5. Aysa Gray, "The Bias of 'Professionalism' Standards," *Stanford Social Innovation Review*, June 4, 2019, https://ssir.org/.

6. See Paulo Freire, *Pedagogy of the Oppressed*, trans. Myra Bergman Ramos (New York: Continuum, 1970). For an excellent summary of Freire's thought see Kim Díaz, "Paulo Freire (1921–1997)," Internet Encyclopedia of Philosophy, accessed May 12, 2020, https://www.iep.utm.edu/freire/.

7. See for example Max Weber, "Wissenschaft als Beruf" [Science as a vocation], in *Gesammlte Aufsätze zur Wissenschaftslehre* (Tübingen: J.C.B. Mohr, 1922), 524–55.

8. See Anthony Cascardi, "The Critique of Subjectivity and the Re-Enchantment of the World," *Revue Internationale de Philosophie* 50, no. 196 (May 1996): 243–63.

9. Hanne De Jaegher, "Loving and Knowing: Reflections for an Engaged Epistemology," *Phenomenology and the Cognitive Sciences* 20 (2021): 847–70, https://doi.org/10.1007/s11097-019-09634-5.

10. See Ed Sarath et al., "Transforming Music Study from Its Foundations: A Manifesto for Progressive Change in the Undergraduate Preparation of Music Majors," College Music Society, November 2014, edited January 2016, https://www.music.org/pdf/pubs/tfumm/TFUMM.pdf.

11. The assertion that *how* we teach is more important than *what* we teach is not new. See Jacques Rancière, *The Ignorant Schoolmaster: Five Lessons in Intellectual Emancipation*, trans. Kristin Ross (Stanford, CA: Stanford University Press, 1991).

12. The continued commitment to "coverage" may be due to a misunderstanding of NASM standards. "NASM advocates for no particular position regarding the overall model for undergraduate music history content," but "traditions and habits tend to move us toward similar models of curricular content" (Don Gibson, "The Curricular Standards of NASM and Their Impact on Local Decision Making," *Journal of Music History Pedagogy* 5, no. 2 [2015]: 76).

13. N. T. Wright, *Surprised by Scripture* (New York: HarperCollins, 2014), 198.

14. Again, subdisciplinary divides have largely kept us from learning from our peers in music cognition and music therapy.

15. Karl Marx, Sigmund Freud, and Friedrich Nietzsche (the so-called "Masters of Suspicion") base interpretations of art on underlying maladies. See Rita Felski, "Critique

and the Hermeneutics of Suspicion," *M/C Journal* 15, no. 1 (2012), http://journal.media-culture.org.au/.

16. I am using "appreciation" in both senses of the term: that is, the aesthetic value of music as well as the kind of introductory course most often taught to nonmajors. Musicologist Carl Engel (1883–1944) "urged educators to think of musicology . . . as a science and to reject music appreciation." Engel wrote in a 1925 article in the *Musical Quarterly*, "Imagine a university, devising courses in law for non-practicing, non-professional students of law!" Quoted in Tamara Levitz, "The Musicological Elite," *Current Musicology* 102 (spring 2018): 29. I also want to recognize the fraught history of music appreciation courses that sacralized musical listening; nineteenth-century values of taste and morality; and reified notions of race, gender, and class. See Julia Chybowski, "Developing American Taste: A Cultural History of the Early Twentieth-Century Music Appreciation Movement," PhD diss., University of Wisconsin-Madison, 2008.

17. Many scholars who employ poststructural frames have simply shifted the object of study and the realm of knowledge from the music (as an autonomous object) to the social theory. Adam Krims, "Disciplining Deconstruction (For Music Analysis)," *19th-Century Music* 21, no. 3 (spring 1998): 304, JSTOR.

18. De Jaegher, "Loving and Knowing," 848.

19. See Hanne De Jaegher and Ezequiel Di Paolo, "Participatory Sense-Making: An Enactive Approach to Social Cognition," *Phenomenology and the Cognitive Sciences* 6, no. 4 (2007): 485–507.

20. De Jaegher, "Loving and Knowing," 862.

21. De Jaegher, 849.

22. De Jaegher and Di Paolo find that "social agents can coordinate their sense-making in social encounters; in other words, they participate in each other's sense-making" ("Participatory Sense-Making," 497).

23. For localizing music curricula, see James Ryan O'Leary and Danielle Ward-Griffin, "Digging in Your Own Backyard: Archives in the Music History Classroom," *Journal of Music History Pedagogy* 7, no. 2 (2017): 1–18; Amanda Black and Andrea Bohlman, "Resounding the Campus: Pedagogy, Race, and the Environment," *Journal of Music History Pedagogy* 8, no. 1 (2017): 6–27; and Crystal Peebles, "Engaging Community in a Twentieth-Century Analysis Class," *Engaging Students: Essays in Music Pedagogy* 5, http://flipcamp.org/engagingstudents5/essays/peebles.html.

24. As a study of how signs can carry meaning, semiotics can help describe the "social effects of music, art, expressive culture, and people's myriad ways of experiencing the world" (Thomas Turino, "Signs of Imagination, Identity, and Experience: A Peircian Semiotic Theory for Music," *Ethnomusicology* 43, no. 2 [spring-summer 1999]: 222). Gender, critical race, and disability studies resist knowledge based on dichotomies and divisions. See Ellen Koskoff, "Gender, Power, and Music," in *A Feminist Ethnomusicology: Writings on Music and Gender* (Chicago: University of Illinois Press, 2014), 76–89; Richard Schur, "Critical Race Theory, Signifyin,' and Cultural Ownership" in *Parodies of Ownership: Hip-Hop Aesthetics and Intellectual Property Law* (Ann Arbor: University of Michigan Press, 2009), 24–41; and Blake Howe, Stephanie Jensen-Moulton,

Joseph N. Straus, Jennifer Iverson, Jessica A. Holmes, Michael B. Bakan, et al., "On the Disability Aesthetics of Music," *Journal of the American Musicological Society* 69, no. 2 (2016): 525–63, https://doi.org/10.1525/jams.2016.69.2.525. Neurodiversity studies challenge, among other things, "brain-bound cognition"; rather, cognition is dynamic, "out-of-the-head," and contextualized in the world. See Inês Hipólito, Daniel Hutto, and Jick Chown, "Understanding Autistic Individuals: Cognitive Diversity Not Theoretical Deficit," in *Neurodiversity Studies: A New Critical Paradigm*, ed. Hanna Bertilsdotte Rosqvist, Nick Chown, and Anna Stenning (New York: Routledge, 2020), 206.

25. See Sara Haefeli, "From Answers to Questions: Fostering Student Creativity and Engagement in Research and Writing," *Journal of Music History Pedagogy* 7, no. 1 (2016): 7.

26. See Freire, *Pedagogy of the Oppressed*, 73, 77.

27. See Ivan Marquez, "Knowledge of Being v. Practice of Becoming in Higher Education: Overcoming the Dichotomy in the Humanities," *Arts and Humanities in Higher Education* 5, no. 2 (2006): 147–61. Marquez argues: "Moving from an almost exclusive focus on knowledge of being to a more balanced one that dissolves the dichotomy between knowledge of being and practice of becoming . . . would allow us to reorganize universities as places where people are given the tools and are trained to become somebody, and to become actors in their lives and in the bigger social context" (159–60).

28. Inspiration: "from Old French *inspiracion* 'inhaling, breathing in.'" Enthusiasm: "from Greek *enthousiasmos* 'divine inspiration, enthusiasm (produced by certain kinds of music, etc.),' from *enthousiazein* 'be inspired or possessed by a god, be rapt, be in ecstasy,' . . . from *en* 'in' + *theos* 'god.'" Enchantment: "'act of magic or witchcraft; use of magic; magic power,' from Old French *encantement*, 'magical spell; song, concert, chorus.'" (Douglas Harper, *Online Etymology Dictionary*, accessed June 2, 2020, https://www.etymonline.com/.)

29. James McKinnon, *The Advent Project: The Later Seventh-Century Creation of the Roman Mass Proper* (Berkeley: University of California Press, 2000), 37.

30. See Harry Triandis and Michele Gelfand, "A Theory of Individualism and Collectivism," in *Handbook of Theories of Social Psychology*, ed. Paul Van Lange, Arie Kruglanski, and Tory Higgins (Los Angeles: Sage, 2012), 498–520.

31. See Robert C. Lagueux, "Inverting Bloom's Taxonomy: The Role of Affective Responses in Teaching and Learning," *Journal of Music History Pedagogy* 3, no. 2 (2013): 119–50.

32. Edward Said, "Identity, Authority, and Freedom: The Potentate and the Traveler," in *The Future of Academic Freedom*, ed. Louis Menand (Chicago: University of Chicago Press, 1996), 227.

33. Said, 227.

CHAPTER 2

Teaching Approaches to Race through Music

A Timely Example from the American South

MOLLY M. BRECKLING

On April 10, 2018, Assistant City Manager of Newnan, Georgia, Hasco Craver, issued a press release regarding an upcoming event, stating:

> The City of Newnan received a Pavilion Rental Agreement from the National Socialist Movement.... Upon review for adherence to stated policies, the City of Newnan executed the Agreement.... The National Socialist Movement [NSM] will be hosting a political rally between 3:00 and 5:00 pm in Greenville Street Park on Saturday, April 21, 2018.[1]

The primary concern stemmed from the fact that the NSM claimed to be the "largest and most active" Neo-Nazi, white supremacist group in the United States.[2] News of the gathering broke days earlier, but this was the city's first public acknowledgment of the event.

A small city of roughly 40,000, Newnan is experiencing a period of exponential growth. Between 2000 and 2010, the population doubled, mostly due to its proximity to Atlanta. As that urban center continues to grow, further-out towns are evolving into suburbs.[3] So, while Newnan is a small southern town, its people do not all conform to the typical southern stereotypes of being "less modernized, less educated, more racist."[4]

Public outcry soon indicated that Newnanites had concerns about the rally.[5] Resident Rachel Cox started a petition for the city to cancel the event; it was signed by over 51,000 people, more than the city's actual population. The petition stated that allowing the rally would make Newnan "toxic for everyone involved" and "seem unwelcoming and hateful with the implied support of Neo-Nazism."[6] Signer Matthew Holl wrote, "This does not represent

Newnan at all. Newnan is being taken advantage of by [the group's] rights [to free speech]." Ronald Smith stated, "Love is greater than hate. Hate must be confronted with love."[7] Nonetheless, the city could not deny the NSM their constitutional right to assemble without possible legal ramifications, as they had paid the fees and completed the necessary paperwork. So, despite community opposition, the rally would take place.

Chosen to commemorate the birth of Adolf Hitler on April 20, the proposed rally date of April 21 marked over seven months since a demonstration in Charlottesville, Virginia, led to violence between those attending the Unite the Right Rally and counterprotesters supporting Antifa, a national conglomeration of militant left-wing antifascism groups. Clashes in Charlottesville culminated in the murder of 32-year-old Heather Heyer and left sixty-five people injured. Citizens of Newnan worried that this rally might also end in violence. *The Newnan Times-Herald* allowed citizens to express concerns, including "This will cost the city several thousands," and "We should be holding our city to a higher standard, one that will never support an agenda of racism and violence."[8]

Tensions increased, even as officials detailed plans to keep citizens and businesses safe. Residents were urged to stay home, and businesses were permitted to close the day of the rally.[9] Seven hundred law enforcement officials were brought in from around the state, and the park reserved for the rally was made inaccessible by car.[10] All Newnanites could do was hold their collective breath and wait.

On April 16, just five days before the rally, the winners of the 2018 Pulitzer Prizes were announced. Among those recognized was an unlikely candidate; rapper Kendrick Lamar won the Music prize for his album *DAMN*.[11] This was the first time in its seventy-five-year history that the award went to a composition of neither Western classical music nor jazz.[12] Almost immediately the Internet exploded with both celebration and protest.

The backlash against the award was painstakingly covered under the Twitter handle @NewMusicDrama. The account and its responses to the negative comments made clear that it supported the decision and found contrary arguments ignorant and offensive.[13] Some protesting against the decision argued that awarding a rap album would diminish the reputation of the Pulitzer:

- "The Pulitzer Prize now has no meaning in classical music. It's over."
- "Kendrick Lamar didn't deserve to win a Pulitzer. Congratulations, America, this is why we can't have nice things."

While not explicitly racist, these kinds of comments clearly sought to maintain the status quo of what bell hooks calls the "white supremacist capitalist patriarchy," dominant in Western art for centuries.[14] Arguments debating the aesthetic differences between rap and Western classical music could not help betraying racial bias.[15]

Still other comments regarding the Pulitzer were more blatantly racist:

- "Rap music is GARBAGE, and a purveyor of it winning the Pulitzer is the ultimate in philistinism."
- "Provocative? Ridiculous? Obscene? Racist? This is considered 'music'? No wonder the Pulitzer has remained a joke (cough—Obama—) and America is in such a state. Appalling."
- "There's one. Great talent. Let's get 'blown' with the homies. Great motivation for kids. Let's give him a Pulitzer."

This latter type of response, combined with the tensions already being felt on campus due to the forthcoming rally, compelled me to bring up the Pulitzer in my music history classroom as a first step in introducing systems of oppression to my students. In fact, the decision to do so was motivated directly by the very weight of the rally in our community. I describe the rally in such detail because the context of my teaching, as I realized, was so incredibly important. Many of my students, after all, were in crisis—they did not know how to position themselves or what would become of our community. And everything they were learning in their college classes, I discovered, was being learned against the backdrop of this very immediate calamity in Newnan. This is, of course, the root of culturally responsive teaching.

In 2017 I lived in Newnan, but I was an instructor at the University of West Georgia, a small public university of approximately 14,000 students in Carrollton, twenty miles to the north. The student body is highly diverse. Fifty percent of students identify as white, thirty-five percent as Black, and seven percent as Latinx, with the remaining eight percent divided among the Multi-Ethnic, Asian, Indigenous, and Other demographics. The music department is relatively small, with approximately ninety undergraduate and twenty-five graduate students enrolled in a typical year. During the spring 2018 term, Music History II had eighteen students enrolled: ten white and eight Black. While little had been said in my presence about the coming rally, I worried about how its proximity might impact the students of color in my classes. Yet it seemed inappropriate to bring the rally up in a music history classroom without context and presumptuous to assume that BIPOC students would feel threatened. Still, I felt an intense responsibility to create a safe space to discuss concerns about the rally, so I decided to use the Lamar Pulitzer controversy as a springboard for a broader discussion about racism in music and in our own backyard. This allowed me to keep the discussion relevant to the course while opening the door to any student concerns.

My interest in this experience lies in unpacking the impulse to tackle these local and heated issues head-on in the context of a music class, following a context-driven focus that is characteristic of critical whiteness approaches in education. When these events happened, I had no illusions of being qualified to teach racial issues. I merely felt an instinctive urge to care for students who might feel attacked by the upcoming demonstration and used the Kendrick Lamar controversy as a subject-appropriate gateway to bring the topic into my classroom. My intent in writing this chapter is not to declare any kind of expertise, but simply to encourage white instructors who struggle with "white fragility" to acknowledge their white positionality, and while living with the complexities, also allow it to inform teaching practices of our chosen fields in meaningful ways.[16] In my experience, our BIPOC students will appreciate us making an effort to reach out compassionately, as long as we are honest and open about our "not-yetness" when it comes to our lived experiences and sophisticated understandings of critical race studies.[17] It also seems imperative in these moments that we recognize the growing body of literature on critical whiteness that is now essential reading for those instructors interested in augmenting their pedagogy in this culturally responsive way.[18]

Not only did I lack training in teaching about racial issues prior to this exchange, this exercise could easily have backfired in the classroom and in my career. As has been widely publicized regarding trigger warnings, some students have been conditioned to fear discomfort in the classroom, leading some instructors to avoid controversial but important topics.[19] As a contingent employee, my contract was renewed yearly. An exercise designed to build my students' comfort could have been misinterpreted and elicited complaints from white students of racial bias or insensitivity that administrators could weaponize against me. These fears are simply the reality of contingent faculty employment. Indeed, I told a colleague what I intended for class that day, and he advised against taking the risk. Nonetheless, I was instinctively responding to what felt like an urgent need to care for my students who I perceived as being attacked in both their neighborhood by the rally and their future career field by the Pulitzer backlash.[20]

Two days after Lamar's Pulitzer prize was announced we started our in-class discussion. I began by asking if students had heard about the award and the surrounding controversy. Responses were mixed, so I read some of the comments. We then examined the Pulitzer rules regarding the music award to learn how prestigious awards are judged, and determine whether or not the rules made any distinctions about style, message, or significance of the music chosen for the award.[21] Clearly *DAMN* conformed to the surprisingly basic requirements for entry, which say nothing about specific musical styles. This part of the process echoed debates over the merits of art vs. popular music, which we had already discussed in other moments in history and further contextualized the Lamar controversy.[22]

We then discussed the problematic history of the Pulitzer. *DAMN* was the first winning piece that was an example of neither Western classical nor jazz music. We discussed Wynton Marsalis's win for his 1997 jazz oratorio *Blood on the Fields* (the first jazz award).[23] We also discussed Duke Ellington being denied the prize in 1965, despite unanimous approval from the nominating committee, when the board claimed they had no suitable candidates and gave no award.[24] Prestigious awards such as the Pulitzer helped to uphold the hegemony of Eurocentric art for decades, and the class found it troubling that over thirty years passed before the disgraceful racist decision regarding Ellington would be recognized.[25]

Our next question was "Why *DAMN* in particular?" Answering this question required a deep dive into the work. As I had only listened to the album a few times, many of my students knew the music better than I did; so I allowed them to guide our critical listening. The album, taken as a complete work, has recurring themes and a structure that take listeners on a guided tour through Lamar's life—his childhood on the streets of Compton; his brushes with violence, gangs, and drugs; his life as a celebrity, dealing with fame and wealth; his spiritual life, and ultimately, hope. Students observed that five of the album's songs include variations of the lyric "Ain't nobody prayin' for me," identified as a kind of leitmotiv. They viewed the concept album like a song cycle, exploring a single topic (poverty and violence in urban black neighborhoods) from multiple perspectives (fear, anger, despair, a call to action, and the centrality of faith and family).

The Pulitzer board called *DAMN* "a virtuosic song collection unified by its vernacular authenticity and rhythmic dynamism that offers affecting vignettes capturing the complexity of modern African-American life."[26] We agreed; it is indeed complex and profound in its depiction of Lamar's life, and, though we disagreed on the message's universality, as few could relate to the described events, we generally determined that the message of *DAMN* was important for its time with its depictions of street violence and references to the Black Lives Matter movement.

The more complex and surprising part of the conversation regarded the award backlash. Students were generally alarmed by the racist comments, but they were quick to denounce these responses as insignificant and lacking in credibility.[27] One student proposed that giving Lamar the award in the first place was perhaps merely a token gesture in response to the Black Lives Matter movement rather than a genuine recognition of quality, and she suggested that the award might be a form of racist tokenism. Another intriguing discussion stemmed from implications that awarding the Pulitzer to a rap album cheapened the award or symbolized a loss of recognition for Western classical music. As music majors, these students are devoting their education to an art that is consistently losing market share and exposure. How will opening the Pulitzer field to popular music impact the future of art music? I was surprised by the lack of concern my students appeared to show at this idea. I learned that my students see less division between art music and popular music than those of previous generations did. This is supported by a 2014 report from the College Music Society, which advocates for the integration of traditional Eurocentric music study with global and popular techniques to encourage students to "discover the structural, textural, design, and aesthetic dimensions of the sonic experience defined as music."[28]

When our two-day discussion ended, I had to wonder if choosing to bring this topic into my classroom was the right thing to do. My intentions might have been good, but did the students see it that way? Did they see the links between this incident in the cultural world and the events about to occur in their neighboring town? I purposefully did not mention the Newnan rally, simply because I wanted to see if they would make the connection on their own. Ultimately, I asked students to comment on the class sessions and whether they saw the parallels with the rally, giving them the opportunity to do so via e-mail or anonymously. While only a handful of students took the time to respond, those who did largely reported finding the discussion respectful and useful. They wrote:

> I wholeheartedly believe that more than just artists, we are people. Sometimes we hide behind our passions and talents rather than challenge the world around us.... The discussion we had in class was very respectful and appropriate, but even if it wasn't, it is necessary to create these dialogues. I think the way you chose to handle social topics was very refreshing and underrated; we have to be people of humanities and not robots that just have useless knowledge.... How can we truly call ourselves musicians without exploring more than what may be standard or in some way doesn't cause a certain degree of discomfort even outside just music?
>
> The discussion we had in class was very productive, and I enjoyed it greatly. The basis of social justice was portrayed well through Kendrick Lamar's album, and talking over some lyrics of his songs and interpreting the meanings behind his words really opened a window into the views of generations of black Americans in the US and the issues that have been/are being faced with. I believe as a class we came up with reasonable conclusions to support the ideas and themes Kendrick Lamar was delivering.
>
> Kendrick Lamar winning the Pulitzer is an example of development not only of what we define as art, but how we interact with it. It is easy to dispar-

age a piece of popular music with, "That's not real music," but what does that mean? On the rally: The first issue that comes up in this discussion is likely for most free speech. As long as no laws are being broken, people are allowed to peaceably assemble for whatever cause they like constitutionally. However, what if the cause is something considered by most to be a hateful one? The issue then becomes whether it is the state's right to silence hate speech. I don't think it is, deplorable a cause as white supremacy may be to me.

I do not know how the activity was perceived by students who didn't respond to my request for feedback. Further, given that this exercise was connected to the urgency of a local event, I have never repeated it.[29] That said, I have used other opportunities in popular music culture to launch discussions in my classroom, such as covering the Halftime Show from the 2020 Super Bowl, featuring Jennifer Lopez and Shakira, as an act of political commentary in my World Music class for general education students. I'm finding that students appreciate the spontaneity and timeliness of discussing something in class that recently took place in "the outside world" that adds to their understanding of our other course material.

For those who would hesitate to bring a topic like this to their classroom, I would not claim to be an expert on inclusive pedagogy. Before this experience, I believed I was providing a welcoming space in my classroom for all, but I had little experience to really even know what that would look like. Since the Lamar class discussion, I have devoted more effort to learning the best methods for approaching students with sensitive issues.[30] I have made it my mission to learn as much as I can about inclusive pedagogy. Some of this work has been in my own reading and with colleagues at my university.[31] Other opportunities have arisen from workshops operated virtually during the pandemic.[32] No matter how much I try to educate myself, however, I will never fully understand what daily life is like for my BIPOC students. The most important task for me as an educator who strives for social justice in the classroom is to learn as much as I can about ways of life that differ from my own and how to honor and recognize those differences.

Bringing topics of racial injustice to the classroom has positive benefits. Studies at Stanford University and the University of Texas at Austin have shown that students belonging to a nondominant group (racial minorities, the LGBTQ community, first-generation college students, the differently abled, etc.), when told during their education that they belong on campus, are more likely to perform as well as their peers from dominant groups than students never encouraged in this manner.[33] Ideally, I like to think that I show all of my students that they are fully equipped to succeed in my classroom and in life every day, but actually taking time to confront head-on the difficulties some students face makes meaningful and explicit my dedication to minoritized students in an environment of care. Sociologist Susan Chase further notes that true inclusivity isn't possible without continued, sustained dialogue. Faculty and students from all populations must be willing to openly and honestly communicate their feelings and educate members of both dominant and non-dominant groups about the issues they face and how these issues can be brought to the fore and discussed in a respectful and productive fashion.[34]

Talking about racial conflict is never easy; I suspect that most people believe their intentions are inherently good and therefore we believe we would never intentionally hurt someone else, but when an instructor claims that they "don't see race," they disregard the experiences of another human being.[35] As much as we might wish to live in a post-racial society, race inherently carries implications for opportunity and acceptance.[36] Instructors may worry that opening a classroom dialogue about race will make students uncomfortable, but to ignore racial diversity amplifies the messages that people of color have received for generations: that they are somehow less than their white neighbors and unworthy of recognition for their achievements. The only way we can learn to be more inclusive is to recognize that we have not been inclusive enough. As William Cheng writes, "If instructors and students are willing to go there—there, meaning beyond the sanitized conventions of polite pedagogy—even musical artifacts from long ago can impart urgent strategies for listening and speaking up."[37]

One further difficulty stems from what Kat Griffith calls the "savior complex," the notion that members of a dominant group must claim responsibility for fighting for the rights of the marginalized, rather than supporting the efforts of those working for their own rights.[38] It is startlingly easy to confuse compassion and activism with condescension. As Judith James writes, "The job of the culturally sensitive human being is to appreciate the other's experience from where he or she is positioned, not from my own privileged position."[39] To want others to enjoy the same opportunities that you enjoy is kind, but to assume that your position of privilege is the only way to win those opportunities is hubris.

The best way to learn about students is to simply ask. My students and I have shared laughs when I asked about a dreadlocks sponge or why some students don't eat casseroles. My students of color have been willing to share their culture with me, as long as I show genuine respect for what they tell me and continue to do my own work on learning about inclusivity. Social psychologists refer to this kind of thinking as "solidarity practice," which Emile Durkheim described as "the interdependence of different individuals . . . [allowing for] a different basis of social life emerging, . . . leaving room for individual differences."[40]

Obviously, in the time that has passed since this class activity took place, the murders of figures such as Breonna Taylor and George Floyd have further galvanized the Black Lives Matter movement and brought the issues of police brutality and systemic racism into even greater focus than they were in 2018. It is impossible to imagine how differently a rally such as that in Newnan would be received if it were announced in today's climate; however, given that NSM leader Jeff Shoep was found guilty of charges of criminal conspiracy in connection with the rally in Charlottesville, the movement has essentially collapsed.

But, what happened with the NSM rally in Newnan? About the best result anyone could hope for. First, a social media group called #NewnanStrong appeared.[41] Citizens of all races banded together to resist the hatred heading our way. St. Smyrna Baptist Church worked with Mayor Cynthia Jenkins to plan a unity gathering, including speakers from the Newnan Youth Council, the Atlanta Muslim Center, and the local Hindu community.[42] The community and Chamber of Commerce planned a counterrally to take place the night before the NSM event. Local downtown businesses stayed open late on Friday evening, and people came together to help them recoup the income they would lose from closing on Saturday.[43] The event became a type of street party. And, fittingly, there was music. At least seven local bands and DJs volunteered to perform for free at the event, lending it a truly celebratory feel.[44] Local daycare centers took children to Greenville Street Park, where the rally was going to occur, and armed them with sidewalk chalk. By the time the Neo-Nazis arrived, the sidewalk on which they spouted their words of hate had been covered with images of hearts and rainbows and words of love and acceptance.

The permit allowed for one hundred, but there were only about twenty-five NSM attendees at the Newnan rally. One hundred Antifa counterprotesters also appeared, and the city had prepared for them, too. Reimplementing a state law from 1951 to discourage Ku Klux Klan activity, wearing of masks in public assemblies became illegal. Eight counterprotesters were arrested for refusing to remove masks.[45] Some news sources interpreted these arrests as evidence that local police were siding with the NSM, but these protesters were told that masks were against state law, yet they still refused to remove them.[46]

When all was said and done, the rally didn't amount to much. It cost the city of Newnan around $110,000 for the added law enforcement and security measures, but, had the rally turned violent, the financial and emotional cost would undoubtedly have been much higher. The outcome doesn't erase the pain caused by groups like the National Socialist Movement. People were still hurt by the white-supremacist rhetoric surrounding this event. We can write this event off as "crazy people, shaking their fists at the sky," but, as Kendrick Lamar states in the song "PRIDE," "Race barriers make inferior you and I." Collectively, we can and should use our pedagogy and course design to help people (students, colleagues, and community members) accept one another and address issues of social inequity. And if we don't feel we have the tools, find them, along with the courage to use them.

Notes

1. "Newnan Officials Release Statement Regarding Planned White Nationalist Rally," Fox 5 Atlanta, April 10, 2018, http://www.fox5atlanta.com/news/.

2. "The NSM: America's Nazi Party," https://www.nsm88.org/about.

3. "Newnan Georgia Population," World Population Review, http://worldpopulationreview.com/us-cities/newnan-ga-population/, 2018 data. As of 2017, 51% of the people of Newnan were born in Georgia, 39% in other states, and 10% in other countries.

4. Todd Leopold, "The South: Not All Bubbas and Banjos," *CNN*, April 12, 2012, https://www.cnn.com/.

5. Winston Skinner, "Cowetans: We Wish Neo-Nazis Would Stay Away," *Newnan Times-Herald*, April 7, 2018, https://times-herald.com/.

6. Rachel Cox, "Newnan: Do Not Host the National Socialist Movement's Rally," Change.org, accessed July 26, 2019, https://www.change.org/.

7. Cox.

8. "Sound Off," *Newnan Times-Herald*, April 11, 2018, https://times-herald.com/.

9. "City Braces for Proposed White-Supremacist Rally," *Newnan Times-Herald*, April 5, 2018, https://times-herald.com/.

10. Jacey Fortin, "Neo-Nazi Rally Draws about Two Dozen People and Upends a Small Georgia City," *New York Times*, April 21, 2018, https://www.nytimes.com/.

11. Joe Coscarelli, "Kendrick Lamar Wins Pulitzer in 'Big Moment for Hip-Hop,'" *New York Times*, April 16, 2018, https://www.nytimes.com/.

12. Coscarelli.

13. Alyssa Rosenberg, "What the Classical-Music World Can Learn from Kendrick Lamar's Pulitzer Prize," *Washington Post*, April 18, 2018, https://www.washingtonpost.com/act-four/.

14. bell hooks, *Feminism Is for Everybody* (Cambridge, MA: South End Press, 2000), 4.

15. Alex Ross, "Toscanini, Trump, and Classical Music as a Tool of Power," *New Yorker*, July 12, 2017, https://www.newyorker.com/.

16. "White Fragility" has been coined by Robin DiAngelo to describe the discomfort white people experience when confronted by issues related to racism. See *White Fragility: Why It's So Hard for White People to Talk about Racism* (Boston: Beacon Press, 2018), 2.

17. Kevin Gannon generously frames "not-yetness" as a state of becoming and of hope in his *Radical Hope: A Teaching Manifesto* (Morgantown: West Virginia University Press, 2020). Gannon builds on the concept laid out by Amy Collier and Jen Ross in "For Whom, and for What? Not-yetness and Thinking beyond Open Content," *Open Praxis* 9, no. 1 (2017): 7–16.

18. See DiAngelo, *White Fragility*, but also James Jupp and Timothy Lensmire, "Second-Wave White Teacher Identity Studies: Toward Complexity and Reflexivity in the

Racial Conscientization of White Teachers," *International Journal of Qualitative Studies in Education* 29, no. 8 (2016): 985–88; G. Gay, *Culturally Responsive Teaching: Theory, Research, and Practice*, 2nd ed. (New York: Teachers College, 2010), among many others.

19. Emma Pettit, "How 3 Professors Use Trigger Warnings in Their Classrooms," *Chronicle of Higher Education*, September 6, 2016, https://www.chronicle.com/; Scott Kaufman, "Are Trigger Warnings Actually Helpful?" *Scientific American*, April 5, 2019, https://blogs.scientificamerican.com/.

20. Bettina Love identifies the act of using "intersections of privilege, leverage . . . , power and support [and a willingness to risk those things] to stand in solidarity and confront anti-Blackness" as being a "coconspirator." *We Want to Do More Than Survive: Abolitionist Teaching and the Pursuit of Educational Freedom* (Boston: Beacon Press, 2019), 117.

21. Entries must have been premiered—either publicly performed or commercially released—during the calendar year in question, and submissions must be either in the form of a musical score with premiere details included or a recording.

22. "Colloquy: Musicology beyond Borders?," convened by Tamara Levitz, demonstrates how even musicologists struggle to distinguish between high and low art (*Journal of the American Musicological Society* 65, no. 3 [2012]: 821–61).

23. Maureen Anderson reflects on long-held racist connotations of anti-jazz rhetoric in "The White Reception of Jazz in America," *African American Review* 38 (2004): 135–45.

24. "The 1999 Pulitzer Prize Winner in Special Awards and Citations: Duke Ellington," Pulitzer Prizes, accessed July 26, 2019, https://www.pulitzer.org/winners/duke-ellington.

25. Ellington was awarded a posthumous Special Citation by the Pulitzer Board in 1999 "in recognition of his musical genius, which evoked aesthetically the principles of democracy through the medium of jazz and thus made an indelible contribution to art and culture" ("1999 Pulitzer Special Awards").

26. "2018 Pulitzer Prizes," Pulitzer Prizes, April 18, 2018, https://www.pulitzer.org/prize-winners-by-year/2018.

27. We had not yet seen comments from within the classical music world, such as those in Randall Roberts, "Kendrick Lamar's Pulitzer Prize Sparks Lively—And at Times Snobby—Conversations on the Aesthetics of Music," *Los Angeles Times*, April 18, 2018, https://www.latimes.com/.

28. Ed Sarath et al., "Transforming Music Study from Its Foundations: A Manifesto for Progressive Change in the Undergraduate Preparation of Music Majors," College Music Society, November 2014, edited January 2016, https://www.music.org/pdf/pubs/tfumm/TFUMM.pdf.

29. At the 2019 national meeting of the Society for American Music, a panel about *DAMN* featured scholarship by Loren Kajikawa, Graham Peterson, and Chris Benham. Their papers would provide powerful tools for teaching *DAMN*.

30. Benjamin Bowser, *Confronting Diversity Issues on Campus* (Newbury Park, CA: Sage Publications, 1993); Howard Ball, S. D. Berkowitz, and Mbulelo Mzamane, eds., *Multicultural Education in Colleges and Universities: A Transdisciplinary Approach*

(Mahwah, NJ: Lawrence Erlbaum Associates, 1998); Jane Bolgatz, *Talking Race in the Classroom* (New York: Teachers College Press, 2005); Susan Chase, *Learning to Speak, Learning to Listen: How Diversity Works on Campus* (Ithaca: Cornell University Press, 2010); Judith James and Nancy Peterson, eds., *White Women Getting Real about Race: Their Stories about What They Learned Teaching in Diverse Classrooms* (Sterling, VA: Stylus, 2013).

31. In spring 2019, I participated in a Faculty Learning Community on Inclusive Pedagogy, meeting monthly with other instructors committed to finding strategies for making our classrooms safe, welcoming, and inclusive places where all students can work, learn, and succeed. Guiding our discussions was *Intersectionality in Action: A Guide for Faculty and Campus Leaders for Creating Inclusive Classrooms and Institutions*, ed. Brooke Barnett and Peter Felten (Sterling, VA: Stylus, 2016).

32. In summer 2020, I completed a minicourse with the Gardner Institute entitled The Humanity of Inclusive Practices.

33. Alta Mauro and Angela Mazaris, "Student Recruitment and Retention at the Intersections: A Case for Capacity Building," in *Intersectionality in Action* (2016), 9.

34. Chase, *Learning to Speak*, 167–97.

35. Judith M. James discusses the trappings of wanting to appear nonracist and overcompensating in "For the Love of Clowns," in *White Women Getting Real about Race*, ed. James and Peterson, 17–32.

36. Part of a practice that Charles Mills calls the "epistemologies of ignorance," white people (and institutions), believing that blatant racism is the most potent kind, seek to stamp it out, and then proclaim that their racism no longer exists. Mills, "White Ignorance," in *Race and Epistemologies of Ignorance*, ed. Shannon Sullivan and Nancy Tuana (Albany: State University of New York Press, 2007), 11–38.

37. William Cheng, *Just Vibrations: The Purpose of Sounding Good* (Ann Arbor: University of Michigan Press, 2016), 48.

38. Kat Griffith, "Of Privilege, Approval, and a Savior Complex," in *White Women Getting Real about Race*, ed. James and Peterson, 45–55.

39. James, "Love of Clowns," 36.

40. Emile Durkheim, quoted in Arto Laitinen and Anne Birgitta Pessi, eds., *Solidarity: Theory and Practice* (Lanham, MD: Lexington Books, 2015), 11.

41. "We Are #NewnanStrong," *Newnan Times-Herald*, April 22, 2018, https://times-herald.com/.

42. Winston Skinner, "Community Responds to Neo-Nazi Rally with Unity Gathering," *Newnan Times-Herald*, April 19, 2018, https://times-herald.com. Local rabbis were invited to participate but declined as the gathering took place on the Sabbath.

43. Kandice Bell, "Businesses Report Record Sales on Friday," *Newnan Times-Herald*, April 26, 2018, https://times-herald.com/.

44. The Shopper, "#Newnanstrong," Winters Media, April 20, 2018, https://www.wintersmedia.net.

45. Meagan Flynn, "Georgia Police Invoke Law Made for KKK to Arrest Anti-Racism Protesters," *Washington Post*, April 23, 2018, https://www.washingtonpost.com/. Antifa supporters frequently demonstrate while wearing black with masks, allowing protest-

ers to appear as a collective anonymous unit. "Seven Things You Need to Know about Antifa," *BBC News*, accessed July 26, 2019, https://www.bbc.co.uk/.

46. Daniel Politi, "Neo-Nazi Counterprotesters Met by Aggressive Militarized Police Force in Georgia," *The Slate*, April 21, 2018, https://slate.com/; Alan Pyke, "Georgia Police Arrest Counterprotesters at White Supremacist Rally, Cite Anti-Mask Law Made for KKK," *ThinkProgress*, April 23, 2018, https://archive.thinkprogress.org/.

CHAPTER 3

Empathy in Opera

COLLEEN RENIHAN

Empathy is a powerful form of care, and more specifically a crucial component of a critical pedagogy rooted in issues of social justice and community care. The push for empathy in pedagogy has arisen out of what's been termed an empathy crisis—empathy is eroding, according to Simon Baron-Cohen.[1] Many suggest that empathy is central for global and social revolution, and in this age of increased polarization and in-group thinking perpetuated by media and social media, our ability and willingness to feel with and for others is crucial. As historian Susan Lanzoni writes, "the lack of empathy on the part of white Americans has long impeded the fight for racial equality."[2]

Empathy is an intervention; it can be radical. But like care itself, empathy is complicated. (See introduction.) It can easily slip into the realm of pity, where the empathizing individual or group operates from a sense of superiority. It is also incredibly difficult to cultivate across barriers and prejudices that people carry with them, and to dismantle the forces (like racism) that keep people from attempting to fully understand one another. In her essay "Empathy and Its Alternatives: Deconstructing the Rhetoric of 'Empathy' in Video Games," Bonnie Ruberg hopes to

> disentangle and delineate the multiplicity of meanings contained within this rhetoric: that is, to resurface the experiences and feelings currently grouped under the umbrella of 'empathy.' Some of these feelings, such as the self-satisfied feeling of allyship, indeed demand stringent critique. However, others—such as feelings of caring, heartbreak, and even a kind of intimate queer entanglement—demonstrate that already contained within the marginalizing rhetoric of empathy lies the potential for envisioning alternative and more socially-just ways of how video games allow players to feel with and for others.[3]

Extending Ruberg's approach to opera, I use the term *empathy* throughout this essay with the acknowledgment that while the very concept of empathy needs to be unpacked and critiqued, its employment as a way in to discussions about affect and audience behavior in opera can be incredibly productive, and resonates powerfully with the ethics of care in music for which this book advocates.

I was spurred to think of empathy and its significance in post-secondary education on my own campus when our community dealt with two events that forced us to have difficult but important discussions about race and empathy. First, a student Halloween costume party featuring appropriated non-Western cultural costumes was publicly criticized for its white-supremacist underpinnings. Second, the ensuing comments and discussion on social media and in the press highlighted long-standing concerns about the climate for persons of color on the Queen's University campus, and ultimately revealed deep-seated racism in the community.[4]

Many felt that a conversation about race at Queen's was long overdue, and the prevalent culture of whiteness concerned many students and faculty. Several town hall meetings were held for students and faculty in the School of Drama and Music, at which students revealed the depth of the hurt caused by what they described as ingrained, systemic racism at the university and within the School. This, in turn, inspired me to think further about how I might try to mobilize conversations about these issues in my own teaching in music theatre and opera, both of which carry long histories of whiteness and of cultural appropriation.

Current work in care ethics and pedagogies of care suggests that empathy is crucial to ethical life and, more importantly, that it is teachable.[5] As Nadine Dolby argues, if educators care about things like social justice, global citizenship, or sustainability, we need to think about how the development of prosocial behaviors and fundamental human qualities might be honed in our classrooms. *The Final Report of the Truth and Reconciliation Commission of Canada* (TRC), which is informing educational policy and educational institutions on how to integrate Indigenous ways of knowing and teaching methods into classrooms, names empathy. Indeed, item 63.3 in the "calls to action" specifically asks educators to build student capacity for "intercultural understanding, empathy, and mutual respect."[6] If our students are exhibiting self-centered behavior, and thus low levels of empathy, how could this be addressed in our curricula? *How can* empathy be taught? And how can it be interrogated for its limitations and shortcomings? While empathy courses have been pervading curricula in a variety of disciplines for a few years now, I want to suggest that music faculty may have a unique opportunity to highlight particular aspects of empathy in our varied learning spaces. And while empathy could easily be explored in courses or units on musical theatre, film music, video game music, popular music, among others, I chose to implement it through a redesign of my undergraduate opera history course, which I taught during winter 2017 following our local discussions about racial empathy during the Town Halls mentioned above. It seemed to me that the kind of engagement that operatic spectatorship demands might be examined fruitfully through the lens of empathy, and as I discovered with my students, opera provides a compelling platform for productive discussions on this topic.

Defining Empathy

The term *empathy* was coined as late as 1909 by British-American psychologist Edward Titchener, though as a concept it has been around much longer. Initially it was an attempt to translate philosopher Robert Vischer's term *Einfühlung* ("feeling into"), subsequently championed by Theodor Lipps, who had changed it from an aesthetic term to one used to account for humans' abilities to imagine another's circumstances. Most theorists situate the roots of the empathy debate in the philosophical thinking of eighteenth-century philosophers David Hume and Adam Smith, particularly in their theories of morality. Hume's writings suggest that empathy is a principle of communication fundamental to human nature—it is for Hume an automatic process. This has been termed low-level empathy, or mirroring.[7] Smith is more direct about what social and developmental psychologists call the "role-taking" or "perspective-taking" component of empathy—its imaginative component. Many refer to this as high-level empathy (also called reenactive empathy, reconstructive empathy, or perspective-shifting).[8] Empathy has been understood, variously, as:

- Feeling what someone else feels
- Caring about someone else
- Being emotionally affected by someone else's emotions and experiences, though not necessarily experiencing the same emotions
- Imagining oneself in another's situation
- Imagining being another in that other's situation
- Making inferences about another's mental states
- Some combination of the above processes.[9]

Some researchers, like Stephanie Preston and Frans de Waal, claim that the distinctions between these forms of empathy are less important than we have made them out to be. Others, like Amy Coplan, believe that these differences are key.[10] Coplan defines empathy as a "complex imaginative process in which an observer simulates another person's situated psychological states while maintaining clear self-other differentiation."[11] Opera offers possibilities for engaging with and performing all three of Coplan's elements (affective matching, other-oriented perspective-taking, and self-other differentiation). It also complicates their understanding in important ways and, as I will show, offers us the opportunity to understand and critique the limitations of the term *empathy* and to consider ways that opera might also serve as a space in which to explore care and interpersonal connection more broadly.

Empathy in Opera: Broad Themes

Teaching opera to students between the ages of eighteen and twenty-two remains a challenge, since, in my experience, they are resistant to the idea that it might be considered a form with any contemporary resonance. Most have experienced opera as representative of old elite European culture, an issue magnified for my few racialized students who feel implicitly outside of the genre, or worse, stigmatized by its representations. I recognize this in my classes by naming it outright, and begin by introducing opera as a historical genre with a great deal to teach us about representation, power, and expression that comes from particular times, places, cultures, and sets of experiences. Notwithstanding, I emphasize that opera is an art form that harbors great contemporary possibility in its ability to take on current political, social, environmental, and interpersonal issues and stimulate conversation among performers and spectators.[12] Finally, I advance it as a form with a great deal to teach us about empathy.

Opera's theatrical component draws on all of the possibilities for engagement, replication, and imagination of theatre. Music, however, is the element crucial for understanding opera's unique role in the teaching of empathy. Researchers have shown music to be able to evoke responses in listeners through an empathic process that involves both autonomic responses to music as well as intentional imaginative work on the part of the listener.[13] Empathy has factored in research on music and the endogenous opioid system (endorphins), music and mirror neurons, the ethnomusicology of affect, the history of musical subjectivity, and sociological studies of music and collective action. Music facilitates intersubjectivity, social bonding, and group cohesion on a variety of levels, thereby enacting a kind of empathy. As Eric Clarke, Tia DeNora, and Jonna Vuoskoski have concluded in their impressively wide-reaching study on music and empathy:

> Music and musicking, then, can be viewed as a rich environment in which more or less active participants [either listeners and/or makers] can engage with the real and virtual subjectivities of other real and virtual participants, and in doing so come to experience (and perhaps increasingly understand) the cultural perspective that those others (real or virtual) inhabit. Music is in this way both a *medium* for engagement with others (who may be more or less empathic or antagonistic) and an *environment* in which to explore and experiment with a range of more or less projected, fantasized, and genuinely discovered subjectivities.[14]

The way in which theatrical performance and music (in opera) lead one through the processual aspect of experiencing events is key to its ability to position the events as central to personal imagining, in Murray Smith's definition. We imagine that they are taking place—we "mentally *simulate* experiencing [them]."[15] And through the eyes of a character on stage whom we observe, we get the opportunity for "other-focused personal imagining" as Smith calls it, or what Coplan names "other-oriented perspective taking."[16] Crucially, the emotional response evoked by fictional characters is nearly indistinguishable from the emotional response evoked by "real world" objects (or scenarios).[17] This research underscores the exciting opportunities for real-world impact that encountering empathy in the context of opera could have, and the rich pedagogical potential inherent in approaching the teaching of opera in this way.

Pedagogical Applications in an Undergraduate Opera Course

During the second week of classes, I divided students into groups and had them each read a particular short piece on empathy; I wanted them to engage with what I thought were some of the most salient points about empathy and its potential implications for opera. These included an academic article on how operatic music invokes emotional responses from listeners, Paul Bloom's now famous article "Against Empathy" in the *Boston Review* about the drawbacks of empathy, an episode of the NPR podcast *Hidden Brain* on the process of empathizing with the enemy, and a popular science article on how mirror neurons function in the brain.[18] Each group became "experts" on their topic, and taught the rest of the class about it. We then brainstormed ramifications for and questions about opera on big whiteboards around the classroom: did the music have something to do with its ability to cultivate empathy? Were audiences more or less likely to empathize with characters they had something in common with? and so forth. This was a challenging exercise, because not all students were music majors. But with my collaborative support, and some group discussion, we arrived at some interesting conclusions, and I think students thought more deeply about some of the ways that opera "works" for and with its audiences.

Having established some solid groundwork on empathy and a shared knowledge of its potential workings in opera (or, at least, some questions about how it might play out), we then studied various operatic examples in a roughly chronological presentation, as I typically do. I led students in discussions about how certain aspects of empathy played out in these case studies, and students often had intriguing contributions to make after having become "experts" on their empathy topics. I will present some highlights from these discoveries in what follows.

Points of Interest: Opera and Empathy

Though I will not have space to discuss each in length, I will provide a summary of some of our major discoveries or fruitful avenues for the consideration of empathy in opera. I have organized this section thematically since it might help spark ideas on the part of future instructors thinking about integrating empathy in their teaching about opera, musical theatre, film music, video game music, and so forth.

Music and Affective Matching

Affective matching occurs when an observer's affective states are "qualitatively identical to a target's though they may vary in degree."[19] In other words, the observer must experience the same type of emotion (or affect) as the target.[20] One form of affective matching occurs through a process called "emotional contagion" that neuroscientists have attributed only recently to mirror neurons. Mirror neurons were first discovered in the 1990s in Italy, and first in research with macaque monkeys. They are activated both when an individual performs a particular kind of action, and *when an individual observes another performing that action*. The first mirror neurons to be noticed were motor activated, but in the early 2000s, evidence of affective experience mirroring emerged.[21]

There is a great deal of literature linking music with the induction of an experience of affective matching in its listeners.[22] Emotions, after all, are often communicated nonverbally, and there is some evidence that emotion is expressed facially and vocally in similar ways cross-culturally.[23] Music elicits social bonding, synchronization, or as Tarr, Launay, and Dunbar call it, self-other merging, which in the context of empathy is central.[24] Music's potential for entrainment, the aligning of one's beat with another's, or synchronization in general, can elicit a kind of empathy with that other—thus spurring implications for studies of empathy in both listeners and performers.[25]

Our discussions focused on how the music participates in the eliciting of empathetic responses from spectators. One point I focused on was affective matching: The subconscious function of contagion or mirroring speaks to music's immersive and manipulative properties, which we explored in the context of Mozart's music and various directorial choices for the character of Don Giovanni. We watched various productions' stagings of the duet "La Ci Darem La Mano" and explored the ways that Giovanni musically seduces the listener (along with Zerlina, of course) to empathize with him as a predator. We explored what was at stake when we are coerced to empathize with a predator in this instance. With care surrounding the issue that many students would themselves have been victims of sexual violence, we discussed the ways that art and music are complicit in perpetuating certain aspects of rape culture. The empathic manipulation at work in an opera like *Don Giovanni* might also be an issue raised in future discussions about how programming certain operas (such as *Don Giovanni*, but of course there are many more) is highly questionable if we consider the very real work of contagion and mirroring, and if audience care is indeed a concern.

This led us to question music and narrative voices in opera—in other words, to ask who is manipulating us and to what end in a given operatic moment. Does operatic music prevent the self-other differentiation that Coplan identifies as key to the empathic process? As Coplan describes it, we need to keep clear "where the self ends and the other begins *and* where the other ends and the self begins,"[26] and as we discovered, the music for many operatic characters works actively against this process, resulting in what Coplan would call fusion or enmeshment.[27] Along the same lines, we also discussed the response to John Adams's empathetic portrayal of both the Israelis and Palestinians in *The Death of Klinghoffer*, thus highlighting the political ramifications of these aesthetic choices. In other examples, like Jeanine Tesori and Tazewell Thompson's opera *Blue*, audience members indicate being viscerally moved by the mournful singing of the grieving mother, as discussed in a presentation by National Sawdust+ that included excerpts of the opera along with writings of James Baldwin and Ta-Nehisi Coates.[28] Because wailing and keening are operatic in ways—most obviously as emotionally laden vocal expressions that exceed the parameters of everyday vocal expressivity—the medium presents an opportunity for a group of listeners to sit with and absorb the emotional impact of a mother mourning her deceased son. Opera thus presents opportunities for understanding and challenging racism, when taught through the lens of empathy, understanding, and compassion.

The Structure of the Aria

In the context of empathy, discussions surrounding the dramatic function of the aria took on a more significant focus, because my class realized more fully that these were moments where operatic characters revealed themselves to the audience in a focused and intentional way. The music could then be heard as supporting a particular emotional state, and as affecting the listener as a result. Stephen Davies argues that emotional contagion is more likely to occur if one's attention is focused intently on another person.[29] In film, this can be achieved with a close-up on facial features; in opera through music and through the operatic close-up: the aria. We are hardwired to relate to individual cases (think of the use of children's images in humanitarian aid organization campaigns, for example)—as psychologist Paul Slovic explains, "the mind is very much geared to respond to a single person in need—whether it's ourselves or a single person in front of us."[30] Which person in the opera we empathize with could be yet another question to explore.

Performers and Empathy

Though most of our considerations were from the perspective of the audience, it is also useful to consider ways that empathy and compassion might be modeled or experienced from the performer's perspective. Research is sparse on the issue of empathy between a performer and the character they are playing. Amy Cook looks at how actors access empathic relationships with their characters by actually feeling the emotions themselves, drawing on twentieth-century acting theory, including the work of Stanislavski, and Erin Heisel looks at this as the most intimate form of empathy in opera.[31] A recent post-performance talk with cisgender baritone Philip Addis focused on empathy; he shared that he felt an incredible empathy for playing a trans person—what he called "*being* in that body" for a few weeks—in the opera *As One*. Singers, after all, are putting themselves in the shoes of another person, and acting and reacting as that person. Addis's is thus an experience that might be considered on several levels given the need for more support for trans singers in opera, and the wealth of emerging research on vocal pedagogy on teaching trans singers in music departments. An interesting discussion for performance majors might be raised about the challenges of maintaining self-other differentiation (the crucial third component of Coplan's definition of empathy) in order to actually sing difficult roles without becoming overcome by emotion.[32] Another discussion might involve researching emerging accounts of more and more trans folx being cast in operas, especially in trans roles, as well as the necessity of featuring BIPOC performers in BIPOC roles—which Anna Netrebko's blatant and continued appearances in blackface in *Aida* ask us to consider.

The Operatic Other

Perhaps the most important aspect of cultivating empathy, compassion, and care in an operatic context (and given the challenges to which I was responding while undertaking this pedagogical project) is the cultural understanding and prosocial behaviors that can come from imagining another's experience. The imagination required in other-oriented perspective-taking is crucial, since this imagining distinguishes this process from that of sympathizing, where the imagining of another's position is not required. This is ultimately the distinction between self- and other-oriented perspective-taking: there is often a significant difference, for example, between how I would react to and/or feel in a particular situation, and how the target would feel in a given situation.[33]

Indeed, empathy is subject to certain biases including the fact that reconstructing a target's subjective experiences has been proven to be more difficult when the target is different from ourselves in some significant way.[34] But one can see how this could be especially productive in an operatic context, and with a group of students for whom understanding the perspective of those who are different from themselves is a foreign concept. Indeed, the predominant whiteness of my class (and of my university's student body in general) meant that this was an important, if at first stilted, conversation to have, which we did.

In what was perhaps the most interesting and important aspect of empathy in our immediate community context, we explored the concept of in- and out-group empathy, and the idea that we relate more easily to, and empathize with, others who are most like ourselves. There is a great deal of literature on the idea that empathy is constrained by social factors, most notably attitude and group membership.[35] We discussed the many ways characters are "othered" in opera, such as Cio-Cio San in *Madama Butterfly*, and the effects on our perception of them and our ability to empathize with them and, by extension, other individuals from the minoritized group(s) to which they belong. (See Hung's discussion in chapter 8 in this volume.) We also addressed the "hot-cold empathy gap" with respect to our inability to recall what it's like to be influenced by a specific state of being or affect after we have recovered from it.[36] We wondered whether there was a way to reactivate the "hot" affective state in order to increase one's empathetic response to others—and realized that perhaps music and theatre are primed to do this.

At the same time, Clarke and colleagues point to research that suggests that music, even when encountered in passive circumstances, has the potential to positively influence people's unconscious attitudes toward cultural others.[37] And thus we decided that perhaps opera can provide an opportunity to learn to be more empathetic toward those we perceive as being different from ourselves. Indeed, a striking 2012 study by Michael Inzlicht shows that if we force mimicry, unconscious bias can be reduced—a striking suggestion, which implies that a theatrical medium that invites empathy with others, like opera, could bridge the empathy gap. There is also evidence that the accuracy or efficacy of one's empathic project will be more successful and accurate dependent upon the level of knowledge of the target individual's life and situation. This provides support for the development of audience-education programs like preconcert talks that provide context for operatic productions and open up discussion on difficult topics. (See Everett and Magarotto's discussion in chapter 9 in this volume.)

A significant challenge with empathy, of course, is that it risks embedding ideas of normative, privileged, or dominant positionalities, and a kind of consumerism of marginalized experiences. My students and I had rich discussions about these risks, along with some alternative ways to frame the affective engagement we were having with these works, vis-à-vis our understanding of viewpoints and experiences beyond our own.

Live vs. Mediated Empathy

Given that much opera is consumed digitally, and that nearly all of the opera my students and I would engage with was digital and virtual, live vs. mediated empathy was an interesting line of inquiry to pursue. A study of the live vs. digital performances of opera provides several rich avenues for discussion on the topic of how technological mediation might impact empathic behavior. In my class, this involved a visit to the movie theatre to experience a *Live from the Met* broadcast, along with a study of some of the literature on liveness. We then discussed how the mediated nature of the experience impacted empathy (for instance, we considered the intermission backstage interviews with the stars of the show). Dr. Iacoboni, one of the preeminent specialists on mirror neurons, has written about the idea that mirror neurons work best in live contexts; "Virtual reality and videos are shadowy substitutes," he explains.[38] But this notion continues to be strongly contested by the steady stream of emerging research on the impact and immersive opportunities in virtual and augmented reality game and performance worlds, as well as by live streaming of operatic performances, all of which became much more ubiquitous during the pandemic.[39] It is particularly interesting that empathy as a rhetoric has become highly corporatized in the video game market—as Ruberg writes, "affect is presented as a commodity: an experience that can be bought and sold, or which can boost further sales," a rhetoric that is supported by many playing games, and that is challenged by scholars and marginalized game developers.[40] It would be illuminating to have students compare some of the empathy-focused video games to operatic examples in order to understand what makes opera different and/or unique, where empathy is concerned.

Possibilities for Opera as Empathy

Thinking about opera through the lens of empathy has the potential to upend traditional work-focused approaches common in teaching opera. It might offer a non-work-centered approach to teaching opera, something many instructors are looking for in an attempt to open up the field to broader perspectives and issues. Specifically, it might meaningfully connect the study of music and culture to broader issues of relationality, empathy, and cultural competencies by compelling us to reconsider operatic spectatorship as an arena where opinions, outlooks, and relationships in the so-called "real world" can be transformed. This is striking if we consider the implications. As my students and I discovered together, operatic performance gives us the opportunity to rehearse, and indeed *perform*, new empathetic alliances. This was indeed an empowering discovery.

When I teach this course again, I will plant more intentional seeds and include reflection assignments about things students could do to actively mobilize these ideas both in their work and in the ways in which they navigate the world outside our classroom. I hope also to problematize and nuance our understanding of empathy further, as new research is published that supports and troubles traditional so-called empathic modes of engagement within various performance genres. As Joanna Quinn explains—vis-à-vis realizing the justice sought by the Truth and Reconciliation Commission which has been very much on the hearts and minds of Canadians since its publication in 2015—"reconciliation is the intersection of empathy and justice and the discovery or rediscovery of facts surrounding gross abuses of human rights."[41] And yet, in the context of the TRC and other calls for the dismantling of racism, we are reminded that ultimately, we must be prepared to move beyond an affective form of empathy to empathy-induced action.[42]

Notes

1. Simon Baron-Cohen, *Zero Degrees of Empathy: A New Theory of Human Cruelty and Kindness* (New York: Penguin, 2011).

2. Susan Lanzoni, "Why Empathy Is the Key to Dismantling White Racism," *The Washington Post*, February 22, 2019, https://www.washingtonpost.com/outlook/.

3. Bonnie Ruberg, "Empathy and Its Alternatives: Deconstructing the Rhetoric of 'Empathy' in Video Games," *Communication, Culture & Critique* 13 (2020): 54–71; 54.

4. See Eric Andrew-Gee, "Costume Party Highlights Racism at Queen's University, Critics Say," *The Globe and Mail*, November 22, 2016, https://www.theglobeandmail.com/.

5. Edith Stein, a doctoral student of the philosopher Edmund Husserl and author of *On the Problem of Empathy*, proposed a definition of empathy that first emphasized that it is an educable skill.

6. Truth and Reconciliation Commission of Canada, *Honouring the Truth, Reconciling for the Future. Summary of the Final Report of the Truth and Reconciliation Commission of Canada* (Winnipeg: Truth and Reconciliation Commission of Canada, 2015), 331.

7. See Karsten Stueber, *Rediscovering Empathy: Agency, Folk Psychology, and the Human Sciences* (Cambridge, MA: MIT Press, 2006).

8. For a discussion of reconstructive empathy, see Alvin Goldman, "Two Routes to Empathy: Insights from Cognitive Neuroscience," in *Empathy: Philosophical and Psychological Perspectives*, ed. Amy Coplan and Peter Goldie (New York: Oxford University Press, 2011), 31–44; for perspective-shifting, see Peter Goldie, "Anti-empathy," in Coplan and Goldie, *Empathy: Philosophical and Psychological Perspectives*, 302–17.

9. See Amy Coplan, "Understanding Empathy: Its Features and Effects," in Coplan and Goldie, *Empathy: Philosophical and Psychological Perspectives*, 4.

10. Stephanie Preston and Frans de Waal, "Empathy: Its Ultimate and Proximate Bases," *Behavioral Brain Science* 25, no. 1 (2002): 1–20. Cited in Coplan, "Understanding Empathy," 5. Coplan offers a rather restrictive definition of empathy that seems to resonate with many of the major contemporary thinkers on the issue, and I follow her theory here since she is a philosopher whose work engages with studies in both cognitive science and philosophy and who has also published on the question of empathic engagement with narrative fiction. See Amy Coplan, "Empathic Engagement with Narrative Fictions," *The Journal of Aesthetics and Art Criticism* 62, no. 2 (2004): 141–52.

11. Coplan, "Understanding Empathy," 5.

12. See, for example, Naomi André, *Black Opera: History, Power, Engagement* (Chicago: University of Illinois Press, 2018).

13. See, for example, Jerrold Levinson, "Musical Expressiveness as Hearability-as-Expression," in *Contemporary Debates in Aesthetics and the Philosophy of Art*, ed. Matthew Kieran (Oxford: Blackwell Publishing, 2006), 192–206; Klaus Scherer and Marcel Zentner, "Emotional Effects of Music: Production Rules," in *Music and Emotion: Theory and Research*, ed. Patrik Juslin and John Sloboda (Oxford: Oxford University Press, 2001), 361–92.

14. Eric Clarke, Tia DeNora, and Jonna Vuoskoski, "Music, Empathy and Cultural Understanding," *Physics of Life Reviews* 15 (2015): 72.

15. Murray Smith, "Empathy, Expansionism, and the Extended Mind," in Coplan and Goldie, *Empathy: Philosophical and Psychological Perspectives*, 100.

16. Smith, "Empathy, Expansionism, Extended Mind," 101; Coplan, "Understanding Empathy."

17. See Alex Neill, "Fiction and the Emotions," *American Philosophical Quarterly* 30 (1993): 1–13.

18. Andrei Miu and Felicia Rodica Baltes, "Empathy Manipulation Impacts Music-Induced Emotions: A Psychophysiological Study on Opera," *PLoS One* 7, no. 1 (2012), doi:10.1371/journal.pone.0030618; Paul Bloom, "Against Empathy," *Boston Review*, September 10, 2014, https://bostonreview.net/; Max Nesterak, "What Happens When You Empathize with the Enemy?," March 22, 2016, in *Hidden Brain*, podcast, https://www.npr.org/; Jason Marsh, "Do Mirror Neurons Give Us Empathy?," *Greater Good Magazine*, March 29, 2012, https://greatergood.berkeley.edu/.

19. Coplan, "Understanding Empathy," 4. Note that with sympathy, one feels "an emotional response that consists of feeling sorrow or concern for the distressed or needy other (rather than feeling the same emotion as the other person). Sympathy is believed to involve other-oriented, altruistic, motivation" (Nancy Eisenberg, "Empathy and Sympathy," in *Handbook of Emotions*, ed. Michael Lewis and Jeanette Haviland-Jones [New York: Guildford Press, 2000], 678).

20. Coplan clarifies that this precludes situations where, for instance, the observer becomes angry at the way that the target is being treated in a particular situation, even if the target isn't actually feeling anger as a response. On this particular matter, one might also raise the issue of cross-cultural understandings of emotion. The same could potentially be argued for historically removed situations. Still, there is a growing consensus among scientists that at least some emotional types do exist cross-culturally, typically identified

as "basic" emotions (fear, anger, sadness, joy, and disgust). See Coplan, "Understanding Empathy," 7.

21. Quoted in Coplan and Goldie, "Introduction," in *Empathy: Philosophical and Psychological Perspectives*, xxx. Hoffman thinks of emotional contagion as a kind of immature state of empathy, something we experience before we are able to experience full-fledged empathy. Perhaps we might think of it in music, then, as synchronization, entrainment, or a kind of training for the more engaged, top-down process of empathy that occurs in actual empathy.

22. See Tai-Chen Rabinowitch, Ian Cross, and Pamela Burnard, "Musical Group Interaction, Intersubjectivity and Merged Subjectivity," in *Kinesthetic Empathy in Creative and Cultural Practices*, ed. Dee Reynolds and Matthew Reason (Bristol, UK: Intellect, 2012), 109–20; Ian Cross, Felicity Laurence, and Tai-Chen Rabinowitch, "Empathic Creativity in Musical Group Practices: Towards a Concept of Empathic Creativity," in *The Oxford Handbook of Music Education*, ed. Gary McPherson and Graham Welch (New York: Oxford, 2012), 337–53. One can measure music-induced emotions using the Geneva Emotional Music Scale (GEMS)—a self-report instrument that captures the blends of negative and positive emotions most frequently induced by music. See Marcel Zentner and Tuomas Eerola, "Self-Report Measures and Models of Musical Emotions," in *Handbook of Music and Emotion: Theory, Research, Applications*, ed. Patrik Juslin and John Sloboda (New York: Oxford University Press, 2010), 187–223. See also the entire collection: Juslin and Sloboda, eds., *Handbook of Music and Emotion*.

23. See Hillary Anger Elfenbein and Nalini Ambady, "On the Universality and Cultural Specificity of Emotion Recognition: A Meta-Analysis," *Psychological Bulletin* 128, no. 2 (2002): 203–35.

24. See Bronwyn Tarr, Jacques Launay, and Robin Dunbar, "Music and Social Bonding: 'Self-other' Merging and Neurohormonal Mechanisms," *Frontiers in Psychology* 5 (2014): 1–10.

25. Studies on entrainment and synchronization include Michael Hove and Jane Risen, "It's All in the Timing: Interpersonal Synchrony Increases Affiliation," *Social Cognition* 27, no. 6 (2009): 949–60; Scott Wiltermuth and Chip Heath, "Synchrony and Cooperation," *Psychological Science* 20, no. 1 (2009): 1–5. Amy Cook explores the affective and empathic potential of poetic meter in Shakespearean drama; see "For Hecuba or for Hamlet: Rethinking Emotion and Empathy in the Theatre," *Journal of Dramatic Theory and Criticism* 25, no. 2 (2011): 71–87.

26. Coplan, "Understanding Empathy," 16.

27. Coplan, 16.

28. See "National Sawdust+ Presents: An Evening with 'Blue' and 'Between the World and Me,'" June 9, 2020, https://vimeo.com/427500631.

29. Stephen Davies, "Infectious Music: Music-Listener Emotional Contagion," in Coplan and Goldie, *Empathy: Philosophical and Psychological Perspectives*.

30. See Amos Zeeberg, "How Images Trigger Empathy," *The Atlantic*, January 6, 2016, https://www.theatlantic.com/. Research shows that increased activity in the nucleus accumbens, a brain area associated with pleasure and reward, is the reason for increased generosity and empathy. The author believes that with exposure to images, empathy has the potential to grow.

31. See Cook, "For Hecuba or for Hamlet"; Erin Heisel, "Empathy as a Tool for Embodiment Processes," *Empirical Musicology Review* 10, no. 1–2 (2015): 104.

32. See Jenefer Robinson and Robert Hatten, "Emotions in Music," *Music Theory Spectrum* 34, no. 2 (2012): 71–106.

33. The "false consensus effect" involves our assuming that others are more similar to us than they actually are. We assume they feel the same way we feel, think the same way we think, and want the same things we want.

34. Note: there have also been neurological studies that show that the process for self- and other-oriented perspective-taking is different. See Jean Decety and Jessica Sommerville, "Shared Representations between Self and Others: A Social Cognitive Neuroscience View," *Trends in Cognitive Science* 7 (2003): 527–33. Theorists are divided about the significance of making this distinction, but Coplan believes it to be crucial.

35. See, for example, Jennifer Gutsell and Michael Inzlicht, "Intergroup Differences in the Sharing of Emotive States: Neural Evidence of an Empathy Gap," *Social Cognitive and Affective Neuroscience* 7, no. 5 (2012): 596–603.

36. Rachel Ruttan, Maryk-Hunter McDonnell, and Loran Nordgren, "Having 'Been There' Doesn't Mean I Care: When Prior Experience Reduces Compassion for Emotional Distress," *Journal of Personality and Social Psychology* 108, no. 4 (2015): 610–22.

37. Clarke, DeNora, and Vuoskoski, "Music, Empathy and Cultural Understanding," 77.

38. Marco Iacoboni, quoted in Sandra Blakeslee, "Cells That Read Minds," *New York Times*, January 10, 2006, http://www.nytimes.com/.

39. Research on video games and empathy is growing. Video game designer Jane McGonigal's book *Reality Is Broken: Why Games Make Us Better and How They Can Change the World* (New York: Penguin Press, 2011) reveals video games have the potential to solve real-world problems and boost global happiness, and Bonnie Ruberg's "Empathy and Its Alternatives," cited above, includes a great deal of contemporary research that supports the idea that video games provide ample and meaningful opportunities for affective engagement.

40. Ruberg, "Empathy and Its Alternatives," 58.

41. The Truth and Reconciliation Commission's reports can be found at https://nctr.ca/records/reports/. Joanna Quinn is cited in Caleb Snider, "Concrete Change Begins with Empathy, but It Doesn't End There," Federation for the Humanities and Social Sciences Blog, May 31, 2017, https://www.federationhss.ca/en/blog/concrete-change-begins-empathy-it-doesnt-end-there.

42. I am reminded here of Dylan Robinson's powerful challenge of "the assumption that the shared affect—or 'affective contagion' (Brennan 2004)—represented by an audience's tears indicates an experience of positive transformation that is similarly felt by audience members," noting in particular the differences between Indigenous and settler audience members. See *Hungry Listening: Resonant Theory for Indigenous Sound Studies* (Minneapolis: University of Minnesota Press, 2020), 202.

CHAPTER 4

Integrating Well-being and Intersectional Equity across a Revised Music History and Culture Curriculum

JOHN SPILKER

Research in higher education routinely highlights connections between well-being and enhanced intellectual growth.[1] For example, from its inception, the field of critical and inclusive pedagogies places care of self and community at the core of its approaches.[2] This focus infuses recent publications such as *Race, Equity, and the Learning Environment*, *Difficult Subjects*, and *Radical Hope*.[3] Musicology has also signaled the importance of care pedagogy across the broader music discipline: Bonnie Gordon has highlighted continued acts of violence against women, and Loren Kajikawa exposed the damage wrought by white supremacy in our ideologies and practices.[4] Finally, drawing on care ethics, disability studies, and queer theory, William Cheng called for reparative approaches to music-making, teaching, and research.[5] But practical considerations do not always accompany theoretical musings about the deficits of our current teaching contexts. How might these practices and orientations be mobilized in the context of the courses we teach? In this chapter, I argue that despite the problematic and exclusionary nature of music history and world music survey courses, through radical and careful curricular revision attuned to reimagining broader, more applicable musicological skills rather than content coverage, these courses are indeed the very site of transformation for students, colleagues, and the music discipline.

Intervening through well-being and intersectional equity connected to skills and practices in the history and culture curriculum has never been so important. Inviting care into higher-education music builds on the foundation laid by Bianca Williams's concept of "radical honesty," which is "a pedagogical practice of truth-telling that seeks to challenge racist and patriarchal institutional cultures in the academy." She affirms that "radical honesty emphasizes the significance of personal narratives and opens a space for creating strategies that enable scholars and students to bring their 'whole self' to the classroom, while getting rid of the shame that frequently accompanies their bodies in academic settings." Furthermore, Williams advocates, "professors are allowed to be human, and our emotional experiences are even more important in a time when our labor is becoming ever more disconnected from ourselves. It demands that we are honest—with ourselves, trusted colleagues, and our students—when we are experiencing and working through the shame that these disconnects induce."[6] Williams's scholarship shows how care-based approaches are inextricably linked to acknowledging, resisting, and dismantling the "imperialist white-supremacist capitalist patriarchy" operating in higher education writ large and, more specifically, music departments.[7]

Risk, Privilege, Precarity

Benefitting from institutional and systemic inequities, as a white male I experience considerable support when taking risks associated with well-being work in the learning environment. Perhaps I notice my intersectional privilege precisely because care pedagogy requires me to embrace discomfort and eschew the ease white male professors experience. This teaching approach necessitates attention to self-care.

As noted by Williams, minoritized colleagues experience precarity and suppression by design, a reality that Nikole Hannah-Jones amplified in July 2021 in national headlines. She asserts, "all across this country Black faculty, and faculty from other marginalized groups, are having their opportunities stifled."[8] Engaging well-being topics places them at even greater risk, a point amplified by Alyson Cole's work.[9] Discussions of care often center well-being concepts as a universal (read: white) experience, with no risks, only benefits. This prevents us from more fully understanding systemic injustices faced by people with minoritized identities. Precarity has been further intensified by the ways in which care and well-being have recently collided with cancel culture and misunderstandings of conflict, discomfort, and trauma in college classrooms, not to mention state laws like Florida's "Stop Woke Act," which forbids equity and honesty in education.[10] This all requires urgent attention to communal care and the complicated nature of care. (See the introduction.)

Students, especially those from minoritized groups, may also experience precarity as we learn. Informed by collaboration with social work and gender studies colleagues at my institution, I remind students throughout the semester, "I am not a trained mental health professional. Intellectual work with well-being topics is not mental health therapy. You and I should have a plan to (1) notice and manage embodied emotional responses and (2) seek routine care for our mental health. The campus counseling center employs trained professionals to support students." This is rooted in trauma-conscious pedagogy, which, together with disability studies, provides a vital avenue for professional development to deepen care-based practices.[11]

Scaffolding and Integrating Well-being Scholarship

Rooted in scholarship cited throughout this chapter, I support intellectual growth by scaffolding well-being scholarship across four semesters of required music-major coursework: "World Music Cultures," "Music History 1: Gender & Sexuality," "Music History 2: Antiracist Liberation," and "Senior Capstone Seminar." I select well-being content that integrates with the learning experiences specific to each course. Alongside discipline-specific content, students explore care-based scholarship and take notes guided by broad prompts such as: "Identify the structure, thesis, and main concepts of each chapter. Are there one or two concepts you would like to practice currently? How will this facilitate your goals?" During in-class discussions about discipline-specific content, or workshops for the research project, students often note connections between well-being research and course objectives. In fact, they infuse care-based content whenever they see its application to the nexus of lived experience and our shared learning work.

This essay presents an overview of the sequential four-semester course structure and the integrated well-being scholarship that is key to each course. Details of course structure, assignments, or in-class examples lie beyond the scope of this chapter. However, I would gladly share my course materials, which I routinely adapt based on student feedback and my teaching experience. "A Glimpse Inside the Classroom" (later in this chapter) discusses components of some assignments that could be adapted across courses to help students engage well-being scholarship.

In 2013, Kaitlin Beck, a collaborating student-instructor, recommended Brené Brown's work, which presented a starting point for my care-based work. Although pejoratively classified by some as pop psychology, she adapts qualitative social work research for the general reader, which students find accessible. Brown's books can be used to reinforce narratives of whiteness and self-help. Thus, "Continual Work" (later in this chapter) explains how I am adapting my care-based content to reflect ongoing research on intersectional equity.

Supported by a campus-wide initiative, curricular revision provided fertile soil to include well-being and intersectional equity. Topic-based music history courses use a case-study approach to help students cultivate musicological research methods, which they apply to semester-long research projects.[12] Drawing upon varied repertoires, these courses satisfy NASM's flexible guidelines and integrate with components of my institution's revised liberal education curriculum, including: instruction in interdisciplinary inquiry, diversity, research, and writing.[13]

"World Music Cultures" provides second-semester sophomores an introductory framework for the relationships between music and culture using Kay Kaufman Shelemay's *Soundscapes*.[14] Thus, students hopefully begin music history with an understanding that our work remains about music and culture, whether we study twentieth-century Accra or fourteenth-century Aquitaine. Despite this aspiration, ideological tension remains for students; in most curricula they have already spent one to two years in performance and theory working under different assumptions. We take opportunities to discuss these tensions, or differences, since they are not integrated across the bigger picture of their degree coursework, which remains focused on the content, processes, and assumptions of the classical music conservatory. In "World Music Cultures," students complete research assignments related to a fieldwork project with a local music culture. During past semesters, student groups have selected drag shows, open-mic night, coffee house performances, country line dancing, or karaoke. They apply scholarship and instruction on participant-observation fieldwork and library research on their topic.[15]

As students unsettle their preconceptions about music and culture, I take the opportunity for us to unpack the baggage we carry surrounding limiting definitions of "successful" or "authentic" musicking—and studenting, for that matter. Brené Brown's *Gifts of Imperfection* encourages students to cultivate authenticity through "the daily practice of letting go of who we think we're supposed to be and embracing who we are."[16] During college, emerging adults explore core parts of their identity, building skills for this continual iterative lifelong process.[17] Furthermore, students (and faculty) struggle with mental health, perfectionism, and self-imposed unrealistic expectations.[18] Brown's research presents students with concepts and tools to work through challenges presented by the fieldwork project, and the music major writ large. She explores the impact of shame and the power of identifying and letting go of our shame narratives, rather than hiding or ignoring them. Courage includes "speaking honestly and openly about who we are, about what we're feeling, and about our experiences (good and bad)." Compassion recognizes shared humanity, fuels an empathetic relationship between equals, and requires "setting boundaries and holding people accountable." Connection is "the energy that exists between people when they feel seen, heard, and valued; when they can give and receive without judgment; and when they derive sustenance and strength from the relationship."[19] Brown provides ten daily practices for wholehearted living, and students select something to enhance their personal and intellectual growth, recognizing that they might focus on different concepts based on their changing needs during the semester. While all of Brown's practices could apply to music majors, students routinely note that the following offer a welcome perspective shift: "Cultivating Self-Compassion: Letting Go of Perfectionism," "Cultivating Creativity: Letting Go of Comparison," "Cultivating Play and Rest: Letting Go of Exhaustion as a Status Symbol and Productivity as Self-Worth," and "Cultivating Meaningful Work: Letting Go of Self-Doubt and 'Supposed To.'"[20] These topics help them notice uncaring realities in their learning experiences across the siloed subdisciplines within the music major.

As students record observations, analysis, and individual experiences in their fieldwork journal, they often cite Brown's research about courage, compassion, connection, shame, or vulnerability while they reflect and unpack their individual reactions in the field. During in-class workshops on fieldwork-project assignments, they discuss information from Brown's research. It feels challenging and uncomfortable to collaborate with student peers on a project. In short, they prefer more transactional learning activities such as lectures, tests, and working alone to check the learning box, go to work, and get back to their life. Furthermore, participant-observation research with strangers in unfamiliar venues remains daunting, even more so if you embody minoritized identities.

Students discuss the relationships between Shelemay's case studies and their experiences in the practice room, rehearsals, and the concert hall; they also use concepts from Brown's research, such as naming and letting go of shame, comparison, or productivity as self-worth. Therefore, integrating well-being scholarship opens space for students to acknowledge and grapple with the negative emotional impact of music-department policies, practices, and procedures. Faculty take these for granted as normative, yet students increasingly identify them as harmful to their personal and intellectual development.

"Music History 1: Gender & Sexuality" introduces first-semester juniors to concepts from the Medieval through Baroque periods of the music history survey. Using *Threshold Concepts in Women's and Gender Studies*, students learn about the social construction of gender, privilege and oppression, and intersectionality.[21] They apply these concepts to the music and cultures in the course calendar. To build writing and information literacy skills, multiple research assignments culminate in a concert plan designed to educate a local audience about the National Organization for Women (NOW). Through music and spoken word, each concert segment focuses on one of NOW's core issues.[22]

To foreground intersectional equity throughout course design, a topical connection pairs together a U.S. genre from the "more recent" past with European art music of the distant past.[23] For the topic of complaint/protest, we study the Medieval chanson *A Chantar* by the Comtessa de Dia and Maria Coldwell's chapter on joungleresses and trobairitz.[24] This is paired with "Memphis

Minnie-Jitis Blues" and Tammy Kernodle's essay "Having Her Say: The Blues as the Black Woman's Lament."[25] While discussing Memphis Minnie's protest of deplorable living conditions for black Americans, we explore parallels in Beyoncé's 2016 single "Formation."[26]

In this course, many students are uncomfortable and/or unaccustomed to unpacking how our world was (and still is) built, represented, and lived in gendered ways that privilege patriarchy. Brown's *Daring Greatly* helps students embrace discomfort associated with uncertainty, risk, or emotional exposure, which occur any time we step outside our comfort zone to grow.[27] In this course, specifically, students experience these emotions with the readings, robust discussion, collaborative projects, and, frankly, the "different" orientation to the expected music history survey. They develop tools to invest deeply in all aspects of the music major, while simultaneously examining the problematic underpinnings of our institutional culture. For example, Brown explores the impact in our culture of scarcity and "never enough."[28] She discusses the relationship between shame, comparison, and disengagement.[29] Thus, if we want our students to remain engaged, we should invest in tools to combat shame and comparison. To affect equitable change, Brown poses questions to examine institutional culture and address discrepancies.[30] For example, "What behaviors are rewarded? Punished?" and "What rules and expectations are followed, enforced, and ignored?"[31] Applying this information, students have often asked iterations of this question: "Why are revivals of standard musicals in the theater department celebrated for making fresh changes that respond to inequitable gendered realities, while performances of canonic works in the music department continue to reinscribe oppressive gendered norms?"

Brown posits, "to reignite creativity, innovation, and learning, leaders must rehumanize education and work."[32] This involves helping people understand expectations and teaching them how to give and receive feedback in a way that fosters engagement and growth. If leaders prize learning, critical thinking, and transformation, they need to normalize discomfort. Brown tells students, "If you're comfortable, I'm not teaching and you're not learning. It's going to get uncomfortable in here and that's okay. It's normal and it's part of the process."[33] While these concepts may seem countercultural to the study of classical music, *Daring Greatly* helps faculty cocreate and cofacilitate cooperative learning environments. Rather than instructors pushing students to work harder, Brown's social work research teaches faculty and students how to collaborate and learn while noticing and managing discomfort.

As we learn and apply gender studies concepts, students note the relationship with concepts in *Daring Greatly*. They document how gender is constructed "then" and "now" through studying the experiences of musicians in their respective cultures. Students note how varied cultures from the past and present remain structured, albeit in different ways, to privilege dominant groups at the expense of oppressing the "other." They see how social constructs impact the ways innovation, engagement, struggle, learning, and growth are defined and regarded within our music institutions. *Daring Greatly* culminates in Brown's leadership manifesto, which in particular provides tools music faculty and students can apply to shift the culture of patriarchy and white supremacy embedded in our discipline.[34]

"Music History 2: Antiracist Liberation" introduces second-semester juniors to concepts from the classic through contemporary periods of the music history survey.[35] The course builds on the Equal Justice Initiative's (EJI) reparative work of truth-telling and reckoning with narratives and legacies of racial difference and violence by connecting it to student research on music and culture. Students develop writing and information literacy skills in multiple research assignments that culminate in a concert plan designed to educate a Nebraska audience about the EJI.[36] Using music and spoken word, students design multiple concert segments focused on the EJI's reports on slavery, reconstruction, lynching, and segregation.[37]

Acknowledging many students' unfamiliarity and discomfort with racial justice, our work in Music History 2 begins with scholarship that examines how racism operates in the United States, or, in other words, how unspoken assumptions of white supremacy undergird our institutions and ideologies.[38] The next unit, titled "The Story We Tell," provides a five-day intensive overview of the classic period, the nineteenth century, the turn of the century, modernism, and postmodernism. The following two class sessions unsettle the traditional music history survey narrative, treating it as an object of inquiry. First, "The Birth of American Music" from the *1619* podcast invites us to ask "What's Missing from the Story We Tell?"[39] Second, Kajikawa's essay in *Seeing Race Again* helps us understand "Why It's Missing," a possessive investment in whiteness within U.S. music departments.[40] A summer 2020 interview with Bryan Stevenson, EJI's founding executive director, invokes the need for and possibility of racial reconciliation.[41] The *Reconstruction* documentary by Henry Louis Gates Jr. demonstrates repair by teaching information that has been intentionally excluded from our education.[42] Gates also shows how the arts have been marshalled to reinforce white supremacy within the popular imagination in order to justify Jim Crow laws then and black exclusion from political power now. While building knowledge and skills for the concert project, students simultaneously bring one piece of music to each class, using Burnim and Maultsby's *African American Music* as a suggested resource.[43]

In *The Body Is Not an Apology*, Sonya Renee Taylor teaches readers to embody critical consciousness through connections between well-being and systemic oppression. She affirms, "A return to self-love requires our commitment to building shame-free, inclusive communities that uplift one another while honestly addressing body terrorism in all the ways it manifests as oppression based on age, race, gender, size, ability, sexual orientation, mental health status, and all other human attributes."[44] Students recognize the ways that social, political, and economic systems have wrought intersectional oppression on bodies. In other words, "violence, poverty, [and] injustice . . . happen to bodies."[45] We explore how shame, guilt, and apology result from socialized oppressive norms, default bodies, and body hierarchies.[46] Taylor asserts, "We have ranked our bodies against the bodies of others, deciding they are greater or lesser than our own based on the prejudices and biases we inherited."[47] Her fourteen "Unapologetic Agreements" infuse our shared work around racial justice and music. Through structured student-facilitated dialogues, an iterative individual research journal, and the concert project, students embrace "curiosity-driven dialogue," "multiple perspectives," "varied journeys," and "unapologetic inquiry."[48]

Taylor invites readers to "see ourselves and others in the fullness of our complexities and intersections and . . . work to create space for those intersections."[49] Through their concert project, students create space in Nebraska to see the work of the EJI and to value black lives. To help students draw local immediacy and relevance, we examine recent local news about slavery, lynching, and the death penalty.[50] Considering potent connections between present and past, the concert project invites Nebraskans to "understand and accept the bodies of others," a goal of Taylor's concept of radical self-love.[51] Thus, the music history classroom provides an opportunity for students to learn about and situate the traditional survey using racial justice scholarship, and to connect music-making to education about local legacies of injustice and the need for repair and equity.

In **"Senior Capstone Seminar"** students complete research on any topic that supports the next step in their career goals, culminating in a public presentation and dialogue. Guided by our institutional and departmental learning outcomes, they also assess their summative educational experience. Connected to this work, I selected *Rising Strong* because it helps students develop skills to acknowledge, examine, and learn from failure.[52] Since students will soon be launching careers, I am also drawn to Brown's important assertion that "we . . . need a critical mass of badasses who are willing to dare, fall, feel their way through emotion, and rise again. And we need these folks leading, modeling, and shaping culture in every capacity."[53] Honoring the social and emotional complexities of failure, she designed a three-step "rising strong process," explained throughout the book.[54] First, "the reckoning" asks students to notice emotions associated with struggle and failure and examine how failure and the associated emotions are connected to our thoughts and behaviors. Second, "the rumble" asks us to notice stories we create about failures, so we can critique our assumptions. Third, "the revolution" invites readers to assess the learnings born of failure, so we can change our thoughts and behaviors and engage more deliberately in future challenges.

Throughout work on their capstone project, students practice acknowledging and working through the roadblocks and failures that lead to new directions and growth. This happens during in-class workshop discussions and as part of the iterative assignments that culminate in the final presentation and dialogue. A summative essay assignment invites reflection on institutional and departmental learning outcomes. As they write, students often recognize new ways of dealing with situations, informed by how they could have better handled past struggles or failures. Some students express, "I wish you would have assigned this book earlier in our education." While I remain open to the idea, I wonder, "Should they read it sooner? Or is it more impactful after having experienced the past three years of college and thinking about moving into your future?"

A Glimpse Inside the Classroom

Since well-being scholarship integrates with course objectives, content, and skills, students engage it similarly to discipline-specific material. Assignments and in-class activities facilitate student understanding, analysis, and application of the well-being reading. This approach keeps well-being on the same plane as discipline-specific content while simultaneously normalizing and destigmatizing well-being topics.

Low-stakes writing prompts and verbal welcoming questions may include, "Which well-being concept are you currently practicing this week in your personal development or your research project? Which well-being concept could you practice while preparing for midterms or an upcoming high-stakes presentation or performance?"

Three medium-stakes writing assignments embed well-being scholarship among multiple required prompts. The beginning-of-semester learning plan asks, "Which concepts from this book pique your interest to foster personal and intellectual growth?" A mid-semester vocation reflection includes, "Which concepts from this book help you cultivate facets of vocation?" Students apply interdisciplinary course content to develop their vocation and leadership identities. The end-of-semester learning reflection states, "Discuss how you used concepts from this book to foster personal and intellectual growth."

Anonymous write-and-share exercises open communal space for well-being scholarship. Students respond to prompts on a half-sheet of paper; I collect, shuffle, and pass them back. We read what students wrote to share anonymously with our learning community. A first-day prompt, which students enjoy, states, "Tell us: one thing you're excited about; one thing you're worried about; one thing you can give to care for us; one thing you need from us (that may require extra courage to ask for)." During stressful arcs of the semester, students respond well to this prompt: "Tell us one thing you need to hear from someone you trust so that you will feel more empowered right now." Small-group discussion provides another forum, and two possible prompts include: "How do concepts from the well-being reading apply to the current research project assignment? Design a brief professional development session for students using two to four concepts from the well-being reading." As we collaboratively apply well-being scholarship, students learn that the ways they approach their work and the subject of music is bound inextricably with thinking care-fully about people.

Understanding Resistance

Student responses to well-being scholarship contribute to the fraught complexity of facilitating a productive learning environment, including earnest engagement, disinterest, shutting down, complaining, derailing conversation, minimizing the information, oversharing, or using well-being content to attack peers. I created a handout with helpful guidelines from recent scholarship to frame our class discussions and foster a collaborative learning environment.[55] (See figure 4.1 at the end of the chapter.) Furthermore, I continue to learn facilitation techniques to honor student contributions and maintain focus on the well-being scholarship and its application to course objectives and lived experience.[56]

While many students express feeling support from a white male professor affirming a shared human experience of journey, struggle, failure, and growth, some resist. They may view well-being scholarship as superfluous, "touchy-feely," "new-age nonsense," or nonacademic. Others note that well-being research constitutes nonmusical content and therefore has no place in music classrooms. These responses invite us to explore dissent to understand the sources of conflicting perspectives and approaches. Though all may not agree, we can notice how and discuss why our tightly drawn disciplinary borders resist interdisciplinary content or processes, including care-based work. In some cases, student concerns are fueled by their conversations with colleagues who are beholden to their experience with the music history survey. This further exacerbates our precarity and alienation.

Since the academy and conservatory remain bastions of the "imperialist white-supremacist capitalist patriarchy," pushback is expected, and nevertheless, we persist.[57] Perhaps resistance provides a coping mechanism for students who are not yet ready to learn well-being. Often students come from backgrounds where emotions or well-being remain unwelcome discussion topics. Some are not allowed to acknowledge, discuss, or seek professional treatment for their mental health status. Some experience trauma before or soon after they arrive at college. Thus, engaging well-being scholarship remains radical and vital.

Students register resistance on anonymous mid-semester check-ins (self-administered) and end-of-semester evaluations (university-administered). This feels discouraging, given the urgency of care, and precarious, due to increased emphasis placed on student opinions within our nation's customer-service model of higher education. Negative student comments on course evaluations wreak havoc on the mental health of resilient faculty and impede best practices of teaching and learning. For example, one student used my practice of Williams's "radical honesty" and Brown's vulnerability to question my job performance. They claimed that my self-disclosure of increased depression and anxiety due to divorce compromised my ability to teach well. The institutional emphasis placed on student evaluations exacerbates faculty job precarity; this could be easily ameliorated with more focus on scholarship of teaching and learning together with colleague observations. Job insecurity remains exponentially amplified for the growing force of contingent-labor faculty. For all, it remains a fraught balance to demonstrate to students, faculty, and administrators, "I'm earnestly listening to student concerns and making adjustments, where needed. Here's how my work is firmly rooted in the scholarship of teaching and learning. It's normal to feel uncomfortable, have concerns, or perhaps disagree." Regarding the overreliance on student evaluations as an indicator of success, continued employment, tenure, and promotion, Parker Palmer asserts, "students who have been well served by good teachers may walk away . . . angry that their prejudices have been challenged and their sense of self shaken. That sort of dissatisfaction may be a sign that real education has happened. . . . A marketing model of educational community, however apt its ethic of accountability, serves the cause poorly when it assumes that the customer is always right."[58]

Continual Work

My curricular and pedagogical approaches represent ongoing research and adjustments. Through a process that began in 2012, I am learning that my vocation centers community, collaborative learning, interdisciplinary connections, and intersectional equity, all of which intersect with care. For me, and many others, graduate training required objective systematic rigor in research and writing at the expense of personal proximity or emotional response.[59] Thus, I remained unaware of scholarship that welcomes care pedagogy until I began my work as faculty cocoordinator for new student programs at my institution. My success in that collaborative role with Karri Sanderson, dean of student success and engagement, was only possible through her generous mentoring. Beginning January 2019, sabbatical research on antiracism revealed that BIPOC scholars of critical and inclusive pedagogies have long been doing the work of care. My lack of awareness betrays an education rooted in content, skills, and "white supremacy culture," my segregated socialization, and continued choices to remain in predominantly white spaces until recent years.[60] Connected to my lifelong work of recognizing, resisting, and dismantling white supremacy culture, I am committed to researching well-being scholarship from BIPOC authors invested in intersectional equity.[61]

Turning to the classroom, in order to decenter whiteness, amplify communal care, and underscore the complicated nature of care, I am currently selecting and integrating new sources. For "World Music Cultures," Morgan Harper Nichols draws on her experiences as an autistic musician, poet, and artist to show students how *Peace Is a Practice* rooted in deep breathing, iterative cycles, and communal living.[62] Advocating for embodied intersectional feminism, Taylor's *The Body Is Not an Apology* deepens our work in "Music History 1: Gender & Sexuality." Podcast interviews with BIPOC authors present students with perspectives on equity and care in "Music History 2: Antiracist Liberation."[63] Finally, for "Senior Capstone Seminar," adrienne maree brown's *Emergent Strategy* immerses students in adaptive leadership informed by equity and environmental justice.[64] Assigned materials will change as I continue collaborative learning with students and colleagues.[65]

Conclusion

Integrating well-being scholarship reinforces skill development with discipline-specific content and forms a foundation for intersectional antiracist equity. This valuable body of knowledge centers learning as a process and helps students and faculty develop tools to embrace and work through challenges. Faculty reinforce student success by including ourselves in shared humanity and collaborative processes. Simply put, I remain on the same uncomfortable journey of intellectual and personal growth alongside them. One student wrote: "I have dealt with crippling anxiety since junior high. When you shared on the first day about your struggle with depression and anxiety and coping with meeting new groups of people, I felt reassured for the upcoming semester because my professor knows what depression and anxiety feel like" (used with permission).

As faculty acknowledge national reports about increased student mental health struggles, care pedagogy coupled with intersectional equity work helps

FOSTERING OUR LEARNING COMMUNITY

<u>Rationale</u>

- **Boundaries** should provide for broadening of understandings and challenging of preconceptions.[1]
- How do we **create space for: questions** rather than agreements, fostering **openness around our hidden "isms"** (racism, sexism, classism, heterosexism, etc.), and **encouraging growth**?[2]
- How do we **rely on each other to remember and apply** guidelines during discussions throughout the semester?[3]
- <u>**Class discussion**</u> is practicing how to use empirical evidence to <u>**build arguments**</u> and <u>**frame problems**</u>. We will use the **application** and **analysis** (learning skills) of newly acquired knowledge as a tool for **argument formation** and **evaluation** (learning skills).[4]
- An argument is defined as a series of statements built using theoretical or empirical evidence leading from a premise to a conclusion.
- Opinions do not include empirical evidence to develop a line of reasoning leading from a premise to a conclusion.

<u>**Embracing discomfort**</u> is important to learning and to developing a set of communication skills that will prepare people for productive contributions to public discourse, especially on topics of inequality in the future.[5]

- In order to develop communication skills necessary to facilitate and contribute to productive discourse, people need to acknowledge and feel discomfort, use discomfort to understand social frameworks that create these feelings, and leave these narratives behind as part of growth.[6]
- The ability to communicate across social boundaries is imperative to synthesis, which requires people to compile evidence into new patterns and encourages the formation of alternate solutions to the same problem.[7] (class discussion and research project)

Figure 4.1. Handout: Fostering Our Learning Community

Controversy with Civility[8]

- Conflict is a natural outcome in a diverse group.
- Continued engagement through conflict is important.
- Civility allows room for strong emotion and rigorous challenge.
- Commitment to understand sources of disagreement and to work cooperatively is necessary.

Own Your Intentions and Your Impact[9]

- Learn how you have caused harm, better understand how and why you did so, and learn what role privilege has played in creating the gap between intention and impact, so you can show up better next time.
- The impact of our actions is not always congruent with intentions.
- Positive or neutral intentions do not trump negative impact.
- Although we have some choice in how we respond to and express our emotions, we do not have control over which ones we experience at any given time and to what degree.

Be aware of what factors influence your decisions about whether **to engage and challenge yourself** on a given issue.[10]

- How does privilege keep you from challenging yourself?
- How is your daily life affected if you choose not to challenge yourself?

What are the different ways we **demonstrate respectfulness to each other**?[11]

- How might you firmly challenge the views of someone in a respectful manner?
- How can you respond when you are firmly and respectfully challenged?
- How do cultural understandings shape ideas about respectfulness? (For example, in some cultural contexts interruption, talking over one another, and strong emotions are welcome.)

Figure 4.1. (continued)

What are **<u>the differences between a personal attack on an individual and a challenge to an individual's idea, belief, or statement</u>** that simply makes an individual feel uncomfortable?[12]

- Suggestions could be: "I find that idea/statement/belief to be heterosexist because . . ." or "I felt _____ when you said _________ because . . ."
- Instead of "you're a jerk," "that idea is worthless," and so forth.

How do we (in this learning community) demonstrate respectfulness to each other? (Starting place from our day-two discussion):

- Note that our ideas of "civility," "respect," "nice," and "kind" are complicated by race, ethnicity, gender, socioeconomic status, ability, and other markers of identity.

Notes

1. Jasmine L. Harris, "Uncomfortable Learning," in *Difficult Subjects: Insights and Strategies for Teaching about Race, Sexuality, and Gender*, ed. Badia Ahad-Legardy and OiYan A. Poon (Sterling, VA: Stylus Publishing, 2018), 254.
2. Harris, "Uncomfortable Learning," 255.
3. Harris, "Uncomfortable Learning," 255.
4. Harris, "Uncomfortable Learning," 258.
5. Harris, "Uncomfortable Learning," 253.
6. Harris, "Uncomfortable Learning," 261–62.
7. Harris, "Uncomfortable Learning," 259.
8. Brian Arao and Kristi Clemens, "From Safe Spaces to Brave Spaces," in *The Art of Effective Facilitation: Reflections from Social Justice Educators*, ed. Lisa M. Landreman (Sterling, VA: Stylus Publishing, 2013), 144.
9. Arao and Clemens, "From Safe Spaces," 145–46.
10. Arao and Clemens, "From Safe Spaces," 147.
11. Arao and Clemens, "From Safe Spaces," 147–48.
12. Arao and Clemens, "From Safe Spaces," 148–49.

Figure 4.1. (continued)

students persist to graduation and thrive beyond their college years. If this approach piques your interest and aligns with your vocation, select well-being scholarship that complements your ways of teaching and learning with students. Two of my music colleagues use Angela Duckworth's *Grit* and Carol Dweck's *Mindset*.[66] An English colleague uses Ken Bain's *What the Best College Students Do*.[67] Integrate scholarship that reinforces your learning outcomes and pedagogical processes. Cultivate openness to acknowledge and learn from painful moments of failure and get back up to try again.

Notes

1. George Kuh, Jillian Kinzie, John Schuh, Elizabeth Whitt, et al., *Student Success in College: Creating Conditions That Matter*, 2nd ed. (San Francisco: Jossey-Bass, 2016); Lori Patton, Kristen Renn, Florence Guido, Stephen John Quaye, *Student Development in College: Theory, Research, and Practice*, 3rd ed. (San Francisco: Jossey-Bass, 2016); Kristen Renn and Robert Reason, *College Students in the United States: Characteristics, Experiences, and Outcomes* (San Francisco: Jossey-Bass, 2012); Parker Palmer, *The Courage to Teach: Exploring the Inner Landscape of a Teacher's Life*, 2nd ed. (San Francisco: Jossey-Bass, 2017).

2. bell hooks, *Teaching to Transgress: Education as the Practice of Freedom* (New York: Routledge, 1994); bell hooks, *Teaching Community: A Pedagogy of Hope* (New York: Routledge, 2004); bell hooks, *Teaching Critical Thinking: Practical Wisdom* (New York: Routledge, 2010); Paulo Freire, *Pedagogy of the Oppressed* (New York: Penguin Books, 1970); Paulo Freire, *Education for Critical Consciousness* (New York: Seabury Press, 1973).

3. Frank Tuitt, Chayla Haynes, and Saran Stewart, eds., *Race, Equity, and the Learning Environment: The Global Relevance of Critical and Inclusive Pedagogies in Higher Education* (Sterling, VA: Stylus Publishing, 2016); Badia Ahad-Legardy and OiYan Poon, eds., *Difficult Subjects: Insights and Strategies for Teaching about Race, Sexuality, and Gender* (Sterling, VA: Stylus Publishing, 2018); Kevin Gannon, *Radical Hope: A Teaching Manifesto* (Morgantown: West Virginia University Press, 2020).

4. Bonnie Gordon, "Why We Matter," *Women and Music* 19 (2015): 116–24; Loren Kajikawa, "The Possessive Investment in Classical Music: Confronting Legacies of White Supremacy in U.S. Schools and Departments of Music," in *Seeing Race Again: Countering Colorblindness across the Disciplines*, ed. Kimberlé Williams Crenshaw, Luke Charles Harris, Daniel Martinez HoSang, and George Lipsitz (Berkeley: University of California Press, 2019), 155–74. See all articles in *Journal of Music History Pedagogy* 10, no. 1 (2020).

5. William Cheng, *Just Vibrations: The Purpose of Sounding Good* (Ann Arbor: University of Michigan Press, 2016).

6. Bianca Williams, "Radical Honesty: Truth-Telling as Pedagogy for Working through Shame in Academic Spaces," in Tuitt, Haynes, and Stewart, *Race, Equity, and the Learning Environment*, 72–73, 81.

7. bell hooks, *Understanding Patriarchy* (Louisville Anarchist Federation Federation

and No Borders: Louisville's Radical Lending Library), accessed May 20, 2020, https://imaginenoborders.org/pdf/zines/UnderstandingPatriarchy.pdf.

8. "Nikole Hannah-Jones Issues Statement on Decision to Decline Tenure Offer at University of North Carolina-Chapel Hill and to Accept Knight Chair Appointment at Howard University," *Legal Defense Fund*, July 6, 2021, https://www.naacpldf.org/.

9. The introduction of this volume discusses these topics. See also Alyson Cole, "All of Us Are Vulnerable, but Some Are More Vulnerable Than Others: The Political Ambiguity of Vulnerability Studies, an Ambivalent Critique," *Critical Horizons* 17, no. 2 (2016): 260–77.

10. See Sarah Schulman, *Conflict Is Not Abuse: Overstating Harm, Community Responsibility, and the Duty of Repair* (Vancouver: Arsenal Pulp Press, 2016); Jessica Bennett, "What If Instead of Calling People Out, We Called Them In?" *New York Times*, November 19, 2020, https://www.nytimes.com/; Jessica Bennett, "If Everything Is 'Trauma,' Is Anything?" February 4, 2022, https://www.nytimes.com/; Tim Craig and Lori Rozsa, "In His Fight against 'Woke' Schools, DeSantis Tears at the Seams of a Diverse Florida," *Washington Post*, February 7, 2022, https://www.washingtonpost.com/.

11. Virginia Strand and Jo Ann Coe Regan, steering committee chairs, *Specialized Practice Curricular Guide for Trauma-Informed Social Work Practice* (Alexandria, VA: Council on Social Work Education, 2018), https://www.cswe.org/getattachment/Education-Resources/2015-Curricular-Guides/2015EPAS_TraumaInformedSW_Final-WEB.pdf; Bessel van der Kolk, *The Body Keeps the Score: Brain, Mind, and Body in the Healing of Trauma* (New York: Penguin Books, 2015); Thema Bryant, *Homecoming: Overcome Fear and Trauma to Reclaim Your Whole, Authentic Self* (New York: Tarcher Pergree, 2022); Janice Carello and Phyllis Thompson, *Lessons from the Pandemic: Trauma-Informed Approaches to College, Crisis, and Change* (New York: Palgrave Macmillan, 2021); Phyllis Thompson and Janice Carello, eds., *Trauma-Informed Pedagogies: A Guide for Responding to Crisis and Inequality in Higher Education* (New York: Palgrave Macmillan, 2022); Cia Verschelden, *Bandwidth Recovery: Helping Students Reclaim Cognitive Resources Lost to Poverty, Racism, and Social Marginalization* (Sterling, VA: Stylus Publishing, 2017); Thomas Tobin and Kirsten Behling, *Reach Everyone, Teach Everyone: Universal Design for Learning in Higher Education* (Morgantown: West Virginia University Press, 2018); Leah Lakshmi Piepzna-Samarasinha, *Care Work: Dreaming Disability Justice* (Vancouver: Arsenal Pulp Press, 2018); Robyn Henderson-Espinoza, *Body Becoming: A Path to Our Liberation* (Minneapolis: Broadleaf Books, 2022); Lennard Davis, *Beginning with Disability: A Primer* (New York: Routledge, 2017).

12. See John Spilker, "Adventures in 'Survey Adjacent' Music History Courses," *Musicology Now*, November 16, 2017, https://musicologynow.org/.

13. See Don Gibson, "The Curricular Standards of NASM and Their Impact on Local Decision Making," *Journal of Music History Pedagogy* 5, no. 2 (2015): 73–76. Among other things, he notes that NASM does not require coverage of the six historical periods. Rather, flexible guidelines for content, repertories, methods, and competencies are shared by the entire degree program, not just music history coursework.

14. Kay Kaufman Shelemay, *Soundscapes: Exploring Music in a Changing World*, 3rd ed. (New York: Norton, 2015).

15. Robert Emerson, Rachel Fretz, Linda Shaw, *Writing Ethnographic Fieldnotes*, 2nd ed. (Chicago: University of Chicago Press, 2011).

16. Brené Brown, *Gifts of Imperfection: Let Go of Who You Think You're Supposed to Be and Embrace Who You Are* (Center City, MN: Hazelden Press, 2010), 50.

17. See Sharon Daloz Parks, *Big Questions, Worthy Dreams: Mentoring Emerging Adults in Their Search for Meaning, Purpose, and Faith* (San Francisco: Jossey-Bass, 2011).

18. hooks, *Teaching Critical Thinking*, 121–26; hooks, *Teaching Community*, 93–103.

19. Brown, *Gifts of Imperfection*, 12–13, 16–17, 19.

20. Brown, 55–62, 93–98, 99–104, 111–16.

21. Christie Launius and Holly Hassell, *Threshold Concepts in Women's and Gender Studies: Ways of Seeing, Thinking, and Knowing*, 2nd ed. (New York: Routledge, 2018).

22. National Organization for Women, "Core Issues," accessed January 28, 2021, https://now.org/issues/.

23. "Recent past" is relative to the distant past of, say, the Middle Ages or Renaissance. At the 2017 Teaching Music History Conference, Sara Haefeli suggested that our students' concept of early music likely comprises anything before the 1980s, definitely anything before the Beatles.

24. Maria Coldwell, "Jounglerresses and Trobairitz: Secular Musicians in Medieval France," in *Women Making Music: The Western Art Tradition, 1150–1950*, ed. Jane Bowers and Judith Tick (Urbana: University of Illinois Press, 1986), 39–61.

25. Tammy Kernodle, "Having Her Say: The Blues as the Black Woman's Lament," in *Women's Voices across Musical Worlds*, ed. Jane A. Bernstein (Boston: Northeastern University Press, 2004), 213–31.

26. Beyoncé, "Formation," accessed February 27, 2019, https://www.youtube.com/.

27. Brené Brown, *Daring Greatly: How the Courage to Be Vulnerable Changes the Way We Live, Love, Parent, and Lead* (New York: Gotham Books, 2012), 33–37.

28. Brown, 18–30.

29. Brown, 27–29.

30. Brown, 173–83.

31. Brown, 174–75.

32. Brown, 184–212, quotation on 184.

33. Brown, 199.

34. Brown, 212.

35. An in-depth discussion about this course is found in John Spilker, "Transdisciplinary Antiracism Research and Teaching as a Foundation for Revising Music Coursework," in *Teaching and Learning Difficult Topics in the Music Classroom*, ed. Laura Moore Pruett and Olivia Lucas (Ann Arbor: University of Michigan Press, forthcoming).

36. See https://eji.org/, accessed January 30, 2021.

37. *Slavery in America: The Montgomery Slave Trade* (Montgomery: Equal Justice Initiative, 2018), https://eji.org/wp-content/uploads/2019/10/slavery-in-america-report.pdf; *Reconstruction in America: Racial Violence after the Civil War, 1865–1876* (Montgomery: Equal Justice Initiative, 2020), https://eji.org/wp-content/uploads/2020/07/reconstruction-in-america-report.pdf; *Lynching in America: Confronting the Legacy of Racial Terror Lynching* (Montgomery: Equal Justice Initiative, 2017), https://

lynchinginamerica.eji.org/report/; *Segregation in America* (Montgomery: Equal Justice Initiative, 2018), https://segregationinamerica.eji.org/report/.

38. Currently we read select chapters from Robin DiAngelo, *White Fragility: Why It's So Hard for White People to Talk about Racism* (Boston: Beacon Press, 2018); Ibram Kendi, *How to Be an Antiracist* (New York: One World, 2019); Derald Wing Sue, *Race Talk and the Conspiracy of Silence: Understanding and Facilitating Difficult Dialogues on Race* (Hoboken, NJ: Wiley, 2016); Resmaa Menakem, *My Grandmother's Hands: Racialized Trauma and the Pathway to Mending Our Hearts and Bodies* (Las Vegas: Central Recovery Press, 2017); Isabel Wilkerson, *Caste: The Origins of Our Discontents* (New York: Random House, 2020); Joseph Barndt, *Understanding and Dismantling Racism: The Twenty-First-Century Challenge to White America* (Minneapolis: Fortress Press, 2007).

39. Nikole Hannah-Jones, "The Birth of American Music," September 6, 2019, in *1619*, podcast, episode 3, https://www.nytimes.com/2019/09/06/podcasts/1619-black-american-music-appropriation.html.

40. Kajikawa, "Possessive Investment."

41. Ezra Klein, "Bryan Stevenson on How America Can Heal," *Vox Conversations*, July 20, 2020, https://www.vox.com/.

42. Henry Louis Gates Jr., *Reconstruction: America after the Civil War*, Public Broadcasting Service, 2019, https://www.pbs.org/weta/reconstruction/. The series is based on Henry Louis Gates Jr., *Stony the Road: Reconstruction, White Supremacy, and the Rise of Jim Crow* (New York: Penguin Books, 2019).

43. Mellonee Burnim and Portia Maultsby, eds., *African American Music: An Introduction*, 2nd ed. (New York: Routledge, 2014).

44. Sonya Renee Taylor, *The Body Is Not an Apology: The Power of Radical Self-Love* (Oakland, CA: Berrett-Koehler Publishers, 2018), 87.

45. Taylor, 4.

46. Taylor, 25–56.

47. Taylor, 13.

48. Taylor, 87–91.

49. Taylor, 9.

50. Todd Cooper, "Most Nebraskans Voted to Abolish Slavery as Criminal Punishment. But 32% Voted to Keep It," *Omaha World Herald*, November 6, 2020, https://omaha.com/; Chris Burbach, "Hundreds Gather for Ceremony at Omaha Courthouse on Anniversary of 1919 Lynching and Riot," *Omaha World Herald*, September 29, 2019, https://omaha.com/; Paul Hammell, "Nebraskans Vote Overwhelmingly to Restore Death Penalty, Nullify Historic 2015 Vote by State Legislature," *Omaha World Herald*, November 9, 2016, https://omaha.com/.

51. Taylor, *Body Is Not*, 9.

52. Brené Brown, *Rising Strong: The Reckoning, the Rumble, the Revolution* (New York: Spiegel and Grau, 2015).

53. Brown, xxvii–xxviii.

54. Brown, 37.

55. See Jasmine Harris, "Uncomfortable Learning," in Ahad-Legardy and Poon, *Difficult Subjects*, 248–65; Brian Arao and Kristi Clemens, "From Safe Spaces to Brave Spaces," in *The Art of Effective Facilitation: Reflections from Social Justice Educators*, ed. Lisa Landreman (Sterling, VA: Stylus Publishing, 2013), 135–50.

56. Landreman, *Art of Effective Facilitation*; Oliver Escobar, *Public Dialogue and Deliberation: A Communication Perspective for Public Engagement Practitioners* (Edinburgh, UK: Beacon for Public Engagement, 2011); Marianne Mille Bojer, Heiko Roehl, Marianne Knuth, and Colleen Magner, *Mapping Dialogue: Essential Tools for Social Change* (Chagrin Falls, OH: Taos Institute Publications, 2008).

57. hooks, *Understanding Patriarchy*.

58. Palmer, *Courage to Teach*, 96–97.

59. One can imagine my surprise and delight when a colleague shared with me Susanne Cusick, "On a Lesbian Relationship with Music: A Serious Effort to Not Think Straight," in *Queering the Pitch*, ed. Philip Brett (New York: Routledge, 2006), 67–83. This currently grounds a queerness case study in "Music History 1: Gender and Sexuality."

60. Tema Okun, "White Supremacy Culture," https://www.whitesupremacyculture.info/. Her original 1999 collaborative article of the same name is found here: https://www.whitesupremacyculture.info/uploads/4/3/5/7/43579015/characteristics_of_white_supremacy_culture-_original.jpg.

61. For example, Karen Walrond, *The Lightmaker's Manifesto: How to Work for Change Without Losing Your Joy* (Minneapolis: Broadleaf Books, 2021); Nedra Tawwab Glover, *Set Boundaries, Find Peace: A Guide to Reclaiming Yourself* (New York: Tarcher Perigee, 2021); Shawn Ginwright, *The Four Pivots: Reimagining Justice, Reimagining Ourselves* (Berkeley, CA: North Atlantic Books, 2022); Anneliese Singh, *The Racial Healing Handbook: Practical Activities to Help You Challenge Privilege, Confront Systemic Racism, and Engage in Collective Healing* (Oakland, CA: New Harbinger Publications, 2019); Mary-Frances Winters, *Black Fatigue: How Racism Erodes the Mind, Body, and Spirit* (Oakland, CA: Berrett-Koehler Publishers, 2020); Resmaa Menakem, *The Quaking of America: An Embodied Guide to Navigating Our Nation's Upheaval and Racial Reckoning* (Las Vegas: Central Recovery Press, 2022); Valerie Kaur, *See No Stranger: A Memoir and Manifesto of Revolutionary Love* (New York: One World, 2020); Tarana Burke, *Unbound: My Story of Liberation and the Birth of the Me Too Movement* (New York: Flatiron Books, 2021); Tarana Burke and Brené Brown, *You Are Your Best Thing: Vulnerability, Shame Resilience, and the Black Experience* (New York: Random House, 2021).

62. Morgan Harper Nichols, *Peace Is a Practice: An Invitation to Breathe Deep and Find a New Rhythm for Life* (Grand Rapids, MI: Zondervan Books, 2022).

63. Aiko Bethea, "Inclusivity at Work: The Heart of Hard Conversations," November 9, 2020, in *Dare to Lead*, podcast, https://brenebrown.com/podcast-show/dare-to-lead/; Aiko Bethea, "Creating Transformative Cultures," February 8, 2021, in *Dare to Lead*, podcast, https://brenebrown.com/podcast-show/dare-to-lead/; Oprah Winfrey and Bruce Perry, "Trauma, Resilience, Healing," May 5, 2021, in *Unlocking Us*, podcast, https://brenebrown.com/podcast-show/unlocking-us/; Austin Channing Brown, "I'm

Still Here: Black Dignity in a World Made for Whiteness," June 10, 2020, in *Unlocking Us*, podcast, https://brenebrown.com/podcast-show/unlocking-us/; Jodi-Ann Burey and Ruchika Tulshyan, "Imposter Syndrome," October 11, 2021, in *Dare to Lead*, podcast, https://brenebrown.com/podcast/imposter-syndrome/.

64. adrienne maree brown, *Emergent Strategy: Shaping Change, Changing Worlds* (Chico, CA: AK Press, 2017).

65. For example, I look forward to studying and applying information from these newly released sources: Horace Maxile, Jr. and Kristen Turner, *Race and Gender in the Western Music History Survey: A Teacher's Guide* (New York: Routledge, 2022) and Phillip Ewell, *On Music Theory, and Making Music More Welcoming for Everyone* (Ann Arbor: University of Michigan Press, 2023).

66. Angela Duckworth, *Grit: The Power of Passion and Perseverance* (New York: Scribner Press, 2016); Carol Dweck, *Mindset: The New Psychology of Success* (New York: Random House, 2016).

67. Ken Bain, *What the Best College Students Do* (Cambridge, MA: Belknap Press, 2012).

CHAPTER 5

Care, Carefully

Caring for the Whole Student from Recruitment through Retention

FREDERICK A. PETERBARK

Centering care in music needn't be limited to care in the traditional classroom. When I accepted a position in college recruitment, a reaction I received was, "You wasted your life. You got a degree in performance and teaching, and now you're doing neither." I remember telling them they were wrong. I explained that while I am not a full-time teacher or performer, I do both every day. While I do not teach in a space identified as a classroom, I teach prospective students and families both inside and outside of my office about the college admission process and the prospects of not only a career in the performing arts, but how the area of study will prepare them to pursue a job in any field. I am an educator. But most importantly, I care about students, and I have carefully watched and observed the changes that have taken place in education since I graduated from high school in 2001 and continue to react to them as a dean of enrollment and aid. By sharing my observations and actions with you I hope it helps us all better understand the students we are charged to care for in our colleges and universities and to center the value of care in our work in music and our service to students, regardless of what kind of teaching or mentorship we offer.

To care carefully means moving away from some of the teaching pitfalls that have haunted higher education in the past and, as an administrator, recognizing what modes of teaching and student support are proven to be most inclusive and adaptable and which might create the kind of environment that could bolster and assist students who need more support in place to succeed. My experience as a high school educator early in my career informs the teaching and decision-making in my career in higher-education music-enrollment management. Until the twenty-first century, the process of education was based on a teacher-centered classroom model. Also characterized as "direct instruction," teachers would "assert control over the material that students study and the ways in which they study it—i.e., when, where, how, and at what pace they learn it."[1] In 2001, however, the No Child Left Behind Act pushed the educational pendulum to an extreme, creating the means of assessing the teacher-centered classroom model by creating a law holding schools accountable for how kids learned and achieved, spawning new national education standards and various Standards of Learning (SOL) exams.[2] The law, unfortunately, undercut teachers' ability to use creative means of reaching and motivating underachieving students and/or inspiring and challenging overachieving students. As Robin Harwick writes in a recent article about standardized testing, "The narrowing of the curriculum for the benefit of high scores on standardized tests doesn't promote the development of cognitive abilities. Additionally, it stifles teachers. They can't teach a breadth of topics because they fear that their students won't score as high on the standardized tests."[3] While the idea of nationalizing education standards was motivated by a desire to leave "no child behind," the implementation created a new mantra for teachers and educators: "teach to the test." No Child Left Behind attempted to incentivize success by linking test results to future funding for both teachers and schools. Unfortunately, for some teachers and schools who were already struggling to produce results, the incentive became a catalyst for both criminal and negligent behavior. In 2013, thirty-five educators from the Atlanta Public Schools district were indicted in a major test-cheating scandal. As reported by CNN, "The cheating is believed to date back to 2001, when scores on statewide aptitude tests improved greatly, according to a 2013 indictment. The indictment also state[d] that for at least four years, between 2005 and 2009, test answers were altered, fabricated or falsely certified."[4] To me, this scandal was inevitable and, in hindsight, is no different than our recent experience with COVID-19 and the anxiety many felt regarding the uncertainty of the future.[5] These teachers wanted to ensure their livelihood. Although teachers can, for the most part, control their classroom and the information presented, they cannot control their students' retention of learned information and test preparation through means outside the classroom. Those variables can include whether the student studies, gets a good night's sleep, and does not have other impeding challenges like food deficiencies. Those variables could impact a student's performance on the same exam that could cost a teacher their salary and/or career. Simply put, some teachers cannot afford to take that risk, which results in substandard educational experience for students.

I experienced the depth of the systemic issues caused by standardized testing in my experience as a proctor for one of those exams. While student teaching in Detroit, Michigan, I attempted to report an issue of test language after proctoring a standardized test. The exam question asked students to *explore the strengths and weaknesses of an essay*. I was not completely surprised when the students' heads rose in near unison, as one student raised a hand to say, "I don't understand what I'm supposed to do." It made sense to me that while the students understood the term "explore," they did not comprehend what they were supposed to write. The direction was implicit, not explicit. When I inquired where I should report the issue, I was told that I should call the state testing office. When I made the call to alert the test makers of this issue and that they might consider amending this language in the future, I was put on trial over the phone. I was asked for my name and the school for which I worked. Later that day, I was summoned to the principal's office, where I was chastised for making the call to request a change or clarification. I was told by my superiors that the students were just trying to take advantage of me. From this conversation, I was left feeling like the risk of losing funding was more important than student comprehension and equity within the exam. As a young future educator, I was saddened to experience a reversed hierarchy of care for students and will not make that mistake in my role as dean.

During the 2010s, education witnessed a pendulum counterswing with the idea and implementation of a "student-centered" learning approach, focusing on the student and their experience, allowing for renewed flexibility in education and student preparation. This approach I found so lacking in my early educational experiences is one that has the potential to open up higher education music to more talented musicians moving forward. One former math teacher, Jen Pazirandeh, experienced this flexibility in the implementation of standards-based grading (SBG) at two Californian schools where she worked. Standards-based grading allows students to retake tests to improve their grades and their skills. It is described as "a grading system in which students are evaluated based on their proficiency in meeting a clearly-articulated set of course objectives."[6] Pazirandeh observed that this assessment environment shifted the focus to "learning and retaining rather than cram and forget." She said,

> The most important part, really, was that it was a natural extension of the growth mindset [espoused by Carol Dweck]. If we actually believe that students can improve over time and we want them to try to improve, even after the arbitrarily determined test date, then we must give them the opportunity and incentive to do so. [Standards-based grading] prioritizes mastery. Traditional grading practices prioritize the speed of learning. But, implementation is important—both for teacher workload and for cultivating a supportive relationship with students. Throughout the course, especially including the grading practices, they should hear the teacher's voice: *This is important, you can do it, I won't give up on you.*[7]

Within her implementation, Pazirandeh found that standards-based grading had a larger impact on the middle: "Students who you might expect would earn an A based on their previous math grade were already going to earn that A; students coming in with a 2.5 (C/C+) improved slightly, but not that much. Probably because they did not take advantage of the opportunities. Students coming in with a B math average though improved the most—over half a letter grade higher on average on the final exam compared to B students pre-SBG."[8] Pazirandeh's observations influence my work in music recruitment, by focusing my attention on students in the so-called middle.

I entered the field of music recruitment at the University of Colorado Boulder. Since this is a flagship institution, I was charged with ensuring that at least 60% of the incoming class were residents of the state of Colorado. To meet that charge, I traveled throughout the state visiting numerous high schools—attending countless rehearsals and performances—and shared how students could continue their involvement in music after high school; be it extracurricular, cocurricular, or curricular. Understanding that the cost of college is often a significant financial investment for students, I provided all prospective students with information about how to access financial aid, and informed them all equally of the many opportunities that would be available to them should they enroll, regardless of the level of talent I observed on that day and in that moment in time.

In her article "In the Service of Life," Rachel Remen states, "When we help we may inadvertently take away from people more than we could ever give them; we may diminish their self-esteem, their sense of worth, integrity and wholeness."[9] My recruitment philosophy was not to help students choose CU-Boulder for their collegiate studies, but to serve them as a resource in discovering if Boulder was the right place for them. Like Pazirandeh experienced, some students took advantage of opportunities, while others did not. One memorable student was a Colorado All-State musician. Prior to his senior year, and at the time of his first meeting with a CU-Boulder faculty member, he was not ready to meet the audition requirements. Nevertheless, he took advantage of understanding what was required and surprised the faculty with his level of growth. He is one of the students I was proudest to serve. Unfortunately, such results are not always guaranteed.

When Pazirandeh moved to another school where they were already implementing standards-based grading, she discovered how it became a direct replacement of the standardized testing model. Although the school had provided opportunities for retakes and support for tutoring, they enforced a significant penalty if students failed a standard. Pazirandeh reported, "If a student did not 'pass' any standard, their entire standard grade was set at a 60% (students were also required to pass math classes with at least a 70%) so this was more or less intended to keep students from passing the course if they did not pass one or more standards. This harsh attitude toward passing standards meant students hated standards, parents hated standards, and this school had a high failure rate."[10]

While there was a desire to ensure students understood the material before moving to the next course, Pazirandeh observed that it created "an antagonistic relationship between teachers and students."[11] As with No Child Left Behind, teachers were characterized as doorkeepers rather than shepherds of education. This is still not the care pedagogy model I am seeking at my institution.

As I continue working in the field of collegiate recruitment and admission, I am observing how the student-centered approach is positively influencing colleges and universities and how it is changing the way recruiters and admission officers are caring for students, even before they become members of our academic communities. As a means of retention, admission officers and financial aid professionals are beginning to consider need-informed admission policies.[12] While institutions receive a window into the student's financial support system through such documents as the FAFSA or CSS Profile, offers of admission are still distributed to students who, on paper, do not possess the ability to afford the cost of attendance, even after receiving additional financial aid.[13] Within highly selective degree programs—musical theatre, for example—students believe that an offer of admission can be reason enough to attend and enroll by any means necessary. Some believe that if they can "prove themselves," they can receive additional institutional support. The unfortunate consequence is that their inability to settle their tuition fee bill will prevent them from registering in future semesters and prohibit them from obtaining an official transcript to complete the process of transferring to another institution. In addition, within the study of performing arts, most non–general education courses do not transfer from one institution to another, extending their time and financial investment toward graduation. Rather than place parents and guardians as the person who makes their student's dream come true, or the person who crushes that dream, collegiate institutions are seeking means of preventative care by increasing need-based scholarship funding, expanding financial aid counseling, and/or implementing need-informed admission processes.

The same considerations of care are being applied to the application process as well. In addition to the production of campus events, visits, and tours, application processes have been revised, refocused, and reformatted to reflect what is best for the student. These include, but are not limited to, test-optional policies, preferred pronouns, net price calculators, standardization of degree credit requirements, and clearer admission and transfer pathways. While these new policies better inform applicants as they initiate their applications, an unexpected variable within the "iGen" generation of students has disrupted their enrollment decisions: the smartphone.[14] Having a smartphone provides iGen students not only access to information but also access to social media (#influencers).

While most collegiate application and enrollment decisions were previously influenced by a student's family member(s), counselor, and/or coach, a 2015 survey found that "55% of admitted students said that the way their school of enrollment used social media positively influenced their decision."[15] Applicants are now making decisions influenced by the friends they know, and the people they *follow* on social media. Social media, therefore, is another tool for universities to use in order to introduce their ways of caring to prospective students. Still, at the collegiate level, the iGen generation has impacted the use of the similarity-attraction theory.[16] In the age of social media, we now wonder, who or what is *similar*? This disruption has facilitated a new reality: our student bodies are more complex in diversity and are composed of various smaller groups with similar characteristics whom we must approach with a greater sense of awareness and variety of care. Students are looking for a place they belong, where they feel "at home." A place they will be recognized and *cared* for.

As explained in Carey Business School's 2021 iteration of Johns Hopkins University's "RoadMap for Diversity, Equity, Inclusion, and Belonging," "Some of these aspects of diversity are visible, some are invisible, and some, like identifying as having a disability, may be both. Most individuals have a combination of these diverse factors that influence their perspective and worldview. Recognition of this intersectionality is fundamental to valuing every . . . student, faculty, or staff member in their complete identity. Incorporating an evolvingly complex understanding of what factors affect equity is critically important to implementing a culture of inclusion and belonging."[17] Through this description, music schools can also understand and include other groups within our student bodies (for example, those who have experienced or been impacted by the loss of a family member, cancer, COVID-19, anxiety/poor mental health, and so on). Moreover, we can better understand other traditional groups, such as first-generation, underresourced/socioeconomically disadvantaged, and LGBTQ+ students. Our greatest challenge is to gain more awareness and knowledge regarding the needs of each group so that we can begin to understand how to best care for them.

So how can we gain this knowledge? As Renihan, Spilker, and Wright explore in the introduction to this volume, centering the whole student in the educational experience is key, and can inform all kinds of administrative and curricular decisions throughout the educational process. This is not easily done, however. To begin, the Family Educational Rights and Privacy Act (FERPA) protects the privacy of student records. Still, we can increase our awareness and care of the student by asking questions early on through various strategic means.[18] At the collegiate level, as part of the application process, several universities now ask for a preferred name—in addition to a legal name—which especially assists transgender and transitioning students from publicly disclosing their gender identity. In addition, the practice assists in developing a relationship of respect toward students and their life decisions. Likewise, institutions are beginning to adapt and adjust their essay questions based on current events. For example, during the fall 2021 application cycle, Columbia College Chicago asked, How has COVID-19 impacted your life? Unfortunately, in some states, these caring questions are prohibited due to state laws or propositions. This includes California.

The 2016 approval of Proposition 209 in California forbids asking for and/or collecting data "on race, ethnicity, sex/gender, or national origin." However, questions can be asked indirectly within a limited scope or pertaining to a specified area. For example, UCLA's School of Art and Architecture's World Arts and Culture/Dance Department asks, "How might dance address some of the pressing social issues of our times? How do you see yourself or other choreographers as social change agents?" These kinds of questions, easily edited to serve incoming music students and their teachers, motivate the community as a whole to gain awareness of the care a student might need, as well as the leadership they might provide others. I plan to use questions like them for my incoming students at the Cleveland Institute of Music. Likewise, these questions aim to allow educators to "meet students where they are and take them where they need to go," as Daniel Washington, professor of voice at the University of Michigan, says. Still, there are opportunities to consider and respond to the needs of students directly, although it may require forethought.

While working at Ithaca College, I witnessed my colleague Brad Whittemore carefully consider the needs of low-income students attending the Summer Music Academy. The academy maintained an ongoing partnership with OrchKids to bring three to four students from Baltimore, Maryland, to the academy—in Ithaca, New York—each summer at no cost.[19] Often, institutions believe that when recruiting low-income and first-generation students, providing tuition and housing are the keys to success. In 2018, however, Laura Pappano reported, "when elite admissions offices stepped up recruitment of low-income and first-generation students several years ago, they focused on financial aid, not noticing the culture. As a result, these students suddenly found themselves challenged by the social shock of sharing a campus with 1-percenters with money for eating out, spring break trips, and thousand-dollar designer puff jackets."[20] This is a truth not just for summer camps but for financially disadvantaged college students all over the country.[21] As the OrchKids students arrived in Ithaca, Brad saw that they did not always have necessities (such as laundry detergent and dress clothes) and provided these for the campers. Likewise, my colleague understood this was the first time away from home for these students. To further assist them with the experience, Brad created a mentorship fellowship which allowed for the hiring of an OrchKids intern known to the students, Mateen Milan. The awareness shown to the academy campers extended beyond those from OrchKids. The academy soon began welcoming campers with Tourette syndrome. Brad made every effort to ensure the success of students' social orientation, in addition to their curricular orientation, so they could all participate fully. The actions above align with Tia Brown McNair's urgent call and resources for campus colleagues to become "student ready," rather than bemoaning those students we label as "not college ready."[22]

This anecdote reminds us that we have a need in higher education music to be attentive to the many ways our programs and structures are exclusionary. In what communities will some financially disadvantaged students not feel comfortable? What structures have we put in place that implicitly exclude entire demographics of students from even considering taking part in what we have to offer? And more importantly, what do we have to learn from these students and communities about musicking, and about creative communities?

Similarly, direct care is now needed to address the growing mental health–related challenges that many students face.[23] Some professionals are developing response tools by taking courses through Mental Health First Aid from the National Council for Mental Wellbeing.[24] When asked for his reflection on his experience in the course, Ithaca College Professor Alex Shuhan said,

> [It prompted an] increased awareness of just how important the issue of mental health fragility is in today's world. [People] were all taking the class because they had had experiences they felt they were unprepared for and were hoping that the class would provide insights and strategies for helping themselves, and others close to them, when the stresses of college and young adulthood got the better of them. Also, just being in a room with a small group of participants, with everyone opening up about their own struggles, was cathartic in and of itself. It's always a good thing when people are able to let down their guard in a safe space and show their vulnerability. I think everyone left that day feeling like it had been very much worth their emotional and time investment.[25]

As educators, we most often provide care in emergencies and after trauma. Still, preventative care provides a means of diminishing the number of traumas and emergencies that we will likely encounter year after year. This suggests that any opportunity to build care practices into our diverse teaching and learning environments—at all points along the way—is well worth it.

Student-centered pedagogy has begun to expand and evolve into a whole student approach. Nevertheless, one must be careful not to limit one's consideration to one's own internal experience and interaction with the students.

A well-known child development theory can demonstrate this point, which can then be extended and applied to teaching in higher education. In 1979, American psychologist Urie Bronfenbrenner formulated the ecological systems theory to explain how the inherent qualities of a child and his or her environment interact to influence how the child will grow and develop.[26] Bronfenbrenner stressed the importance of studying a child in the context of multiple environments, also known as ecological systems, in the attempt to understand the child's development. Bronfenbrenner's theory presented the microsystem—the realms of family, classroom, spiritual community, and peer group—as the most influential level of a child's development. Of course, this was before the emergence of social media (MySpace, 2003; Facebook, 2004; Twitter, 2006), which blurred the boundaries between the relationships between the individual and their environment on a variety of levels. Consequently, in 2006, Bronfenbrenner revised his theory as the bioecological model of development, a theory of educational psychology that studies human development over time. The model highlights the ways that the interactions between the individual and their environment, categorized into various systems, shape the individual's development over time.[27] One of the most significant revelations from this activity is the role that privilege plays in defining an individual's experience. I define privilege as the ability to act without awareness. Being conscious of the points raised by Bronfenbrenner's theory can help orient professors to student needs and thus point them toward a caring approach to teaching and relating in higher education music. Again, this can impact the ways we teach students and expect them to learn, but it can and should also impact our recruitment strategies and approaches, our curricula, our policies and practices both pedagogically and administratively.

Caring for students is a constantly evolving project, as I've shown. As I work toward caring in different and more nuanced ways in the various facets of my work, I discover new tools and resources and am inspired by new stories that help light the way. On May 15, 2014, Dr. John M. Wacker, former director of bands at Western State Colorado University in Gunnison, Colorado, died in a car accident at the age of 55. At his funeral, his brother told a story about how John asked him, "What is it that you do?" His brother responded, "I'm a psychology teacher." John asked him the same question two more times, and his brother responded, "I teach psychology." John responded, "No! You teach *kids*." No matter what subject we teach, the level we teach, or who we teach, as educators, "we teach kids," we serve them, and we must care for them, carefully.

Notes

1. "Student-Centered Learning," *The Glossary of Education Reform for Journalists, Parents, and Community Members*, last updated May 7, 2014, https://www.edglossary.org/student-centered-learning/.

2. No Child Left Behind Act of 2001, H.R. 1, 107th Cong., https://www.congress.gov/bill/107th-congress/house-bill/1.

3. Robin Harwick, "Teaching to the Test Harms Students," *Medium*, October 5, 2020, https://medium.com/.

4. Ralph Ellis and Elwyn Lopez, "Judge Reduces Sentence for 3 Educators in Atlanta Cheating Scandal," *CNN*, April 30, 2015, https://www.cnn.com/.

5. Although beyond the scope of this chapter, data science scholar Cathy O'Neil might argue that the issue is more complex. See *Weapons of Math Destruction: How Big Data Increases Inequality and Threatens Democracy* (New York: Broadway Books, 2017).

6. Carol Tomlinson and Jay McTighe, *Integrating Differentiated Instruction and Understanding by Design: Connecting Content and Kids* (Alexandria, VA: Association for Supervision and Curriculum Development, 2006); National Council of Teachers of English, *Formative Assessment That Truly Informs Instruction*, October 21, 2013, https://cdn.ncte.org/nctefiles/resources/positions/formative-assessment_single.pdf.

7. Jennifer Pazirandeh, "Standards Based Grading," Math Department, Monta Vista High School, Cupertino, California (unpublished manuscript, 2011). See also Jon Saphier, Mary Ann Haley-Speca, and Robert Gower, *The Skillful Teacher: Building Your Teaching Skills* (Acton, MA: Research for Better Teaching, 2008), 261; Carol Dweck, *Mindset: The New Psychology of Success* (New York: Ballantine Books, 2007).

8. Jennifer Pazirandeh, "Standards Based Grading."

9. Rachel Remen, "In the Service of Life," *Noetic Sciences Review* 37 (1996): 24, https://cih.ucsd.edu/sites/cih.ucsd.edu/files/mbpti/In_the_Service_of_Life.pdf.

10. Pazirandeh, "Standards Based Grading."

11. Pazirandeh.

12. Also referred to as need-sensitive, need-conscious, or need-aware.

13. FAFSA: Free Application for Federal Student Aid; CSS: College Scholarship Service.

14. "iGen" generation (1992–2012): the first generation of students to spend their entire adolescence with a smartphone (Jean Twenge, *iGen: Why Today's Super-Connected Kids Are Growing Up Less Rebellious, More Tolerant, Less Happy—and Completely Unprepared for Adulthood—and What That Means for the Rest of Us* [New York: Atria Books, 2017]).

15. EDUVentures Insights, "Break through the Noise: Survey of Admitted Students," *Recruitment & Retention* 1.12 (2015): 1–7.

16. "People are attracted to others who are similar, rather than dissimilar" (Ellen Berscheid and Elaine H. Walster, "Rewards Others Provide: Similarity," in *Interpersonal Attraction* [Reading, MA: Addison-Wesley, 1969], 69–91).

17. Johns Hopkins Carey Business School, "Roadmap for Diversity, Equity, Inclu-

sion, and Belonging," Johns Hopkins University, June 2021, https://carey.jhu.edu/sites/default/files/2021-06/2021-2-497-roadmap-deib_v3b.pdf.

18. U.S. Department of Education, "Family Educational Rights and Privacy Act (FERPA)," December 15, 2020, www2.ed.gov/policy/gen/guid/fpco/ferpa/index.html.

19. OrchKids is a year-round, during- and after-school music program, founded in 2008, designed to create social change and nurture promising futures for youth in Baltimore City neighborhoods. See https://orchkids.org/ourprogram/.

20. Laura Pappano, "Low-Income Graduates of Elite Colleges Struggle with Class Issues," *The Hechinger Report*, March 30, 2020, hechingerreport.org/ivy-league-degree-now-what/.

21. See Anthony Jack, *The Privileged Poor: How Elite Colleges Are Failing Disadvantaged Students* (Cambridge, MA: Harvard University Press, 2019); Ryan Shaw and Amy Auletto, "Is Music Education in Tune with the Pursuit of Equity? An Examination of Access to Music Education in Michigan's Schools," *Journal of Research in Music Education* 69, no. 4 (2022): 364–81.

22. Tia Brown McNair, Susan Albertine, Michelle Asha Cooper, Nicole McDonald, and Thomas Major Jr., *Becoming a Student-Ready College: A New Culture of Leadership for Student Success*, 2nd ed. (San Francisco: Jossey-Bass, 2022).

23. See the chapters by Langfitt, Natvig, and Wright in this monograph.

24. National Council for Mental Wellbeing, *Mental Health First Aid*, June 1, 2021, www.mentalhealthfirstaid.org/.

25. Alex Shuhan, personal conversation with author, July 8, 2021.

26. "What Is Bronfenbrenner's Ecological Systems Theory?," *The Psychology Notes Headquarters*, accessed September 1, 2019, https://www.psychologynoteshq.com/bronfenbrenner-ecological-theory/.

27. Urie Bronfenbrenner and Pamela Morris, "The Bioecological Model of Human Development," in *Handbook of Child Psychology: Theoretical Models of Human Development*, ed. Richard Lerner and William Damon, 793–828 (Hoboken, NJ: Wiley, 2006).

CHAPTER 6

Kindness as Universal Design

Rethinking the College Music Classroom from Within

STEPHANIE JENSEN-MOULTON

Prelude: Carrie

Carrie had dissolved into tears twice already during the semester, and it was only the sixth week of the term in her first music course.[1] I had asked around—perhaps other professors had experienced this student differently? I wondered if I was being too easy on her, or maybe the opposite. I wanted to help her succeed in my course, but with this individual I sensed that she needed more support. Yet, as a female professor, I knew that student perceptions could frame me as less rigorous, more likely to accommodate requests for extensions and grade changes.[2] One Monday, Carrie came into class thirty minutes late when everyone was already in the midst of taking a test; in a public voice, she asked me if she could take the test another day, since she hadn't had a chance to study and her ADA accommodation gave her double time.

Until this point in my college teaching career, my general philosophy had been something akin to "strict on paper, kind in person," with an understanding of the syllabus as a contract that protected both the students and me. But in this instance, I worried that the student had been leveraging her accommodation as privilege—not a productive or particularly kind thought on my part, and in fact a rather ugly one. So I changed it up: what would be the kindest, most equitable solution for all involved, including the other members of the class? I asked Carrie to sit the exam that day in the Office of Disability Accommodations, so that she would have enough time to take it, and as she left, again in tears, I wondered with knots in my stomach if Carrie would come back to class the following week.[3] I lost some sleep before she attended my office hours another day, noting that—and these words were indelible to me—no one had ever cared enough about her to establish boundaries, especially when she had asked for special treatment.[4]

I followed Carrie's progress closely, as she would periodically return to me to ask for help with other classes and (sometimes) offer recital invitations. She struggled with the courses that had the most linear formats, especially music theory; but Carrie excelled in flipped and student-centered classrooms. In the meantime, I had been reconsidering my own courses based not only upon this student's experience but that of many others before and after her. What kind of class could benefit all the students in the room, while maintaining both rigor and kindness, and understanding that the two are not mutually exclusive? The long period of COVID-19 disruption has allowed me time to apply the principles of universal design for learning (UDL) to my musicology courses, and to consider specifically how kindness both intersects with and amplifies UDL pedagogy.

Danger: Kind Classroom

Although "kindness" and "danger" seem like contradictory terms, employing kindness as a principle for teaching involves taking unanticipated risks for both the instructor and the students in the classroom. In developing a pedagogy of kindness, I have come to realize that if kindness is at the center of an axis of life skills we hope our students own and value at the end of their university journey, one of the most important prongs is vulnerability, which, indeed, allows for learning, and likewise for risk-taking. As Brené Brown notes, "The perception that vulnerability is weakness is the most widely accepted myth about vulnerability and the most dangerous."[5] When an individual makes a conscious choice to be kind, the reaction from other people might include genuine gratitude, anger, or indifference. As Adam Phillips and Barbara Taylor argue in their recent study *On Kindness*, "Real kindness is an exchange with potentially unpredictable consequences."[6] When kindness is built into the syllabus and methodology of classroom rhetoric and philosophy—as in, built into the lived environment of the classroom—the professor makes herself vulnerable to the response of the students in the room, and the reverse. In addition, no matter what type of teaching experience that instructor may have, the outcome will be different with each cohort.

As college teachers of music studies—conceived broadly as those of us who teach the varied subjects within music departments, conservatories, and schools of music at the university level—many of us receive little to no training in our masters or doctoral programs with regard to scholarship of teaching and learning in our respective subject areas.[7] The field of music is not alone in this, which is why most campuses have centers for teaching and learning that exist to bridge the gap and provide workshops for faculty and staff to hone their classroom skills.[8] Nevertheless, both research-trained academics and conservatory-schooled performers alike would find challenges when confronted with the following, hypothetical undergraduate classroom: some students may have physical disabilities, some may be neurodiverse, others may be international students who are relatively new to the English language, yet all of the students might be academically advanced—let's say this is an honors section of Music Appreciation. Several students also may need double time for exams, as mandated by their education plans with the Office of Disability Services. While student needs in this "sample" class may seem as diverse as the students entering the classroom, advocates for universal design have argued that one plan for a very differentiated class of learners can serve *every* student better, not only the ones who need particular accommodations.

Stripped down to basics, universal design accommodates the "widest range of people possible in the widest range of situations without separate or special design."[9] A typical example of universal design in everyday architecture is the sidewalk cut: while originally conceived to make daily travel easier for wheelchair users, cuts in the sidewalk help a wide variety of individuals, including people pushing carts, caregivers with strollers, those using walkers, and even skateboard riders. While the college music classroom is a different type of built environment—physically, psychically, intellectually—the seven primary principles of universal design can be applied effectively to post-secondary pedagogical practice. Music students benefit particularly from a universal design pedagogy due to its capacity to reduce physical and mental stress in the classroom.[10] I assert that kindness pedagogy, as outlined below, could be considered an eighth element of universal design, seamlessly weaving into the other seven universal design learning practices.

Kindness links with universal design in its capacity to shift the atmosphere of a classroom for all students of all abilities within that space, maximizing tolerance for error while simultaneously creating equity. A conscious application of kindness in pedagogy has been found to reduce attrition and create bonds between students through mutual vulnerability.[11] In highly competitive fields such as music performance, where students must compete with their peers on a daily basis, both kindness and universal design prepare students to enter the twenty-first-century workforce with the crucial skill of collegiality. In music classrooms specifically, the conscious infusion of kindness—which I interchange with compassion and radical kindness in this article—helps to undo the history of injustice and privilege reinforced by the canonical material and the exclusionary practices of concert music so often represented in the standard curricula of higher education music courses for majors and nonmajors. In addition, since universal design has been associated with integration of disabled students into "mainstream" classrooms, kindness pedagogy also addresses and redresses the shadows of institutional educational practices, recognizing that higher education for some neurodiverse and intellectually disabled students is a relatively recent opportunity. Kindness pedagogy as applied in the college classroom also has the potential to subvert and dismantle intellectual gender binaries such as emotion versus reason, calling into question the ableist, racist, classist, sexist assumptions on which we have built traditional methods of assessment (both of students and faculty).[12] Thus, in brazenly embroidering an eighth onto the seven already well-established principles of universal design, I codify a crucial methodology for each of the other principles applicable for classrooms in all subject areas, while recognizing a meaningful and essential professional practice for musicians.

When I first set out to write about this pedagogy and its links to universal design, I anticipated describing several instances I had witnessed of colleagues demonstrating kindness through their actions in the field. These displays of kindness included acts of good will such as bringing a young child to a professional jazz rehearsal, demonstrating work-life balance in real time; conducting from the maestro's podium without belittling or raising one's voice at colleagues; and building a solo instrumental career based upon both extraordinary playing and collegial relationships with contemporary composers. But an exhibition of these manifestations of kind musical practice and leadership, though admirable and worthy of replication, does not probe the question at the heart of this chapter: What has prevented faculty from insisting on kindness in higher education pedagogy, both as a general higher education praxis, and one for music as a field?

"Feeling kind is not enough": Defining Kindness and Its Paradoxes

Kindness as a concept refers to "kin," or the sort of familial connection that allows for deep understanding based on sameness. While the Oxford English Dictionary finds early relationships between kindness and "generation," "nation," and "kin," the modern definition revolves around relationality and conduct based upon quality of action.[13] The relational environment of the college classroom represents the location where learning will (hopefully) take place based upon how the instructor decides to consider quality of action as part of the equation. College teachers' instructional styles vary widely, but the professor teaching a mega-section of one hundred–plus students can decide to apply kindness to her pedagogy as much as the private-lesson instructor can, though the methodology might differ. In order to establish a kind classroom, however, the instructor has to show that she can be vulnerable, and establish that the space of the classroom is one where vulnerability is accepted, appreciated, and even valued.[14] But the "safe space" model of instruction that has become a common phrase in the last decade is often fraught with unacknowledged power dynamics that can undermine the good intentions of even the most well-meaning instructor.[15] As Elizabeth Ozment writes, "Ideal as it may be, there are no truly safe spaces in or outside of the classroom, nor ought that be the ultimate goal for feminist pedagogues."[16] The space that is deemed safe within the classroom often masks white and/or ableist privilege, resulting in an imbalance of power that may leave some students feeling shut down, stonewalled, and disempowered. Ideally, the kind classroom functions in a way that allows for mutual respect, dialogue, and risk-taking; but merely giving lip service to "safe space" can be harmful to the delicate window of vulnerability we have with our students.[17] But is this kind, safe classroom one where students can learn with enough rigor to be successful?[18]

The primary and overarching paradox in any discussion of a practice of kindness is the tension between extrinsic indicators of success and a perceived softness or "lack" associated with acts of kindness. Although kindness has not always been associated with weakness,[19] the dawn of the industrial age gave rise to greater individualist thinking that prevailed over group-centric, interdependent mindsets.[20] Along with this shift in thinking with regard to an individual's relationship to society, public educational environments adjusted to meet the need of an increasingly independent and competitive population of students, particularly in higher education. As Clegg and Rowland write,

> The paradox of kindness is that it can lead to acts that by intention are kind but may involve misjudgment and harm to others, paradoxically therefore kindness may involve regulation. Feeling kind is not enough. Intellectual judgements are involved and not just empathy. Empathy, understood as an affective interpersonal capacity, would limit acts of kindness to particular sorts of imaginary others. Kindness is not simply the projection of one's own needs and desires onto people who are in fact not like us and/or do not share our values, considerable rigour is entailed in working out what would be kind in relation to the realization of the projects of others.[21]

Pedagogical kindness, then, is not simply an exercise in metaphorical throwing of candy to the class; nor does kindness justify the adoption of people-pleasing behaviors that undermine discipline and structure, or overburden one with the weight of others' rightful responsibilities.

My definition of kindness pedagogy operates on five central principles that combine a politics of care[22] and introvert-centered teaching[23] with a straightforward, common-sense approach to teaching a diverse classroom. These tenets serve not only as guideposts for the instructors and the students but also as outcomes, given that not every student or teacher will find each principle equally simple to apply to the changing microcosm of the classroom.

1. Equal care for self and others
2. "Listen first" communication (embrace silence as time to think and learn)
3. Mutual desire to learn from one another
4. Growing socioemotional and intellectual flexibility
5. Mutual goal of course completion with
   a. Personal satisfaction
   b. Professional success

While seemingly simplistic, these tenets, leaves on an affective tree of sorts with kindness at the root (as shown in Figure 6.1), allow for further growth after the close of the course. In addition, they provide a framework for students' communication as they move forward through their student years and onward into the professional world.

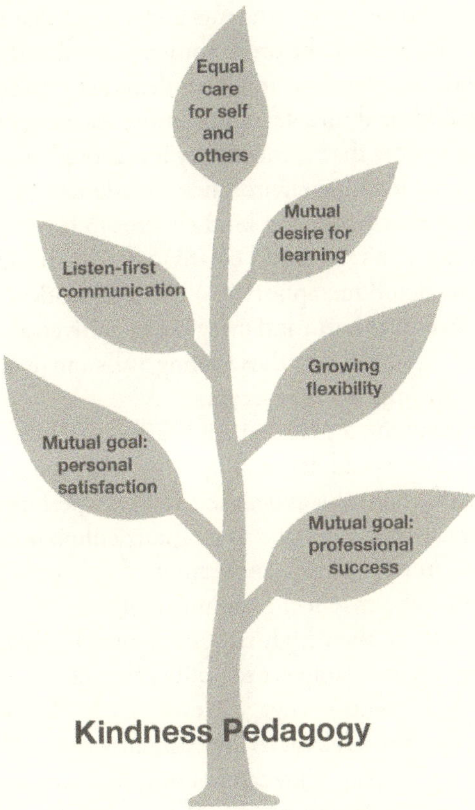

Figure 6.1. Kindness Pedagogy Tree

Kindness as a Principle of Universal Design?

Higher education administration thrives on an ability to assess, collect data, and justify spending. While students may inherently understand that the teachers they keep coming back to are kind, affective qualities are not typically included as criteria on student evaluations for professors, or on peer-to-peer faculty teaching evaluations. Perhaps even more important, affective qualities such as kindness and collegiality cannot be measured and assessed for tenure, promotion, or evaluation of employment status because these qualities are simply too subjective.[24] Still, it's clear that the kindness of the instructor makes a great deal of difference to students, as open-ended comments on student evaluations demonstrate. For example, one student, when asked to describe the strengths of the instructor apart from the course, took the time to note that the instructor was "very kind, patient, understanding, and accommodating."[25] As Clegg and Rowland note, "what is subversive about kindness, and indeed love of the discipline, is that it cannot be regulated and prescribed."[26] In essence, in the kind classroom, students understand that they have permission to be subversive, because the professor is always already in a subversively open affective mode. In what ways might students act subversively in a college classroom that would be desirable and promote learning? Chiefly, students in a kind classroom know that vulnerability is accepted, welcomed, and even valued. In an optimal learning environment, students can embrace the feeling of vulnerability that being in a kind classroom brings, knowing that it will allow for greater risk-taking and creativity.[27] Vulnerability breaks down barriers—both literal and metaphorical—between students such as canons, policies, and practices that harm and marginalize; universal design is a system that engages the energy created by those falling walls and uses it to build better, more accessible environments for everyone.

Imagine, for a moment, a practical application of kindness in a high-risk music course. Students would define "high-risk" as a course that makes them feel nervous, worried, or anxious about their ability to perform at their best. For some students, the ear-training/sight-singing curriculum presents as high-risk, while for others, an improvisation course might feel like the high-risk course. Still other students, who may feel uncomfortable with writing long papers, find history classes to be their high-risk moment. The Reacting to the Past role-playing pedagogy, for example, exemplifies the subversiveness of the kind classroom, requiring students to engage in everyday intellectual risk-taking. In embodying their roles for weeks at a time, students come to embrace vulnerability through character play. They can not only be outrageous but also make incredible errors out in the open, because they're doing it in the body of that historical figure. This allows for a holistic learning process among peers that builds a deeply connected classroom where kindness continues even after the semester ends. Reacting to the Past connects directly with UDL because, as a curricular choice, it provides multiple means of representation, expression, and engagement for students, creating a more equitable and flexible platform for learning with a large tolerance for error and low need for physical effort.

Universal design for living finds its basis in these seven original principles: "Equitable Use, Flexibility in Use, Simple and Intuitive Use, Perceptible Information, Tolerance for Error, Low Physical Effort, and Size and Space for Approach and Use."[28] When applied to everyday designs and situations, the application of these principles makes the built environment not only accessible for people with a wide range of physical and cognitive abilities but also simply a better and kinder, more thoughtful world "without adaptation or specialized design."[29] Above, I used the example of the sidewalk cut, but another example might be the way subtitles help everyone understand a film or video text, while also serving as captioning for Deaf and hard-of-hearing audiences. The important part of the universal design system is that it isn't meant to be specifically adaptive: it's just better for everyone. The principles of UDL have their basis in that same idea—the creation of a learning environment not adapted specifically to one learner's needs, but which will best serve all the learning needs in the room.

Universal design for learning aligns logically with kindness pedagogy, but not necessarily with the college music classroom in its current incarnation, largely because UDL seeks to move beyond the traditional (often soloistic) performance or content markers that are highly valued by music faculty. Based on three tenets that reflect the seven principles of universal design for living, UDL seeks to provide:

- Multiple means of representation—give learners various ways of acquiring information and knowledge
- Multiple means of expression—provide learners alternatives for demonstrating what they know
- Multiple means of engagement—tap into learners' interests, offer appropriate challenges, and increase motivation.[30]

Each of these ideas addresses a mode of learning engagement on the part of the student. In giving learners several ways to acquire knowledge through different means of representation, the instructor addresses the different ways in which students learn, or the "how" of learning that can be so different from student to student. By providing multiple ways for students to express what they have learned in the classroom, instructors may encourage students to celebrate and embrace difference, where a more typical mode of assessment might create disparities among learners with differentiated histories. Finally, the affective state of the classroom depends so much on connection with the instructor, and student engagement links directly with "why" students want to learn and succeed in a course.

Taking a step back, these principles of UDL were created during a time when advocates of disability education recognized a need to desegregate schools and integrate disabled students into "mainstream" classrooms.[31] It is important to acknowledge the regrettably dark history of disability education in the United States and the West generally, given that American schools and colleges still bear some of the marks of the terrible past. As Margaret Price writes, "Scholars of Disability Studies who engage the topic of education tend to struggle with its chimerical nature: sometimes 'schools' are abusive prisons, sometimes pathways to greater social justice, and it is not always easy to tell the difference."[32] The modern Western classroom has often been a location for intelligence testing, reinscription of medical diagnosis, and classification into groups or segments based on those data. Regrettably, the determining criteria cannot be uncoupled from biases associated with race, class, gender, physical ability, and mental illness. The school is therefore a location for "interventions and cures to take place,"[33] in the tradition of nineteenth-century asylums. The effort for educators to move away from this model has involved a rethinking of education for every student. Major legislation from the 1970s (the Rehabilitation Act, 1973, and the Individuals with Disabilities Education Act, 1975) impacted who attended school and levels of accessibility, but also in many ways led to continued classification and segregation. The diagram below provides a gross simplification of the trajectory of education for disabled students in the United States since the nineteenth-century:[34]

> Asylum → Institution → Specialized School/Workshop/Institution → Special Needs Class → Integrated Class/UDL Class/Participatory-Inclusive Design Class

While some disability advocates have rightly called UDL "aspirational," arguably any method beyond one-on-one schooling has an element of the aspirational. I would, however, contend that kindness pedagogy is applicable across all categories of higher education, from musicology to chemistry to philosophy. With regard specifically to the history of disability education and UDL, scholars of disability studies have considered a design called "participatory" or "inclusive," which Jason Palmieri also refers to as "human-centered."[35] Importantly, even the binary of instructor/student ceases to function in Palmieri's model, as both retain their humanity.

Nevertheless, the most significant hurdles for implementation of UDL in higher education can be in the very experience of the instructors themselves, or in other terms, in the rewriting of specific courses in ways that the professors find unfamiliar.[36] Asking instructors to completely reenvision an entire course might be too overwhelming, but working assignment by assignment can be a practical step towards converting a course to the UDL approach. A great start is to think of that phrase "multiple means": how can I offer the content of my course in multiple ways and means of representation, expression, and engagement? Most of this work involves changing types of assignments in the course; the balance of assessment in a UDL course should shift from primarily test-based or writing-based to having some assignments based on group work, low-risk writing (such as blog entries or chat comments), oral presentations, and other forms of demonstrating knowledge.

One example of a replacement assignment that has worked well in college courses is accepting podcasts or video essays in lieu of final papers. While not appropriate for every course (especially if the point of the course is writing!), the podcast or video essay can demonstrate the same outcomes: (1) deep knowledge acquisition on a particular topic; (2) analysis of and insight about that topic; (3) research on and citation of primary and secondary sources; (4) preparation and production of a final product of some depth and length; and (5) ability to speak cogently using technical vocabulary with reference to the subject. I've enjoyed asking students to record oral histories with their relatives and friends about American music events they've attended during their lifetimes. For some students, writing a final paper might inspire fear and dread to the point of noncompletion; these students may have had inadequate preparation in writing, or they may bring a neurodiverse profile to class that does not make writing their best or preferred mode of communication. For some of these students, a podcast is the right final project, and one that will require just as much—if not more!—work as a final paper. In addition, it will require them to meet the same outcomes as the students writing the final paper.[37]

In another variation on this theme, I've assigned students small-scale oral history documentaries of 10–12 minutes in length (recorded via Zoom or similar) in lieu of final papers. Featuring a primary interview with a relative or friend about an American music event they've attended during their lifetime, students begin with a brief series of questions we devise together as a class over the course of the semester that connect with our course content. Post-pandemic, many students have been reluctant to reengage socially, and the process of learning and practicing interview techniques has helped them not only to complete their final projects but also to meet their classmates and converse at surprisingly deep levels about subjects ranging from their favorite Brooklyn clubs to the loss of close relatives to living with anxiety.

While altering final projects or shifting assignments are not the only ways to "do" UDL, these are examples that have helped instructors change the nature of their courses, step by step. But what happens when, in a music school setting, performance majors must complete performance-centered tasks? For example, performance majors typically play an end-of-semester jury exam which determines a significant percentage of their grade for the term. How can a course design be "universal" when major aspects of music curriculum find their basis in individualism and solo grading? One answer lies in the type of music students study, and how they choose to study that music.

Kindness, Individualism, and the Music Classroom

Along with the shifts in the nature of both higher education generally and the types of jobs music students aim to acquire upon graduation, both music curricula and pedagogy have needed to change.[38] Whereas in the late twentieth century and even at the beginning of the twenty-first century, many students attended college-level music schools to pursue a performance career—perhaps auditioning for an orchestra or opera company, perhaps as a soloist or member of a chamber ensemble—the dismantling/defunding of numerous ensembles and the complexity of making a living in the arts has led many music programs to differentiate their curricula.[39] In addition, the dawning realization that music curricula have been centered around a white European male model of composer-centric history and theory has also brought about significant and positive change.[40] Nevertheless, even with all of these alterations, the last bastion is the music field's extraordinarily ableist mode of teaching and learning. While it's difficult to make an argument that all music curricula should move away from "sight" singing simply because many cannot participate in such a venture, I'd like to consider the connection between designing our curricula and pedagogy universally so that every exercise is accessible to every student with kindness.

Questions such as "Can a Deaf student major in music composition?" and "Can a blind student with a tactile disability—no access to Braille—major in music?" are on my mind, because they are real questions posed to me and to the members of my department in the past year. With the technology available to disabled musicians, they are able to create music that gets them in the door for the audition, and further, through it with musical skill and talent. The problem for college music departments and conservatories is in whether or not the curriculum, the classes we offer, and the professors that teach those classes are ready to teach the students who are here to be taught.[41] While some might argue that budget can be an obstacle,[42] I offer that kindness is at the heart of our willingness to make the music major a major for all.

Consider the importance to the music major of music notation writing, the musical score, and the ability to read Western music notation. Despite the primacy of electronic musical production and varied musical cultures performed and remembered through the oral tradition, Western notation remains at the center of the undergraduate music major at a majority of public higher education institutions. For some students, Western notation is essential to their practice of music, particularly those who will continue to participate in art-music performance traditions in some form. But for many students who enter higher education with a deep knowledge of music composition softwares, electronic media, and studio musical practice; for those whose musical practice will progress in a folk music setting; for those who sing with a non-notational practice ensemble and plan to make a lifetime of music doing so; what is our obligation to their work? I suggest that both UDL and kindness pedagogy offer strategies for engagement with these thorny issues that require our attention and commitment as we move forward as a discipline.

The Urgency of Kindness Pedagogy

No matter where or when college teachers find themselves in a classroom, the infusion of kindness will make that classroom a better, safer, more productive environment for learning, and students will carry that feeling of care with them when they leave the classroom and move into their larger world. For music students who have engaged their individual talents to pursue higher education, becoming more community-minded as they grow intellectually can only improve their chances for success as a colleague, entrepreneur, and human being.[43] The kind music professor subverts and challenges a patriarchal and ableist nineteenth-century conservatory system, creating transformative classroom experiences that reach every student in lasting, changing ways.

Notes

1. Student's name has been changed at her request; permission for use of anecdote granted via personal communication.

2. Amani El-Alayli, Ashley Hansen-Brown, and Michelle Ceynar, "Dancing Backwards in High Heels: Female Professors Experience More Work Demands and Special Requests, Particularly from Academically Entitled Students," *Sex Roles* 79 (January 2018): 138. The authors' study reveals how gender explicitly determines student expectations of nurturing behaviors, friendship, and the giving of special treatment and favors in a higher education setting. The authors also discuss student (mis)perceptions of female professors' vulnerability.

3. When faculty receive official confirmation of a student's Americans with Disabilities Act–mandated disability accommodation, there should be no question about our willingness to follow that directive, which indeed equalizes and makes accessible the academic playing field. What is at stake here is the culture of privilege that can exist among any of our students, regardless of any other attribute.

4. With regard to courage in human interactions, Brené Brown comments, "One of the greatest (and least discussed) barriers to compassion practice is the fear of setting boundaries and holding people accountable" (*The Gifts of Imperfection: Let Go of Who You Think You're Supposed to Be and Embrace Who You Are* [Center City, MN: Hazelden Publishing, 2010], 16).

5. Brené Brown, *Daring Greatly: How the Courage to be Vulnerable Transforms the Way We Live, Love, Parent, and Lead* (New York: Penguin Random House, 2012), 32.

6. Adam Phillips and Barbara Taylor, *On Kindness* (New York: Picador, 2009), 13.

7. Situating myself as a musicologist teaching in the discipline since 2003, I have experienced a positive shift in the field toward interest in musicology pedagogy in the past decade, with the establishment of the AMS's Music History Pedagogy Study Group, its annual conference, and this year, a peer reviewed journal; the SAM, SMT, and SEM have also established similar pedagogy study groups. See Teaching Music History, https://www.teachingmusichistory.com/; the SAM Pedagogy Interest Group, https://www.american-music.org/page/InterestGroups; the Music Theory Pedagogy Interest Group, https://societymusictheory.org/interest-groups/music-theory-pedagogy-interest-group; the SEM Section on Education, https://semed.weebly.com/; all accessed July 28, 2022.

8. Thomas J. Tobin and Kirsten Behling, *Reach Everyone, Teach Everyone: Universal Design for Learning in Higher Education* (Morgantown: West Virginia University Press, 2018), 199.

9. Rosemarie Rossetti, "The Seven Principles of Universal Design," *Action Magazine*, December 2006, http://www.udll.com/media-room/articles/the-seven-principles-of-universal-design/.

10. Tobin and Behling, *Reach Everyone*, 142. In this example, the authors recount the story of a Deaf student whose professor adopted the practice of using captions on all video content. While this was a relatively small accommodation, it had unexpectedly positive student impacts.

11. Matthew James Capp, "The Effectiveness of Universal Design for Learning: A Meta-Analysis of Literature between 2013 and 2016," *International Journal of Inclusive Education* 21, no. 8 (2017): 794.

12. Sue Clegg and Stephen Rowland, "Kindness in Pedagogical Practice and Academic Life," *British Journal of Sociology of Education* 31, no. 6 (November 2010): 719; see also Ibram Kendi's discussion of scholastic achievement through the lens of race in *How to Be an Antiracist* (New York: One World, 2019), 93.

13. "Kindness," *Oxford English Dictionary Online*, June 2016, https://www.oed.com.

14. Brown, *Daring Greatly*, 186–87.

15. Badia Ahad-Legardy and OiYan A. Poon, eds., *Difficult Subjects: Insights and Strategies for Teaching about Race, Sexuality, and Gender* (Sterling, VA: Stylus Publishing, 2018), 12.

16. Elizabeth Ozment, "Embracing Vulnerability and Risk in the Classroom: The Four-Folder Approach to Discussion-Based Community Learning," *Journal of the Scholarship of Teaching and Learning* 2 (2018): 138.

17. Ozment, 141.

18. Brown, *Daring Greatly*, 197.

19. Greek philosopher Marcus Aurelius noted that kindness should be man's "greatest delight," setting kindness as a foundational human principle of western thinking (Phillips and Taylor, *On Kindness*, 4).

20. Phillips and Taylor, *On Kindness*, 6.

21. Clegg and Rowland, "Kindness in Pedagogical Practice," 723–24.

22. For a wonderfully creative, controversial, and intelligent discussion of the politics of care, see William Cheng, *Just Vibrations: The Purpose of Sounding Good* (Ann Arbor: University of Michigan Press, 2016). Cheng details an intellectual and creative case for a politics of care in the field of musicology, now. He writes: "In a world where injuries run rampant, what if care *is* the point?" (36); and further, "Doing good would involve reaching out and reaching back, lending help to those in need, and seeking opportunities for care and repair" (40).

23. I base this aspect of my teaching philosophy on work by Susan Cain, who has researched the underutilized power of introverts and the ways that modern society—particularly since WWII—has been structured around extroverts, while the greatest innovations of our time have been developed by introverts. For more, see Susan Cain, *Quiet: The Power of Introverts in a World That Can't Stop Talking* (New York: Broadway Books, 2013), and Cain's TED Talk "The Power of Introverts," March 2012, https://www.ted.com/talks/.

24. Sandra Acker and Michelle Weber, "Uneasy Academic Subjectivities in the Contemporary Ontario University," in *Identity Work in the Contemporary University*, ed. Jan Smith, Julie Rattray, Tai Paseta, and Daphne Loads (Boston: Brill Sense Publishers, 2016), 70.

25. Anonymous Brooklyn College feedback comment, MUSC4435, TR3, spring 2022, "Disability in America, Instructor, Stephanie Jensen-Moulton," accessed August 3, 2022, https://websql.brooklyn.cuny.edu/facultyevaluations/show_nonpub_comments1.jsp.

26. Clegg and Rowland, "Kindness in Pedagogical Practice," 733.

27. Ozment, "Embracing Vulnerability," 136. It should be noted, as well, that this type of pedagogy has largely been found in feminist classrooms and documented specifically as feminist pedagogy.

28. Centre for Excellence in Universal Design, "The 7 Principles," National Disability Authority, Dublin, Ireland, accessed August 1, 2019, https://universaldesign.ie,/What-is-Universal-Design/The-7-Principles/.

29. Tobin and Behling, *Reach Everyone*, 21.

30. Kurzweil Education, "Three Principles of UDL," accessed August 1, 2019, https://www.kurzweiledu.com/udl-three-principles-p4.html.

31. Margaret Price, "Education," in *Keywords in Disability Studies*, ed. Rachel Adams, Benjamin Reiss, and David Serlin (New York: New York University Press, 2015), 66.

32. Price, 64.

33. Price, 64.

34. Price, 66.

35. Jason Palmieri, "Disability Studies, Cultural Analysis, and the Critical Practice of Technical Communication Pedagogy," *Technical Communication Quarterly* 15 (2006): 51.

36. Tobin and Behling, *Reach Everyone*, 199.

37. Instructors can employ the same grading criteria for the podcast or video essay as for the paper, but I have found it helpful to provide strict timing and quality parameters. For example, if the required length for the paper is three pages, the podcast should be no longer than five minutes (the approximate time it would take a student to read three pages of text). Students should have access to high-quality examples. For videos, the same applies. Also, help the students know where you'd like media submitted (Dropbox? Blackboard?), and in what format. In all settings, it's important to provide resources for students including where to find software, links for online tutorials, and contact information for IT support (both online and in person). The best of all worlds is that department tech person or tech-savvy work-study student who can help students format their projects.

38. Robin Moore, "Music Curricula for the 21st Century: Guiding Principles," College Music Society, accessed January 20, 2020, https://www.music.org/index.php?option=com_content&view=article&id=2747:music-curricula-for-the-21st-century-guiding-principles&catid=231&Itemid=3288; Jason Hanley and Susan Oehler's work on teaching popular music also deserves notice. See "Perspectives of Popular Music Pedagogy in Practice: An Introduction," *Journal of Popular Music Studies* 21, no. 1 (March 2009): 2–19.

39. For a detailed discussion linking music history pedagogy and universal design, listen to "Decolonizing the Music Curriculum with Andrew Dell'Antonio at the Big XII Teaching and Learning Conference," July 30, 2019, in *Think UDL*, podcast, https://thinkudl.org/episodes/.

40. In one memorable example, Music theorist Dr. Rachel Lumsden recently took on the teaching of a dusty old European "Masterworks" course at the University of Florida, where she renamed the course "Mistressworks" and rewrote the content to feature exclusively compositions by women and trans writers (Skype conversation, December 21, 2019). Many other such examples exist, both gradually and quite wholly infusing curricula with a much-needed shift in mindset.

41. Tia Brown McNair, Susan Albertine, Michelle Asha Cooper, Nicole McDonald, and Thomas Major Jr., *Becoming a Student-Ready College: A New Culture of Leadership for Student Success* (San Francisco: Jossey-Bass, 2016), 5.

42. With the tightening of state and federal support for higher education, private lessons that, in the twentieth century, had been taught by full-time appointments/lines, are now primarily taught by part-time/adjunct faculty. If students who have limited training (but great potential) enter college for additional one-on-one training, and this training is needed in "new" areas such as popular music, gospel, improvisation, etc., faculty and chairs must make a solid case for funding additional part-time faculty to fill these roles. In order to make this happen, faculty and chairs must first acknowledge the demand that is present and the students who are making their desire to learn and grow known.

43. Brown McNair et al., *Becoming a Student-Ready College*, 48.

PART II

Unmeasured Pedagogical Horizons

CHAPTER 7

Connecting Students and Artistic Communities

Understanding Agency, Fostering Empathy, and Expanding Representation in the Classroom

MARK KATZ

The best thing about my courses, student evaluations tell me, is not me. The best thing, students say, is the artists—the professional, nonacademic musicians who have a regular place in our classroom. I'm OK with that. I'm happy to be outshone, because my collaboration with these artists has been crucial to my development as a teacher and has allowed me to better serve my students. To be clear, I am not talking about having the occasional guest speaker or performer. Rather, I have designed these courses around the participation of artists; their voices and perspectives shape the courses' content and direction. This type of pedagogical collaboration is challenging and risky, but the rewards are immense. For some students, these artists represent aspects of their identity that I do not. For others, the collaboration exposes them to people, perspectives, and ways of living they have never encountered. Many of the artists I work with have faced discrimination, economic inequality, and financial hardship, and their lived experience highlights issues of social justice for the students more directly and bracingly than I can. As students have told me, their engagement with these artists can be empowering, inspiring, and revelatory. This pedagogical approach is meant to center care, which demands the actions I name in the title of this essay: understanding agency, fostering empathy, and expanding representation.

To highlight my collaborative approach, and the rich student learning that comes from it, I'll focus on two courses I have taught at the University of North Carolina at Chapel Hill: The Art and Culture of the DJ and Hip Hop Diplomacy.[1] I taught The Art and Culture of the DJ six times between 2007 and 2018, always for undergraduate non–music majors. Enrollment ranged from about thirty to forty students, a higher than optimal number for the hands-on aspects of the class but a size that responded to consistently high demand. The course description in the syllabus, which has stayed largely the same over the years, is as follows:

> At heart a DJ, or disc jockey, is someone who plays recordings, whether on the radio, in dance clubs, at parties, or as part of a musical group. However, there is much more to DJing than simply playing records. In this course we will explore the art and culture of the DJ in order to understand the important and often misunderstood role of the DJ in modern musical life. In particular, we will explore the ways in which DJing challenges traditional notions of music, musicianship, and musical instruments and examine the DJ's role as a cultural arbiter. Readings and discussion will be supplemented by guest lectures and performances and demonstrations by professional DJs. In addition to learning about the history of the DJ, students will also create a DJ mix, observe DJs in a club setting, and learn some basics of DJ equipment and technique.

The course is part historical survey, spanning technological developments from early recording to digital DJ systems as well as covering DJ-centric musical genres, among them disco, hip hop, house, techno, and dubstep. There is also a creative and interactive component, which has students producing mixes, learning how to use DJ equipment, and observing DJs at work. The course description rather downplays the participation of DJs: "Readings and discussion will be supplemented by guest lectures and performances and demonstrations by professional DJs." The reason is practical, and raises an issue I'll return to: from semester to semester I don't know how much funding I might be able to secure to pay visiting DJs, and the amount of funding I have dictates the extent of their participation.

I have taught Hip Hop Diplomacy four times between 2018 and 2022, once as a graduate musicology seminar for ten students, and three times for undergraduates from a variety of majors with enrollments between 23 and 35. Here is the course description of the spring 2020 offering for undergraduates:

> Focusing on the period following the 9/11 terrorist attacks, this course explores the U.S. government's use of hip hop as a form of people-to-people diplomacy, the interaction of citizens of different countries meant to establish dialogue, shape public opinion, and influence policy. At heart, this course is about the intersection of music and power. We will explore the power of music to bridge cultural divides, facilitate understanding, and build community. We will also seek to understand the fraught power relationships—between art and the state and between the United States and the international community—revealed in the practice of hip hop diplomacy. The course will follow my work as found-

ing director of Next Level, a State Department–funded hip hop diplomacy program that has visited more than 30 countries since 2014 and will be conducting residencies during the semester.

In all versions of the course, a variety of hip hop artists visited the class, and a major assignment required students to interview an artist who had participated in a State Department–funded program. Moreover, as I'll explain, I developed a pedagogical approach to the class that was directly shaped by my work with hip hop practitioners and informed by hip hop culture.

I don't have to make the case that hosting guest artists in the classroom can enhance student experience. It's easy to see why students would enjoy witnessing performances in an intimate setting, where they have also the opportunity to interact with the artists. As Kaishan Kong, a scholar of intercultural communication, notes in a review of the pedagogical literature on guests in the classroom, "Guest speakers enrich education by providing first-hand knowledge, offering career-specific information and broadening range of ideas."[2] In this essay, I want to amplify this assertion by arguing for the value of treating guests like coteachers, making their perspectives and involvement integral to one's pedagogy.

In teaching The Art and Culture of the DJ, I saw an important shift in the course's shape and impact when, in 2014 and 2016, I not only brought DJs in as guests but cotaught the class with them. In both years, I worked with DJ A-Minor and DJ SK, artists who have a wealth of experience DJing a wide variety of events and venues, whether bars, dance clubs, fashion shows, sporting events, or weddings. They attended every class session, demonstrating genres and techniques and discussing music and relating their experiences as DJs. They held office hours in the Beat Lab, a space in UNC's Department of Music that houses DJ and beatmaking equipment; students, as part of their participation grade, attended office hours to receive hands-on instruction.[3] A-Minor and SK also contributed suggestions for listening and reading assignments and commented on the mix assignment, in which students assembled a twenty-minute set designed for a particular venue or occasion (such as a dance club, gallery opening, wedding, or fashion show). I was responsible for creating the syllabus, lecturing on DJ history and culture, grading, and maintaining the course website. I also served as moderator, leading the discussion and guiding the flow of each session.

Having A-Minor and SK as coteachers drove home a central point of the course: that DJs are (or more accurately can be) musicians and that DJ technologies should be understood as musical instruments. With performances, demonstrations, and workshops, students quickly appreciated the difficulty of DJing and the artistic sensibilities and choices involved in nearly every aspect of a DJ's work. Moreover, students came to understand the perspectives, careers, and lived experiences of these DJs with a depth that a single visit could never communicate. For example, students were surprised to learn the extent to which success as a DJ depended on entrepreneurial hustle and acumen as much as musical taste and skill, seeing firsthand the harsh reality of the twenty-first-century gig economy. In one semester we organized a dance party as a collaborative class project. Students worked on contracts, sponsorships, promotions, catering, lighting and decorations, and more. It was an intensive, instructive, eye-opening experience that I, not a professional DJ, couldn't have overseen alone. One student told me that because of the regular presence of the DJs and the hands-on nature of the course, he learned more about entrepreneurship in that semester than he had in his various business classes.

Another crucial outcome of the DJs' consistent participation in the class was the opportunity to delve into sensitive issues of great relevance to university students. Sexual assault is sadly too common in dance clubs, where darkness, close physical contact, copious alcohol consumption, and libidos meet. Club DJs constantly witness nonconsensual physical contact on the dance floor and have perspectives on the matter born out of long experience. Each semester we spent multiple sessions talking about dance clubs as both safe and unsafe spaces, and the presence of DJs opened up difficult conversations. Many students (particularly those who identify as women) related the numbingly common experience of being groped on the dance floor. Some students (particularly those who identify as men) were shocked to hear these reports. Discussion often turned to issues of consent and bystander intervention. The DJs talked about their strategies for discouraging predatory behavior and offered sound advice to students.[4] When we organized the dance party we also designed clever posters encouraging consent that students placed around the dance floor and in bathrooms.[5]

Queerness and the history of queer contributions to DJ culture were also important topics of discussion in the class. As a cisgender, heterosexual man it is important that I acknowledge both the centrality of queer culture to the history of dance music (in which DJs have always played a vital role) and its pernicious erasure from narratives about the music.[6] At the same time, I cannot speak from personal experience on these matters. Nor could A-Minor or SK, also cisgender, heterosexual men. But two other DJs—PlayPlay, a trans man, and VSPRTN, a queer Black man, could and did speak from their perspectives.[7] (PlayPlay was a frequent guest before I hired them to teach the course while I was on leave. VSPRTN held weekly lab hours one semester and was a regular presence in the classroom.) Representation matters, and having these two artists play prominent roles in the course meant that LGBTQ students and students of color saw people like themselves in positions of authority, a rare

Figure 7.1. Courtesy Patrick Phelps-McKeown

occurrence in a university setting (or anywhere for that matter). Students, of course, also learn from one another. A university-supplied open-ended question on my student evaluation form one semester asked, "How did the diversity of your classmates contribute to your learning in this course?" Here are some of the responses: "Gave me insight onto how others feel at clubs, as opposed to how straight, white men feel." "I like how we addressed the importance of representation in class." "The Pulse nightclub discussion we had was really powerful." This last comment refers to our discussion of the horrific 2016 mass shooting at the gay nightclub in Orlando that left forty-nine people dead and fifty-three wounded.[8] One student stunned us when he related how he had been living in Orlando at the time and was at the club the night before the shooting; he talked to us about the devasting impact of the shooting both on him personally and on the queer community. I credit PlayPlay and VSPRTN for making such conversations possible, both because they have influenced me to be a more sensitive facilitator and because of the work they have done, symbolically and pedagogically, in my courses.

Anthropologist Amber R. Clifford-Napoleone writes of the value of exploring music through the lens of sexuality: "Using sexuality to study music is an opportunity not only to make our students better thinkers, but also to demonstrate that sexual diversity has always been there, that the study of music is not separate from that diversity but woven within it, and that we as music scholars will refuse to embrace the phobias and oppressions that exist around us." "It is not just good pedagogy," she concludes, "it is good humanity."[9] Moreover, when PlayPlay, VSPRTN, or any of the other collaborating artists held the floor, I happily moved out of the spotlight. In doing so, we collectively effected a visible power shift in the classroom, conveying a message about who can be authorities in a university setting. This is an important message to send, especially from white male professors who are overrepresented in the academy. As women's studies professor Tamara Agha-Jaffar writes, "Such an approach dismantles patriarchal power relations in the classroom."[10]

The presence of musicians in the Hip Hop Diplomacy course was different from that in the DJ class, but no less powerful. Each time I offered it, hip hop artists who participated in Next Level, a cultural diplomacy program that I directed from 2013 to 2019, visited the class, speaking to and often performing for us.[11] These musicians directly and indirectly influenced the class. First, in this course I did something I had never done before: I developed a pedagogical approach that drew directly from hip hop culture and practice. Second, I asked students to interview artists who had participated in the Next Level hip hop diplomacy program.

Here is how I explained my pedagogical approach in the syllabus:

> PEDAGOGICAL APPROACH
>
> "I hope these guys don't think they're coming to teach us hip hop. I hope they're going to learn as well and build with us." Ngoni Tapiwa, aka Upmost
>
> The statement above comes from a 2014 interview with Zimbabwean hip hop artist Upmost, who expressed his concerns about the Next Level program coming to his community. When Upmost said he hoped that we were com-

> ing to *build with* Zimbabwean hip hop, he was drawing on a crucial concept in hip-hop culture. To build with someone is to collaborate, to work toward something that can be achieved collectively, but not individually. To build with someone is different from teaching someone, or to use a hip hop term that suggests domination, *schooling* them.
>
> I prefer to build with students rather than teach them. Although I am an expert in the subject matter, I will not simply be dispensing my knowledge or wisdom. I want to model the type of diplomacy that Next Level aspires to, one that is fundamentally collaborative, culturally sensitive, and mutually respectful. Practically speaking, this will mean that students will often take the role of discussion leader/moderator and will provide constructive feedback on the draft chapters of the book I am writing on hip hop diplomacy.[12]

In addition to empowering the students to lead discussion and help shape the direction of my book, the concept of building also led us to sit in a circle in emulation of a cypher, a hip hop practice in which rappers or dancers improvise in the round. It was, in fact, Toni Blackman, a rapper and poet who visited our class, who inspired the classroom cypher.

The impact of building, as a concept and philosophy, affected the course in less observable ways as well. In the graduate seminar I promoted building as a model for critique. Graduate students are often encouraged by their professors to be sharp-eyed and sharp-tongued critics, to find flaws in arguments, to problematize and complicate the work of others. I asked students to adopt a simultaneously skeptical and charitable stance toward others, to see their commentary as building with others or building upon what other scholars have done before them. I particularly encouraged this approach when it came to the question of complicity. It is easy to call hip hop artists who participate in State Department diplomacy programs complicit with the bad actions of the U.S. government, particularly in its oppression of marginalized people at home and abroad. This is an especially stinging critique of hip hop, which has given voice to marginalized people and has a history of challenging power structures. I did not dismiss this critique. But I did ask students to consider why artists would be motivated to engage with the State Department, to appreciate the artists' agency, and to try to understand how they operate within larger, often oppressive systems.

In a paper, graduate student Meli Kimathi wrote beautifully about the challenge of navigating power structures and the issue of complicity in the lives of hip hop artists: "Hip hop was born of the sort of tensions cultural diplomacy seeks to address, conflicts between dominant power structures and subordinate groups over rights and freedoms, economic and health outcomes, and political voice. Hip hop practitioners, then, contend with daily cognitive dissonance around inhabiting and preserving their culture in inhospitable environments, requiring constant calculations of agency, complicity, and potential to 'play oneself' or 'be played.'"[13] She clearly saw the broader context in which Asheru, a rapper she had long admired and whom she interviewed, lived his life and conducted his career. In reading interviews with hip hop artists and interviewing the artists themselves, students came to hold more nuanced and charitable views of the artists' actions. In the classroom and in academia in general it is all too easy to judge the actions of others without acknowledging or accounting for their agency. But when the subjects of classroom discussion are sitting right in front of students (in person or virtually) or when students conduct interviews with them, it becomes difficult to ignore the complexities of their humanity. For me, this appreciation of agency is one of the most powerful benefits of engaging in sustained collaboration with artists in an academic setting.

The interview assignment proved powerful in other ways as well. Many students reported coming away inspired by the artists—by their talent, their wisdom, their passion, and their hustle. Some were inspired by seeing real people (as opposed to celebrities) making lives for themselves in the arts. Others responded to aspects of the artists' identities. They were inspired by the presence of powerful and talented women and people of color in the classroom, something that I cannot model for them. The artists facilitated many points of connection. Undergraduate student Chiazo Agina, who grew up in California with Nigerian parents, was moved by her conversation with Junious Brickhouse, an African American dancer (and now director of Next Level) who led a residency in Nigeria. Her interview with Brickhouse, she explained, "advanced my own belief that the complexities of identity are entrenched systems stemming from oppression and that both African Americans and Africans have a lot to learn from each other. As someone who also believes in the arts but struggles with seeing them as a viable career path, speaking to Junious was incredibly enlightening. Ultimately, I was incredibly grateful to conduct this interview and hope that I will continue to have these difficult discussions with more people as I myself attempt to navigate my own identity."[14]

Agina's classmate John Cho Edmonds summed up the importance of connecting with artists in writing about his interview with rapper Mahogany Jones: "Whatever we flesh out in the ivory tower means little without affirmation from lived experience, and it means everything coming from Mahogany Jones," an artist whose talent and integrity he greatly admired.[15]

In describing the benefits of this collaborative approach, I don't want to give the impression that nothing more is required than getting artists into the classroom and then letting the magic unfold. There are significant challenges and risks to this work. To begin with, it's no simple matter to secure the participation of outside artists. Two aspects of my courses may make their collaborative nature difficult to replicate. First, both arose out of book projects that had significant ethnographic components.[16] Because I had interviewed a few hundred artists for these books and developed strong relationships with many of them, I have enjoyed access to a robust network from which many of my classroom guests and collaborators were drawn. Second, both courses have at times been supported by grants. Typically, my department has little or no money available for classroom guests, and I assume that this is norm at universities everywhere. I acknowledge, then, the demands of identifying, engaging, and paying guest artists and coteachers. But it is worth both the effort and expense, and I hope that this essay can help teachers convince administrators and granting agencies to fund this kind of classroom collaboration.[17]

There are additional challenges once the artists are in the classroom. My collaborative work is constantly an exercise in ceding professorial authority and control. For anyone accustomed to being the sole authority figure and the dominant voice in the classroom, it takes practice and sensitivity to know when to jump in and when to hang back, when to clarify or even argue and when to leave one's dissenting views unspoken. Sometimes the artists violate unspoken academic norms (or the ones a particular professor subscribes to), whether connected to attire or speech or student interaction. The effect can be refreshing and break down barriers, or it can be offensive and disrespectful. There's an unpredictability to these collaborations, and one must be comfortable with uncertainty. To make this work, I have to be ready to improvise, to be prepared to explore new topics at a moment's notice, or conversely, to steer a wandering discussion back on track. I need to be willing to expose my ignorance and to settle for being the least cool teacher in the room. Moreover, it takes a great deal of work outside the classroom to achieve and sustain a positive, productive collaboration. For me, it means raising money; lobbying or persuading colleagues and administrators to support or approve of my work; dealing with the intricacies of university finances and human resources policies; planning syllabi and assignments with the artists; helping my collaborators navigate academia; and a whole lot of e-mail.

There's no doubt that it would be simpler to plan and teach courses by myself. My experience, however, always demonstrates that collaboration is worth the effort, both for myself and for my students. I learn and grow from each experience. I am never bored. I have been a full-time professor for twenty-three years and have yet to experience a midcareer rut. I also value the relationships, sometimes friendships, that have developed out of these collaborations, which I appreciate not only for themselves but also because they ward off academic insularity.

The real payoff of this work, however, is its effect on students. When students can see the subjects of their study in their complete, glorious, and sometimes contradictory humanity, they understand—much more powerfully than

I could communicate—the complexities of personal agency and the fraught, always shifting relationship between agency and structure. When students hear the artists' stories, when they learn of their joys and triumphs, their compromises and their regrets, they are challenged to see the world through the eyes of others and hone their empathic faculties. This work can also enhance diversity and representation—in terms of gender, race, sexuality, and socioeconomic status—in the classroom. For some students, working with these artists means interacting with those they would never encounter otherwise. For others, it's about seeing their own identities reflected in the classroom. At its best, this intensely collaborative approach is—to borrow from one of my students—an affirmation of lived experience, which is a central goal of humanistic education and artistic engagement as well as a valuable way to understand and practice care.[18]

Notes

1. Since writing the initial draft of this essay, I have taught two additional courses using the same approach, Music in the Community, a thirty-five-person class for nonmajors (fall 2021), and Music, Technology, and Culture, a fourteen-person class for upper-level music majors (spring 2021).

2. Kaishan Kong, "Different Voices: Guest Speakers as Pedagogy in a Culture Class," in *Transnational Perspectives on Innovation in Teaching and Learning Technologies*, ed. Emmanuel Jean-Francois (Leiden, Netherlands: Koninkijke Brill, 2018), 263.

3. I created the Beat Lab in 2012 when, as department chair, I repurposed a room that had been used to store instruments and outfitted it with DJ and beatmaking equipment (e.g., turntables, DJ controllers, drum machines, and MIDI keyboards) that I had obtained through grants, through private donations, and from Red Bull, the energy drink company that has had a long history of sponsoring DJs and DJ-related events. Creating the Beat Lab would undoubtedly have been more challenging had I not been chair and had I not had funding from nondepartmental sources.

4. The DJs' strategies included signaling security to attend to problematic situations, calling individuals out on the microphone, and (in the case of fights), playing War's "Why Can't We Be Friends?" The DJs also provided practical advice to the students, for example, pretending to be friends with someone who is being accosted and drawing them away from the predator and making sure that inebriated friends (or strangers, for that matter) never leave a venue alone. I also assigned readings on the subject, including Chantelle Fiddy, "We Need to Talk about Sexual Harassment in Nightclubs," *Mixmag*, April 13, 2015, https://mixmag.net/.

5. This form of feminist and queer activism was inspired by Queen Plz and PlayPlay, two DJs who posted such signs at Party Illegal, a regular event they hosted in Durham, North Carolina, known for its safe and welcoming atmosphere, particularly among LGBTQ people. Two of the posters, created by their colleague Patrick Phelps-McKeown,

read "DON'T TOUCH OTHER PEOPLE WITHOUT THEIR CONSENT thank you :)" and "I KNOW THAT ASS IS INCREDIBLE BUT YOU GOTTA ASK BEFORE YOU TOUCH IT." Other posters were inspired by the book *Learning Good Consent: On Healthy Relationships and Survivor Support*, ed. Cindy Crabb (Chico, CA: AK Press, 2016). My thanks to Queen Plz (Laura Friedrich) for sharing the posters and Crabb reference.

6. This issue came up in assigned readings as well, particularly in Luis-Manuel Garcia's "An Alternate History of Sexuality in Club Culture," *Resident Advisor*, January 28, 2014, https://ra.co/features/1927.

7. Women artists also spoke to students on many occasions. These include Dr. Dakar, Queen Plz, DJ Ripley, and Suzi Analogue. VSPRTN was not the only DJ of color who visited the class. A-Minor is Black, as are Suzi Analogue, DJ Bro-Rabb, GrandWizzard Theodore, J-Live, DJ Nabs, Rasta Root, and DJ Trife, who have visited my classes in the past. DJ Rang, a frequent guest, is Indian American.

8. To inform this discussion I had students read Tim Lawrence, "Life and Death on the Pulse Dance Floor: Transglocal Politics and the Erasure of the Latinx in the History of Queer Dance," *Dancecult* 8 (2016): 1–25.

9. Amber Clifford-Napoleone, "Teaching Music & Difference—Let's Get It On: Pedagogy, Sexuality, and Music," *Musicology Now*, August 28, 2018, http://www.musicologynow.org/2018/08/.

10. Tamara Agha-Jaffar, "Theory to Praxis in Women's Studies: Guest Speakers and Service-Learning as Pedagogy," *Feminist Teacher* 13 (2000): 1.

11. These artists included rappers J-Live, Pinqy Ring, and Toni Blackman, dancer Junious Brickhouse, DJ Trife, and beatmaker Jaci Caprice. More information on these artists can be found at https://www.nextlevel-usa.org/artists.

12. The book I refer to is *Build: The Power of Hip Hop Diplomacy in a Divided World* (New York: Oxford University Press, 2019). Although this approach was not directly inspired by Paulo Freire, it connects with elements of his 1968 classic *Pedagogy of the Oppressed*. The hip hop concept of building resonates with Freire's theory of dialogue, as when he writes that "dialogue cannot be reduced to the act of one person's 'depositing' ideas in another. . . . It is an act of creation; it must not serve as a crafty instrument for the domination of one person by another" (Freire, *Pedagogy of the Oppressed*, trans. Myra Bergman Ramos [New York: Bloomsbury, 2012], 89).

13. Meli Kimathi (unpublished class assignment, February 12, 2018). The last sentence refers to lyrics from the 1996 song "Ya Playin Yaself" by Jeru the Dmaja.

14. Chiazo Agina (unpublished class assignment, December 4, 2018).

15. John Cho Edmonds (unpublished class assignment, December 3, 2018).

16. Mark Katz, *Groove Music: The Art and Culture of the Hip-Hop DJ* (New York: Oxford University Press, 2012) and *Build: The Power of Hip Hop Diplomacy in a Divided World*.

17. All the guests and coteachers I mention in this essay participated in person. During the coronavirus pandemic, I continued to engage artists in the classroom, but their participation was virtual. Recognizing the value of their time and expertise and the

financial hardship many of them endured, I paid them the same amount for virtual visits as I would for in-person visits. In the past I had not offered honoraria for virtual visits, but will do so in future, post-pandemic courses.

18. In a development that occurred as this volume was moving into production, UNC-Chapel Hill's Department of Music hired producer Suzi Analogue, who had previously served as guest in my courses, to begin teaching in the fall 2022 semester. She became the department's first full-time faculty member who is a hip hop artist. This hire represents another potential and positive outcome of connecting students with artistic communities in that artists who begin as visitors can, through this process, eventually become colleagues.

Bibliography

Agha-Jaffar, Tamara. "Theory to Praxis in Women's Studies: Guest Speakers and Service-Learning as Pedagogy." *Feminist Teacher* 13 (2000): 1–11.

Clifford-Napoleone, Amber R. "Teaching Music & Difference—Let's Get It On: Pedagogy, Sexuality, and Music." *Musicology Now*, 28 August 2018. http://www.musicologynow.org/2018/08/.

Crabb, Cindy, ed. *Learning Good Consent: On Healthy Relationships and Survivor Support*. Chico, CA: AK Press, 2016.

Fiddy, Chantelle. "We Need to Talk about Sexual Harassment in Nightclubs." *Mixmag*, 13 April 2015. https://mixmag.net/.

Freire, Paulo. *Pedagogy of the Oppressed*. Trans. Myra Bergman Ramos. New York: Bloomsbury, 2012.

Garcia, Luis-Manuel. "An Alternate History of Sexuality in Club Culture." *Resident Advisor*, 28 January 2014. https://ra.co/features/1927.

Katz, Mark. *Groove Music: The Art and Culture of the Hip-Hop DJ*. New York: Oxford University Press, 2012.

———. *Build: The Power of Hip Hop Diplomacy in a Divided World*. New York: Oxford University Press, 2019.

Kong, Kaishan. "Different Voices: Guest Speakers as Pedagogy in a Culture Class." In *Transnational Perspectives on Innovation in Teaching and Learning Technologies*, ed. Emmanuel Jean-Francois, 262–84. Leiden, Netherlands: Koninkijke Brill, 2018.

Lawrence, Tim. "Life and Death on the Pulse Dance Floor: Transglocal Politics and the Erasure of the Latinx in the History of Queer Dance." *Dancecult* 8 (2016): 1–25. Accessible at https://dj.dancecult.net/index.php/dancecult/article/view/906.

CHAPTER 8

Toward Socially Responsible Music History Pedagogy

A Rant, Some Theories, and a Few Resources

ERIC HUNG

Letting the Butterfly Go

On March 16, 2021, a gunman went to three Asian spas in the Atlanta area, and murdered eight people. Six of them were women of Asian descent. A survivor interviewed by the South Korean newspaper *Chosun Ilbo* stated that, at Gold Spa, the gunman said, "I'm going to kill all Asians."[1] In explaining his motives to the police, the perpetrator denied that his actions were racially motivated. According to Captain Jay Baker of the Cherokee County Sheriff's Office, "He does claim that it was not racially motivated." He added that the gunman "apparently has an issue, what he considers a sex addiction, and sees these locations as a temptation for him that he wanted to eliminate."[2] Even if we take the perpetrator's words at face value—and we should not—we are forced to ask, "Given that sex work occurs at many places, why are Asian spas his primary locations of temptation? More generally, why is there so much demand for Asian spas that perform sex work in North America?"

The answer lies, in large part, in the stereotype of the hypersexualized yet submissive Asian woman. Often referred to as the "lotus flower," "china doll," or "geisha doll," this fetishized Asian woman was a product of European and U.S. imperialism, and is maintained first and foremost through culture. Primary examples are the many manifestations of *Madame Butterfly*: Pierre Loti's novel, John Luther Long's short story, David Belasco's play, Giacomo Puccini's opera, films directed by Sidney Olcott and Chester Franklin, and so on. More recently, there is Claude-Michel Schönberg and Alain Boubill's *Miss Saigon*. This stereotype was also maintained through law. The first restrictive federal immigration law in the United States, the Page Act of 1875, effectively barred "Oriental" women from entering the country on the assumption that they were coming for "lewd and immoral purposes."[3] In enforcing what is essentially family separation legislation, "Immigration officials apparently operated on the premise that every Chinese woman was seeking admission on false pretenses and that each was a potential prostitute until proven otherwise."[4]

In this essay, I argue that sound pedagogy and radical care involve thinking not just about the well-being of our students, but also about how our teaching alters the relationships students have with the historic and contemporary communities—particularly marginalized communities—we explore in our classrooms. In many instances, we are introducing students to populations they have never encountered. At other times, we are presenting contexts that can trigger positive or negative memories for some students, and alter others' ideas about these communities. To be ethical instructors, we need to consider how our pedagogy potentially benefits or harms the groups about whom we teach. This is an issue that some music education researchers and (ethno)musicologists who teach repertories outside the Western classical canon have engaged in for several years.[5] Until very recently, however, this conversation has not seriously impacted Western music history classrooms.[6] Here, I diagnose our general reluctance to think about the effects of our teaching on marginalized communities through applying theories of "colorblind teaching" (Milton Reynolds), "information poverty" (originally developed by Elfreda Chatman, and recently elaborated by Amelia Gibson and others), and "research refusal" (Eve Tuck and Wayne Yang). I also provide a way forward through applying a feminist ethics of care, particularly through adapting Michelle Caswell and Marika Cifor's model for radical empathy in archives for music history pedagogy.[7]

It is within this framework that I address Puccini's *Madama Butterfly*'s continuing popularity in music history courses and, by extension, on operatic stages. In most music history texts written for students and the general public, Asian musical traditions and composers before the late twentieth century are conspicuously absent; they only make ghostly appearances in discussions of orientalism. To put it another way, Asian music is only considered useful when it serves a subservient role as a tool to freshen up Western musical language. In the 2019 edition of *A History of Western Music*, Peter Burkholder writes that, for Puccini, "The exoticism of America, Japan, or China was just another form of realism, with the added appeal of the unfamiliar and far away." Later on, when he discusses how Cio-Cio-San presents different personas to Pinkerton, he felt the need to judge the old Japanese practice of *seppuku* when he states that Cio-Cio-San "inadvertently [let Pinkerton] see a *darker side of Japanese culture* and of her own personal history: her father's ritual suicide" (emphasis added).[8] When teaching *Madama Butterfly*, serious discussions of the racism and colonialism that are at the root of musical exoticism since the nineteenth century are absent in most music history classrooms. Also absent is the fact that the opera reinforces a stereotype that continues to harm people of Asian descent in North America today.[9]

This approach to teaching exoticism is one reason why music history classrooms frequently continue to be what Milton Reynolds calls a "site of colorblind production and socialization."[10] He argues that bypassing discussions of race and racism causes two major problems. The first is "conceptual impoverishment," which limits the tools our students can use to make sense of historical events and their own experiences. He writes, "conceptual impoverishment fosters ignorance by intentionally abstracting historical events from the systems and structures of power and subjugation that produce these outcomes."[11] The second problem is "affective under-skilling," which restrains the development of our students' critical thinking skills and emotional intelligence. If racism (or sexism, ableism, homophobia, intersectionality, and so on) is not considered a relevant or admissible topic in classrooms, what we get are "the predictable patterns of social anxiety, agitation, evasion, and consternation that emerge in conversations regarding race among people who have been socialized to be colorblind."[12]

The above approach to teaching *Madama Butterfly* also brings out another issue that is very common in academia. In this environment, "The Subaltern can speak, but is only invited to speak her/our pain."[13] In some ways, this opera can be interpreted as a powerful indictment of American imperialism and racism. Unfortunately, few music history teachers take their students there. Instead, we focus on Cio-Cio-San's pain, and the Japanese characters' lack of agency. In this opera, the only people with the power to alleviate this pain are White Americans. This departs significantly from the historical context of Meiji-era Japan, the period during which the opera was set. At that time, the country instituted drastic reforms in all sectors to counter American imperialism.

Finally, my objection to standard narratives about *Madama Butterfly* is heightened by the fact that this opera has long been one of the very few discussions of Asia in music history surveys. The 2019 edition of *The Norton Anthology of Western Music*, for example, includes just three works that are based significantly on the cultures from the world's most populous continent. Besides *Madama Butterfly*, there is Book 1 of John Cage's *Music of Changes* (which used the *I Ching* as a compositional tool) and the first movement of Bright Sheng's *Seven Tunes Heard in China*, which is also about a young woman who is seeking love. If our courses explore a variety of Asian narratives and include the voices of many people of Asian descent, then the inclusion of *Madama Butterfly* is not a huge problem. When we seriously discuss how racism, sexism, and colonialism combined to create the "lotus flower" stereotype, teaching this opera can even be positive. Unfortunately, we so rarely discuss how Cio-Cio-San represents a stereotype that continues to affect the lives of Asian American women and influenced the murderer of eight people in Atlanta.

Moving Past Information Poverty

In thinking about why *Madama Butterfly* and other highly problematic works continue to be taught and staged with regularity and often without serious conversation, I find Elfreda Chatman's theory of "information poverty" to be helpful. Chatman argues that our society is made up of various information communities, and that each shares some sort of common lived experience (for example, race, ethnicity, gender, sexual orientation, class, disability, political orientation, religion, profession), which in turn forms "expected norms of behavior and ways to approach the world."[14] These norms—mostly unspoken codes—divide us into insiders and outsiders, and this bifurcation significantly hinders information sharing. This problem is somewhat alleviated by the fact that most people belong to multiple information communities, and therefore understand several sets of norms. That said, 1.5-generation immigrant children who must code-switch between their school-world and their home-world can tell you just how difficult translating between these two information communities can be. Similarly, musicians in multicultural ensembles can discuss how difficult it is for performers of different traditions to communicate effectively. After all, they trust dissimilar types of sources, and have radically different codes of expectations.

Chatman's original theory focused on the information poverty of people with low incomes. Following recent scholars who have extended her theory, I believe that intellectual elites who are trying to understand the cultures of marginalized populations can also be information poor.[15] Chatman's theory of information poverty involves six propositions—four of which are relevant to our current discussion.

Proposition 1 states, "People who are defined as information poor perceive themselves to be devoid of any sources that might help them."[16] Many academics say that diversifying a syllabus is difficult because they are unable to reach local musicians who are willing to talk to us, or because there simply are not enough resources that are readily accessible to both faculty and students. Given the vast amount of information and contacts available through the internet, what could this mean? One possibility is that we don't have enough time to devote to this issue given heavy teaching loads, requirements for research and service, and the need for contingent faculty to hold multiple positions. To alleviate this barrier, I encourage faculty who have greater job security to devote some of their research time to the creation of resources that can help less privileged faculty members become less information-poor. A second possibility is that some communities are not interested in sharing their insider knowledge. In this situation, we should ask very difficult questions about why we want to teach these traditions. Another possibility is that resources are available, but not easily accessible because of paywalls, language issues, information overload, and so on. Some of these problems are easier to solve than others. A fourth (and I suspect the most common) possibility is that, although resources are available, they do not fit academic norms. The resources are not articles in peer-reviewed journals or do not use the methodologies we view to be legitimate or the jargon we understand. This should—but rarely does—lead us to question our norms.

Chatman addresses this reluctance in propositions 3–5, which state:

- "Information poverty is determined by self-protective behaviors which are used in response to social norms";
- "Both secrecy and deception are self-protecting mechanisms due to a sense of mistrust regarding the interest or ability of others to provide useful information"; and
- "A decision to risk exposure about our true problems is often not taken due to a perception that negative consequences outweigh benefits."[17]

This theory acknowledges that there are significant risks associated with challenging the social norms of your information community. In the case of music academia, overhauling your courses requires you to confront those who want to hold on to established norms as well as your own insecurities about the availability, accuracy, and relevance of the information that insiders are willing to provide you. This leads to four forms of self-protecting behavior. Chatman calls the first "risk-taking," which refers to not sharing information because you think that no one cares about the problem you perceive, or that people will use what you reveal against you. In the case of music history pedagogy, you might decide not to raise issues about including *Madama Butterfly* in the course because you don't want to upset your colleagues, or perhaps you fear that they will come to see you as this "woke" troublemaker who is impossible to work with. The second is "secrecy," which refers to the process of actively shutting down or dismissing the information you receive. Chatman describes the third, "deception," as "a deliberate attempt to act out a false social reality."[18] This often occurs when one is trying to act more like an insider than one actually is. The final self-protecting behavior is "situational relevance," which involves downplaying the relevance of information supplied by an outsider. The end result is that many academics remain information poor when it comes to the needs and desires of students from marginalized populations. We end up perpetuating conceptual impoverishment and affective under-skilling in our teaching, and this can ultimately harm communities we examine in our courses. *Madama Butterfly* remains on the syllabus and is taught without serious considerations about racism and sexism because we have not listened to information outsiders who are telling us about the harm that the "lotus flower" stereotype continues to have on Asian American women.[19]

How can music academics move beyond being information poor about historically marginalized communities? And how can we deliver a music history curriculum that takes into account the well-being of different communities we discuss in our courses? Here, I argue that in determining course content—as well as course policies and pedagogical techniques—we need to move away from a masculinist framework that focuses on individuality and genius and toward a feminist ethics of care, a concept popularized through the research of psychologist Carol Gilligan. In her book *In a Different Voice*, Gilligan concluded that—based on interviews with many women—dominant theories about ethics, which focused on free will, individual choice, rights, and rationality simply did not speak to many of her subjects. Because most women are socialized into caregiving roles from an early age, many discussed the importance of relationships, contexts, and emotion in their ethical decisions.

In applying a feminist ethics of care to music history courses, we begin not with lists of exceptional and representative works of key artistic movements. Instead, I propose that we begin by focusing on three sets of affective relationships. The first is the relationship between the instructor and the students. Here, some of the questions we need to ask are:

- How can I present materials in a way that is personally meaningful to many students?
- How will I help my students develop deep critical thinking and discussion skills on issues that are highly relevant to their lives?
- How will I help my students emotionally process difficult and potentially triggering issues?

The second is the relationship between the instructor and the historical communities that we examine in a course. Here, we need to consider:

- What am I trying to accomplish by presenting this historical community to my students?
- If I am dealing with materials related to trauma or communities with strict protocols about cultural ownership, is it ethical to teach (or how do I ethically teach) this topic?
- How will I present the perspectives of the historical communities and subjects I am teaching, and how will I present other views about these communities?

Finally, the third relationship is between the instructor and contemporary communities. Among the issues we need to address are:

- How does my pedagogy potentially benefit or harm this community?
- If there is very little potential benefit or a good chance of harm, why should I teach this material?
- When I am teaching topics that are especially relevant to certain communities, how should I engage them? And how do I get their voices into my classroom?

An Example Module: Music and Incarceration

It is now time for me to discuss a few resources that can help instructors develop more socially responsible approaches to teaching Japanese and Japanese American experiences (or experiences of other marginalized cultures) in Western music history courses. One difficulty many instructors encounter is resistance from students who are reluctant to engage in discussions about colonialism, racism, sexism, and other forms of systemic discriminations. One strategy that has helped me is Julia Rose's commemorative museum pedagogy (CMP).[20] Developed by a public historian who was working to incorporate the experiences of the enslaved in tours and education programs at plantations, CMP focuses on the psychology of museum visitors and workers. Rose argues that—to be successful—educators who raise difficult topics need to recognize that learners generally go through five states: reception (when they are ready to learn something new), resistance (when they fight the new information), repetition (when they need to hear something again), reflection (when they need some time to think), and reconsideration (when they rethink their preconceived ideas). Rose points out that learners rarely proceed through these phases in a linear fashion. Encounters with a surprising artifact or a random thought can lead them to jump from one state to another in unexpected ways. Ultimately, greater attention to learners' psychological states can help instructors convince students to be open to new ideas and frameworks for thinking about difficult issues.

Another challenge for instructors is finding works that can naturally raise issues about the experiences of Japanese Americans and other immigrants. Here, I suggest two works. The first is Takuma Itoh's *American Postcards: Picture Brides (Hawaii 1908–1924)*, which is the focus of one episode of *Who's an Immigrant?*, a forthcoming podcast by the Music of Asian America Research Center. Here, I explore how this work considers issues that continue to affect Japanese American and other immigrant communities, including racist immigration legislation, family separation policies, the idea of Asians and Latinx people as "perpetual foreigners" and "liminal citizens," and ideas about the

American dream. The second is Tōru Takemitsu's *November Steps*. In an essay on Beyond Tokenism, a website dedicated to helping music history instructors develop equitable and relevant pedagogies, Kunio Hara reflects on how he uses this work to demonstrate the challenges of cross-cultural communications. This exercise shows his students that music is not a universal language, and that exoticism has cast a long shadow in Western classical music.[21]

To close, I argue that the seminal moment of Japanese American history—the World War II incarceration of 120,000 Japanese and Japanese Americans who lived on the West Coast and Latin America in concentration camps throughout the Western and Central United States—can be embedded into a unit on another hot-button topic: mass incarceration. I developed this module through exploring the three sets of affective relationships above. As presented, the module is for a course on twentieth-/twenty-first-century music. It lasts for four weeks, with the class meeting twice a week for 75–90 minutes. It can, however, be easily adapted for the music history survey, an American music course, or a topics seminar. You can also lengthen and shorten the module.

For this unit, I define incarceration broadly, as "being confined for an extended period to a specific facility through the actions of a state." This includes prisons, concentration camps, prisoner-of-war camps, facilities for undocumented immigrants, Native American residential schools, and so on. In terms of affective relationships with students, I chose this topic first because of its relevance. Incarceration has been a hot political issue for several years, so many students would likely have already thought about the issue. It is also likely that some students will have a personal connection to incarceration. Second, because I can discuss so many different historical situations and ways music has been used (for example, for healing, as a weapon, to resist, for educational purposes, to build solidarity), I can help students broaden their thinking, sharpen their critical thinking skills, and learn how to discuss intellectually and emotionally difficult issues with others.

With regard to affective relationships with historical and contemporary communities, incarceration is a good topic to teach not only because so many formerly incarcerated people want these experiences shared, but also because the issue deeply affects so many segments of society. By ethically teaching this topic, we can learn to analyze the effects of past, current, and proposed policies, and to support and advocate for marginalized voices that are often neglected because they lack certain credentials and use methodologies that policy and academic elites do not favor. In creating this unit, I tried to center these voices and the needs of their communities. Because no group is monolithic, it is also important to present different and opposing viewpoints from within the same community. In implementing this module, one of the most efficient ways to find potential collaborators is to reach out to relevant local organizations.

Ideally, you would be able to bring them into your classroom (physically or virtually) and to pay them for their services. If no budget is available, I think it's still important to reach out. Sometimes, there are volunteers who want to share their stories and programs free of charge. You can use some of the online materials that they have available. Below, I will mention organizations that are based in the greater Philadelphia area, where I live.

Music and Incarceration Module

Learning Goals

1. To improve students' critical thinking and discussion skills when confronted with intellectually and emotionally difficult subjects; and
2. To introduce students to major musical genres of the twentieth and twenty-first centuries.

At the end of this module, students should be able to:

1. Outline the key ways states have used incarceration over the past century;
2. Critically analyze the consequences of key incarceration policies and the functions of the arts programs that are related to incarceration; and
3. Apply the critical thinking and discussion skills they learned in this unit to other intellectually and emotionally difficult subjects.

Unit Assignment

Create a "Critical Karaoke" mini-podcast on an incarceration-related musical work. The mini-podcast should examine several of the key concepts discussed in this unit and demonstrate good analytical and discussion skills. It should also cater to your target audience (you can choose your target audience).

Schedule

Part 1: Introduction of Music and Incarceration

Guest: Speaker from the Reentry Think Tank (an organization that "connects returning citizens with artists and advocates to transform the stereotypes, social services, and platforms that impact our lives and communities") or Eastern State Penitentiary (a prison museum dedicated to advocating against mass incarceration)

In-Class Activity: The session begins with the instructor outlining the broad definition of incarceration and asking the students to share what they know about the key questions below. The remainder of the session is devoted to the guest speaker. If a guest speaker is not available, I would assign relevant online videos that introduce the history of incarceration in the country where you reside. I would then use class time to conduct a small-group activity, during which students will look for and talk to each other about music they can find on the internet about incarceration.

Key Questions: How has your country used incarceration over the past century? What problems does incarceration solve or fail to solve? What problems does incarceration make visible or hide? What roles can art play in the lives of the incarcerated and in advocacy?

Part 2: Music for Entertainment, Rehabilitation, and Education

Class #2: Music by Inmates in the Early Twentieth Century

View: (1) Instructor's video lecture on late nineteenth- and early twentieth-century string band music and on music in prisons and concentration camps in the early twentieth century; (2) Excerpts from *The Goree All Girl String Band*, a musical by Michael Bradley and Artie Sievers

Read: Gnagy, Caroline (Caroline Casey), "As If They Were Going Places: Class and Gender Portrayals through Country Music in the Texas State Prison, 1938–1944," in *Country Boys and Redneck Women: New Essays in Gender and Country Music*, University Press of Mississippi, 2016, pp. 126–45

Key Questions: What are the different functions of music programs in prisons during the early twentieth century? What do you think the members of the Goree All Girl String Band were trying to achieve? Who benefits and what might be harmed by their music?

Class #3: Different Approaches to Prison Education

Guest: A music educator who teaches in prisons, preferably in the local area

Listen: Excerpts from Mozart's *Don Giovanni*

Read: (1) Polzonetti, Pierpaolo, "Don Giovanni Goes to Prison: Teaching Opera behind Bars," *Musicology Now*, Feb. 2016 (https://musicologynow.org/don-giovanni-goes-to-prison-teaching-opera-behind-bars/); (2) Gordon, Bonnie, "The Perils of Public Musicology," *Musicology Now*, Feb. 2016 (https://musicologynow.org/the-perils-of-public-musicology/); and (3) Cohen, Mary L., and Catherine M. Wilson, "Inside the Fences: Pedagogical Practices and Purposes of Songwriting in an Adult Male U.S. State Prison," *International Journal of Music Education*, vol. 35, no. 4, Nov. 2017, pp. 541–53

Key Questions: What functions do music education programs serve in prisons? What educational approaches are appropriate and what are not? Why? If you had the opportunity to start a music education program in a prison, how would you decide what you would do?

Class #4: Theorizing Music-Making by Inmates

View: Matthew D. Thibeault, "Oral History of Learning Jazz Improvisation with Play-Along Media While Incarcerated" (https://www.youtube.com/watch?v=BqO_Cdq9BOQ)

Read: (1) McGraw, Andrew Clay, "Feeling the Feels: Spinozist Ethics and Musical Feeling in an American Jail," *Culture, Theory and Critique*, vol. 61, no. 2–3, 2020, pp. 267–82; and (2) Harbert, Benjamin J., and Consuela Gaines, "Sounding Lockdown: Singing in Administrative Segregation at the Louisiana Correctional Institute for Women," *Popular Music and the Politics of Hope: Queer and Feminist Interventions*, Routledge, 2019, pp. 299–316

Key Questions: What are the different effects of music on people who were incarcerated? How were the subjects in the Thibeault video and the McGraw and Harbert/Gaines articles similar and different? What methodologies were used in each research project? Based on what you have examined in the past two weeks, which rang particularly true, and what questions do you have for each author?

Part 3: Music as Weapon, Resistance, and Identity Formation in Incarceration

Class #5: Music as a Tool in War

View: Instructor's video lecture about the use of music as a weapon in war, ethnic conflicts, and protests

Read: Cusick, Suzanne G., "'You Are in a Place That Is out of the World': Music in the Detention Camps of the 'Global War on Terror,'" *Journal of the Society for American Music*, vol. 2, no. 1, Feb. 2008, pp. 1–26

Key Questions: In what ways can music be used as a weapon? What are the possible effects of "musical warfare"? Should the use of music as a weapon in warfare be controlled in some way (for example, similar to chemical and biological warfare)? If so, how and why? If not, why not? Should artists be able to limit how their works are used?

Class #6: Music in Indian Residential Schools and the Truth and Reconciliation Commission

View: Instructor's video lecture on the history of Indian residential schools in North America

Listen: Susan Aglukark, "Bridge of Dreams"; Andrea Menard, "100 Years" and "My Neighborhood"; and excerpts from *Songs from the Indian Residential School Legacy* (Truth and Reconciliation Commission of Canada)

Read: (1) Diamond, Beverley, "The Doubleness of Sound in Canada's Indian Residential Schools," in Levine, Victoria Lindsay, and Philip V. Bohlman, editors, *This Thing Called Music: Essays in Honor of Bruno Nettl*, Rowman and Littlefield, 2015, pp. 267–79; and (2) Diamond, Beverley, "Resisting Containment: The Long Reach of Song at the Truth and Reconciliation Commission on Indian Residential Schools," in Martin, Keavy, et al., *Arts of Engagement: Taking Aesthetic Action in and beyond the Truth and Reconciliation Commission of Canada*, Wilfrid Laurier University Press, 2016, pp. 239–66

Key Questions: What were Indian residential schools in Canada and the United States, and how did they use music? How was music a weapon at these schools, and how effective was this weapon? How did residential school students/survivors and their descendants use music as a tool of resistance?

Class #7: The Incarceration of Japanese Americans During WWII (aka what we should teach instead of the *Butterfly*)

Guest: Participant in the Tsuru for Solidarity Movement

View: (1) Excerpts of oral histories by survivors of the Japanese American incarceration on Densho; (2) Emiko Omori, "Tsuru for Solidarity History"

Listen: Anthony Brown, *E.O. 9066*

Read: Robertson, Marta, "Jitterbuggers, Sugar Plums, and a Geisha: Dancing Nexus in Japanese American Incarceration Facilities of World War II," *Perspectives on American Dance: The Twentieth Century*, University Press of Florida, 2018, pp. 30–55

Key Questions: Why were Japanese Americans on the West Coast of the United States put into incarceration camps during World War II? How did Japanese Americans who were incarcerated use music to form, morph, and express their identities? How was music used to educate Americans about the Japanese American incarceration in the aftermath of the Civil Liberties Act of 1988? Was Anthony Brown's *E.O. 9066* an effective educational tool? How is music used in the "Tsuru for Solidarity" movement?

Class #8: Music and Dance beyond Incarceration

View: Excerpts from the documentary *Music from the Big House*

Read: (1) Redmond, Shana L., "Song Uncaged: Prison Temporality and Black Pop Culture Escape," *Souls: A Critical Journal of Black Politics, Culture, and Society*, vol. 16, no. 3–4, 2014, pp. 227–41; and (2) Buis, Johann S., "Music and Dance Makes Me Feel Alive: From Mandela's Prison Songs and Dances to Public Policy," *Torture: Journal on Rehabilitation of Torture Victims and Prevention of Torture*, vol. 21, no. 3, 2013 (https://irct.org/index.php/publications/torture-journal/117)

Key Questions: For Redmond and Buis, how has music and dance created during incarceration influenced cultures and policies outside prisons? What methodologies did the authors use to make their points? Can we apply their findings to the other examples we discussed in this unit?

Conclusion

In 1993, Molefi Kete Asante wrote, "To teach from an African American perspective does not mean one has to be an African American; it means one must attempt to understand the centric position of the African American people."[22] In this essay, I extend Asante's point, and argue that—for music history instructors to create equitable curricula—we need to be able to grasp and to accurately represent the centric positions of many different musical cultures. To accomplish this, we need to move beyond solely relying on academic journals and books, which primarily publish pieces that use a limited set of methodologies. Instead, we need to be open to worldviews, including those that make us uncomfortable; adopt a feminist ethics of care; and consider forming affective relationships with community members, who can and should become central to our teaching. These relationships will allow us to share authority with organizations and representatives from our communities to create effective course content and curricula. Only then will we approach equity in music history pedagogy.

Notes

1. Hwang, Ji-yoon, "애틀랜타 총격 범인, 아시아인 다 죽이겠다 말해" [Atlanta shooter tells me I'm going to kill all Asians], *Chosun Ilbo*, March 17, 2021, https://www.chosun.com/international/us/.

2. Baker's statement was widely quoted, including in Bill Chappell, Vanessa Romo, and Jaclyn Diaz, "Official Who Said Atlanta Shooting Suspect Was Having a 'Bad Day' Faces Criticism," NPR, updated March 18, 2021, https://www.npr.org/.

3. Page Act, ch. 141, 18 Stat. 477, 477, 43rd Cong., 2nd sess. (1875).

4. Judy Yung, *Unbound Feet: A Social History of Chinese Women in San Francisco* (Berkeley: University of California Press, 1995), 23–24.

5. See, for example, Ted Solís, ed., *Performing Ethnomusicology: Teaching and Representation in World Music Ensembles* (Berkeley: University of California Press, 2004); Juliet Hess, "Performing Tolerance and Curriculum: The Politics of Self-Congratulation, Identity Formation, and Pedagogy in World Music Education," *Philosophy of Music Education Review* 21, no. 1 (2013): 66–91; Kay Kaufman Shelemay, "The Ethics of Ethnomusicology in a Cosmopolitan Age," in *The Cambridge History of World Music*, ed. Philip V. Bohlman (New York: Cambridge University Press, 2013), 786–806; Felicia Miyakawa and Richard Mook, "Avoiding the 'Culture Vulture' Paradigm: Constructing an Ethical Hip-Hop Curriculum," *Journal of Music History Pedagogy* 5, no. 1 (2014): 41–58; David Ake, "On the Ethics of Teaching 'Jazz' (and 'America's Classical Music,' and 'BAM,' and 'Improvisational Music,' And . . .)," in *Improvisation and Music Education*, ed. Ajay Heble and Mark Laver (New York: Routledge, 2016), 19–31; Alejandro Madrid, "Diversity, Tokenism, Non-Canonical Musics, and the Crisis of the Humanities in U.S. Academia," *Journal of Music History Pedagogy* 7, no. 2 (2017): 124–29. Despite this work, it is important to recognize that severe problems in these fields persist. See, for example, Danielle Brown, "An Open Letter on Racism in Music Studies, Especially Ethnomusicology and Music Education," *My People Tell Stories*, June 12, 2020, https://www.mypeopletellstories.com/blog/open-letter.

6. See, for example, Dave Molk, "Teaching Inequality: Consequences of Traditional Music Theory Pedagogy," *NewMusicBox: The Web Magazine*, December 2019; Robin Attas and Margaret Walker, guest eds., *Intersections: Canadian Journal of Music/Revue Canadienne de Musique* 39, no. 1, Decolonizing Music Pedagogies (2019).

7. Michelle Caswell and Marika Cifor, "From Human Rights to Feminist Ethics: Radical Empathy in the Archives," *Archivaria* 81 (2016): 23–43.

8. J. Peter Burkholder, Donald Jay Grout, and Claude V. Palisca, *A History of Western Music*, 10th ed. (New York: W.W. Norton, 2018), 695–96.

9. Kunio Hara explores how an instructor can use *Madama Butterfly* to open difficult topics in "Reframing Musical Exoticism: Ideas for Teaching Puccini's 'Madama Butterfly,'" Beyond Tokenism: Dismantling, Rethinking & Reframing Narratives in Music History Pedagogy, accessed July 27, 2021, https://musichistoryredo.wordpress.com/redoing-mh-pedagogy/reframed-narratives/.

10. Milton Reynolds, "Shifting Frames: Pedagogical Interventions in Colorblind Teaching Practice," in *Seeing Race Again: Countering Colorblindness across the Disciplines*,

ed. Kimberlé Crenshaw, Luke Charles Harris, Daniel Martinez HoSang, and George Lipsitz (Berkeley: University of California Press, 2019), 354.

11. Reynolds, 354.

12. Reynolds, 360.

13. Eve Tuck and K. Wayne Yang, "R-Words: Refusing Research," in *Humanizing Research: Decolonizing Qualitative Inquiry with Youth and Communities*, ed. Django Paris and Maisha Winn (Thousand Oaks, CA: Sage Publications), 226.

14. Elfreda Chatman, "The Impoverished Life-World of Outsiders," *Journal of the American Society for Information Science* 47, no. 3 (1996): 194.

15. See, for example, Maija-Leena Huotari and Elfreda Chatman, "Using Everyday Life Information Seeking to Explain Organizational Behavior," *Library & Information Science Research* 23, no. 4 (2001): 351–66; Amelia Gibson and John Martin, "Re-situating Information Poverty: Information Marginalization and Parents of Individuals with Disabilities," *Journal of the Association for Information Science and Technology* 70, no. 5 (2019): 476–87; Åse Garten Galtrud and Katriina Byström, "Information-Rich, but Time-Poor: Exploring Members of Parliament's Approaches to Information by Chatman's 'Small World' Conception," *Journal of Documentation* 76, no. 2 (2020): 409–23.

16. Chatman, "Impoverished Life-World," 197.

17. Chatman, 197.

18. Chatman, 201.

19. Susan McClary's critique of *Madama Butterfly* particularly resonates with me. See Susan McClary, "Mounting Butterflies," in *A Vision of the Orient: Texts, Intertexts, and Contexts of* Madame Butterfly, ed. Jonathan Wisenthal, Sherrill Grace, Melinda Boyd, Brian McIlroy, and Vera Micznik (Toronto: University of Toronto Press), 21–35.

20. Julia Rose, *Interpreting Difficult Histories at Museums and Historic Sites* (Lanham, MD: Rowman and Littlefield, 2016). I apply Rose's theory to public musicology in "Opening Difficult Conversations in Public Musicology," *American Music*, forthcoming.

21. Kunio Hara, "Notes on *November Steps* by Tōru Takemitsu," Beyond Tokenism: Dismantling, Rethinking and Reframing Narratives in Music History Pedagogy, accessed July 27, 2021, https://musichistoryredo.wordpress.com/redoing-mh-pedagogy/reframed-narratives/.

22. Molefi Kete Asante, "Where Is the White Professor Located?," *Perspectives on History*, September 1993, https://www.historians.org/perspectives.

CHAPTER 9

Public Musicology as Care, or How Should We Respond When the Duke of Mantua Tells Us That All Women Are Fickle?

WILLIAM A. EVERETT AND MATTEO MAGAROTTO

In our public musicology roles, whenever we perform or discuss musical works with problematic elements, if we do not acknowledge such issues, we become complicit with the biases they (re)present.[1] This is a difficult and often uncomfortable responsibility. Wouldn't it be easier just to hum Verdi's gleeful melody to a text that says "all women are fickle" in *Rigoletto*, revel in the beautiful melodies of a Puccini opera in which the Japanese protagonist is exploited by her American husband, or laugh at the transvestism of Prince Orlofsky in Strauss's *Die Fledermaus* than to realize the social institutions of power, especially wealthy white male privilege, that are foundational to each of these examples? Issues of privilege and oppression, gender-based bias, racism, or "othering" are often enmeshed in musical works of the Western classical tradition.

Public musicology offers a context in which these and similar issues embedded in musical works can be productively addressed. Preconcert presentations and public talks place a musicologist in contact with a (usually) receptive audience: the setting is eminently *social*, and, says philosopher Margaret Urban Walker, "moral understandings are typically effected through social ones."[2] (Written program notes lack direct interaction but are nonetheless a component of a concert's social experience.) This chapter proposes that public musicology should be concerned not only with the circulation of musical knowledge but also with the analysis of ethical issues of social injustice as an unavoidable facet of musical history. Public forums can contribute to an awareness of and attention to ethical problems inherent in the classical canon by creating opportunities for conversation about a work's conflicting meanings. The hope is that awareness will then inform how audiences engage with repertoires and how they themselves can continue discussions about music's ethical issues.

To this end, tenets of care ethics and care pedagogy are especially relevant. The idea of an "ethics of care" emerged within gender studies from the revolutionary work of Carol Gilligan and subsequent publications by Nel Noddings and others.[3] Noddings defines caring as "a connection or encounter between two human beings—a carer and a recipient of care, a cared-for."[4] This "caring for" is directly relevant to our work not only in the familiar pedagogical context of a classroom but also in a "public pedagogy" setting.[5] Our caring also includes "caring about": we can express concern *about* an issue and discuss its repercussions with audiences. Musicologists can care for members of the audience by sharing their own caring-about attitudes; a public musicology of care aims to create other carers. As we explore in this chapter, public musicology also involves recognizing the various—often conflicting—needs for care in our audiences.

Pursuing this goal requires sensitivity and savvy. We acknowledge that dominant social groups make up the majority of classical audiences and that it is not typically *these* listeners (especially wealthy, white, male, cisgender, straight, nondisabled individuals) who are directly affected by ethical problems in the music. Caring for the dominant group is not as urgent as caring for marginalized communities and identities. But while we aim to reduce the harm caused by racism and sexism in Western music, we are addressing audiences largely consisting of dominant groups. A productive intervention cannot disregard this social reality, and a confrontational or paternalistic stance is unlikely to foster progress. To organize an entire preconcert event as a militant critique risks alienating an audience, especially those who have come to hear music they love and are often unaware of its problematic elements. Indeed, if an "ethics of care starts with people *as* they are and *where* they are, taking account of their positionality and standpoints,"[6] public musicologists should consider the actual social profile, climate, and expectations of the event at hand. Some audience members may not appreciate "being lectured to" (a comment heard after a panel discussion on opera and #metoo). Why can't they just enjoy *Madama Butterfly* as they always have done? After all, it overflows with absolutely beautiful melodies—why can't that be enough?[7] We do not defend such attitudes, but neither can we ignore them if we wish to recruit caring allies. Many attendees will welcome critical perspectives, but it is a good strategy to assume the presence of opposing attitudes as well. More broadly, many in the audience "may be privileged without realizing, recognizing, or even wanting it."[8] Thus the preconcert speaker may start by validating the audience's desire for aesthetic fulfillment, leading with an engaging contextualization of the music and presentation of its qualities, establishing trust and a convivial atmosphere, then weave the critical elements into the discussion. Unless one proposes to jettison a problematic work altogether—which we find unproductive—a public talk would be more efficient and caring if it gave audiences the chance to reflect on the ethical issues involved.[9]

This essay will offer some ideas about how to discuss issues of gender and "othering" with a focus on the standard operatic repertory and one example from a canonic musical. It is not meant to be a musical history of such issues, nor is it meant to be even remotely comprehensive. Instead, we offer a few models with hopes that other public speakers may find their own ways to apply these models, as well as come up with their own ideas on how to address difficult issues in caring ways for the public. Before continuing, we must acknowledge our identity as two cisgender white men who aim to discuss issues of gender inequality, racism, and "othering"—injustices we have never personally endured; *Madama Butterfly* does not directly harm *us*, so we must decenter our perspective. As Eric Hung writes in his contribution to this collection, it is mostly the dominant groups who must listen "to information outsiders who are telling us about the harm that the 'lotus flower' stereotype [in *Butterfly*] continues to have on Asian American women." Having acknowledged realistically that most musicologists (including most authors in this collection) and most Western music listeners belong to privileged groups, the goal is to promote caring-about attitudes stemming from historic-critical awareness and ethical sensibility. We aim to increase the number of caring allies in the fight for equity.

Gender

Music has, for centuries, been a highly gendered medium. In the European and "Western" tradition women faced and still face limitations as musicians, composers, and scholars.[10] One thinks for example of Maria Anna ("Nannerl") Mozart or Fanny Mendelssohn Hensel in comparison to their more famous brothers. The exclusive male membership of professional orchestras lasted well into the twentieth century, and gender bias still exists.[11] When it comes to musical genres with texts, such as opera, song, and choral music, problematic issues concerning gender seem to infuse the repertory. How do we address these aspects, and how can we offer examples of works that reflect other attitudes?

In opera, the emphasis on vocal prowess helps to explain why many audience members find no difficulty in celebrating the performance of a famous aria even when its text is objectionable. When a renowned tenor dazzles listeners with his ringing high notes and expansive dynamic range, the content of what he is "saying" (extra-diegetically) recedes to the background.[12] One strand of feminist criticism has accused the entire operatic genre of being a system of gender stereotyping and oppression. Literary critic Catherine Clément describes opera as a genre in which women are systematically "undone": oppressed, abandoned, or killed—whether literally or metaphorically.[13] Taking a different stance, Carolyn Abbate considers the musical dimension, arguing for a degree of authorial force in women's voices, and she highlights the potentially subversive role and empowerment that women in opera can achieve through their singing.[14] Opera plots, nonetheless, often portray women as victims, confirming the patriarchal reality. Simply agreeing on this fact, however, will not take us far, nor is censorship desirable. Removing problematic musical works from public life is covering up the issues they embody, pretending they do not exist. Rather, when patriarchal attitudes are enacted on stage—accompanied by the strong emotional impact music affords—they can become especially vivid for the public; this experience can be productive as long as we describe explicitly and critically the attitudes involved.

One sexist stereotype often encountered in opera is that of woman's inconstancy. This *topos* may inform a work's entire plot (as in Mozart–Da Ponte's *Così fan tutte*) or individual numbers. The idea of woman's fickleness is openly asserted in "La donna è mobile" from Verdi's *Rigoletto* (1851)—an emblematic example of mismatch between content and effect (Table 9.1 shows the original text with an English translation).

One may presume that modern audience members would not endorse the message of this aria, but sadly such a stereotype is still alive and well. How should we understand the impulse to applaud performances of such a misogynist text?[15] Is it a matter of not noticing the misogyny (particularly for non-Italian speakers), not minding it, or not regarding it as problematic in the first place?

Several dramatic and musical factors contribute to veiling the aria's discriminatory language. For starters, given that the character who sings the aria is the opera's villain (the lecherous Duke of Mantua), listeners are not expected to side with him. They can praise the *singer* despite the *character*, a split favored by the nature of operatic spectacle, especially when the aria is performed in a concert setting. Excerpting an aria from the original work obscures its intended dramatic significance and instead emphasizes the singer and composer as heroic figures and the music as a manifestation of "pure beauty"—a worship ritual in which neither the Duke nor Gilda are any longer evoked. Although the singer in a concert performance is still uttering "all women are fickle," the semantic content of the words falls under the radar, becoming almost an accessory to Verdi's infectious melody. Moreover, the poetic language ("piuma al vento" / "muta d'accento") sounds deceptively graceful.[16] Verdi's musical setting boasts

Table 9.1. Francesco Maria Piave, "La donna è mobile," from *Rigoletto* (1851), music by Giuseppe Verdi, Act 3, scene 1 (translation by Matteo Magarotto).

La donna è mobile	Woman is fickle
qual piuma al vento,	like a feather in the wind,
muta d'accento	she changes her tone
e di pensiero.	and her mind.
Sempre un amabile	Always a lovable
leggiadro viso,	beautiful face,
in pianto o in riso	in crying or in laughter
è menzognero.	is lying.
La donna è mobil	Woman is fickle
qual piuma al vento,	like a feather in the wind,
muta d'accento	she changes her tone
e di pensier.	and her mind.
È sempre misero	Always is miserable
chi a lei s'affida	he who trusts her,
chi le confida	he who, unwary,
mal cauto il core!	confides his heart to her!
Pur mai non sentesi	Yet one never feels
felice appieno	fully happy
chi su quel seno	who on that bosom
non liba amore!	does not drink love!
La donna è mobil	Woman is fickle
qual piuma al vento,	like a feather in the wind,
muta d'accento	she changes her tone
e di pensier.	and her mind.

the hallmarks of the crowd-pleasing operatic hit: a merry, mostly diatonic waltz, with simple tonic/dominant underpinning and an easily memorable tune. The music surreptitiously invites us to join with the Duke's jolliness, cherishing the festive mood for its own sake. Perhaps we'll exit the theater humming the tune, or even singing, smilingly, that a woman's beautiful face is always lying. Musical beauty may obliterate ethical sensitivity. As Robinson, paraphrasing Clément, puts it: "Operatic music is an opiate that lowers our critical guard and allows us to entertain views that our good liberal selves would disavow were they presented in naked prose."[17]

It thus becomes part of our responsibilities as public musicologists to alert concertgoers to such indulgent impulses and underscore the moral/musical dissonance at play in these instances. But how do we accomplish this goal? In the case of *Rigoletto*, our program notes may address the issue by including remarks such as:

> The celebrated aria "La donna è mobile" invites us to share in a moment of jovial spirit with the Duke; but what does it mean for us today to declaim happily that "woman is fickle," that "her face is always lying"? This is the power of

> Verdi's melodic gift: the carefree simplicity of the music can make us oblivious to its message. While Verdi's original (male) audiences may have endorsed the long-held sexist view that women are by nature unreliable, it has now become one of many saddening aspects of European cultural history. The morally bad and the musically beautiful can coexist; art has many layers. Let us not forget the society and beliefs that it documents.[18]

A message of this sort would care for the public by both acknowledging the music's appeal and caring about the ethical issue.

Another way to foreground ethical problems is to set canonic works alongside contemporary ones with different sensitivities. For example, Ellen Reid and Roxie Perkins's opera *p r i s m*, winner of the 2019 Pulitzer Prize in music, explores the physical and psychological aftermath of a young woman who is a survivor of sexual assault. Placing *p r i s m* in dialogue with *Rigoletto* could result in uncomfortable yet relevant remarks about violence, trauma, and the chronic oppression of women that still persists. We can think of two scenarios for such a dialogue. First, if we have the chance to give a presentation about *p r i s m*, we could play side by side selections from this work and a canonic opera (for example, "La donna è mobile"), and let the grating contrast between the two worlds play out. We could also quote the composer directly: "[Sexual assault] was something that Roxie Perkins, the librettist, and I had both experienced personally and it felt like something that we wanted to delve into together. As you can imagine, going so deeply into something that is so difficult is really challenging. There's something about the piece that makes people who haven't experienced sexual assault understand just a little bit more what it might be like."[19] Second, when discussing a repertory opera, nothing prevents us from mentioning contemporary examples like *p r i s m* to highlight how women's experiences are now, rightfully, receiving attention in a caring manner.

Demeaning stereotypes and sexual violence are not the only problematic gender-associated aspects of opera. The commodification of women as prizes appears in works such as Carl Maria von Weber's *Der Freischütz* (*The Free Shooter*, 1821), with a libretto by Johann Friedrich Kind, in which the head forester offers his daughter Agathe in marriage to the winner of a shooting context; the winner proves to be Max, after help from Samiel (the devil) and a probation period. The *topos* involved here is not openly derogatory (such as woman's fickleness) but rather a seemingly lofty image of woman's purity, conveyed by the representation of Agathe as a white dove. This elevated position of the main female character does, however, limit a woman's place to the angelic stereotype and to a passive role in a doubly patriarchal exchange in which a male ruler "gives the hand" of the daughter to a male hero. *Der Freischütz* is not alone in this regard; Wagner's *Tannhäuser* (1845) and *Die Meistersinger von Nürnberg* (*The Mas-*

tersingers of Nuremberg, 1867) also have plots in which women become prizes. Then there is the image of the woman who sacrifices herself out of love for a man, or perhaps even for all humanity. Examples of this *topos* include the title character in Bellini's *Norma* (1831), Senta in Wagner's *Der fliegende Holländer* (*The Flying Dutchman*, 1843), and Brünnhilde in Wagner's cycle *Der Ring des Nibelungen* (*The Ring of the Nibelung*, 1869–1876). Women are also driven to suicide by oppression or exploitation: consider the likes of the title characters in Puccini's *Tosca* (1900) and *Madama Butterfly* (1904). And mad scenes for women are more prevalent in opera than those for men: how many Lucias are there for every Wozzeck, referring to Donizetti's *Lucia di Lammermoor* (1835) and Berg's *Wozzeck* (1925)? Addressing the hows and whys of such depictions can result in engaging and enlightening interactions with audiences.

Issues of gender in opera extend beyond representation of women. For example, in performances that include cross-dressing, such as Johann Strauss's *Die Fledermaus* (1874) and Engelbert Humperdinck's *Hänsel und Gretel* (1893), it is possible to discuss aspects of gender expression and even the transgender experience. Like the false idea of color blindness, gender blindness is an impossibility on stage. While it is customary to laugh at camp performances of women playing Count Orlofsky in *Die Fledermaus*, nowadays these interpretations and reactions should be reconsidered. We can present historical and musical reasons for such depictions, but many who attend a performance may react only to what they see in the moment.[20] The topic should be approached with special sensitivity, the caring-for dimension becoming even more critical: transgender audience members may feel that their identities are being slighted, disempowered, or negated if such topics are not addressed. The same approach we suggested in the context of *Rigoletto* earlier could also be applied here: discussing a contemporary opera in tandem with the canonic work. For example, the 2014 chamber opera *As One*, with music by Laura Kaminsky and libretto by Mark Campbell and Kimberly Reed, features a transgender narrative that could be contrasted with *Die Fledermaus* or indeed any opera that features a trouser role. *As One*'s main character, Hannah, played initially by a baritone and then by a mezzo, is a transgender woman whose story includes violence, isolation, and eventually a sense of belonging and community.[21] One significant aspect of contemporary opera that public musicology can emphasize is its exploratory and reparative cultural work in giving voice to gender(ed) identities previously discriminated against or ignored.

Othering

As with gender, discussions of how specific musical tropes can be used to represent particular ethnic groups can offer a multitude of opportunities to discuss race and the inherent whiteness embedded in classical music repertories. For example, in Mozart's *Die Entführung aus dem Serail* (*The Abduction from the Seraglio*, 1782), the music of the Turkish characters exhibits all the eighteenth-century aural stereotypes of eastern Mediterranean music: cymbals, triangles, and bass drum; the repetition of surface-level motifs; static harmony; and scales with altered pitches (often lowered 7, lowered 2, or raised 4). When considering iconic arias such as Osmin's "Rage Aria" in Act 1 ("Solche hergelauf'ne Laffen" ["Such Jumped-up Dandies"]) or during the same character's solo passage in the Act 3 vaudeville finale, the problematic connection of violence with Muslim culture through musical means emerges. By contrast, the music that accompanies Pasha Selim (a speaking role) in the Act 3 finale is ordered and noble, befitting the Europeans in the opera and, as we learn, Selim's own experience. He can be Enlightened because he spent time in Europe and embraced European (that is, white) thought. Selim is emblematic of the "noble Turk," as opposed to Osmin, who becomes the oppositional "violent Turk."[22]

Presenting these passages as examples of a dominant whiteness being inscribed into musical works might, for some people, disrupt the pure enjoyment of the work. However, not addressing such representations normalizes them and makes us as presenters complicit with the inherent racist messages. A thoughtful and wide-reaching approach is essential when caring about aspects of race: we must acknowledge that our audience members' needs will vary, and that caring for someone from a dominant group who does not want to hear about an opera's racial complexities should take second place to caring for audience members from marginalized communities for whom these representations are painful to see and hear. As several recent scholars have noted, discussing race is unavoidably difficult and uncomfortable, and we will make grievous mistakes.[23] But to ignore race and racism is irresponsible. We have the responsibility to acknowledge the problematic nature of racial depictions that magnify stereotypes and reinforce racism. Recognizing biases and calling out damaging pigeonholing are important steps in the ongoing task of creating a more just and antiracist society.

One recent opera that directly addresses race and issues of authority in a white world is Jeanine Tesori and Tazewell Thompson's *Blue*, which had its premiere at Glimmerglass Opera in 2019. The story concerns a young African American adult, unarmed, who is shot and killed by a white police officer. To complicate the situation, the young man's father is a police officer, so it was one of the father's work colleagues who killed the young man. As a reflection of the tragic reality of anti-Black police brutality, *Blue* is another example of how contemporary opera offers particularly valuable and relevant material for social justice discourse. The presentation strategy we suggest in this case is similar to those previously discussed: juxtaposing selections from *Blue* with examples from another (canonic) opera, like Mozart's *Die Entführung aus dem Serail.*

The dimension of race interacts with other aspects of identity in a person's experience. To highlight this intersectionality—the overlap of identity categories subject to discrimination—public musicology can draw from critical race theory in exploring musical theater and opera.[24] For example, in Jerome Kern and Oscar Hammerstein II's canonic musical *Show Boat* (1927), Queenie is African American and female, placing her in a perceived position below her husband Joe, who is an African American male, and the other female characters, most of whom are white. Joe has more agency as a male than his wife since he gets to sing the iconic "Ol' Man River" while Queenie's main musical number, "Queenie's Ballyhoo," is often performed with comic bravura that sounds in direct contrast to Joe's wise-seer persona. Likewise, Parthy is an older white woman who suffers oppression (through an absence of musical numbers in traditional productions) because of her gender and age. *Show Boat* thus brings intersectionality to the fore in a particularly poignant manner.[25] In a public presentation, we can begin with Kimberlé Crenshaw's words on the intersection of race and gender prejudice, then show excerpts from the musical to demonstrate how Queenie is "musically discriminated" against as woman and socially discriminated against as Black.[26]

Opera, too, often foregrounds gender and race in intersectional ways. Bizet's *Carmen* (1875) performs the cultural opposition of Self versus Other, here embodied intersectionally as Genteel-Male (Don José) versus Romani-Female (Carmen).[27] Public talks, podcasts, or program notes can point out how the opera conveys Othering by means of literary and musical codes, with the goal of critiquing these codes. To merely explain musical codes, however, may come across as essentializing the Other. Our goal should be, instead, to critique these binaries as a reductive perspective of nineteenth-century society derived from its dichotomous understanding of Self versus Other. We might begin our presentation by noting how the Other in *Carmen* conflates the erotic and the exotic, dimensions marked as alluring but ultimately dangerous from the perspective of nineteenth-century European middle classes. We can further qualify the exotic dimension by listing the negative moral associations conjured by the term "gypsy," a derogatory and ill-informed term that obfuscates Romani identity.[28] Then we could invite the audience to ponder how the "alluring" musical style of Carmen's singing differs from that of the male characters. Diatonic music and marches such as Escamillo's *Toreador* song stand for male-European-authoritative, whereas chromatic melodies such as those of Carmen's *Habanera* and *Seguidilla* stand for female-seductive-exotic-subaltern.[29] Furthermore, Bizet employs a common musical emblem for the exotic (the augmented second) as the defining interval of the "fate motive" associated with Carmen, further linking the Other and danger. These contrasts are introduced early in the prelude to Act 1 and subsequently infuse the narrative. We may ask the audience to listen closely to how these codes shape the characters' identities and their interactions throughout the opera. We could conclude by proposing a provocative interpretation of Carmen's murder as a symbolic annihilation of the moral and sexual danger that the Other brings to genteel society as it was understood during the time of the opera's premiere.[30]

The construction of the Other has been a European cultural and political phenomenon that, since the eighteenth century, has allowed the West to justify its fascination with (romanticized) foreign cultures, particularly Islamic and Asian cultures from North Africa to the Pacific Ocean, its stereotyping and exoticizing representations, and its colonial oppression. In public presentations about "exotic" operas in the canon we can introduce Edward Said's notion of "Orientalism" to situate these works within European colonialism and its underlying racial prejudices.[31] We aim to show our audiences that colonialism is inextricably linked to these operas, that they do not exist (or can no longer exist) in a purely aesthetic space.

From the seventeenth to the early twentieth centuries, operatic representations of the "East" reinforced for Europeans the Orientalist perspective. Here too, often-produced canonic works can offer public musicologists chances to engage in critical pedagogy. The two Puccini operas set in Asian countries—*Madama Butterfly* (1904) and *Turandot* (1926)—well represent Orientalism in music. They also discriminate intersectionally in their conflation of ethnic and gender stereotypes, perhaps most evident in the portrayals of Cio-Cio-San (in *Butterfly*) and Liù (in *Turandot*) as exoticized projections of the angelic woman ideal or as hypersexualized "lotus flower" stereotype—what Ralph Locke has described as the "archetypally beautiful, loving, gentle, and submissive Oriental female."[32] The submission here is taken to extremes, as the two women end up killing themselves: Butterfly out of desperation due to Pinkerton's betrayal and Liù, under torture, out of love for Calaf. Musically, Puccini employs the inherited orientalist codes of nineteenth-century opera, primarily the pentatonic scale. As Locke observes, however, in *Turandot* this Eastern musical signifier appears in a number of guises to advance the narrative: the gradual dilution of Liù's pentatonic idiom (as heard in Act 1's "Signore, ascolta!") toward a more Western idiom conveys her "humanizing or de-Orientalizing."[33] This reading suggests that the Orientalist depiction was a rigid mold, that the Other remains distant until it is reshaped in the familiar European musical vernacular. This process is similar to what happens in *Carmen*, and it would be possible to analyze these two operas in terms of "normalizing," according to white European norms, the Other.

There is no denying the emotional impact and beauty of much of the music from the canonic works discussed in this chapter. When we discuss these works in public forums, however, we cannot ethically sanitize their culturally problematic aspects. Our public presentations, therefore, may work best when we acknowledge both the aesthetic qualities that draw listeners in and the inherent ethical problems of the works at hand. Public musicology offers numerous opportunities to promote social justice through principles of care pedagogy. By caring about difficult questions surrounding gender and race (among others) that are explicit or implicit in musical works and by demonstrating this concern in terms of caring for our diverse audiences, we can contribute to the larger purpose we share with other humanistic disciplines: the fostering of historical-cultural awareness and sensitivity on issues of systemic discrimination and oppression. If we remain conscious that these are difficult and delicate topics and if we avoid dogmatic lecturing in favor of fostering open-ended conversations, we may plant fruitful seeds for more ethically conscious listening experiences.

Notes

1. William Everett is grateful to Bryan Vandevender for his illuminating conversations on this topic.

2. Margaret Urban Walker, *Moral Understandings: A Feminist Study in Ethics* (New York: Oxford University Press, 1997), 17.

3. Carol Gilligan, *In a Different Voice: Psychological Theory and Women's Development* (Cambridge, MA: Harvard University Press, 1982); Nel Noddings, *Caring: A Feminine Approach to Ethics and Moral Education* (Berkeley: University of California Press, 1984); Tony Monchinski, "The Ethic of Care," in *Education in Hope: Critical Pedagogies and the Ethic of Care*, Counterpoints 382 (New York: Peter Lang, 2010), 45–84.

4. Nel Noddings, *The Challenge to Care in Schools: An Alternative Approach to Education* (New York: Teachers College Press, 1992), 15.

5. See William Cheng, "Care-Oriented Musicology," *Musicology Now*, August 26, 2016, https://musicologynow.org/care-oriented-musicology/.

6. Monchinski, "Ethic of Care," 48 (italics in the original).

7. For a compelling examination of the tension between aesthetic enjoyment and ethics, see William Cheng, *Loving Music till It Hurts* (New York: Oxford University Press, 2020).

8. Christie Launius and Holly Hassel, *Threshold Concepts in Women's and Gender Studies*, 2nd ed. (New York: Routledge, 2018), 95.

9. For the philosopher Erich Hatala Matthes, ethical art consumption is not necessarily a matter of avoiding or "cancelling" problematic art but a matter of engaging sensibly with the problems that it raises. *Drawing the Line: What to Do with the Work of Immoral Artists from Museums to the Movies* (New York: Oxford University Press, 2021).

10. Foundational work on music and gender includes: John Shepherd, "Music and Male Hegemony," in *Music and Society: The Politics of Composition, Performance, and*

Reception, ed. Richard Leppert and Susan McClary (Cambridge: Cambridge University Press, 1987), 151–72; Richard Leppert, *Music and Image: Domesticity, Ideology, and Socio-Cultural Formation in Eighteenth-Century England* (New York: Cambridge University Press, 1988); Susan McClary, *Feminine Endings: Music, Gender, and Sexuality* (Minneapolis: University of Minnesota, 1991); and Marcia Citron, *Gender and the Musical Canon* (Cambridge: Cambridge University Press, 1993).

11. The case of the Vienna Philharmonic is notorious. The orchestra accepted the first permanent woman member only in 1997.

12. Paul Robinson has noted that even when a listener is familiar with the text, in a live performance "those textual readings have a way of receding from consciousness, as we gradually forget the language of operatic texts we once knew—something that never quite happens with the music." Paul Robinson, "A Deconstructive Postscript: Reading Libretti and Misreading Opera," in *Reading Opera*, ed. Arthur Groos and Roger Parker (Princeton: Princeton University Press, 1988), 344.

13. Catherine Clément, *Opera, or the Undoing of Women* [1979], trans. Betsy Wing (Minneapolis: University of Minnesota Press, 1988).

14. Carolyn Abbate, "Opera; or, the Envoicing of Women," in *Musicology and Difference: Gender and Sexuality in Music Scholarship*, ed. Ruth Solie (Berkeley: University of California Press, 1993), 225–58.

15. Robinson argues that "the meaning of opera is at bottom musical" and thus "any interpretation of opera derived exclusively, or even primarily, from the libretto is likely to result in a misreading" ("Deconstructive Postscript," 328). However, examining the libretto not for operatic interpretation but as a document of its culture remains relevant.

16. In modern Italian, *accento* means a grammatical accent or regional inflection. As a term for the act of speaking itself, it now sounds old-fashioned and high-brow. Regarding the meaning of *muta*, Matteo Magarotto admits to have previously understood the word as an adjective ("dumb") and the line, therefore, as the harshly misogynous "dumb in speaking and in thought." Although that interpretation is probably erroneous, the fact that a (distracted) Italian speaker can hear it that way suggests an intriguing ambiguity.

17. Paul Robinson, "It's Not Over until the Soprano Dies," *New York Times*, January 1, 1989, https://www.nytimes.com/.

18. Our discussion can also provide operatic counterexamples, such as Despina's "In uomini" from *Così fan tutte*, an indictment of *male* infidelity. We are grateful to the anonymous reviewer who suggested this example.

19. Quoted in Tom Huizenga, "Readjusting Your Reality: Ellen Reid Wins Music Pulitzer for '*p r i s m*,'" *NPR*, April 15, 2019, https://www.npr.org/sections/deceptive cadence/2019/04/15/713625417/readjusting-your-reality-ellen-reid-wins-music -pulitzer-for-p-r-i-s-m.

20. For an analysis of this role in terms of its cultural-historical moment, see Camille Crittenden, *Johann Strauss and Vienna: Operetta and the Politics of Popular Culture* (Cambridge: Cambridge University Press, 2000), 146–47. Stereotypical camp still surfaces in modern times. See for example Philip Gentry's critique of the King George character in Lin-Manuel Miranda's *Hamilton*: "Hamilton's Ghosts," *American Music* 35, no. 2 (June 2017): 271–80. We thank Loren Kajikawa for this reference.

21. A commercial recording of *As One* is available (Bright Shiny Things BSTC-1027 [2019]).

22. For a perceptive analysis of the Pasha character, see Timothy Taylor, "Peopling the Stage: Opera, Otherness, and New Musical Representations in the Eighteenth Century," *Cultural Critique* 36 (1997): 65–81.

23. Among these works are Ijeoma Oluo, *So You Want to Talk about Race* (New York: Seal Press, 2018); Crystal Fleming, *How to Be Less Stupid about Race* (Boston: Beacon Press, 2018); Robin DiAngelo, *White Fragility* (Boston: Beacon Press, 2018) and *Nice Racism* (Boston: Beacon Press, 2021); Ibram Kendi, *How to Be an Antiracist* (New York: One World, 2019); Emmanuel Acho, *Difficult Conversations with a Black Man* (New York: Flatiron Books, 2020); and John McWhorter, *Woke Racism* (New York: Portfolio/Penguin, 2021).

24. Kimberlé Crenshaw introduced intersectionality in the legal field with her article "Demarginalizing the Intersection of Race and Sex: A Black Feminist Critique of Antidiscrimination Doctrine, Feminist Theory and Antiracist Politics," *University of Chicago Legal Forum* 1 (1989): 139–67.

25. See William Everett, "Oscar Hammerstein II and the Performativity of Race and Intersectional Oppression in American Musicals from *Show Boat* (1927) to *Carousel* (1945)," *Arti musices* 50, nos. 1–2 (2019): 355–75, especially 357–60.

26. For further examples concerning Black women, especially from the operatic repertory, see Naomi André, *Black Opera: History, Power, Engagement* (Urbana: University of Illinois Press, 2018).

27. Libretto by Henri Meilhac and Ludovic Halévy after the novel by Prosper Mérimée.

28. See Adriana Helbig's remarks at http://www.columbia.edu/itc/music/NYCO/carmen/gypsies.html.

29. See Susan McClary's "Sexual Politics in Classical Music," in *Feminine Endings: Music, Gender, and Sexuality* (Minneapolis: University of Minnesota, 1991), 57–58.

30. McClary sees a parallel between Carmen's physical annihilation and the "purging" of her chromatic music to reestablish diatonic order and achieve tonal closure at the end ("Sexual Politics in Classical Music," 62).

31. See Edward Said, *Orientalism* (New York: Vintage Books, 1978).

32. Ralph Locke, "Reflections on Orientalism in Opera and Musical Theater," *Opera Quarterly* 10, no. 1 (1993): 52.

33. Locke, 54.

CHAPTER 10

Listening with Care to Nonhuman Musicality and Material Culture

KATE GALLOWAY

Wood, hide, hair, fiber, and the flesh of the pads of her fingers: Kela stroked the hide surface of a Hopi hand drum. Ben ran his fingers through the animal hooves of a Northwest Coast Salish Cowichan ceremonial dance staff; resonant clattering filled the archaeology and anthropology lab as the over forty hooves collided with one another.[1] The Northwest Coast Salish Cowichan dancing staff serves a ceremonial and a musical function. The hooves percussively clatter and sound out each time the staff strikes the ground to signal significant places in a rhythmic cycle or transitions in the choreographic movement and gestures. Human flesh activated the material afterlives of these nonhuman animal bodies made musical.

What does it mean to listen beyond the human and extend care-oriented musicology and categories of musical difference to the nonhuman environment? I examine what listening with care to the nonhuman communicates about notions of musicality that extend beyond the human. At stake in the consideration of the ethical dimensions of nonhuman perspectives and listening to strategies used to represent, embody, and stage animals in musical materials and performances is the ability to articulate and identify the complex connections between humans and animals through music, and human understandings of animals in music-making. By extending our pedagogy in ways that care about and are sensitive to definitions of musicality that are less anthropocentric we can develop an inclusive interspecies approach to musical difference and listening subjectivities. This approach shows students how to attend to the varieties of sounds and music they encounter in their daily lives and critique, analyze, and value them as music. This posthuman shift goes beyond the call for multinational or multicultural listening, complicating the category of "human" vis-à-vis the animal world and taking up what Ana María Ochoa Gautier refers to as "acoustic multinaturalism," which both relativizes and interrogates the constructions of nature and humans, especially in relation to posthumanism and nonhuman materialism in music studies.[2]

While the human musical experience of these objects remains important, it is just as important to consider and foreground the musicking objects themselves and the active participation of nonhuman actors in music-making. What would a short history of Beethoven's pianos sound like alongside the standard Beethoven narratives we encounter in textbooks? When we analyze John Cage's *Sonatas and Interludes for Prepared Piano*, how would a detailed comparative sensory ethnography of each object placed on and between the strings of the piano at the premiere compared to those used in subsequent performances inform our understanding of the relationship between timbre and materiality? And what if we recalibrated the positionality and presentation of animal performers in studies of seventeenth-century Venetian opera that continues to illustrate how animals operated in the spectacle of operative tourism while also casting them as key performers alongside human performers, such as the bear in the narrative and onstage action of Francesco Cavalli's *La Calisto*?

By extending the sociocultural study of music to nonhuman musicality, we come to understand how listening across different sound cultures shapes how we represent others and listen to voices that typically are devalued, go unheard, or are silenced altogether. The case studies that I draw from in this chapter are just a few of the possible pedagogical approaches that promote kinesthetic and embodied learning with the vibrant nonhuman musicality and matter of music practices. As Jane Bennett concludes, what is "needed is a cultivated, patient, sensory attentiveness to nonhuman forces operating outside and inside the human body,"[3] and these forces inform students' understanding of the complexity and diversity of human and nonhuman musical life and listening practices in an interconnected world. A pedagogy oriented to care and well-being incorporates approaches to music as a form of knowledge that is connected to history, culture, and positionality, but it is also a form of knowledge that is activated and used to heighten our sensitivity and awareness of the world around us.

As we shift our point of view and point of audition, we illustrate how different species and individuals of the world see and listen to the world. For example, when I instruct students to make a recording where they improvise with a nonhuman animal of their choice, I ask them to be self-reflexive throughout their process and consider the ethics of multispecies improvisation, issues of consent and agency, and the hierarchical power dynamics of these performances. One student, Kate, guided by these directives, purposefully chose to improvise with her longtime companion, a bearded dragon. However, she wanted to ensure his voice—a combination of sounds made by his body during movement and

Figure 10.1. Students engaging in multisensory ethnographies with items from special collections and archives and the archaeology and anthropology collections.

his breath—was audible. She carefully placed contact microphones in his terrarium in ways that would not negatively disrupt her nonhuman companion (for example, she left a clear path for him to access water and did not affix microphones to his body).

By extending the analysis of music to nonhuman performers and musicality we gain a better understanding of how listening across sound cultures shapes how we listen to and represent voices that typically go unheard or are silenced. In *Exposed: Environmental Politics and Pleasures in Posthuman Times*, Stacy

Alaimo calls for an integrative environmental stance in which we think, experience, feel, act, and perform as and with the nonhuman materiality of the world.[4] In one class meeting, for instance, I guide students through a comparative discussion where we discuss terms such as *performance*, *virtuosity*, *technique*, *skill*, and *musicality*, after listening to the anonymous audio of three YouTube videos of theremin performances. I do not reveal the identities of the theremin performers until we have exhausted our discussion and defined the aforementioned terms in relation to the three audio examples. I then reveal our performers' identities: a human, a cat, and a rabbit.[5] Following this reveal we extend our discussion to include issues of agency, intentionality, and musical knowledge and interrogate how we might have automatically anthropomorphized all three performances by assuming the human animal or nonhuman animal identity of each performer. I challenge students to readjust their perception of the status of human actors in the history and study of ethnomusicology and musicology and develop sensory attentiveness to the reciprocal relationships among human and nonhuman forces.

Musical Artifacts as Assemblages of Nonhuman Matter

While working with musical artifacts from the archaeology and anthropology collections, students analyzed the ways human performers activate and interpret musical objects assembled from the materiality of nonhuman bodies. By designing exploratory activities and projects centered on the sensory knowledge conveyed by the objects, things, and technologies of music—the grain of the page, calligraphic rhythms, embossed textures, nonhuman actors, and material lives of sound objects—students hear sound and music using other sensory modes, engaging with music and other forms of aural culture through tactile, visual, and kinesthetic stimuli. In these material culture labs, the students are learning how to analyze objects in relation to their role within the ecology of music-making and developing valuable multisensory diagnostic skills that are essential tools in fieldwork. For instance, students analyze Hopi musical instruments from the collections using their senses to understand the connections between nonhuman materiality and human music-making. The activity handout for the lab asks students to respond to the following questions to guide their sensory analysis while exploring a single object from the collection.

When we take the objects, things, and materials of music seriously in our teaching, performing, and understanding of music cultures, agency is no longer only something humans have, but rather something, as Bennett writes, "seen as differentially distributed across a wider range of ontological types."[6] Any material object, network, or assemblage of things has a capacity for action

1. ARTIFACT DESCRIPTION—Material
   What material is the artifact made out of? Is the material natural or human-made? Describe the general material.
2. ARTIFACT DESCRIPTION—Characteristics
   Are there particular markings or characteristics of note? Describe the appearance of any special qualities of the artifact.
3. USES OF THE ARTIFACT
   Who made the artifact? How? When? Why?
   Who used the artifact? How? When? Why?
4. COLLECTION OF THE ARTIFACT
   Who collected the artifact? How? When? Why?
5. WHAT DOES THIS ARTIFACT TELL US?
   What does the artifact tell us about the lifestyle and/or technology of the people who made and used it?
   What does the artifact tell us about the time period(s) in which it was made and used?
   What does the existence of this artifact in an archaeology and anthropology collection tell us about the collectors and collecting trends of the nineteenth and twentieth centuries?
6. IS THERE A SIMILAR CONTEMPORARY OBJECT THAT RELATES TO THIS ARTIFACT?

Figure 10.2. Activity handout for the archaeology and anthropology collections

and shaping cultural understanding and experience. Bennett argues that it is essential that we "readjust the status of human actants: not by denying humanity's awesome, awful powers, but by presenting these powers as evidence of our own constitution as vital materiality. In other words, human power is itself a kind of thing-power."[7]

The majority of the musical instruments from the archaeology and anthropology collections are Hopi instruments from Wesleyan University's Melville Collection of Carey (Professor of Mathematics at Clark University) and Maud Melville, residents of Worcester, Massachusetts, who traveled with their children in their Ford Model T in 1927. Their trip included a three-week stay on Hopi lands in northeastern Arizona where they collected items as tourists rather than professional art dealers or ethnographers. However, they were systematic in their collection, acquiring objects of cultural, functional, and aesthetic value in the Hopi community. In the midst of my class visits, Jessie Cohen, then curator and education facilitator of Wesleyan's archaeology and anthropology collections, was actively engaged in efforts to honor the Native American Graves Protection and Repatriation Act (NAGPRA) by repatriating objects of cultural patrimony removed from Indigenous communities and ancestral lands. It was important to Jessie and me to highlight the role of repatriation and the relationships of these objects to the communities they were removed from because we wanted to clearly identify how musical objects and things are part of a cultural and social ecology of music-making and expressive culture.[8] In "The Social Life of Musical Instruments," Eliot Bates teases out the myriad of situations "where instruments are entangled in webs of complex relationships—between humans and objects, between humans and humans, and between objects and other objects."[9] These networks and entanglements of human and nonhuman, living and nonliving musical bodies surfaced during conversations with students concerning their kinesthetic engagements with the nonhuman material culture of music.

At the outset of each materiality lab in the archaeology and anthropology collections, students were provided with little background information for each object. Prior to revealing material and contextual histories of each instrument, the students evaluated their item using their senses. They were asked to describe the article and consider what materials the artifact was made out of, consider whether the material was natural or human-made, and craft a description they would use to describe the object and its materials to someone not present to experience the artifact firsthand. They were also asked to describe the artifact's characteristics, attending to whether there were particular markings, characteristics of note, or special qualities that defined its appearance and how it sounded. Who made the artifact: How? When? Why? Who used the artifact: How? When? Why? As each student continued the exploration and sensory ethnography of their artifact, they began addressing what the artifact told them about the lifestyle and/or technology of the people who made and used the object. As they touched, smelled, looked at, and listened to this collection of musical instruments and sound-making artifacts, each student gradually came to the realization that the music and sound produced by these objects in their intended performance context would not be possible without the nonhuman materials they were each assembled from.

The materiality of the Salish ceremonial dance staff, the sensory vignette from the opening of this chapter, reveals to its ethnographer evidence of its use, adaptation, and repair within the community. The hooves are threaded to the head of the staff with pieces of leather, rawhide, twine, and, more recently,

Figure 10.3. Students engaging in multisensory ethnographies with artifacts from the archaeology and anthropology collections.

nylon rope. These different threading materials reflect the length of time this artifact has occupied an important place in Northwest Coast Salish performance practices, as it was repaired over time rather than being discarded and replaced. The students, Ben and Kate, counted at least fifty individual hooves on the Salish ceremonial dance staff, imagining the herd of deer whose lives are now archived in this staff and re-sounded each time it strikes the ground. Each time they sounded the staff in the lab they could see and hear the sounds of these animals to whom the hooves once belonged. To Ben and Kate, the Salish ceremonial dance staff also represented the respect Indigenous communities pay to the nonhuman world, ensuring that every part of the animal is used and goes unwasted.

As Dylan stroked the hide drumhead of the Hopi hand drum, he noted that the sound that the drum produces now must contrast with how it sounded when it was first made. The hide has since aged, dried, and slackened. He imagined what the drum would have sounded like when the hide of the drumhead was first tuned following a laborious process from animal hide to drumskin: skinned, shaved, dried, stretched, and carefully tuned. He admitted to me that he had not really considered the material origins of the instruments in his life. Now he hears each animal body and the sites where valuable metals and hardwood from old-growth trees are extracted using human technologies. Dylan made the astute observation that the timbre of an instrument is shaped by its material components, and materials sourced from nonhuman animals are dynamic, shifting in accordance with their surrounding conditions (for instance, humidity and temperature), maintenance, and age.

Silenced Specimens and Field Guides That Sound

In special collections and archives, students explored how the aurality and musicality of nonhumans and their environments is heard through the typographic, letterpress, and visual choices made by artists of the book through a close reading of select archival artists' books (Figure 10.4).[10] The purpose of this assignment was for students to use artists' books as a case study to explore the materiality and sensory knowledge of music and sound on the written page, investigating the ethics and representational strategies exercised in the depiction of nonhumans' sounding and the environments they live in among human beings. My colleague Suzy Taraba, director of special collections and archives, and I focused on artists' books that express the sonic experience of the nonhuman.[11]

These print and multimedia books encourage users to use their senses to understand the connections between nonhuman materiality, sonic environments, and human music-making. In my experiential learning activities using

Figure 10.4. Students working with field guide and artists' books in special collections and archives.

items from this collection of artists' books, students evaluated the typographic design of letterpress artists' books that remediate aural culture, identifying the techniques or formal strategies used to convey sound and music, or ideas of sound, music, and the environment. Using the grain of the page, calligraphic rhythms, embossed textures, embedded sound objects, interactive mechanisms, and unconventional materials that extend beyond the printed book, these artists challenge users to hear sound and music using other sensory modalities. These resources are not musical in the traditional sense, but we asked ourselves: How can they provide information about the soundscape and/or music illustrated? How can we sense and interpret music and sound in these texts and images?

These questions and experiences that emerged from these discussions and active learning activities taught students important aspects of care as students evaluated their self, community, and the nonhuman other in relation to one another, global music-making, and cultural sustainability. This pedagogical approach challenges students to develop an ethics and practice of care that foregrounds equity and inclusion that account for notions of musicality and representation outside of their personal experience, thus opening new considerations and conversations for care-pedagogy discourse. This way it is not only during catastrophic moments in the global climate crisis that students pay attention to their sensory engagement with the world, such as the widespread affective responses to the 2019–2020 Australian wildfires. Our care and consideration of the value of nonhuman animals and things must extend into our everyday consciousness just as the continually valued lives and mattering of humanity is ubiquitous.

Field guides and artists' books question how we listen to images, and how these multisensory, unique, handmade art objects that utilize the form of the book inform users' understanding and experience of sonic environments. Artists' books are unusual or special in both their form and content. These works of art challenge conventional understandings of the book format and often tackle social and political issues. They are important not only for their content but for their unique forms. Through their use of handmade paper, original drawings or photographs, unconventional formats (for example, fold-out panels or inclusion of supplementary objects), unusual bindings, and distinctive use of materials (for example, pop-up illustrations, unconventional pigments and textures created by soils and spices, or the integration of audio using QR codes), many artists' books challenge the reader to think about the nature of the book and the act of reading in new ways.

In our two special collections materiality labs, students examined how nonhuman and human environments and nature are represented in other material arts formats: the first was a survey of bird field guides from the nineteenth

Figure 10.5. Examples of the aurality of the visual language in field-guide artists' books

century to the present and the second was a focused study of artists' books that represented and remediated nonhuman soundscapes through a variety of sensory modes and approaches to the art of the book. Through their survey of the history of bird field guides, students documented how representational practices shifted and the techniques used to depict visual and auditory cues to aid in species identification. Students analyzed the descriptive words used to represent the aurality of different species, the use of onomatopoeia, calligraphic textures and lines and different colors that visually depict timbre, pitch range, ornamentation, and texture, and often the stark silence used to illustrate extinct species that no longer sing and we can no longer hear (Figure 10.5), as illustrated in Sara Nicholls's experimental *A Field Guide to Extinct Birds*.

For one activity, students were placed in pairs and assigned a "mystery book" from the curated series of artists' books selected for the material culture lab. As each pair explored their assigned book for the first time and participated in a sensory ethnography of it, they responded to the following set of questions in the activity handout. Upon completion of their worksheet, each pair shared their findings to the class and guided everyone through the distinctive features of their assigned artists' book.

1. Who is the artist, author, or other creator of the book? Is it the work of one individual or a group project?
2. What is the title?
3. When and where was the book published, printed, or made?
4. What is its subject matter?
5. What sounds or music (or types of sounds or music) are presented in or evoked by the book?
6. How is nature or the environment presented in the book?
7. What techniques or formal strategies are used to convey sound (or music) or ideas of sound (or music)? Consider all aspects of the book, including typography, visual elements, materials, structure, accompanying media, and so forth.
8. What connections can you make between nature and sound through the book?
9. How does the book connect to a text or concept explored in class related to sound and nature?

One of the artists' books that caught the attention of the students' ears was *ReSound*. Designed and executed by graduate students in the Art and the Book Program of the Corcoran School at George Washington University in the fall of 2015 under the guidance of instructor Sarah McDermott, *ReSound* explores visual responses to sound within the landscape of Washington, DC, using letterpress, screen printing, and digital printing techniques. Focusing on the human experience of traversing the city, the book combines these printed responses with journals, maps, and process descriptions. Developed as a collaborative book arts experiment, the artist collective wanted readers to be able to experience the sounds that inspired the visual representations in the book and listen back to the soundscape. They included a series of QR codes linked to the audio recordings they made, thus archiving and mapping their field recordings and soundwalks into the pages of the artists' book. Many of the students interpreted *ReSound* as representing an exercise in close listening and playful responses to the spatial, social, and musical nuances of the sonic environment.

We listened with care to images of avian soundmakers native to specific bioregional environments as we explored a series of nineteenth- and twentieth-century field guides, listening to the textual and visual indicators of bird vocality on display across the pages of each volume. We gazed and listened in wonderment until one student began to contemplate how each documentarian was able to coax the bird to remain still while they sketched and painted their detailed portrait, examined their characteristic defining features, and recorded sensory information in their fieldnotes that would provide birders with the necessary information to locate and identify other specimens of these species in the wild.

They were dead. In order to have a still, accommodating subject that allowed the documentarian to fully examine and archive their subject, each specimen had to be carefully killed using processes that would not impact its representational features and be preserved for extended study. Their voices silenced. However, textual evidence of the vibrant animate previously alive vocality is preserved in the descriptive text featured alongside the illustrations and field mark diagrams. A generation of wildlife artists, including figures such as Robert Bateman, would kill, freeze, and preserve their subjects and take color photography of the nonhuman animal's habitat, providing the artist with the time and access to craft a detailed studied depiction of the animal. Members of the seminar briefly mourned the avian lives sacrificed for their education and the enjoyment of the amateur birder in the field. This activity and the experiences that emerged from it teach students aspects of care that illustrate that care for human and nonhuman life has a mutual connection where one thing depends on another. All lives are grievable. Attending to the cost for nonhuman animals does not indicate a lack of care about the impact on human beings.

Although animal studies is a rapidly growing interdisciplinary field devoted to examining, understanding, and critically evaluating the complex relationships between humans and other animals,[12] the scholarship in the field has rarely drawn on the aurality of these multifaced relationships to understand how nonhuman animals figure in our lives and we in theirs in cultural practices of making music. Textual and visual analysis grounds many of the existing critical approaches to the study of animals and their representation, including John Berger's foundational chapter "Why Look at Animals" in *About Looking*.[13] But what can the inclusion of sound, music, and listening contribute to the studies of animals and their representation and how these representational politics have been used to support and perpetuate systems of human difference?

Why listen to animals? How do we listen to and value the musicality of different animal species? If we listen to nonhuman specimens and the material artifacts of music, what do those soundings and silences tell us about music, our own music-making, and our aesthetic judgements? According to Rachel Mundy in *Animal Musicalities: Birds, Beasts, and Evolutionary Listening*, "Specimens became a way to know who fit and who didn't, a map of nature that extended from animal skins to anthropological artifacts."[14] Specimen collections in natural history collections also contained the music of humans and other animals. In these spaces of study and display (primarily visual) they were organized, institutionalized, and ascribed value based on a sonic categorization system where specimens were "arranged to display racial and cultural development" in "silent" exhibits: muted specimens that were "the musical analogue of the stuffed bird skins and preserved beetles arrayed in the natural history museum's specimen drawers."[15] The narratives of these displays were human-organized understandings of natural history and knowledge, and when nonhuman specimens of music and sound were included—most often birdsong—the politics of inclusion were shaped by what would be of interest to human visitors to the museum in the early decades of the twentieth century. Mundy develops the concept of the "sonic specimen" to refer to the new forms of sonic information placed on display that were advanced alongside the new developments for species identification by naturalists and biologists at that time. Mundy sketches out different instances where sonic specimens were used like biological specimens to determine biological identity, measure relatedness, and craft colonial narratives of evolution, "mapping development onto sound in the same way that naturalists mapped evolutionary change onto preserved animal bodies."[16]

The field-guide market is crowded with guides to birds marketed to a diverse audience of birders, from those that instill bird knowledge in children and young adults to those geared toward the seasoned birder who spends extended time looking and listening in the field. Field guides aid expert and hobby bird enthusiasts in sensing different species that are an important part of the ecology of the environment they are situated in. Taking the time to look, listen, and identify is in itself an act of care. It is an act of care that slows the ear and the eye, values delicate details, and transforms everyday sensory encounters into educational practices. The adoption of a new way of thinking about and listening to musicality that includes a range of musicking beyond the human teaches important lessons in observing, listening, and reciprocity.

Field guides reveal a long history of entraining humans to sense the nonhuman. Following its publication, John James Audubon's *Birds of America* became one of the most popular and memorable field guides in circulation.

With its spectacular full-page detailed depictions of North American bird species, *Birds of America* was the ideal coffee-table book in the homes of many upper-middle—class and elite households; it was far from portable or practical for actual use in the field, however. This ornate, detailed, and ubiquitous field guide set the aesthetic and organizational precedent for future field guides: the use of illustrations by artists rather than field photography, diagrams that contextualized the species within its natural habitat, and detailed descriptions that provided the birder with the necessary information to use their entire sensorium for field identification.

The first field guide for birds, however, originates not with Audubon's ubiquitous *Birds of America*, but rather with Florence Merriam Bailey, the sister of a naturalist who in 1889 began documenting and identifying all the birds she encountered in the San Diego region. While she was unable to complete a comprehensive anthology of all bird species in the area, her collected notes were published in *Audubon Magazine* and in the foundational book *Birds through an Opera-Glass*.[17] Although the book addresses only seventy common bird species, it is the manner of her address and her target audience that is of note. *Birds through an Opera-Glass* is an accessible book written for everyday use and geared toward women and youth who are interested in the natural world. The text is lighter, anecdotal, and much less pretentious than many of the prominent field guides authored by men that followed, yet the detailed descriptive text full of multisensory language (including copious auditory language) that draws on the birder's entire sensorium in the identification process is a model for the literary genre. This was one of the first attempts at something that would help bird lovers identify birds. Nicholls's *Field Guide for Extinct Birds* combines the language and field mark lexicon of standardized field guides with the imaginative and evocative language of Merriam Bailey's *Birds through an Opera-Glass* and other naturalist "in the field" publications authored by women.

Epilogue: Materiality, the Stuff of Sound, and Care

Practices of specimen collection, study, and display inside and outside the classroom reveal fascinating details concerning musical valuation and knowledge. Taxidermic field-guide images and natural history displays reveal a value-based system of musical difference that sets human musicking apart from all other forms of animal musicking and places value upon certain forms of nonhuman musicking over others. Placing the sciences in dialogue with the arts and humanities, Mundy's study stands out in its breadth of subject matter, stretching from Darwin to digital birdsong field guides to argue that these practices of musical taxonomy continue to influence how we categorize, evaluate, and listen to musical sounds according to species, races, and cultures. In dialogue with Mundy's approach, I strive to bring a range of different examples of the material culture of music and nonhuman musicality into our discussions in order to understand the histories of collection, study, display, and aesthetic valuation in global music histories. My pedagogy and classroom discussions are enhanced by Mundy's implicit challenge to her readers to rethink our learned musical valuation and knowledge that privileges anthropocentric definitions of musicality and musical excellence. For instance, my students and I use this knowledge to scrutinize how certain genres, performances, and stylistic choices were historically racialized, gendered, and categorized on nonhuman terms (for example, critical reviews of African American women jazz singers who were historically described as canaries and other species of songbirds). By listening across species and their different modes of sonic creativity, students come to understand how human-conceived definitions of music are hierarchical and exclusionary, and how nonhuman animal references and qualities were historically mapped onto instances of human music-making that were devalued on the basis of gender, race, and/or socioeconomic factors.

Listening with care to nonhuman musicality and the soundscapes we cooccupy and cocompose can prompt us to ask challenging questions about nonhuman musicality and human understandings of nonhuman animals in music-making. A care-oriented music history pedagogy that extends the conversation to include more-than-human extends the current discourse addressing how human culture needs to listen to diverse auralities. And this expanded listening palette might involve using other sensory modes to hear the nonhuman world and listen anew to the human. An expanded listening palette includes attending to the array of sounds that interact with your own soundmaking in the soundscape, taking into consideration how the texture, density, surface moisture, and the kind of species used for a traditional Anishinaabe hand-drum head impacts the sonic qualities of a performance, or exploring instances of human improvisation with nonhuman animal vocalists and developing a multispecies vocabulary for interspecies performance. By approaching music studies from this perspective, listeners develop an understanding of the complexity and diversity of human and nonhuman musical life and listen critically to humanity's contributions to our shared sonic environments.

Notes

1. I use only the first name of each student involved in this research or a pseudonym upon request by the student. Interviews were conducted with students who volunteered to participate after final grades were submitted and during a semester when they were not enrolled in one of my classes or in an independent study with me.

2. Ana María Ochoa Gautier, "Acoustic Multinaturalism, the Value of Nature, and the Nature of Music in Ecomusicology," *boundary 2* 43, no. 1 (2016): 107–41. See also Claire Jean Kim, *Dangerous Crossings: Race, Species, and Nature in a Multicultural Age* (Cambridge: Cambridge University Press, 2015).

3. Jane Bennett, *Vibrant Matter: A Political Ecology of Things* (Durham: Duke University Press, 2010), xvi.

4. Stacy Alaimo, *Exposed: Environmental Politics and Pleasures in Posthuman Times* (Minneapolis: University of Minnesota Press, 2016).

5. The videos used in this exercise include "Bunny Momo Plays Theremin by Ear," YouTube, April 16, 2019, https://www.youtube.com/; "Cat Plays Theremin," YouTube, September 14, 2013, https://www.youtube.com/; and an excerpt of "The Haunted Theremin of Carolina Eyck | Reverb," YouTube, October 31, 2018, https://www.youtube.com/.

6. Bennett, *Vibrant Matter*, 9.

7. Bennett, 10.

8. See Frank Gunderson, Robert Lancefield, and Bret Woods, eds., *The Oxford Handbook of Musical Repatriation* (Oxford: Oxford University Press, 2019), particularly the essay by Trevor Reed, "Reclaiming Ownership of the Indigenous Voice: The Hopi Music Repatriation Project," 627–54.

9. Eliot Bates, "The Social Life of Musical Instruments," *Ethnomusicology* 56, no. 3 (2012): 364.

10. See for example, Sarah Nicholls, *A Field Guide to Extinct Birds* (self-published, 2015); Sarah McDermott, *ReSound* (Washington, DC: Marginalia Press Corcoran College of Art and Design, 2015); Shawn Sheehy, *Beyond the 6th Extinction: A Fifth Millennium Bestiary* (n.p.: Paperboy Press, 2007).

11. I would like to thank Suzy Taraba for her openness to pedagogical collaboration and the access she provided to a range of material culture of sound and music during the years we worked together.

12. See Margo DeMello, *Animals and Society: An Introduction to Human-Animal Studies* (New York: Columbia University Press, 2012); Lori Gruen, *Entangled Empathy: An Alternative Ethic for Our Relationships with Animals* (New York: Lantern Books, 2015); Lori Gruen, ed., *Critical Terms for Animal Studies* (Chicago: University of Chicago Press, 2018); Kari Weil, *Thinking Animals: Why Animal Studies Now?* (New York: Columbia University Press, 2012).

13. John Berger, *About Looking* (New York: Pantheon, 1980).

14. Rachel Mundy, *Animal Musicalities: Birds, Beasts, and Evolutionary Listening* (Middletown, CT: Wesleyan University Press, 2018), 42.

15. Mundy, 42–43.

16. Mundy, 43.

17. Florence Merriam Bailey, *Birds through an Opera-Glass* (Boston: Houghton Mifflin, 1899).

PART III

Self-Care, the Root of Teaching

CHAPTER 11

Curriculum Changing Culture

Improving the Mental Health of University Music Students

NATHAN A. LANGFITT

The twenty-first century, thus far, has been a critical time for mental health care on college campuses across the country. Students are seeking help more than ever before, as decades of outreach and education around destigmatizing mental health care has started to take hold. It is also true that the acuity of student mental health needs has never been so severe.[1]

The factors that are impacting student mental health today are a combination of expected considerations such as being away from home for the first time, social anxiety, and the negative impacts of perfectionism. Students who hold marginalized identities may be even more impacted. In some cases, the very system (in this case, the academy) that has been structured to educate and foster students could also be the very thing that is causing them distress. As a result, institutions must develop strategies and interventions that train musicians to cope with the emotional impact of the discipline's demands, while also looking critically at how their own environment and culture could be impacting student mental health.

When examining the environments in which musicians work and learn, it becomes abundantly clear that musicians are routinely placed in situations that often negatively impact their mental health. Job scarcity creates a hypervigilance that leaves musicians unable to trust they will be able to satisfy their most basic needs. The competitive nature of the profession makes relationships with others complicated. Working within unbalanced power structures and in spaces where they lack agency over their contribution can lead to feelings of burnout, which is increasingly viewed as comparable to depression.[2]

Despite all of this, an essential element to our narrative as musicians remains that music benefits the mind and soul. The irony of this discrepancy cannot be ignored. We advocate for music programs in schools with the promise that student participation will improve the lives of young people.[3] Most musicians, myself included, consider music as a personal savior of sorts, as it provided a purpose or sense of community during vulnerable adolescent and early adult years. Given this cherished place that music retains in our culture and personal histories, it can be difficult for musicians to reconcile the transformational experience of studying music with the lasting negative health impacts of existing in the profession. Because it can feel like heresy, or a lack of dedication, to discuss the negative side of being a musician, individuals often suffer in isolation, unwilling or feeling unable to be open about their inner experience, anxiety, and distress.

The students we praise and label as our successes are not always the most skilled, most talented, or hardest workers. They are often the students who possess the most resilience to the pressures and demands of the curriculum, programming, and culture of schools of music. Resilience is complex in its own right, as there is a fine line between someone developing a comfort and flexibility toward failure and someone becoming numb and emotionally hardened, letting negative experiences simply bounce off of them. Our goal as a profession should not be to get the student simply to a level where they can win an audition. Rather, we should develop musicians who have the nonmusical skills to sustain a lasting career. Developing more psychological flexibility, comfort with failure and disappointment, healthy work/life balance, and a greater sense of self-compassion will help students persevere through many audition processes, but also avoid burnout, therefore maintaining longer, healthier careers. These same goals also apply to our students whose goals are in academic, teaching, and research spaces. Music majors who are able to get appropriate amounts of sleep, exercise, and time to relax are less likely to report symptoms of burnout.[4]

When I have worked with faculty and staff in trainings on this topic, someone usually asks if I am advocating for an easier music school. This is usually the same person who supports the common notion that a career in music is inherently taxing, and therefore the school must meet (or even exceed) this level of rigor to ensure that students are prepared. It is not the difficulty that renders music school potentially unhealthy, but instead the music school's demands, as well as the expectations and behaviors that have been normalized within a school's culture. American music schools are full of implicit and explicit rites of passage, which can lead to academic hazing.[5]

My personal experience as a mental health professional and student-affairs administrator has come at two large state flagship R1 campuses that are known regionally and nationally for the size and quality of their music programs. I point this out to note that the mental health issues to be discussed here exist within all sizes and scopes of music schools. The two institutions I have worked for are fortunate in that they have the resources to create robust mental-health and student-affairs services that are often custom-tailored to the lived experience of creative and artistic students. Smaller institutions often have to centralize student-support services at a broader campus level, which means they can be less accessible, harder to navigate, and less likely to be aware of the unique issues that music students endure. Addressing mental health is a complex issue on any campus, and further research needs to be done to address how smaller schools of music can better support student mental health.

After a brief history of research on musician mental health, I will discuss each of the specific stressors connected to music school that I have discussed with students the most frequently in counseling sessions. I will then propose ways in which faculty, staff, and schools of music as an institution can reconceptualize their role in student mental health in order to become stronger advocates for real and lasting change.

Historical Context

In 1987 the International Conference of Symphony and Opera Musicians (ICSOM) commissioned a study to survey the musicians of forty-eight major American orchestras and opera orchestras, and to draw conclusions about the medical problems of their members. Drawing from over two thousand responses, the study found that 27% of musicians were using beta blockers (a medication designed to treat heart problems but often used by musicians to manage performance anxiety), and that 70% of those were doing so without a prescription. Seventeen percent of respondents experienced depression at some point, and 24% had struggled with stage fright (or performance anxiety). The study is frequently cited and encouraged a significant increase in research on musicians' health issues.[6]

A 1989 research study surveyed music students from Texas State University, University of Miami, and the Manhattan School of Music to identify their greatest sources of stress as music majors. The top five issues of concern from the surveyed students were stress, preperformance nerves, progress impatience, burnout, and job insecurity. The study also discovered that 72% of respondents indicated a preference for a counselor with knowledge of the discipline in order to relate to discipline-specific challenges.[7]

James Young and John Hipple (1996) surveyed the presenting problems of music students seeking help at a university counseling center. Their results showed that of the music majors seeking counseling, slightly less than 50% of the students experienced the symptomology necessary to diagnose depression. Twenty-six percent of the respondents reported suicidal thoughts. In addition to these clinical concerns, 47% of surveyed students were discouraged about their future, 41% were unsure of their career choices, and 35% believed that no one understood them.[8]

In 2002 the Music Educators National Conference published *The New Handbook of Research on Music Teaching and Learning*, and included multiple chapters pertaining to performing-arts medicine and musician health. The chapters reference the risk that comes from psychological stress in musicians and how this stress, left untreated, could lead to physical problems as well. The student-teacher relationship was also mentioned as a contributing risk factor that should be addressed. Regarding the options available to improve musician mental health, Alice Brandfonbrener and Richard Lederman agreed that change would be most effective if implemented during the teaching of music. The chapter also advocates that many other musician health issues could be alleviated by addressing student stress reduction.[9]

In 2004, the Health Promotion in Schools of Music Conference brought together experts from music and medical disciplines to discuss the improvement of health outcomes for music students. The conference dedicated a special committee to mental health issues. The resulting report called for a literature review, published materials for educational institutions, collaborations with mental health agencies, curriculum for music-education majors about identifying burnout in students, curriculum and instruction about performance anxiety, instruction and materials for music students for maintaining positive mental health, and development of measures to better understand music-student mental health.[10]

Stressors Connected to Music School

In addition to the developmental, environmental, and preprofessional pressures placed on all college students, there are mental health concerns that most music students experience. As with the general student population, some of these struggles are unavoidable realities of the environment. Changes made to programming, pedagogical structures, and support systems would provide better support as students learn about music.

Adolescent psychology has long examined the effects of the "top dog phenomenon": the idea that students who are in the oldest grade on their campus experience a more favorable experience than students who are the youngest on a campus, and that the transitions between campuses can create increased stress.[11] While this phenomenon has usually been described in relation to the transition from middle school to high school, it provides an apt comparison for the transition of the senior year of high school to the first year of college for a music student. The incoming first-year music student likely spent their senior year of high school being lauded with all-state honors, winning concerto competitions, and being viewed as a student leader in their band, choir, or orchestra. Arriving at college and suddenly being average among peers, who comprise those same high achievers, presents a jarring experience. Thus, students who are already overwhelmed with starting college may also question their sense of value and likelihood of success in their music degree. All students experience increased levels of stress during the transition into college.[12] However, the expectation of prior preparation placed on first-year music students differs from expectations of students who are majoring in fields that don't require years of prerequisite skill development. The sequence of most music curricular structures requires direct admission into the school of music in order to finish in four years. For students who have been tracking toward a music degree for some time, the direct admission also creates an additional pressure to arrive ready to perform at a high level. Colleen Conway and colleagues described tension from students as they struggle to manage their time between the demands of homework, instrumental practice, and self-care.[13]

Due to the immersive nature of a music major's precollege training, music students often conceptualize the postsecondary experience and their emerging adulthood differently, which is likely to impact their mental health needs in ways not seen among students in other disciplines. Examining some of the factors in a music school provides a better understanding of student mental health and how to better address it and support students.

Starting Age

Musicians develop an occupational identity at a younger age in part because they start their training at a young age. Daniel Isbell surveyed preservice music teachers and found that secondary socialization (music teachers and mentors) held a more significant correlation to occupational identity formation than primary socialization (family and caretakers).[14] Teachers and instructors (in the school of music, and also including precollege ensemble directors and lesson teachers) create a complex network of implicit and explicit rules and customs based on their own training and experiences that are passed down from teacher to student. Whether this is intentional or not, it creates a system of rigid expectations that can be challenging for developing minds to interpret and come to terms with. Young students, eager to be successful, will often take the word of their teacher as absolute truth, leaving them without opportunities to develop their own personal identity. Claudia Spahn and colleagues found that first-year music majors identify with their major more strongly than students in other disciplines. This same study found that music majors scored higher for anxiety symptoms than medical students and student athletes.[15]

Many developmental milestones could potentially even be impacted or perhaps delayed by the demands of such rigorous musical achievement. Students ages fifteen to sixteen involved in artistic programs (defined as music, art, drama, and writing) are more likely to experience depressive symptoms than students not studying in the arts.[16] In therapy sessions with music students, I often hear stories of regret for not having played sports as a child, developed other interests, or formed deeper relationships, all because these normal childhood experiences were deemed distracting by teachers and parents. These students arrive on campus and meet peers who did not spend their childhood in a practice room, and for many of them, this is the first moment they realize just how different their lives have been to this point. This overidentification with music and lack of diversified interests is one of the most critical reasons that a young musician may question their self-worth or value independent from music.

Volume and Rigidity of Coursework

Due to the sheer number of courses required to earn a degree in music, it is rare that a music student enters college as an undecided student, opting into music after an exploratory first or second year of school. It is also rare to find music students double-majoring or taking a class outside of the prescribed coursework for enjoyment, curiosity, or development. Many college students in disciplines other than music see their first one or two years of college as a time to explore and clarify their interests and values. Due to the rigidity and insular nature of music curricula in many performance-track degree plans, this kind of exploration is viewed as unrealistic and/or superfluous.

Faculty and staff in music programs constantly remind students that jobs are scarce. However, some music schools struggle to prepare students for this reality by limiting their skill development with overly rigid coursework, and by doubling down on performance-track training. Many of the music students I have worked with in a counseling setting sought my help because they realized that they did not have the skills necessary to be a successful professional musician, but they felt trapped in their major due to the inflexible design of the curriculum. Often schools of music have created an implicit culture that those who become professionals in other fields have failed in some way.

One-to-One Relationships

The success of a music student is often based on their relationship with one specific instructor, the faculty member responsible for that student's instrumental or voice lessons. This instructor holds an extraordinary amount of power in the life of the student, impacting their standing within the school, their ensemble assignments, and their eventual career outcomes. In many cases, this person also decides if a student will receive scholarship funding. For students who possess a healthy mentor-mentee relationship with this professor, it often serves many beneficial roles supporting the students' success. If this relationship becomes fraught, it can create a multitude of problems for the student. During counseling sessions, I have observed students spending an inordinate amount of time and energy fretting about how they are perceived by their primary faculty mentor.

Quality one-on-one instruction is invaluable to the musical development of a student. However, having one person serve as such a significant gatekeeper role to collegiate and professional opportunities creates pressure on the student to uphold a level of diligence and performance that is potentially unsustainable. Faculty awareness and openness to dialogue about this issue can help reduce anxiety for students. I often encourage faculty to name to their students the power that they hold in instructional roles and address the stress that may be created by this.

During counseling sessions, I have heard students describe the many ways in which they prioritize pleasing their primary professor over their own health and wellness needs. Thus, they are less likely to speak up about being ill, having personal struggles, or needing to take a momentary break from their musical practice. In my experience, faculty members can serve as some of the most effective referrals to campus mental-health-care services, since the student holds their opinion in such high regard. To create a productive and sustainable collective mental health culture in schools of music, faculty who closely mentor students should receive additional training on interpersonal relationship dynamics, mental health, and student development. Although the individual relationships developed in a music school can be potentially harmful, they also serve a vital and beneficial function. C. L. Barney Dews and Martha Williams found that music students in distress seek the help of their teachers before parents and mental health professionals.[17] In their study, students only reached out to friends more often than their teachers. This again speaks to the powerful role that faculty serve in the life of music students, and how this mentorship could be consequential to a student's growth in musical prowess and the development of their health-seeking capacities.

Mental Health Issues Connected to Physical Pain

Playing-related injury and physical pain from practice and overuse is ubiquitous to the musician experience, and like mental health it is seldom discussed.[18] Christine Zaza found that 43% of students at a Canadian music school had some form of a playing-related health problem throughout their tenure.[19]

As research continues to develop about the brain-body connection and the relationship of physical pain to emotional suffering, it is increasingly clear that the physical stressors of music training will relate to students' mental health. *Medical Problems of Performing Artists* is a thorough resource for anyone seeking additional information about physical ailments and mental health issues that could come from a career in music.

Isolation

When I speak to other mental health professionals about working with musicians, there is a persistent assumption that one of the strengths musicians possess is a tight-knit sense of community. My nonmusician colleagues often picture musicians working collaboratively, spending the majority of their time working in groups. They are surprised to learn that music students spend the overwhelming majority of their time isolated in a practice room. To the music community, long, narrow hallways containing hundreds of practice rooms is a normal feature of university facilities. I once toured a music building with another therapist colleague, and their reaction to the hallways of practice rooms addressed this key misunderstanding about how musicians spend their time. When this therapist saw all of these musicians in small rooms, alone, and understood how many hours they would spend there, they noted the resemblance to a psychiatric hospital. While this assessment may seem dramatic, it speaks to a core element that makes the school of music experience distressing for students: since they spend large amounts of time in isolation, when they do emerge to collaborate and socialize, it can be challenging to be open with peers and teachers about their internal experience. Students can struggle with forming interpersonal relationships due to this isolation.[20]

Research from the School of Music at the University of North Texas investigated perceived social support of music majors as compared to nonmajors.[21] Social support from significant others, family, and friends provides a critical coping agent and protective factor from anxiety and depression. In this study, music majors perceived significantly less social support from significant others than their non-music-major peers. Additionally, students who reported less social isolation reported less of the debilitating impact of performance anxiety.

Supporting All of Our Students

It is important to remember that layers of distress created by being a music student will be experienced even more aversely by our students who hold any multitude of marginalized identities, as their lived experiences have potentially been fraught with additional stressors. These students may also experience the isolation, pressures, and marginalization of musicians in more acute ways, thus increasing all of the risks discussed above. This point in and of itself is crucial in considering the implications of the inequities in music programs. Further research on the intersection of musician mental health, gender, race, and culture is needed, and could serve as a vital resource to better support all of our students.

Students experiencing isolation, when accompanied by anxiety or depressive symptoms, will assume they are the only person suffering, and because of this, there must be something wrong or broken about them. The healing process includes identifying, accepting, and embracing what we perceive to be broken. A critical step also includes establishing a culture where students feel safe to be honest about their mental health and how it interrelates with their own background and experiences. For example, a studio professor could dedicate real time to checking on how students are faring, and facilitate an open dialogue for students to discuss the ways they are hurting and struggling. When students perceive that it is safe to suffer, they will be one step closer toward understanding that it is safe to heal or ask for help.

Vulnerability and openness from faculty and staff can help a student's comfort level to acknowledge and work through their own issues. Students often idealize and idolize their faculty, and this often creates myths that mentors have been highly successful in their careers because they are better or stronger than others, and experienced little to no suffering along the way. Some of the most meaningful therapy I have provided to music students occurred because a faculty member shared with them the helpful impact from their own therapy.

Training faculty and staff on mental health and student development is an essential step. Understandably, faculty often do not feel skilled or qualified to handle many student disclosures. Faculty worry they may become the therapist, and possibly end up in a situation where they cannot provide adequate help. Faculty fears are heightened when students disclose about suicidal ideation, trauma, or abuse. Faculty should set clear boundaries about their role, while also connecting the student with on-campus mental health resources. It can feel uncomfortable to tell a student that you care about them and want to support them but also know the care they need is with a mental health professional. Initially students may be upset or disappointed to be connected to mental health care; however, the long-term benefits usually result in the student being grateful to the faculty or staff member who helped them start this process.

As musicians, we are often conditioned to put our career above everything else, which can lead to important conversations about prioritizing health. I once had a student experience their first manic episode in my office, and they were only open to getting help if it could be the next day, as they had an important rehearsal in two hours. As the student explored their motivations for refusing therapeutic help in the moment, it boiled down to pleasing their faculty at all costs. The student was also concerned that missing this rehearsal could impact their position in the hierarchy of the studio. As I tried to persuade the student to connect with the necessary type and level of help required for a manic episode, they continually returned to concerns about their music-making, upcoming performances, fellow ensemble members, and the professor, thus completely ignoring their individual health. This situation is reminiscent of a scene in the film *Whiplash*, where the main character has been bloodied and injured by a car crash, but still insists on arriving at the performance and attempting to play. Mental health is sometimes not as apparent as a physical injury, including to the person experiencing it. Changes to increase support for students will only come with a deliberate culture shift from not only schools of music but from the profession as a whole.

Every school of music should have a protocol in place for how to manage and support a student in crisis. Many institutions already possess such protocols and services, such as 24-hour crisis hotlines, an established walk-in procedure to the counseling or health center, and the posting of crisis-hotline phone numbers in areas where suicide attempts are common. Since music students spend many hours in the music buildings, music units can help their students by posting the phone numbers of on-campus mental health resources throughout commonly-used spaces.

Curricular Changes to Encourage Mental Health Promotion

Building mental health promotion into the curriculum shows students that the institution values this topic, and may empower more students to get help. In 2000, the Freiburg University of Music in Germany implemented a study involving health promotion and prevention curriculum that addressed both physical and mental issues experienced by musicians. Students without health promotion and prevention curriculum deteriorated at higher levels than students who were receiving the intervention. Additionally, music students endured more psychological and physical distress than non–music students of their same age.[22]

At the University of Texas at Austin, I developed a mental-health skills-building series titled *Resonate with Resilience*. It aimed to create open dialogue about the stressors that music students experience. Over the course of six, ninety-minute sessions, students explored their feelings around performance anxiety, perfectionism, career uncertainty, and their personal relationship to practicing and their musical craft. Students completed activities designed to help them explore their values, develop a deeper well of self-compassion, and learn mindfulness meditation techniques to address anxiety. Students signed up for the workshop series voluntarily, and all efforts were made to protect their confidentiality. The group would not have been a success, however, without the enthusiastic support of the faculty and leadership of the Butler School of Music at UT.

One of the key suggestions from the 2004 Health Promotion in Schools of Music (HPSM) project included schools of music developing occupational health courses for music majors. Manchester discussed such courses developed by eleven institutions.[23] These offerings could serve as a starting place for ideas on how health providers and music faculty could collaborate to develop more of these types of courses.

Music units would better equip their students for a successful career by increasing dialogue about mental health and becoming more active stakeholders in systemically improving student mental health throughout the unit. Music students would benefit from coursework and other learning experiences infused with supportive coping skills, a growth-oriented mindset, and an internal resource of self-compassion for the inevitable adversity within a career in music. Music units can assist in this process by critically examining the ways in which they teach and the culture they explicitly and implicitly perpetuate. Faculty, staff, and administrators can lead the work of self-study and define healthier values for our teaching institutions and our profession. Our students are capable of making extraordinary music. Among those in the student's educational support system, faculty, staff, and administrators can approach the often difficult topics of mental health with openness, curiosity, and kindness. We can model care for the mind and heart with the same rigor and commitment we grant to the music that resonates through our halls.

Notes

1. Center for Collegiate Mental Health, *2018 Annual Report*, Pennsylvania State University, January 2019, https://sites.psu.edu/ccmh/files/2019/01/2018-Annual-Report-1.30.19-ziytkb.pdf.

2. "Burn-Out an 'Occupational Phenomenon': International Classification of Diseases," World Health Organization, May 28, 2019, https://www.who.int/mental_health/evidence/burn-out/en/.

3. Merja Hietolahti-Ansten and Mirja Kalliopuska, "Self-Esteem and Empathy among Children Actively Involved in Music," *Perceptual and Motor Skills* 71, no. 3 (1990): 1364.

4. Christian Bernhard, "A Survey of Burnout among College Music Majors: A Replication," *Music Performance Research* 3, no. 1 (2010): 31–41.

5. Clifford Madsen, "Instruction and Supervision of Graduate Students in Music Education," *Research Studies in Music Education* 21, no. 1 (2003): 58–71.

6. Martin Fishbein, Susan Middlestadt, Victor Ottati, Susan Straus, and Alan Ellis,

"Medical Problems among ICSOM Musicians: Overview of a National Survey," *Medical Problems of Performing Artists* 3, no. 1 (1988): 1–8.

7. C. L. Barney Dews and Martha Williams, "Student Musicians' Personality Styles, Stresses, and Coping Patterns," *Psychology of Music* 17 (1989): 37–47.

8. James Young and John Hipple, "Social/Emotional Problems of University Music Students Seeking Assistance at a Student Counseling Center," *Medical Problems of Performing Artists* 11, no. 4 (1996): 123–26.

9. Alice Brandfonbrener and Richard Lederman, "Performing Arts Medicine," *The New Handbook of Research on Music Teaching and Learning*, ed. Richard Colwell and Carol Richardson (Oxford: Oxford University Press, 2002), 1009–21.

10. Kris Chesky, William J. Dawson, and Ralph Manchester, "Health Promotion in Schools of Music: Initial Recommendations for Schools of Music," *Medical Problems of Performing Artists* 21, no. 3 (September 2006): 142–44, https://doi.org/10.21091/mppa.2006.3027.

11. Dale Blyth, Roberta Simmons, and Diane Bush, "The Transition into Early Adolescence: A Longitudinal Comparison of Youth in Two Educational Contexts," *Sociology of Education* 51, no. 3 (1978): 149; Amy Schwartz, Leanna Stiefel, and Micah Rothbart, "Do Top Dogs Rule in Middle School? Evidence on Bullying, Safety, and Belonging," *American Educational Research Journal* 53, no. 5 (2016): 1450–84.

12. John Schulenberg, Arnold Sameroff, and Dante Cicchetti, "The Transition to Adulthood as a Critical Juncture in the Course of Psychopathology and Mental Health," *Development and Psychopathology* 16 (2004): 799–806; Lynn Towbes and Lawrence Cohen, "Chronic Stress in the Lives of College Students: Scale Development and Prospective Prediction of Distress," *Journal of Youth and Adolescence* 25, no. 2 (1996): 199–217.

13. Colleen Conway, John Eros, Kristen Pellegrino, and Chad West, "Instrumental Music Education Students' Perceptions of Tensions Experienced during Their Undergraduate Degree," *Journal of Research in Music Education* 58, no. 3 (2010): 260–75.

14. Daniel Isbell, "Musicians and Teachers: The Socialization and Occupational Identity of Preservice Music Teachers," *Journal of Research in Music Education* 56, no. 2 (2008): 162–78.

15. Claudia Spahn, Sandra Strukely, and Andreas Lehmann, "Health Conditions, Attitudes toward Study, and Attitudes toward Health at the Beginning of University Study: Music Students in Comparison with Other Student Populations," *Medical Problems of Performing Artists* 19, no. 1 (2004): 26–33.

16. Laura Young, Ellen Winner, and Sara Cordes, "Heightened Incidence of Depressive Symptoms in Adolescents Involved in the Arts," *Psychology of Aesthetics, Creativity, and the Arts* 7, no. 2 (2013): 197–202.

17. Dews and Williams, "Student Musicians' Personality Styles."

18. Fishbein et al., "Medical Problems."

19. Christine Zaza, "Playing-Related Health Problems at a Canadian Music School," *Medical Problems of Performing Artists* 7, no. 2 (1992): 48–51.

20. Elma Kanefield, "Psychological Services at the Juilliard School," *Medical Problems of Performing Artists* 5, no. 1 (1990): 41–44; David Sternbach, "Stress in the Lives of Music Students," *Music Educators Journal* 94, no. 3 (2008): 42–48.

21. Erin Schneider and Kris Chesky, "Social Support and Performance Anxiety of College Music Students," *Medical Problems of Performing Artists* 26, no. 3 (2011): 157–63.

22. Mark Zander, Edgar Voltmer, and Claudia Spahn, "Health Promotion and Prevention in Higher Music Education," *Medical Problems of Performing Artists* 25, no. 2 (2010): 54–65.

23. Ralph Manchester, "Health Promotion Courses for Music Students: Part 1," *Medical Problems of Performing Artists* 22, no. 1 (2007): 26–29; Ralph Manchester, "Health Promotion Courses for Music Students: Part 2," *Medical Problems of Performing Artists* 22, no. 2 (2007): 80–81; Ralph Manchester, "Health Promotion Courses for Music Students: Part 3," *Medical Problems of Performing Artists* 22, no. 3 (2007): 116–19.

CHAPTER 12

Teaching the First-Generation College Student in the Music History Classroom

A Student-to-Professor Perspective

REBA A. WISSNER

I remember it vividly: it was August 2005. As a first-generation college freshman and commuter student at a public university, I returned home from my first day of classes with only one class that day. My mother greeted me and asked about my first day of college. Overwhelmed, I dropped my two heavy bags of textbooks and cried. I would not take my first music history class for another two years. At that point, I knew that being a first-generation college student would have distinct disadvantages in the music history classroom that I would not face or even foresee in other music classes.

The music history classroom is a place where listening, performing, analyzing, and critical thinking converge. For the typical music student, music history classes can be challenging—sometimes even daunting—especially since college is often the first time that they navigate study of music's history. However, for those students who are the first in their families to attend college, these classes present special challenges, including exacerbating a lack of self-esteem, the high cost and presentation of course materials, unfamiliar concepts due to life and musical experiences, and the potential dismissal of musical experiences and traditions that are framed as "other" to the "core" music curriculum. Finally, the backlash that some students receive from their parents for studying music cannot be ignored, since anxiety over education pathways and career outcomes is prevalent for many of these students.

In our efforts to address the needs of the various student populations in our classrooms, one type of student is frequently ignored: the first-generation college student (FGCS). Often, FGCS do not identify themselves as such unless prompted, either because of insecurity or because they do not feel that being the first in their family to attend college is significant. Unlike race and gender, college status is invisible and is often perceived as unremarkable.[1] I never disclosed because I believed that it did not matter; I now know that it did. Knowledge of my FGCS status would have helped my professors better support me in my learning, and would have helped me to understand my own learning.

This chapter continues conversations in higher education about how faculty can address FGCS' unique needs in the music history classroom. I consider the literature on aiding FGCS and examine the challenges particular to this environment.[2] Some of the unique challenges FGCS meet in music history concern confidence in performing on an instrument or voice and/or in sight-reading; the ability to afford textbooks, anthologies, recordings, and other materials; the learning curve to critically listen to music, read musical scores, and analyze primary sources as steps to completing research projects and homework assignments; learning to understand music in a completely new and analytical way; and seeing music history as relevant for music majors. As a FGCS-turned-professor, I offer suggestions and practices for addressing these needs, moving from what I needed to what I, as a faculty member, do to aid these students. I focus on the practices that I employ to mitigate these students' challenges and foster an environment of compassionate learning where we support students' identities and experiences to ensure their success.

First-Generation College Students: An Overview

A FGCS is defined as someone who is the first in their family to attend a two- or four-year college and whose parents and siblings have no education beyond high school.[3] Sometimes they are referred to as first-in-family students, in contrast with those who are not, referred to as continuing-generation college students (CGCS).[4] We should also consider immigrant students who, while they may not be the first in their family to attend college, are the first in their families to attend college in their new country. Research shows that FGCS have disadvantages compared to CGCS, including lower retention and graduation rates.[5] But compared to their CGCS peers, they have several advantages including independence, self-reliance, and high intrinsic motivation.[6]

College culture is unfamiliar to FGCS.[7] We know that FGCS have different experiences than CGCS.[8] Many of these students perceive themselves as lacking a sense of belonging and feel "that their input is not needed or even noticed."[9] This perception can lead to anxiety and poor performance.[10] Therefore, faculty must show these students that they *do* belong and their input *is* valued. This notion that one can make space for students not filled with content is what Parker Palmer calls "teaching from the microcosm."[11] To teach from the microcosm means to teach a discipline's big ideas through small data samples, which, in the case of music history, is to look at small samples from the field, whether literature or cases.

There is a large FGCS population in American college classrooms—in 2018, one-third of college students in the United States identified as FGCS.[12] Many FGCS also identify as low-income and/or minoritized students who are often less prepared for college than CGCS.[13] Further, FGCS access to college prep courses is more difficult due to race, class, or socioeconomic status.[14] Indeed, "first-generation students are often unaware that preparation for college begins in high school."[15] Therefore, they often do not seek advanced placement courses or ask for help with finding appropriate extracurricular programs due to financial constraints, time, and/or lack of knowledge of their existence and importance. These kinds of programs help students to stand out in the admissions process and prepare them for future study.

Student social capital and academic engagement are particularly problematic for FGCS. We know "low-income and first-generation students are less likely to be engaged in the academic and social experiences that foster success in college, such as studying in groups, interacting with faculty and other students, participating in extra-curricular activities, and using support services."[16] Students who are of high socioeconomic status and/or CGCS typically choose liberal arts majors, including the arts, while FGCS and/or low-income students do not.[17] Therefore, it is unusual for a FGCS to become a music major.

The challenges for FGCS music majors are compounded if they are also first-generation musicians. For example, as Jeffrey Arlo Brown opines, "Once musicians from non-musical families do make it to higher education, they are met with a new set of challenges. Ear training . . . is something that the children of musicians tend to master through osmosis. For first-generation musicians it is a nasty crucible."[18] These students must learn an entirely new skill set that includes theory, ear training, and music history, in addition to piano skills and instrument or voice technique. This is exacerbated if they are from musical families who improvise or play by ear and for whom musical priorities and values differ from those in the Western art-music canon.

Strategies for First-Generation Students in the Music History Classroom

Teaching FGCS is the subject of several recent studies, some of which include tips for working with such students.[19] To best serve FGCS, we must enact support systems; the classroom is the best place to begin. The effort placed into helping these students determines whether or not they academically succeed.[20] As Palmer believes, "good teaching cannot be reduced to technique; good teaching comes from the identity and integrity of the teacher."[21] My argument begins from this perspective. The teacher's identity and disclosure are often overlooked as crucial pedagogical components.

I am a first-generation college graduate. My pronouns are she/her/hers. I was born and raised in the Bronx, New York, in a low-income family. I am from a mixed-religion home (Catholicism and Judaism) but am Jewish. My parents are second-generation Americans. I have several chronic illnesses that sometimes present challenges. I spent eight years as adjunct faculty, teaching six to eight classes per semester, typically at four colleges in two states while working as a freelance editor. As an adjunct, my low income prevented me from living on my own, so I spent eight years living with my parents.

Identifying with one's students and experience should inform one's pedagogy.[22] Bianca Williams calls this disclosure "radical honesty," or what "emphasizes the significance of personal narratives and opens a space for creating strategies that enable scholars and students to bring their 'whole self' to the classroom, while getting rid of the shame that frequently accompanies their bodies in academic settings."[23] Radical honesty is composed of three principles: honesty ("truth-telling"), valuing narratives and personal experiences, and acting.[24] The professor's disclosure of identity and experience directly correlates with student success because it allows the students to come to terms with their own identities, position, and privilege, gives them a voice, and removes the shame/stigma of their experiences.[25]

One recent study confirmed that many college faculty teach how they were taught.[26] But this is often not the best or most useful solution; one must listen to students and their needs, but one may not know the students' needs if one does not ask.[27] Distributing student surveys or asking students for short personal essays on the first day of class shows students from the beginning of the course that the instructor cares about them and their success.[28]

In the spirit of care, I conducted a survey of FGCS experiences in the music history classroom to augment my experiences.[29] I recruited participants through social-media channels and listservs. Definition of a FGCS was presented on the survey's informed consent form page. One survey question asked participants to identify their roles so I could see how the answers of faculty and nonfaculty differed. Of the forty-nine people who answered this question, twenty-four were current music students, eighteen were music faculty, and seven were music major alumni.

Of the forty-eight participants who answered the disclosure question, forty-three did not disclose their FGCS status. Those who did, only did so because it came up in conversation; like me, they did not feel it necessary, likely because FGCS are indistinguishable from their CGCS peers.[30] Regarding whether music history courses contained inherent challenges different from nonmusic courses, twenty-five respondents answered yes while twenty-three answered no. One respondent likened music history courses to "a mix of skills learned in more typical STEM studies but requir[ing] a musical ear." For the question about whether there are inherent challenges in the music history classroom different from other music classes such as music theory and ear training, of the forty-eight respondents who answered, thirty stated no and eighteen stated yes. Those who stated yes cited research requirements and necessary background and interdisciplinary knowledge that they felt they lacked.

According to a 2015 study of 204 North American higher education institutions, most students begin the history sequence in either their sophomore or junior year.[31] In the survey I conducted, however, fifteen participants stated they first took it in their freshman, sophomore, or junior year. Only two responded that they took their first music history class as a senior, and one said as a graduate student. As Table 12.1 shows, FGCS faced many barriers in the music history classroom. There were forty-eight respondents to the question: "What barriers did you face as a first-generation college student in your music history classes? (Select all that apply)." For those who answered "other," the responses included: "lack of musical training before college," "ability to access concerts and musical events," and "working while a full-time student." Many students noted that barriers arose from financial limitations and not knowing what to expect from college.

The greatest barrier was the lecture. The role of the lecture has been hotly debated with many arguing it has outlived its usefulness. In traditional lectures, students are not typically encouraged to think independently or actively use and apply information. Lectures often last beyond the typical adult attention span, and present other structural problems to learners.[32] The lecture was, by far, the most frequent pedagogical method in music history classes, with "multiple self-guided projects during class time" ranking at the very bottom of the list of methods.[33] Many survey respondents (twenty-two of forty-six who commented) stated that less lecture and more participatory activities would have been useful. One respondent remarked that they had to acclimate to the lecture format, while another stopped attending lectures because they felt "distant." Another respondent noted that music history felt vague and "anchorless" because it lacked the music-making in ear-training courses. The lecture for some students was daunting because music history is interdisciplinary and requires mastery of a lot of material, some of which is unfamiliar or outside of their own cultural traditions. With lecture, this information moves quickly and is hard to meaningfully absorb in real time.

The plethora of information presented in class is hardly surprising. On average, music history professors provide ten facts for every fifteen minutes of lecture.[34] Therefore, music history classes may be stressful for students not used to this type of learning. The researcher of one study on music majors' stress

Table 12.1. FGCS Survey Data Responses

Answer Choices	Responses	Number of Respondents
Density of material	41.67%	20
Following scores	22.92%	11
Textbooks	33.33%	16
Understanding the lecture	27.08%	13
Cost of materials	39.58%	19
Classroom environment	14.58%	7
Listening skills	37.50%	18
Study skills	41.67%	20
Research skills	39.58%	19
Other (please specify)	14.58%	7

levels noted that in students' stress data logs of triggers, one student had logged six entries, with two of them specifically about their music history midterm.[35]

The use of interactive activities in class brings "attentive caring," where the students are brought into the present through the professor's interest and care, making them more eager to learn.[36] There were forty-six responses to the question about what would have made participants' experiences as FGCS in the music history classroom easier. Of these, twenty-two responded with more interactive learning. There are two reasons for this: less passive listening and more community interaction aids learning.[37] Active learning activities are often fun, encouraging student engagement and learning.[38] The survey respondents' opinions here are consistent with the Institute for Higher Education Policy's recommendation for "redesigning developmental and/or general education as a means to advance first-generation students to discipline-specific courses."[39]

Some survey responses indicated practices that benefit not only FGCS but also all music students. This is consistent with the principle of universal design for learning (UDL): what benefits one, benefits all.[40] For example, of the forty-six respondents, nineteen noted that lower materials cost would have been helpful.

Many survey respondents believed that acquiring necessary musical skills was also important. Twenty-one out of forty-six respondents noted that taking a one-semester course on the necessary score reading, active listening, and research skills for music history would have benefitted them. I was lucky: my undergraduate institution offered a course that was a one-hour weekly corequisite with the first semester of the sequence and was taught by the same instructor. This kind of course reflects the "embed[ding of] developmental coursework alongside credit-bearing courses and student success courses and support structures to aid success."[41] One respondent noted that it was specifically because of the research requirements that they did not do well in music history. Another equated research skills with self-guided learning for which they were not prepared. Yet another said they did not notice any deficits in their writing until they started writing long music history papers. Several respondents also noted difficulty in achieving listening skills.

Recommendations

We can do a few things to improve our courses based on the survey feedback. We could embed skills acquisition in existing credit-bearing courses like music history. We could encourage disclosure by having students submit a twenty-five- to fifty-word biographical sketch on the learning management system before classes begin with a set of leading questions about their hobbies, career aspirations, and favorite music.[42] This helps build relationships between faculty and students, which aids FGCS retention.[43] One study showed that FGCS building meaningful interactions with professors, such as aiding them in research or creating student-faculty partnerships, promotes student success including higher GPAs.[44]

Embedded peer tutoring can benefit FGCS.[45] According to my survey, eleven of the forty-six respondents noted that peer tutoring or peer partners would have been beneficial. At one of my former institutions, all music history courses have an embedded tutor, a student who previously took the course and did well. However, not many of the students use this opportunity, despite knowing about it on the first day. One way to encourage students to use support systems might be to incentivize tutoring.

Having a peer partner in the course could also be beneficial. This works particularly well for music majors because by the time they get to the music history sequence, most students know others from ensembles, studios, or other classes.[46] Peter Burkholder advocates for peer learning in graduate music history courses; this would also benefit undergraduates.[47] Students reluctant to be matched with a peer partner could form relationships with other students if faculty use the think-pair-share technique as part of class. Pairing students helps them to build relationships and friendships, creating a sense of belonging crucial for FGCS retention.[48] Our social nature is directly connected with successful learning. This link with emotion and positive student outcomes connects to pedagogical caring.[49]

We can also encourage use of open-access materials. Initiatives such as *Open Access Musicology (OAM)* and IMSLP scores or recordings work toward addressing this problem.[50] Some universities are moving toward no-cost courses, and many universities ask their faculty to place required textbooks on reserve. Affordable and Open Educational Resources (OERs) are increasingly utilized; some states have passed legislation on their use.[51]

Much of the necessary pedagogical redesign in music history courses could take the form of hands-on activities such as a gallery walk, LEGO polyphony, and transcription,[52] which feature culturally relevant material, or material that matters to students and their identities; this sometimes means incorporating composers and music outside of the Western art-music canon. Consequently, "for first-generation students, the inclusion of culturally relevant material and supports can strengthen retention, as these efforts build confidence and familiarity throughout the college and classroom experience," which is also consistent with the National Association of Schools of Music (NASM) guidelines.[53] FGCS' involvement level in classroom activities correlates with improvement levels in critical thinking and writing skills by the close of their junior year; this is not the case for CGCS.[54]

When lecture is necessary, one might consider using "interactive lecturing," where active learning activities blend with lecture to achieve course learning goals and reduce cognitive load.[55] Interactive lecturing is a variant of "the music lecture as Gestalt," where the whole is approached before an in-depth examination of the parts.[56] In my approach to interactive lecturing, I divide my classes into three tiered learning sections: listen, see, act. Tiered learning works well when covering subjects such as the evolution of music notation.

When teaching students Renaissance music notation, I present the listen portion of the material as lecture. In the see portion, I show the students a short video on moveable musical type. The act portion includes two parts. First, I split the students into groups and give them a long LEGO plate and a set of LEGOs with mensural notation written on the side; clear LEGOs represent rests. The students use the rhythms to compose "rhythmic polyphony" by stacking rows on the plates, each row representing one part. The students must understand that the values are immutable so that everything must line up. Once each group finishes, they put one person on each part and clap the piece for the class. The second part of the act portion occurs once they understand how the rhythm works. I teach them how to transcribe the notation and have them work in pairs to transcribe two easy examples. Having students do participatory activities not only builds community among students but also allows the instructor to check understanding.

I use technology to address students' insecurity on etiquette or engage shy students. Technology is effective for teaching FGCS because they are actively engaged with their courses and university writ large, including staying connected with student-support programs, but it can also be a barrier.[57] With Padlet, I can keep a pad up on the screen for students to ask questions during the lecture part of the class in real time without having to identify themselves. For review sessions or quick check-ins, I use Kahoot. This is useful because after class, I can pull a spreadsheet showing how my students answered, check for problems, and reach out to the students.

Conclusion

The strategies presented here are unique to the music history classroom because they consider the specific learning outcomes of music history classes, but some could work for other academic music courses. As a shy student who felt that there was no place for me in the music history classroom, these are strategies that would have not only allowed me to better engage with the material but also offered me a stake in the classroom activities and made me feel more comfortable. It is not coincidental that some of the strategies presented here are also consistent with suggestions for the reworking of pedagogical design laid out in a report on FGCS success.[58]

We must care for our music history students, whether they are underrepresented and/or minorities, have disabilities and/or neurodivergence, and/or are FGCS. This creates a student-centered model that does not focus on perceived deficits; "this vision of student capacity to learn or preparation to learn is inseparable from a vision of education for equity, social justice, and democratic well-being. It embraces all categories of difference that students embody."[59] Although the individual students' needs are as varied as the students, I have provided a list of ways that we can best serve our FGCS music majors given the specialized nature of the music history classroom. While these techniques would help FGCS, they remain best practices to serve all students, regardless of race, income, or status. To promote a caring learning environment, we must constantly reevaluate not only our pedagogical methods but also our students and ourselves.[60] We should also ponder whether FGCS need care so they can better assimilate to college or if colleges must rethink their reasons for exclusivity in the first place. Ultimately, we should reframe the study of music history so that it becomes personally meaningful to students.[61] Those of us who are FGCS are ideally situated to model success and care, encouraging FGCS to also care for themselves.

Notes

1. Lee Ward, Michael Siegel, and Zebulun Davenport, *First-Generation College Students: Understanding and Improving the Experience from Recruitment to Commencement* (San Francisco: Jossey-Bass, 2012), 1–2.

2. Kallie Clark, *Decoding College: Stories, Strategies, and Struggles of First-Generation College Students* (Molena, GA: Rowe Publishing, 2017); Cynthia Demetriou, Judith Meece, Deborah Eaker-Rich, and Candice Powell, "The Activities, Roles, and Rela-

tionships of Successful First-Generation College Students," *Journal of College Student Development* 58, no. 1 (2017): 19–36; Sarah O'Shea, Josephine May, Cathy Stone, and Janine Delahunty, *First-in-Family Students, University Experience, and Family Life: Motivations, Transitions, and Participation* (London: Palgrave Macmillan, 2017).

3. The First Scholars Program of the Suder Foundation, accessed August 2, 2019, http://www.firstscholars.org. There are several definitions of FGCS and this definition is only one.

4. O'Shea et al., *First-in-Family Students*, vii.

5. Alice Araujo and Andrea Anastasiou, "The Role of Generational Status, Program Affiliation, and Cultural Background in the Performance of College Students," in *The Invisibility Factor: Administrators and Faculty Reach Out to First-Generation College Students*, ed. Teresa Heinz Housel and Vickie Harvey (Boca Raton: BrownWalker Press, 2009), 47.

6. Lisa Nunn, *33 Simple Strategies for Faculty: A Week-by-Week Resource for Teaching First-Year and First-Generation Students* (New Brunswick, NJ: Rutgers University Press, 2018), 4.

7. Jeff Davis, *The First-Generation Student Experience: Implications for Campus Practice, and Strategies for Improving Persistence and Success* (Sterling, VA: Stylus Publishing, 2010), 29–30.

8. Ernest Pascarella, Christopher T. Pierson, Gregory C. Wolniak, and Patrick T. Terenzini, "First-Generation College Students: Additional Evidence on College Experiences and Outcomes," *Journal of Higher Education* 75, no. 3 (2004): 265.

9. Cia Verschelden, *Bandwidth Recovery: Helping Students Reclaim Cognitive Resources Lost to Poverty, Racism, and Social Marginalization* (Sterling, VA: Stylus, 2017), 79.

10. Verschelden, *Bandwidth Recovery*, 45.

11. Parker Palmer, *The Courage to Teach: Exploring the Inner Landscape of a Teacher's Life*, 10th anniversary ed. (San Francisco: Jossey-Bass, 2007), 120.

12. Emily Forrest Cataldi, Christopher Bennett, and Xianglei Chen, "First-Generation Students: College Access, Persistence, and Postbachelor's Outcome," National Center for Education Statistics, February 2018, https://nces.ed.gov/pubs2018/2018421.pdf.

13. Valerie Garcia, "First-Generation College Students: How Co-Curricular Involvement Can Assist with Success," *Vermont Connection* 31 (2010): 47; Alfred Schademan and Maris Thompson, "Are College Faculty and First-Generation, Low-Income Students Ready for Each Other?" *Journal of College Student Retention: Research, Theory & Practice* 18, no. 2 (2015): 195.

14. J. Engle, "Postsecondary Access and Success for First-Generation College Students," *American Academic* 3 (2010): 25–48; Suzanne Mudge and Daniel Higgens, "College Access Programming: Removing Higher Education Barriers for Underrepresented Student Populations," *International Journal of Learning* 17, no. 1 (2011): 123–39.

15. Rashunda Stitt and Denise Winsor, *A Narrative Inquiry: The Experience of First-Generation College Students* (London: SAGE Publications, 2014), 3.

16. J. Engle and V. Tinto, *Moving beyond Access: College for Low-Income, First-Gen-*

eration Students (Washington, DC: Pell Institute, 2008), 3, http://www.pellinstitute.org/files/COEMovingBeyondReportFinal.pdf.

17. Ann Mullen, "Choosing Majors, Choosing Careers: How Gender and Class Shape Students' Selection of Fields," in *Clearing the Path for First-Generation College Students*, ed. Ashley Rondini, Bedelia Nicola Richards, and Nicolas Simon (Lanham, MD: Lexington Books, 2018), 233. One study, however, suggested the opposite. See Lian Niu, "Family Socioeconomic Status and Choice of STEM Major in College: An Analysis of a National Sample," *College Student Journal* 51, no. 2 (2017): 298–312.

18. Jeffrey Arlo Brown, "Friction: On Being a First-Generation Classical Musician," *VAN Magazine*, July 24, 2019, https://van-magazine.com/friction.

19. Gail Horowitz, *Teaching STEM to First Generation College Students: A Guidebook for Faculty and Future Faculty* (Charlotte, NC: Information Age Publishing, 2019).

20. Ward, Siegel, and Davenport, *First-Generation College Students*, 86, 88.

21. Palmer, *Courage to Teach*, 10.

22. Paolo Freire, *Pedagogy of the Oppressed*, 30th anniversary ed., trans. Myra Bergman Ramos (New York: Continuum, 2000); bell hooks, *Teaching to Transgress: Education as the Practice of Freedom* (New York: Routledge, 1994); bell hooks, *Teaching Community: A Pedagogy of Hope* (New York: Routledge, 2003); Palmer, *Courage to Teach*.

23. Bianca Williams, "Radical Honesty: Truth-Telling as Pedagogy for Working through Shame in Academic Spaces," in *Race, Equity, and the Learning Environment: The Global Relevance of Critical and Inclusive Pedagogies in Higher Education*, ed. Frank Tuitt, Chayla Haynes, and Saran Stewart (Sterling, VA: Stylus, 2016), 72–73.

24. Williams, 73.

25. Williams, 76–77; 79.

26. Amanda Oleson and Matthew Hora, "Teaching the Way They Were Taught? Revisiting the Sources of Teaching Knowledge and the Role of Prior Experience in Shaping Faculty Teaching Practices," *Higher Education* 68 (2014): 29–45.

27. Maggie Berg and Barbara Seeber, *The Slow Professor: Challenging the Culture of Speed in the Academy* (Toronto: University of Toronto Press, 2016), 45–46.

28. Barry Cherkas, "A Personal Essay in Math? Getting to Know Your Students," *College Teaching* 40, no. 3 (1992): 83–86; Thomas Hawk, "Getting to Know Your Students and an Educational Ethic of Care," *Journal of Management Education* 41, no. 5 (2017): 671.

29. My institution's institutional review board approved this survey in April 2019.

30. Kerry Landers, *Postsecondary Education for First-Generation and Low-Income Students in the Ivy League* (New York: Palgrave Macmillan, 2018), 4. For more on this pedagogy of disclosure, see Mary Natvig's chapter in this volume.

31. Matthew Baumer, "A Snapshot of Music History Teaching to Undergraduate Music Majors, 2011–2012: Curricula, Methods, and Objectives," *Journal of Music History Pedagogy* 5, no. 2 (2015): 32.

32. Thomas Buchanan and Edward Palmer, "Student Perception of the History Lecture: Does This Delivery Mode Have a Future in the Humanities?" *Journal of University Teaching & Learning Practice* 14, no. 2 (2017): 1.

33. Buchanan and Palmer, 37.

34. Matthew Baumer, "Quizmasters, Lecturers, and Facilitators: A Qualitative Study of Methodologies in Music History Survey Courses," in *The Norton Guide to Teaching Music History*, ed. Matthew Balensuela (New York: W. W. Norton, 2019), 176.

35. Scott Edgar, "Music and the Social and Emotional Challenges of Undergraduate Instrumental Music Students," *Update* 37, no. 3 (2019): 52.

36. Yusef Waghid, *Toward a Philosophy of Caring in Higher Education: Pedagogy and Nuances of Care* (Chom, Switzerland: Palgrave Macmillan, 2019), 52–53.

37. Joshua Eyler, *How Humans Learn: The Science and Stories behind Effective College Teaching* (Morgantown: West Virginia University Press, 2018), 73.

38. Michael Tews, Kathy Jackson, Crystal M. Ramsay, and John W. Michel, "Fun in the Classroom: Examining Its Nature and Relationship with Student Engagement," *College Teaching* 63, no. 1 (2015): 24; Sarah Rose Cavanagh, *The Spark of Learning: Energizing the College Classroom with the Science of Emotion* (Morgantown: West Virginia University Press, 2016), 6.

39. Institute for Higher Education Policy, "Supporting First-Generation College Students through Classroom-Based Practices," September 2012, 15, http://www.ihep.org/publication/supporting-first-generation-college-students-through-classroom-based-practices/.

40. Thomas Tobin and Kirsten Behling, *Reach Everyone, Teach Everyone: Universal Design for Learning in Higher Education* (Morgantown: West Virginia University Press, 2016), 5–6.

41. Institute for Higher Education Policy, "Supporting First-Generation Students," 15. Also see John Spilker's essay in this volume.

42. Spencer Benson, "First Generation College Students: A Journey without Maps," *Scholarly Teacher*, March 13, 2019, https://www.scholarlyteacher.com/post/guiding-first-generation-students/.

43. Demetriou et al., "Activities, Roles, and Relationships," 34.

44. Young Kim and Linda Sax, "Student-Faculty Interaction in Research Universities: Differences by Student Gender, Race, Social Class, and First-Generation Status," *Research in Higher Education* 50, no. 5 (2009): 447; Alison Cook-Sather, Melanie Bahti, and Anita Ntem, *Pedagogical Partnerships: A How-To Guide for Faculty, Students, and Academic Developers in Higher Education* (Elon, NC: Elon University Center for Engaged Learning, 2019), https://www.centerforengagedlearning.org/books/pedagogical-partnerships/.

45. Institute for Higher Education Policy, "Supporting First-Generation Students," 14.

46. However, students who know others but are shy or introverted may still find these interactions difficult.

47. Peter Burkholder, "Peer Learning in Music History Courses," in *Teaching Music History*, ed. Mary Natvig (London: Routledge, 2002), 205–23.

48. Ian Pratt, Hunter B. Harwood, Jenel T. Cavazos, and Christopher Ditzfeld, "Should I Stay or Should I Go? Retention in First-Generation College Students," *Journal of College Student Retention: Research, Theory & Practice* 21, no. 1 (2017): 3.

49. Eyler, *How Humans Learn*, 73, 129.

50. See Open Access Musicology, accessed March 23, 2021, https://openaccessmusicology.wordpress.com/about/International Music Score Library Project (IMSLP) https://imslp.org/.

51. To see if your state has such legislation, visit SPARC, "OER State Policy Tracker," accessed August 2, 2019, http://www.sparcopen.org/our-work/state-policy-tracking/.

52. Reba Wissner, "Using Gallery Walks for Engagement in the Music History Classroom," *Engaging Students: Essays in Music Pedagogy* 6 (2018), http://flipcamp.org/engagingstudents6/essays/wissner.html; and Reba Wissner, "Teaching Christian Chant in a Jewish Music Context," *Journal of Music History Pedagogy* 8, no. 2 (2018): 1–18.

53. Institute for Higher Education Policy, "Supporting First-Generation Students," 16; National Association of Schools of Music, "The Basic Value of Music Study: Ideas for Spreading the Word" (1999), 18, https://nasm.arts-accredit.org/.

54. Pascarella et al., "First-Generation College Students," 273–74.

55. Elizabeth Barkley and Claire Howell Major, *Interactive Lecturing: A Handbook for College Faculty* (San Francisco: Jossey-Bass, 2018), 16; Christine Harrington and Todd Zakrajsek, *Dynamic Lecturing: Research-Based Strategies to Enhance Lecture Effectiveness* (Sterling, VA: Stylus, 2017), 9.

56. Jamie Fister, "The Music Lecture as Gestalt," in *The College Lecture Today: An Interdisciplinary Defense for the Contemporary University*, ed. Lee Trepanier (Lanham, MD: Lexington Books, 2019), 145.

57. Heather Rowan-Kenyon, Ana M. Martínez Alemán, and Mandy Savitz-Romer, *Technology and Engagement: Making Technology Work for First Generation College Students* (New Brunswick, NJ: Rutgers University Press, 2018), 11–12.

58. Institute for Higher Education Policy, "Supporting First-Generation Students," 15.

59. Tia Brown McNair, Susan Albertine, Michelle Asha Cooper, Nicole McDonald, and Thomas Major Jr., *Becoming a Student-Ready College: A New Culture of Leadership for Student Success* (San Francisco: Jossey-Bass, 2016), 134.

60. See Sandra Yancy McGuire, *Teach Students How to Learn: Strategies You Can Incorporate into Any Course to Improve Student Metacognition, Study Skills, and Motivation* (Sterling, VA: Stylus, 2015).

61. George Kuh, "Making Learning Meaningful: Engaging Students in Ways That Matter to Them," *New Directions for Teaching and Learning* 145 (2016): 51.

CHAPTER 13

New Waters in Music

Recognizing and Processing Trauma While Trying to Diversify a School of Music's Curriculum Offerings

AMANDA CHRISTINA SOTO

Journalist Aaron Cantú describes the image (Figure 12.1) of the Mexico/New Mexico border as follows: "The border line glows red like a re-opened scar ripping through flesh-colored earth, a reminder that the process of colonization is never complete so long as there are people around to resist it."[1] This image was featured on the poster advertising the Decolonizing Nature Conference held in Albuquerque in 2017, where activists, scholars, and members of the public converged to confront the threat that colonialism's legacy posed to our earth. I experienced and continue to experience similar threats to my identity as I navigate the landscape of music in academia as a native Tejana (Texas-Mexican American) who grew up in the southernmost Texas-Mexico *frontera* (borderland). I grew up minutes away from the Rio Grande, which separates Texas and Mexico—a river that is not a place of physical or spiritual nourishment, but a river that represents sadness, separation, division, hostility, pollution, and the death of people and of animals. There are few places along the riverbank to admire its beauty because of border walls, border patrol compounds, and barricades. The dichotomy and the inherent messiness of the borderlands is reflected in my personal experience navigating my musical studies from public school through to my experiences as an associate professor of music education at a large public university in Central Texas. As I will explore in this chapter, the scars that I acquired along the way were reopened as I pushed for change within the curriculum of a school of music. I found myself at a point where I could no longer suppress the trauma that I had been living with for so long, and am now learning to find a way to process this trauma, and heal myself in the process.

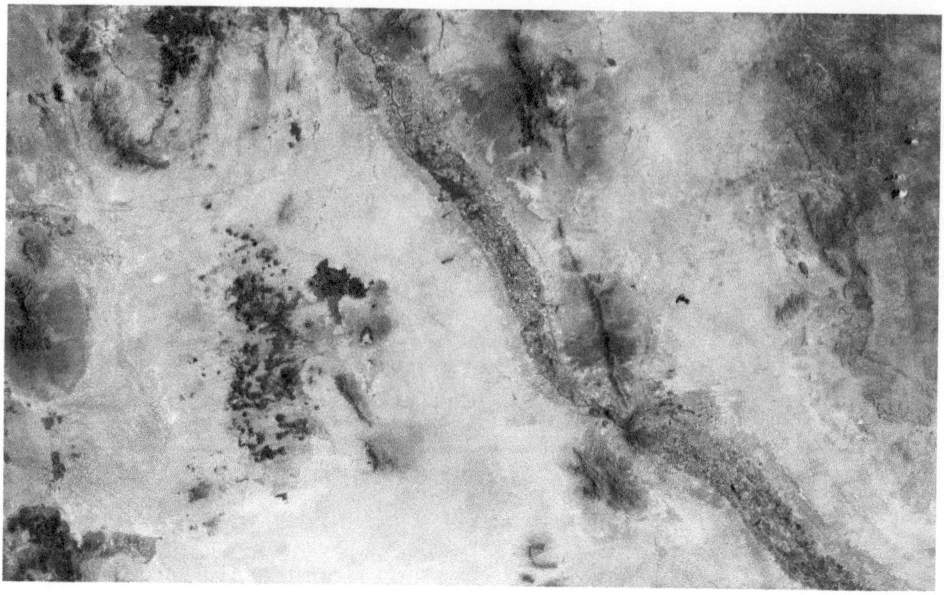

Figure 13.1. Decolonizing Nature: Resistance | Resilience | Revitalization 2017 Conference image (Mexico/New Mexico borderland, NASA Landsat, courtesy of NASA Goddard Space Flight Center and U.S. Geological Survey)

Introduction

This essay unpacks the challenges of being a *Tejana* (Texas-Mexican) music faculty member at a school of music in the southern United States. Drawing from personal experiences and my professional experience, I explore and consider the ways my past influenced and continues to influence my teaching and research in higher education, and I consider the inherent trauma I have been carrying as a result of these experiences. Finally, I consider strategies for an intersectional reenvisioning of inclusion and diversity that include acts of care for both faculty and students who find themselves to be outsiders in their schools of music.

Out of the Frontera (Borderland)

Just in the way we need to understand our students' full selves—their histories and musical backgrounds—in order to best teach them in a careful way, as the editors write in the introduction to this volume, it is also imperative that we as instructors acknowledge our fullest selves when considering how we came to this work in music. Growing up, I was entrenched in Mexican, American, and

Texan culture and worked to assimilate as a second/third-generation Mexican American. I made it out of my small town in the "Valley" and worked my way through schooling to secure and receive tenure as an associate professor in music education in a large public university in Central Texas. My musical experiences have been complicated and unique. From birth I was surrounded by the sounds of conjunto, Tejano, and mariachi music, but was also exposed to Mexican pop star Juan Gabriel, who sang popular Spanish-language music. I was also surrounded by the sounds of American popular music of the 1980s and 90s and knew every lyric to every song sung by Karen Carpenter and the Beatles. Music was always present in my household, at church, within family functions, and at school. My cultural music was not offered formally in my public school music education. I began playing the flute in sixth grade band and continued through high school, where I served as the drum major for two years. At the same time, I was active on the dancing scene at quinceañeras, weddings, celebrations, dance halls, and anywhere there was a Tejano group performing. My friends and I would even make our way into parties at the local dance hall with our fake presents just to get in and dance to the awesome conjunto or Tejano group that was hired.[2] I had, effectively, two musical lives, and unfortunately, I felt that one was better than the other. I always held my band music and classical art music in high regard, while I thought my cultural music was just for fun and not that important. I later came to realize that those feelings were reflected in the way that I saw myself and my family's culture as I struggled hard to be American or "white" throughout high school and in college.

My life was forever changed during my undergraduate studies when I was able to take several ethnomusicology courses, participate in an Ewe Ghanaian drumming ensemble, and experienced several study-abroad programs in the United Kingdom and in Ghana. It was then that I realized there was so much more music to study, explore, and feel connected to than the music that I performed and taught in the instrumental band setting. Those experiences changed my life path, and I made the switch to major in ethnomusicology for my master's degree in the Pacific Northwest. It took me moving across the entire country to be able to study and learn about my own cultural music (conjunto) within the formal university system.

Finding a Home

It can be lonely when you are one of two faculty of color within a school of music. This was the case at my first university job. Even though everyone was nice, I still felt out of place. It was luck that brought me into contact with the faculty in the modern languages department, who I could connect with on a deeper level and was supported by through my time there. Microaggressions from the community, racist comments on some student evaluations, and backlash from trying to incorporate a multicultural music education course in the curriculum made that teaching experience a very traumatic one, which made me seek refuge in the support of an Ombudsman, and a therapist with whom to work through the trauma.

Shortly after that experience I applied for a position at another university, in response to a search. After doing some research, I realized that there was an active and progressive Latin music studies program with degrees in both mariachi and salsa. I was also called to this position since it was physically close to family and to my area of research, while being culturally familiar. I applied and fortunately got the job. My third day on the job, I met up with the director of the Latin music studies (LMS) area and have been part of the LMS faculty ever since. It was a breath of fresh air to be able to be in LMS faculty meetings where English and Spanish would be spoken. It was amazing that we could speak truthfully to the issues and barriers that we were encountering with regard to the music genres we were working within. Sometimes tamales (traditional Mexican food made of masa mixed with other ingredients and steamed in a corn husk) would show up at a meeting or mariachi musicians would appear at an informal faculty gathering. I finally felt like I belonged and fit in. I cannot tell you how wonderful it was to hear the sounds of mariachi and salsa in a music building. I never thought I would hear them in this space. I had found my home—and had not needed to assimilate to be there.

Processing Historical Trauma

One Friday morning, I found myself observing a mariachi rehearsal and was amazed by the level of musicianship from our students. I then attended the Latin Music Seminar class that took place directly after the mariachi rehearsal. They had some guest conjunto musicians who gave a lecture-demonstration. It was toward the end of this class that tears started to form. I struggled to compose myself. I then realized why I was crying. I was sad and angry that it had taken this long to have music that defined me culturally being played and part of a class in a university school of music. I quickly left after the class was over and went to my office and just sobbed. Even though I was aware of the discrimination and of the exclusion of my cultural music from school-of-music ensembles and from the curriculum at most institutions, I had not really processed it on a deeper level. My scar had been reopened and I was bleeding. I am still processing it as I write this essay so that I may come to a place of healing and peace.

Supporting Faculty

It is important for faculty who are being marginalized within the academy to understand and process their trauma. It is of course worth mentioning how unfathomable it is that so many faculty of color need to acknowledge and then heal from the traumas experienced as the result of the exclusive spaces that schools of music often are. This personal account resonates powerfully with Loren Kajikawa's "The Possessive Investment in Classical Music," in which he notes the ways that most U.S. schools of music were "built on a culture of exclusion,"[3] a pervasive attitude in which non-Western practices, techniques, and even musics are relegated to the periphery of both the curriculum and the schools.

I was/am mad because my culture was worthy of study and was/is being excluded in the curriculum and degree programs. I was/am mad because I never learned about my own musical culture besides the informal knowledge I soaked in being around it. I was/am mad that because of this I thought of my culture, my music, and myself as being lesser than other musical cultures and than others.

Most significantly, I was/am mad as I think about the other Mexican American children or children from other cultures that have gone and are going through the same trauma that I went through. This has been difficult to process and I find it difficult to continue on in a system that still perpetuates these ideologies. I often struggle daily with the choice to stay in an academic and music education system when there has been little change. I personally process this trauma by talking about it with my colleagues, students, family, and friends. I am processing it through writing this essay. I process it through counseling. I will continue to process it through creating concrete systemic change to curriculum and degree programs whenever I can. This work is triggering and painful as it reopens old scars and sometimes creates new ones. It is exhausting but necessary work.[4]

Deans and directors should be aware of this trauma and emotional baggage that faculty of color struggle with even if they do not discuss it. There are several ways to support diversity work and faculty of color:

1. Do not overload faculty of color with service obligations;
2. Factor in time for faculty to mentor and do the extra work to support their students of color, and count diversity efforts as part of the tenure and promotion requirements;
3. Give equal or more support (financing, space, and time) to classes and ensembles that support diversity in the school of music, recognizing the inherent inequalities in the system that values band, choir, and orchestra;

4. Give space for writing and support by checking in with faculty and asking them what they need and telling them about the resources that are available to them—like faculty development leave funding for special projects;
5. Give them clear expectations for tenure or other job requirements and help mentor them through the process—reviewing third-year and tenure portfolios, giving suggestions, and so forth;
6. Do a comprehensive and supportive review of their teaching practices rather than rely on student evaluations alone because of inherent bias in the system;[5]
7. Support and mandate curriculum changes that are in line with state diversity goals;
8. Be culturally and musically competent in all musics;
9. Value and support nontraditional research;
10. Support conference travel and network-building events for this faculty cohort in particular;
11. Work to reevaluate existing structures at all levels in the university, and to dismantle the inequities built within them;
12. Do not forget to equally support the nontenure and adjunct faculty of color.

Faculty of color will clearly see the environment they are working in once they begin the job. Make sure that you reach out to them personally and check in with them so that you can communicate your support for them so that they feel comfortable asking for help.

Supporting Students

In addition to processing our own trauma as faculty members in music, we need to assist our students in recognizing and processing their trauma. Students are now more aware of the inequities that exist in our society given the current climate, but too often forget the ones that exist in their own school, faculty, or department of music. I have discussed these issues with my students in class, often drawing on ideas of culturally responsive pedagogy to address these issues of inequity in my teaching. Drawing on the first chapter of Vicki Lind and Connie McKoy's book *Culturally Responsive Teaching in Music Education*, I ask my students the following questions: "Do you believe that the music you associate with your own ethnic and cultural heritage was reflected in the music curriculum you studied at any educational level? If so, how? If not, describe if or when you became aware of the omission."[6] This is often surprising for my students because many times they become aware of this gap when I ask this question during their junior year of college. It is imperative that students are able to dissect, unpack, and discuss these issues within all of the music and music education courses, thus positioning themselves and their own complex musical histories and experiences within the music curriculum. My students should learn to use a critical lens when evaluating music curriculums and programs. We analyze the Orff, Kodály, Feierabend, and Dalcroze/Eurhythmics music teaching methods through the lens of culturally responsive teaching and pedagogy. I have them strategize ways in which to modify key elements within those methods in order to be culturally responsive and student centered.

I acknowledge that I do this work now because I have tenure. Previously I was too afraid to include these topics in my courses because of past experiences. As I strive to incorporate these topics and needed discussions in my classes, I have learned that students are talking about this within their social circles and are having these important discussions outside of the classroom. They want to talk about it and deal with it but are afraid to bring it up to the professors because of inherent power dynamics in institutions such as those we work in in higher-education music. We as (tenured, nonprecarious) faculty can express that it is a safe place to come and ask questions, to challenge the status quo, and to express unpopular opinions about what is happening in the school of music or in the field of music education in general. I let them know that they do in fact have power and can ask for change.

Faculty can provide support to assist students to work through their unbelonging. Faculty can share their personal stories, show emotion, and direct students to resources and organizations that can professionally help them. Faculty can also let the students know that they see, hear, and understand their concerns and communicate the actions they are taking to make a change. Creating a music education organization or club that is used to discuss equality and inclusion in music education can be another way for students to discuss these issues and to send a message to the administration that things need to change. I let the students know that these feelings are normal and that it is important to acknowledge them and to learn how deep they may be buried. I share my personal story of how I suppressed those emotions because I wanted to hide the scar. I am learning not to cover up my scars but to reveal them and tend to them because they are a part of who I am and who I will become.

Imposter Syndrome

I have often felt incompetent or unworthy because I always felt behind musically or academically when I compared myself to classmates during my undergraduate and graduate studies. I often attributed my shortcomings to a lack of personal worth and felt I was not smart, talented, or driven enough and felt like an imposter. I have always questioned whether I truly earned an acceptance into an education program, award, or scholarship or whether it was because of my ethnicity.[7] These thoughts still run through my head in my professional career. Even though I was privileged compared to others in my secondary education, I was unaware of the privileges that others had in music and education. I had to come to grips with the fact that I had almost no private music instruction, a beginner-level instrument with many problems, and very little instruction in music theory, aural skills, history, composition, and improvisation. It took a while to understand that my academic schooling in kindergarten through twelfth grade also had many gaps. It has been a long journey of wading through these muddy and dirty ideas about myself in order to realize my worth, strength, and abilities.

I do my best to explain to the students how the system has failed them or has made their journey more difficult. As I now sit on the other side of the fence of a professor, I have a clear understanding of the game and what it entails. I try to pull the curtain back for my students and try to explain the game to them and how to play it. I do my best to build up their confidence and to let them know that they are worthy of being here and they have the power and ability to do anything they choose. I try to explain to them that almost everyone needs assistance in various ways and/or extensions in one way or another. I try to explain the unfairness of the process and give them guidance on how to navigate the system since many are unfamiliar with it. I try to let them know of the various support services and rights that they have as students.

Most students like to believe that they will be successful if they just fall in line with the societal and program expectations, study hard, get good grades, and complete all expectations. However, systemic barriers and systems work to keep some students in the dark and struggling.[8] In order for our students to successfully navigate the system, it is imperative that they are educated about the inherent inequities within the curriculum and degree programs, financial barriers, available jobs, and other obstacles they will uniquely face. They can learn this through classroom lectures and discussions, professional development outside of the classroom, and an examination of the system of music education in their own state and community, and through personal conversations.

Colliding Worlds: Hispanic Musicking under the Classical Western Paradigm

Even though there has been much advancement in establishing music degrees in both mariachi music education and a graduate performance degree in either mariachi or salsa, the struggle to exist and expand is continuous. As the Latin music studies area is housed within a classical Western school of music at my institution, it has been relegated to the margins in thought and practice when resources are allocated. This next section will provide some historical context and briefly describe some of the challenges the LMS area has faced as it has tried to carve out a spot in an already crowded table that is a traditional Western school of music by creating a mariachi specialization within our program. I will then share suggestions for working within and around the margins.

Hispanics make up 40.2% of the population of Texas, and of that 40%, 86% are of Mexican descent.[9] Hispanics outnumbered whites in Texas in 2021.[10] Within the Texas public schools, Hispanics account for 52.7% of over 5 million enrolled.[11] With this shift in demographics in the state of Texas, it is not a surprise to see the proliferation of mariachi ensembles in public schools and within university music programs across the state of Texas and beyond, as well as their relevance and meaning for students involved in them.

Mariachi music education took root in Texas in the late 1960s in the San Antonio area. It was not until 2007 that the University Interscholastic League (UIL) allowed mariachi ensembles to participate as a medium ensemble as part of the solo and ensemble events that take place in the twenty-eight UIL regions in Texas.[12] The chamber-ensemble contest offered mariachi ensembles a chance to participate in UIL,[13] but historically mariachi ensembles favored participating in the Mariachi Vargas Extravaganza held annually and other mariachi festivals sponsored by the Texas Association of Mariachi Educators (TAME). Recently, UIL began a state mariachi festival that required mariachi ensembles to participate at a regional-level concert contest to qualify for the state festival. It began with fifty-five schools in 2016 and rose to over seventy high schools participating by 2019.[14] TAME also includes an all-state mariachi ensemble composed of musicians who auditioned from across the state and perform at the annual music-education convention. Furthermore, as the number of mariachi ensembles in public schools increases, so does the need for qualified and teacher-certified mariachi music educators. Many of the school mariachi groups have been taught by mariachi musicians who were hired at a paraprofessional level or are certified music teachers with either some or no experience with mariachi. Our Central Texas university has been producing state-certified music teachers with a specialty in mariachi music since 2005, when they offered a mariachi certificate, which later developed into a minor for music education degree students at the undergraduate level.

This school of music is centrally located in Texas, serves over 38,000 students, and is a Hispanic Serving Institution with over 44% Hispanic enrollment. The school of music has about 600 students with about 300 music education students, over 30 ensembles, and over 90 faculty. The Latin music studies area offers a mariachi minor for undergraduate students in music education in addition to a master of music in performance in either mariachi or salsa. Since 1997, there have been two mariachi and two salsa ensembles. The LMS area houses a mariachi vocal studio, a youth mariachi program, and several large events that raise scholarship money and provide a festival and workshops for local area mariachi programs. The new music education mariachi concentration degree allows for students to take private studio lessons with mariachi musicians (instead of classical studio lessons), for the mariachi ensemble to count as their major ensemble (not requiring them to take mariachi and another large ensemble), and for students to audition and enter as mariachi musicians who are both proficient in vocal and instrumental abilities. It provides mariachi instrumental and vocal techniques courses alongside mariachi arranging and rehearsal technique courses.

There were several reasons why we decided to create a mariachi concentration for music education students. The mariachi minor created many barriers and inequities for the students who were there to really study mariachi but could only do so under the instrumental or vocal concentration umbrella. First, our students' major ensemble had to be band/marching band, choir, or orchestra. This caused undue stress as students were also enrolled in mariachi each semester, had three times the number of performances in mariachi than in the other ensemble(s) they participated in, and had to pay for the ensemble credit. There were also scheduling issues that impacted the enrollment in mariachi and salsa ensembles. Many of the students had never played in an orchestra or band or sung in a choir and were learning to be bimusical along the way as they struggled to get through intense music theory, aural skills, and music history courses. Many of our students would transfer in from community colleges and were not able to get the minor or were overloaded with too many credits and would have to pay out-of-state tuition if they decided to do the minor. Furthermore, students were studying Western classical music and playing techniques in their studio lessons, with the exception of the mariachi vocal students, which added another barrier and frustration. Since they had to audition in classical music (a genre they were often not very proficient in) to enter a studio, they often did not receive performance scholarships or sometimes were denied entry into the studio or school of music. Undocumented students would also drop out because of limited financial support and because of the social and political climate that would impact their ability to even secure a music teaching job.

LMS faculty were also on constant overload because there were not enough faculty to cover the two mariachi and the two salsa ensembles. The director was responsible for overseeing four ensembles, overseeing the youth mariachi, teaching many of the courses for the degrees, securing funding, hosting community events, preparing the students for the many performances throughout the year, and competing in national competitions. The operating budget was much smaller than the budgets for band, choir, and orchestra, and it was a constant struggle to make everything work. Even with all of the setbacks and obstacles, the director always found a way through due to his devotion of his life to the program, utilizing community and human resources that he had access to after working and living in the area for over twenty-five years, and always hustling to secure additional funding.

Every year was a constant battle to fight for resources and to constantly prove the department's worth. It reminded me of a central theme from the series *Game of Thrones* and a powerful statement that Tyrion Lannister made in season five, episode nine: "It's easy to confuse 'what is' with 'what ought to be,' especially when 'what is' has worked out in your favor." It reflects part of the "is-ought" fallacy articulated by Scottish philosopher David Hume in his book *A Treatise of Human Nature* (1739), which is when an "assumption is made that because things are a certain way, they should be that way."[15] Change within the music core and music education curriculum is incredibly difficult because the original foundation of music study has been rooted in a particular system that certain people benefit from. It is difficult to let go of those benefits. Tyrion's quotation encapsulated all the feelings, actions from faculty and administrators, and the obstacles in our fight for a real seat at the table. The feeling that "we are allowed to exist" is one that has been felt throughout the LMS faculty. Even with this feeling, there is a determination and belief that this fight is important, as the director has strived to create a paradigm shift where Latin music is treated equally with the other genres within the School of Music. As we have started on this pathway by being one of the first in the country to offer performance and music education degrees in both mariachi and salsa, the hope is that the support and resources will follow in order for the program to grow and to serve as an example to other universities that hope to replicate this in other genres.

Even though my personal history and experience prepared me for the challenge of passing a mariachi concentration for our music education students, I was not prepared for the emotional toll it eventually took on me. My scar, which had turned into a scab, was ripped open and the bleeding began again. Some of this comes with the process of proposing a new concentration, but much of the pain comes from the way we were treated and the many microaggressions and issues of discrimination we experienced (outside of the music education faculty) along the way. Justifying our existence and musical culture triggered and brought to the forefront the emotional baggage that I still carried with me. Even though it has finally been passed, it still feels like we continually run into issues of funding and staffing with little support to get this new and progressive concentration off the ground.

Reflecting on this Intervention

We know that socially constructed meaning is not an individual matter: it is social. Ideology is not based on individual thought but is supported and followed by communities or societies, and as professors and scholars we perpetuate ideology through curriculum (content), pedagogy, and everyday actions.[16] When we think about antiracist and culturally relevant pedagogies, the work of

Gloria Ladson-Billings (1994), who created a pedagogy of culturally relevant teaching, has come to the forefront in education.[17] This relevant pedagogy ensures that students become academically successful because the teacher's lessons and methodology are informed by the students' backgrounds and knowledge so that students do not have to assimilate in order to be successful. Assimilation should not have to be the key that unlocks success. Integration and change needs to also be woven through the cultural and social aspects of a school of music and go beyond just course curriculum. It was fascinating to see the various components of Ladson-Billings's culturally relevant pedagogy emerge from my research on bi- and/or multimusicality and mariachi pedagogy at the collegiate level. I feel that the implementation of this pedagogy has contributed to the success of this group and area. Even though I will not speak to all the points within each of the tenets, I would like to highlight some that contributed to the various strategies that align with concepts inherent in creating culturally relevant pedagogies.

The most significant was that both faculty members were Mexican American, meaning they could relate to the students on a number of different levels and had cultural and socioeconomic understanding that came through in their use of both the English and Spanish language, their instruction, and their interaction with their students. This understanding allowed them to create a sense of home and strong community within the ensembles and area and enabled the directors to anticipate the struggles or issues some of these students could and do encounter. The director went the extra step to educate students, parents, and directors about the application and audition process, he worked with people in the school admissions office to accept academically borderline students, he worked with community agents who assisted with fundraising and other types of support, he used the department budget to hire student workers and to give them performance grants, and he coordinated events like *Feria del Mariachi* that enabled middle school and high school students to experience campus life. Finally, he provided a lot of emotional support for his students, who kept in touch with him even after they graduated as he helped them get jobs and continued the mentorship during their first few years of teaching.

It was very clear through interviews with the students that they culturally connected with the mariachi genre and found great pride in performing this music. Many conveyed that they would practice mariachi more or could be more expressive and musically competent when performing mariachi as opposed to classical music because they were more culturally connected to it. Some mentioned they were actually learning more about their culture because it was never discussed at home or within the context of their public-school music education. The director also discussed the importance of being professional and doing their best because they have to educate students and faculty in the School of Music about what mariachi is and what it can be if treated the same as other genres. Students discussed the many microaggressions they received from students and faculty, confirming the need for this.

Schools of Music as Microcosms

Our school of music environments are not removed from the cultural contexts in which they are embedded—in fact, they often reflect them. In 2016, we were reminded of this, and lived through a divisiveness on campus that reaffirmed the ongoing need for this work and for this conversation. Indeed, the river that flows through our campus came to represent in many ways the different banks and camps, and the need for bridges.

While the students felt at home in the mariachi music environment, they became particularly aware of their position as minority, Hispanic, and mariachi musicians in the period following Trump's election to office. Our campus made national news because a particularly racist flyer was posted across campus the day after he was elected.[18] Some of our mariachi students were physically and verbally assaulted and were told to "Go back to Mexico." Many protests took place on campus in response to the flyers and how they were poorly handled by the campus president.[19] In response to this, the director decided to have a musical protest response through the program selections for their next performance. He said,

> "Popurri Revolucion" was performed by our top mariachi in the fall of 2017 at the Mariachi Vargas Extravaganza collegiate ensemble competition where they placed first. The songs in this work come out of the classic repertoire of music from the Mexican Revolution. First of all, as always, we prepared and exposed the students to classic repertoire from Mexico, in this case the music of the Mexican Revolution. And secondly, it provided some valuable historical perspective to stimulate discussions about the current political landscape and the important role this new generation plays as Mariachi students, Hispanics, Texans, and Americans.[20]

This performance and experience served as a vehicle for processing their collective trauma from the events that took place the year prior. Students also expressed how they learned more about their own history and culture and connected the curriculum to their lived reality.

These experiences, along with changes to the curriculum, have provided comfort to students and faculty. They are akin to the waters of a river that can wash and clean the scars and provide nourishment to aid in the healing process. It is the same river that ebbs and flows and changes its path. Our Latin music studies area has been trying to chart a new water pathway and reclaim a space within a Western school of music through change in the curriculum and culture. The work to exist is extremely difficult because we were forced to work within a colonized structure and were bound to the university and music core curriculum. It has been an ongoing struggle to merely exist. It is this very struggle that takes an emotional, psychological, and physical toll that is layered on top of the normal stresses of academia. This leads to faculty burnout and faculty eventually leaving academia altogether. The area and faculty should receive enough support for the area to thrive, especially when it is used as the face of diversity for the school of music and for the university if that is truly a goal they all espouse.

My own long and ongoing struggle to navigate these traumas is evidence that this work does not happen overnight. It takes a constant effort to continually push for change over many generations. The hope is that the new water representing our music and culture can chart new pathways that slowly wedge their way into the cracks of a Western school-of-music system that over time will freeze and start to break it apart from the inside. Even though there are many more challenges and hurdles to come, we hope that we are carving a healing pathway, the way a river does: a pathway toward reclaiming our space, our music, and our culture with the hope of offering emotional, spiritual, and musical nourishment to those who have been a part of the musical and cultural landscape for generations.

Notes

1. Aaron Cantú, "Unfinished Business: Decolonizing Nature Conference Pits Imaginative Defiance against a Reactionary Agenda," *Santa Fe Reporter*, April 21, 2017, https://www.sfreporter.com/.

2. Conjunto music is a regional style of music that originated in South Texas and was influenced by music from Northern Mexico and from European immigrants in Texas. Bajo sexto and the accordion were the original instruments of the ensemble. Tejano music incorporates conjunto music and other modern popular genres and includes additional instruments and the use of synthesizers.

3. Loren Kajikawa, "The Possessive Investment in Classical Music: Confronting Legacies of White Supremacy in U.S. Schools and Departments of Music," in *Seeing Race Again: Countering Colorblindness across the Disciplines*, ed. Kimberlé Williams Crenshaw, Luke Charles Harris, Daniel Martinez HoSang, and George Lipsitz (Berkeley: University of California Press, 2019), 158.

4. Challenges experienced by racialized faculty are discussed in Nigel Brissett, "Teaching Like a Subaltern: Postcoloniality, Positionality, and Pedagogy in International Development and Education," *Comparative Education Review* 64, no. 4 (2020): 577–97; Flova Anthias, "Intersections and Translocations: New Paradigms for Thinking about Cultural Diversity and Social Identities," *European Educational Research Journal* 10,

no. 2 (2011): 204–17; Bryant Keith Alexander and John Warren, "The Materiality of Bodies: Critical Reflections on Pedagogy, Politics and Positionality," *Communication Quarterly* 50, no. 3–4 (2002): 328–43.

5. Aeron Haynie, "Equity-Minded Faculty Development," *To Improve the Academy: A Journal of Educational Development* 37, no. 1 (2018): 5562, https://doi.org/10.1002/tia2.20070.

6. Vicki Lind and Constance McKoy, *Culturally Responsive Teaching in Music Education: From Understanding to Application* (New York: Routledge, 2016), 20.

7. Gabriella Gutiérrez y Muhs, Yolanda Flores Niemann, Carmen G. González, and Angela P. Harris, eds., *Presumed Incompetent: The Intersections of Race and Class for Women in Academia* (Logan, UT: University Press of Colorado, 2012).

8. See, for example, Tachelle Banks and Jennifer Dohy, "Mitigating Barriers to Persistence: A Review of Efforts to Improve Retention and Graduation Rates for Students of Color in Higher Education," *Higher Education Studies* 9, no. 1 (2019): 118–31.

9. Alexa Ura, "Hispanic Texans May Now Be the State's Largest Demographic Group, New Census Data Shows," *Texas Tribune*, September 15, 2022, https://www.texastribune.org/.

10. Elena Bruess, "Hispanics Are Now Texas' Largest Demographic Group, Data Shows as Hispanic Heritage Month Begins," *San Antonio Express*, September 15, 2022, https://www.expressnews.com/.

11. Texas Education Agency, "Enrollment in Texas Public Schools, 2021–22" (Document No. GE22 601 05), June 2022, https://tea.texas.gov.

12. Daniel Sheehy, *Mariachi Music in America: Experiencing Music, Expressing Culture* (New York: Oxford University Press, 2006).

13. https://www.uiltexas.org/.

14. Bradely Kent, "Mariachi—Newest State Music Event in Texas," National Federation of State High School Associations, May 24, 2017, https://nfhs.org/.

15. Department of Philosophy, Texas State University, "Is Ought," accessed October 2, 2022, https://www.txst.edu/philosophy/resources/fallacy-definitions/.

16. Pat Russo, "Teaching for Social Justice," SUNY Oswego Center for Urban Schools, accessed July 22, 2019, https://www.oswego.edu/center-for-urban-schools/.

17. Gloria Ladson-Billings, *The Dreamkeepers: Successful Teachers of African American Children* (San Francisco: Jossey-Bass, 1994).

18. Rick Jervis, "Texas Campus Tense with Incidents Since Donald Trump Election," *USA Today*, December 16, 2016.

19. Jordan Buckley, "At Texas State, Student Activists Make Their Voices Heard," *Texas Observer*, January 25, 2017, https://www.texasobserver.org/.

20. John Lopez (retired Latin music studies director) in discussion with author, December 2017.

CHAPTER 14

Lessons in Student- and Self-Care from Trauma

A Personal Narrative

LAURA MOORE PRUETT

In this essay I offer a personal history of physical and mental trauma and recovery, and the lessons I have learned from my experiences, which can be applied in the classroom setting and beyond. The lessons are simple, but profound: in sum, we must care for ourselves and for our students to be effective pedagogues. In a post-COVID-19 world, and in a nation currently grappling with systemic racism and the dismantling of white supremacist ideologies, these lessons are even more crucial to identifying and upholding the most important reasons why we do what we do as academics and professors.[1]

I serve as director of a small but growing music program in the Department of Visual and Performing Arts at Merrimack College, an Augustinian liberal arts institution north of Boston, Massachusetts. I am well aware of the advantages and security I enjoy in the context of higher education in the humanities as well as the many forms of privilege that currently shape my life: white, cisgender, upper middle class, married with children, homeowner, full-time tenured position. In addition to my privileges, I've experienced hardships as well. By the time I started my graduate studies, I had been grappling with depression, anxiety, and panic disorder for two years.[2] Writing a dissertation exacerbated these conditions, which impacted both my emotional and physical health and my marriage. With continued therapy and medication and a lot of exercise, including yoga (I even got certified to teach yoga, which I did for several years), however, I was ultimately able to accomplish that goal. But overall, my life has been relatively peaceful and largely predictable. I successfully earned tenure and promotion and took over as chair of my department; we bought a house and cars, went on vacations and visited family, and continue to pay off our student loans. Considered in the light of broader U.S. economic statistics, my life has been privileged and well above average. I acknowledge my awareness of the dissonance between my daily existence and the much harsher realities of that of the majority of U.S. citizens.

After tenure, I felt freer to turn a large part of my academic focus to pedagogy, especially new methodologies I began adopting in my classes to enliven discussions, enrich our learning, and engage the varied interests of my students. I began presenting on curricular design at the 2016 conference of the American Musicological Society and the 2017 conference of the Society for American Music.[3] In the summer of 2017 I read Will Cheng's groundbreaking book *Just Vibrations*.[4] His thoughts on reparative work and "doing good" in the field of musicology shifted my thinking about my life's work in a way I had not anticipated. The idea of my teaching and research making a difference in someone's life was revolutionary to me—I had never really thought of my academic work as having a humanist meaning and function. By spring semester 2018 I was primed to make substantive changes in my classroom and in my publications; I was ready to shift from the singular focus on the analytic research agenda I had learned was core to being a musicologist to incorporating reparative modes of thinking and writing that placed difference and engagement at center stage. I was energized, excited, ready to make things happen.

Brain and Bones: Physical and Emotional Trauma

Then April 2018 delivered a physical injury with a complex recovery, giving me personal experience with challenges to ability and the connected issues of mental health. We had begun a modest home renovation project early in the year and had just welcomed a German high school graduate into our home; a friend of a friend, she would be staying with us for about five weeks that spring. Five days after her arrival, I came home from a Wednesday full of teaching and meetings. Heading upstairs to check on the renovation progress in the bathroom, I noticed that our ceiling fan in the master bedroom was set on its highest level. I reached up to pull the chain to adjust it, and the heavy, glass globe-shaped cover surrounding the light bulbs—which must have been loose—fell out of its fittings and struck me in the head, just above my right temple, before falling to the ground and shattering into a million fragments. It hurt. A lot. At first, I assumed I'd be fine; but the pounding headache, ringing in my ears, and light and sound sensitivities persisted beyond our children's bedtime, and after consulting with a neighbor (a nurse), we decided to go to the emergency room at our closest hospital. There, a CT scan ruled out bleeding in the brain, and the ER physician told me I had a concussion. She recommended "cognitive rest" until I began feeling better.[5]

In practice, what this meant was that each evening, I went to sleep convinced that I would feel better the next morning, only to be newly devastated when I woke up again with searing pain at the slightest sound, hypersensitivity to light, and dejection at knowing I couldn't return to teaching that day. I didn't teach on Friday, my next scheduled teaching day. I didn't teach the entire next week, and by the following weekend, it was clear that I wasn't going to be able to manage to return to the classroom anytime soon. With great regret, profound shame, and a sense of deep loss, I arranged for others to take over my classes for the last few weeks of the semester. In one case this was straightforward; I cotaught a course in Music and Politics with my colleague in political science, so she "simply" took over all the grading for our forty-student course, including their research papers and final exams. My other course that spring was The Architecture of Music (form and analysis). Since there were no other full-time music professors at my institution, our choral director took over with mixed success.

While the students rallied and the last five weeks of the semester carried on without me, I spent the days in my bed (or those of friends and neighbors, as the renovation continued), shades drawn, avoiding screens and sounds and reading large-print, extremely fluffy fiction. As an introvert, I am naturally very comfortable in quiet solitude, but weeks on end with no opportunities for intellectual stimulation had a significant impact on my mental health. I'd creep downstairs for dinner with my husband and children; they'd whisper and fidget in the dimmed light, trying not to hurt Mami's ears, and I'd eventually go back up to my room and cry, both from the physical trauma and the emotional shame and frustration.[6]

I began resuming the activities of my "normal life" after extensive concussion treatment including ocular therapy, physical therapy, and progressive extension of exposure to light and sound. Over the summer I continued my self-care but simultaneously started to build up my mental and physical strength. As August approached, I was motivated by the coming semester and the chance to begin anew, to press the reset button. I had big plans for my Music History course, a complete overhaul designed around the interdisciplinary framework of gender and sexuality. My other course was always a delight to teach: an honors section of my Concept Album course, which challenges students to be more flexible thinkers and use their creativity. These are skills that many honors students at Merrimack aren't always particularly comfortable learning and exercising. I was excited for both classes as well as returning to my regular duties as department chair.

Our family decided to ring in the new school year with a spontaneous, last-minute camping trip to New Hampshire for the Labor Day weekend. The campsite is a favorite of our neighbors; in fact, they were there the same weekend, just a few sites away. We had a glorious two days, including a spectacular and challenging hike to Arethusa Falls on Sunday with friends. On our way back to the campsite, however, we were in a one-car accident on a two-lane mountain road. At the small local hospital, I had X-rays and first learned the phrase "tibial plateau fracture"; my left tibia had been broken just below the kneecap. The doctor recommended I return to Boston for any further treatment, bandaged me up, and sent me on my way. After a harrowing night in a hotel and with the help of many friends and neighbors, we eventually made it home.

I did not teach my classes that first week. I sent an e-mail to my students explaining the situation, and pulled together some online assignments to keep them on track until I was able to return to school. One week after the accident I had surgery to implant a steel plate and seven screws into my left leg. And I returned to the classroom, in a wheelchair, the following Monday—two weeks after both the accident and the start of the semester.[7] For the next six weeks I had to use the wheelchair or crutches to get around. With the help of lots of physical therapy I was eventually able to adjust to using one crutch and ultimately took my first unassisted steps shortly before Christmas, about twelve weeks later. Even into the 2019 spring semester I continued to use a cane, especially on snowy and icy days, to get across campus. In late May 2019 I had a second surgery to remove the hardware, and I continue in my physical rehabilitation as I complete this chapter in June 2021. I still experience pain in my leg and knee on a daily basis. My ultimate goal is to return to running and complete a half-marathon in 2022 to celebrate my forty-fifth birthday.

The recuperation process after surgery, while less isolating than that of the concussion, was similarly miserable. After one day of teaching, I would return home exhausted and convalesce for the next forty-eight hours before doing it again. I wasn't able to drive for at least six weeks, so I relied on colleagues and my husband to get me back and forth. The smallest tasks seemed difficult or impossible, and I spent much of my resting time alone in a state of mourning, ruminating on all I felt I had lost—my career trajectory, my social life, my very sense of self-identity. Gradually, though, and with the help of therapy, spiritual direction, and perceptive and empathetic friends and family, my thoughts shifted to embrace all I had begun to learn as a result of both of these traumatic experiences: information about the ways in which the brain and bones work and heal; an altered and perhaps healthier perspective on my life and work (along with the illusions of control associated with both); and finally, ways in which my compulsory self-care could inform and enhance the academic endeavors of teaching, research, and service.

Care in the Classroom and Takeaways: Applying the Lessons of Trauma

The first logical outcome: I now explore ways of engaging in the work of care for students and self-care for ourselves as professors. Along with tenure, my position at a liberal arts Augustinian institution affords me a privileged place from which to experiment with methods of care in my classes and daily life. As an integral component of its Augustinian identity, Merrimack College works to foreground a focus on social justice and in particular Catholic social teaching, the seven themes of which issue a global call to care for self and others.[8] Furthermore, my interdisciplinary classes (such as Music and Politics, Music and Spirituality, and Music History and Gender) present opportunities in which tensions among diverse student identities can be made strikingly manifest and can significantly impact the quality of our discussions and group work.[9] In such courses, the application of care pedagogy—or, as the editors of this volume define it in the introduction, "the cocreation, with our students, of just, equitable, and reparative communities and spaces that empower all participants"—makes practical sense in relation to both the interdisciplinary foci and the understandable tensions that can arise during discussion. In addition, care pedagogy has the potential for wider application not only across classes in music but across the academic institution.

One contrast between my two accidents was the length of time before I returned to the classroom. Doing so a week out from invasive surgery was, in hindsight, a mistake. Frankly, I should have considered the possibility of taking the entire semester off, and I would encourage any professor who is struggling with physical, emotional, or any kind of temporary or permanent disability to reflect deeply on those kinds of choices before making them. I again acknowledge my privilege: such a decision could have been logistically relatively simple for me to make; my husband has a full-time job with benefits, our children are not babies but school-age, and they are all able-bodied. That said, full-time academics sometimes don't realize all the workplace benefits that may be available to them. Have a frank discussion with your human resources department to find out what options may exist to assist you before making major decisions about your potential workload.[10]

I resumed teaching again too soon because I was selfish: I created those classes and I wanted to teach them myself. To be sure, there were benefits to being back on campus. I gleaned energy from working with the students and colleagues within the supportive academic atmosphere of my delightfully collegial department; my work provided a distraction from my constant pain and immobility and positively shaped my rehabilitation process. But these benefits were gained at the cost of an immense physical drain on my weakened body.

On a very basic level, my physical limitations made classroom teaching complicated and frustrating. I am a physically active teacher; I walk, circulate, gesticulate, dance, jump. Being confined to a wheelchair and later a chair behind a desk felt like imprisonment.[11] I hated being still so much that I eventually started using my crutches as pointers. By the 2019 spring semester I was more mobile, and thankfully so: my two classes were in buildings almost a mile apart. Even using a cane, I sometimes needed to ask a student to accompany me across campus to navigate icy sidewalks with confidence.

My experiences with physical injuries and subsequent recoveries have also influenced the ways in which I respond to students in my classes who present with physical, emotional, or other traumatic circumstances. It is simple, and technically correct, to refuse students any accommodations until they present paperwork from the accessibility services office. Yet the process for accommodations can be lengthy and stressful in itself, making it challenging to accomplish for students already in difficult circumstances. Can we give our students more grace and opportunity, while still honoring the institutional processes and resources?[12] In spring 2019 I had a student recovering from a major concussion; my willingness to work with his mostly-invisible disability differed from how I would have handled his situation previously. We came up with ways to address his difficulties in completing various tasks, including extensions, extra review meetings, and eliminating one especially challenging assignment from his requirements altogether.[13] Many student-athletes routinely attend class with ice packs on shoulders, knees, or elbows; braces and compression sleeves, and, in some cases, crutches. For these students, it's not only the physical injury itself, but also the potential limitations from team play that can be emotionally debilitating.[14]

We must remember that every student has invisible or visible, diagnosed or undiagnosed extenuating circumstances that deeply impact their ability to work in our classes. When we assume that "the kids are all right," nobody wins. Low-stakes assignments early in the semester can both help students build confidence and give teachers an initial touchpoint of their students' abilities and challenges. As one student in Music History commented, "In the beginning of the semester, I didn't feel very confident doing the first few listening journals. However, the comments that were added onto the journal once they were returned were most helpful, and I really appreciated how you gave me time and breathing room for my music skills to develop." This student had not spoken to me about their anxiety about the assignments, but appreciated the opportunities for learning and growth at their own pace. Including such low-stakes and reflective assignments can serve to ease generalized anxiety for many students.

"A therapeutic method for my mental health": Student Responses to Care Pedagogy

Capped at eighteen students, my honors course for non–music majors, The Concept Album in Popular Music, traces the evolution of the concept album, looking back as far as nineteenth-century song cycles and program symphonies and culminating in current-day examples of the genre, including works by Kendrick Lamar, Taylor Swift, Janelle Monáe, and Beyoncé. One of the collaborative group projects requires students to complete the first several steps of producing an original concept album. The students discuss and sometimes argue before settling on an overall concept for their album; each person then writes a poem or set of lyrics related to that theme. Depending on the skill sets of that semester's students, they also work to create an album title and an album cover with text, colors, and images that reflect the concept. Sometimes they even write, perform, and/or record a song or two. This assignment requires students to be creative and to move way outside of their preferred classroom comfort zones. In my experience, honors students at Merrimack are by and large much more comfortable with clear-cut directions and rubrics detailing expected outcomes, so this kind of project can be unsettling for many of them.

In the fall 2018 semester, the class eventually settled on the concept of "mental health." For college-age young adults, this topic provides opportunities for self-reflection, personal growth, and perhaps even healing. The topic is also naturally fraught with the possibility for classroom tension, but the benefits outweigh the discomfort.[15] Student comments in end-of-semester reflections included the following:[16]

> *"The creative album project I enjoyed far more than I anticipated and I truly enjoyed doing the project revolv[ing] around mental health. . . . With my own experience with anxiety I thought that my poem was pretty powerful and it felt good to write down on paper. It also made me feel empowered because I was able to share something so personal that it made me realize how far I have come in my journey with mental health." (health science major)*
>
> *"The final outcome was extremely meaningful because it was really cool to see how we came out of this class with a beautiful album with meaningful lyrics about mental health. After discussing concept albums all semester we had finally create[d] our own." (business administration/economics double major)*
>
> *"I thoroughly enjoyed working on the creative project. I have never really truly expressed myself through poetry. . . . I thoroughly enjoyed the class and I feel inspired to write daily poems as a therapeutic method for my mental health. Thank you." (biology major)*
>
> *"There was not a part of this project that I found too difficult. I think the only thing that I was a bit hesitant about was whether or not I should have been so open in the poem that I wrote. Everything that I wanted to write about came to mind immediately after we were given this assignment, and I wrote the poem less than an hour after class ended. What I wrote meant a lot to me, but I had no idea if anybody else would be as open or transparent as me or if they would*

just write something to complete the assignment. Even though my poem wasn't too depressing or anything, it did explain a lot about what I go through, and it took a lot to present that to the class, and I was very happy to see that I was not the only person who got detailed about struggles with mental health. . . . The main thing I learned about this project is that the best writing or compilation of creative works comes from what people truly want to write about. Mental health, in our generation, has become a stigma that we are no longer afraid to address, and I think that people's poems showed that very well." (exercise science major)

While this particular project was perhaps more focused on poetry and processes of design than the sounds and elements of music, I would argue that lyrics and design can be powerful tools for self-expression, both in terms of what we choose to listen to and also how these students chose to articulate their own feelings. They can also allow nonmusicians to deepen their connection with music by participating in segments of the creative process that feel less formidable than writing songs. During the exam period, we invited the director of the honors program to our classroom, where the students described the process of creating this final project, read a few poems, and performed some of the music that resulted. She confided to me later that she had never witnessed such emotional depth and student investment in a final project before. This class and project occurred well over a year before the COVID-19 pandemic and its increased impact on our collective trauma levels; yet even as an early, tentative endeavor in the implementation of care pedagogy it serves as a concrete example of assignments that can inspire students to emotionally and creatively invest in work with reparative potential.

The other course I taught in fall 2018 was Music History I: Antiquity to the Baroque. Despite the accident, or perhaps in part because of it, I stuck to my original plan to revamp the course with a new lens of gender and sexuality studies. While we weren't able to accomplish all the projects I had conceived, we did successfully combine learning goals from the fields of music and gender studies in an interdisciplinary fashion and in ways that students found effective.[17] Care pedagogy techniques that I utilized in this class included a deeper sensitivity and giving name to the range of intersectional identities and biases we all brought into the classroom; given that students had not anticipated the gender and sexuality framework, they ultimately responded positively to my "radical honesty" and the cultivation of a safe space in which to do our collective work of music listening, analysis, and engagement.[18] First meeting them in a wheelchair, a week out from major surgery, compelled me to a new level of candor and authenticity. I could not successfully pretend to play the role of a professional, polished professor, but had to appear as I was—human and flawed, literally broken. This openness, I believe, emboldened them to share their own vulnerabilities and insecurities in a way that positively informed our interdisciplinary engagement.

Final Reflection

The pedagogy of care has recently become both an academically fundamental area of study within the discipline of music as well as, for me, painfully personal. From my vantage as a relatively recent interloper in the field of care pedagogy, I believe it is vital that we examine, evaluate, and utilize this component of our careers and teaching as much as the content of our academic research and teaching. The more recent global and national crises of the COVID-19 pandemic and the important work being done to dismantle systemic racism in the United States in 2021 bring this need into even stronger focus by shining a spotlight on our collective trauma, grief, and pain in the entire human race. We cannot effectively teach without caring for our students and ourselves; why would we even want to try? Let us treat one another with care, with concern,—dare I say, with love; we will all be the better for it.

Notes

1. See Loren Kajikawa, "The Possessive Investment in Classical Music: Confronting Legacies of White Supremacy in U.S. Schools and Departments of Music," *in Seeing Race Again: Countering Colorblindness across the Disciplines*, ed. Kimberlé Crenshaw, Luke Charles Harris, Daniel Martinez HoSang, and George Lipsitz (Berkeley: University of California Press, 2019), 155–74, for a powerful commentary on the history of systemic racism within the post-secondary music education system. In addition, the essay by Travis Stimeling and Kayla Tokar, "Narratives of Musical Resilience and the Perpetuation of Whiteness in the Music History Classroom," *Journal of Music History Pedagogy* 10, no. 1 (2020): 20–38, was among the first to consider this issue specifically within the music history classroom.

2. I had my first panic attack as a junior in college, during a rehearsal surrounded by seventy-plus lustily singing choir members. I tasted pennies in my mouth and, frantic, headed to the hospital with the departmental assistant; when the doctor explained what a panic attack was (this was in 1997, before panic disorder was well documented in the popular press), I proceeded to have another one. My privilege again played a significant role: I was able to immediately begin treatment that included both medication and therapy; I learned about my related conditions of depression and anxiety; I was able to continue these treatments throughout graduate school and beyond; and I am blessed with a supportive husband and extended family, who helped to connect my experiences to our long familial history of depression.

3. "Music and Interdisciplinarity at the Liberal Arts Institution," a presentation for Master-Teacher Roundtable: Interdisciplinary Strategies, sponsored by the AMS Committee on Career-Related Issues, American Musicological Society Annual Conference,

Vancouver, British Columbia, Canada, November 2016, and "'I Did It My Way': An Alternative Concept for Teaching American Music," a research poster for the Society for American Music Annual Conference, Montreal, Québec, Canada, March 2017.

4. William Cheng, *Just Vibrations: The Purpose of Sounding Good* (University of Michigan Press, 2016).

5. Concussion recovery research varies in its estimates of length of recovery time; the innovative and individualized UPMC treatment methods and recommendations on returning to normal life and work/school can be found at https://rethinkconcussions.upmc.com/. However, most ER physicians do not have specialized training in concussion recovery, so the generalized recommendation I received to "rest until you feel better" was both typical and not particularly helpful.

6. For more on shame and silence, see Brené Brown, *The Gifts of Imperfection: Let Go of Who You Think You're Supposed to Be and Embrace Who You Are* (Center City, MN: Hazelden Press, 2010), especially Guidepost #1, "Cultivating Authenticity: Letting Go of What People Think," 49–54.

7. An incredibly sensitive and useful resource that I encountered long after my initial injuries is Andrew Dell'Antonio's chapter "Cripping the Music History Classroom: Disability, Accommodation, Universal Design for Learning," in the *Norton Guide to Teaching Music History*, ed. Matthew Balensuela (New York: Norton, 2019), 247–60. It is listed along with many other helpful resources at the "Pedagogy Resource" page of the Music and Disability Studies blog at https://musicdisabilitystudies.wordpress.com/pedagogy/, accessed July 7, 2021.

8. Among the seven tenets are "Life and Dignity of the Human Person," "Call to Family, Community, and Participation," "Option for the Poor and Vulnerable," and "Solidarity." See a summary and links to more information at the website of the United States Conference of Catholic Bishops, "Seven Themes of Catholic Social Teaching" (Publication No. 5-315, 2005), http://www.usccb.org/beliefs-and-teachings/what-we-believe/catholic-social-teaching/seven-themes-of-catholic-social-teaching.cfm.

9. For further guidance on strategies to engage in classroom dialogue on uncomfortable topics, see Brian Arao and Kristi Clemens, "From Safe Spaces to Brave Spaces: A New Way to Frame Dialogue around Diversity and Social Justice," in *The Art of Effective Facilitation: Reflections from Social Justice Educators*, ed. Lisa Landreman (Sterling, VA: Stylus Publishing, 2013), 135–50, and Jasmine Harris, "Uncomfortable Learning: Teaching Race through Discomfort in Higher Education," in *Difficult Subjects: Insights and Strategies for Teaching about Race, Sexuality, and Gender*, ed. Badia Ahad-Legardy and OiYan A. Poon (Sterling, VA: Stylus Publishing, 2018), 248–65.

10. Clearly, these are incredibly complex and personal decisions. In addition, different options may not be available at all institutions; if they are available, there may be limitations that can start to impact eligibility for health care; and they are usually only available for full-time faculty, not contingent.

11. I am acutely aware that this verbiage may be triggering for those with permanent or temporary physical limitations or who identify as within the disability community. Yet it is the most authentic way for me to articulate my lived experience; by giving name to it in this way, I hope not to dismiss or trivialize the reality for any such individuals.

For more information on disability studies within the study of music, see Alex Lubet, *Music, Disability, and Society* (Philadelphia: Temple University Press, 2011), and Blake Howe, Stephanie Jensen-Moulton, Neil Lerner, and Joseph Straus, eds., *The Oxford Handbook of Music and Disability Studies* (Oxford: Oxford University Press, 2015).

12. I fully recognize that faculty in less secure positions than my own may need to protect their own boundaries (i.e., avoid additional uncompensated labor) and/or exercise caution against providing insufficient or nonsanctioned accommodations.

13. The assignment involved public presentation of a research topic before a mid-size peer audience, including taking questions afterward; the student was not able to handle such an environment, so we had him present his topic for the two coteachers alone, thus still reaching the course learning goals successfully and satisfactorily.

14. See Ray Wooten, "Healing into Life after Sport: Dealing with Student-Athlete Loss, Grief, and Transition with EFT [Emotional Freedom Techniques]," *Journal of Creativity in Mental Health* 1, no. 3 (2005): 89–102, and Catherine Cody Wooten, "A Heuristic Inquiry into Female Student-Athletes' Experiences of Identity Loss after Retirement from Sport" (Ph.D. diss., St. Mary's University, 2018), https://commons.stmarytx.edu/dissertations/29/.

15. Brené Brown, *Daring Greatly: How the Courage to Be Vulnerable Transforms the Way We Live, Love, Parent, and Lead* (New York: Gotham Books, 2012). See especially chapter 6, "Disruptive Engagement: Daring to Rehumanize Education and Work," 184–213.

16. Note: These student comments were not anonymous but included as part of a final reflective assignment. All students gave explicit permission to me to feature their reflections here.

17. The gender and sexuality framework for the course was initially based on a similar course offered by coeditor John Spilker at Nebraska Wesleyan University, and pairs more traditional music history texts and compositions with readings, recordings, and contemporary performances that center the general concepts of gender and sexuality as a dual lens through which to consider the history of Western music. Student reflections included the following comments: "I found that the integration of both music history and modern day gender studies was a very effective combination, as it simultaneously shined light on two very distinct topics. . . . Overall I feel confident covering the general idea of sex/gender identity." "I feel like my thoughts were curbstomped when I realized that this class was going to explore the gender and sexuality of music throughout history. The thought about finally learning about everything that is not a white man in music history excited me so much, because that's all I was ever really taught. . . . I really feel as if this course taught me way more than I was expecting to learn. I came in with an attitude that I already knew everything, and boy was I wrong. This course slapped me left and right, up and down, but in a good way."

18. For more on intersectionality, see Kimberlé Crenshaw's seminal essays "Demarginalizing the Intersection of Race and Sex: A Black Feminist Critique of Antidiscrimination Doctrine, Feminist Theory and Antiracist Politics," *The University of Chicago Legal Forum* 140 (1989): 139–67, and "Mapping the Margins: Intersectionality, Identity Politics, and Violence against Women of Color," *Stanford Law Review* 43, no. 6 (1991):

1241–99. The powerful reflection by Bianca Williams quoted elsewhere in this volume, "Radical Honesty: Truth-Telling as Pedagogy for Working through Shame in Academic Spaces," in *Race, Equity, and the Learning Environment*, ed. Frank Tuitt, Chayla Haynes, and Saran Stewart (Sterling, VA: Stylus Publishing, 2016), deserves mention again here, especially the "introductory monologue" she uses to begin her first class each semester, pages 73–74. In introducing her intersectional identity as teacher and human to her students, she invites students to simultaneously consider their own intersectional identities and confront their implicit biases from the very first shared moments of the semester.

CHAPTER 15

Mental Health and the Pedagogy of Self-Disclosure

MARY NATVIG

"We are profoundly failing our students. They seem in many ways so accomplished, so engaged with the world, yet they are also extraordinarily anxious, depressed, and overwhelmed."

—Brian Rosenberg

Case Study
Part 1

Several years ago, a friend revealed that she was four years old the first time she experienced what she now knows was a depressive episode. It periodically recurred when she was left with an overnight sitter or when she made her own childhood journeys into the world: slumber parties, summer camp, even visiting out-of-town relatives. As a college freshman, unexplained despondency plagued her the entire first semester. She withdrew after winter break, not able to overcome the dark cloud of hopelessness and misery, which her parents attributed to homesickness.

The Campus Crisis: Demographics, Depression, Anxiety, and Stress

Forty-some years ago, during my friend's freshman year, there was little awareness of mental health problems on campus or support for students experiencing anxiety (60.7%), depression (48.6%), or stress (47%), the most prevalent mental health disorders reported on campuses today.[1] Now, in the third decade of the twenty-first century, the professional and popular press have declared a mental health crisis among teens and students on college campuses.[2] We know that these issues affect retention, recruitment, and, most importantly, the health and well-being of our students.

Caring for our students means being aware of both academic and personal pressures that face them. Caring for our students means knowing them, and the first step is to understand their demographics. About 3.2 million teens (12–17) have had at least one major depressive episode, and over six million teens have had an anxiety disorder.[3] Seventy-five percent of lifetime mental health cases begin before age 24.[4] Among people aged 18–25, 10.5% have had thoughts of suicide and 7.5% have had a serious mental illness.[5] While increasingly more students arrive on campus having been treated and medicated for mental health issues, once on their own, many do not continue with prescribed treatments.[6]

White college students and students of color have similar rates of mental illness, but students of color are less likely to be diagnosed or to seek counseling due to stigma and lack of diversity or cultural competency among college counselors.[7] Among Black, Asian, and Latinx students, *imposter syndrome* often precipitates psychological distress,[8] and for Black students specifically, racism and discrimination are strong factors.[9] Black music students, who are immersed in studying works composed, performed, and taught primarily by white people, are, by virtue of their major, exposed daily to the emotional and spiritual pain of living as a Black person in America, identified as "double consciousness" over a hundred years ago by W. E. B. Du Bois.[10] The standard university music curriculum is inherently white, and decolonizing our courses, embracing a wider array of genres, and hiring faculty of color are more than political or social justice issues (though these are important). They are a means of caring for our students' very lives.

While feelings of sadness and/or apprehension are part of life's journey, depression and anxiety disorders interfere with everyday life in significant ways; they can be chronic and/or situational and require psychological intervention. Neither indicates weakness, nor can they be overcome with willpower, happy/calming thoughts, or "snapping out of it." Depression and anxiety often occur together, and though there is no single cause for either disorder, components such as genetics, illness/disability (of self or family members), grief, stress, change, and race/ethnicity are risk factors. Social environments also contribute: school shootings, racial violence, conspiracy theories, social media, skyrocketing student debt, and COVID-19 have made our students' experiences significantly different from those that many of us who now teach at the university level experienced in our college years.

Case Study
Part 2

After her first semester in college, my friend came home and enrolled at a local university. Embarrassed and ashamed, she usually lied about the reasons she had left her first school. Shortly thereafter, she was thrilled, but also apprehensive, to be accepted at the Aspen Summer Music Institute. A major depressive episode began soon after she arrived in Colorado, and in the first week, in a mental fog, she walked dangerously close to the front of a moving bus—not by accident. And she knew that back in her dorm were prescription pills which, if taken all at once, would end her misery.

My friend was not homesick. Sporadic episodes of despair continued. In graduate school she sought help at the campus health center but was told, "You're not sick enough; your grades are too high." After checking the "depression" box on her medical forms, a university physician erased it and advised her to never reveal mental health problems. In her early thirties she was finally diagnosed and treated for two depressive disorders.

Music Students and the Stress—Burnout—and Depression/Anxiety Continuum

Psychological studies within the last twenty years show that professional and collegiate musicians exhibit greater than average rates of mental health problems.[11] David J. Sternbach, a professional musician, teacher, and psychotherapist who has worked with musicians for over thirty years, warns us to be particularly concerned about increasing levels of stress among college musicians, who are more vulnerable than the general adolescent.[12] Our students spend long hours playing in multiple ensembles, taking lessons, and practicing in isolation, making them more prone to introversion and self-criticism than their peers, which Sternbach cautions can be destructive in excess.

First-year students in particular are inundated with new, often unfamiliar ways to engage with music, which suddenly becomes different from what it was in high school—moving from extracurricular to curricular. Theory and history classes, methods courses, world music, master classes, class piano, and so on fill their schedules (and music programs notoriously undervalue credits vs. hours). Time practicing and performing increase at the college level, even for those previously diligent. With crushing financial burdens, many students work an outside job. All of this contributes to overwhelming schedules, little downtime, and stress.

Addressing any kind of psychological problem in its early stages is essential. Long term, untreated stress turns into burnout, a condition of "emotional exhaustion, depersonalization, and lack of perceived personal accomplishment."[13] Studies point to higher rates and more significant symptoms of burnout among music majors than non–music majors.[14] Burnout, in turn, is associated with or can lead to numerous other conditions, both medical and psychiatric: chronic fatigue, insomnia, impaired concentration/attention, chest pains/difficulty breathing, weakened immunity, loss of appetite/weight loss, anxiety (which may lead to panic attacks), lack of productivity or poor performance, and emotions such as anger, pessimism, apathy, hopelessness, irritability, loss of enjoyment, and isolation.[15] Burnout is also associated with depression and anxiety.

Case Study
Part 3

In her room in Aspen, my friend thought about the good Samaritan who pushed her away from the bus and the pills in her room. She decided, once again, to leave her dreams behind and run from the feelings of despair. Her parents, however, wanted her to "stick it out." Thinking it was the right thing to do, they forbade her from coming home. But they did ask the family physician to call her. After their conversation he told her parents: "Bring her home immediately. Your daughter is suicidal."

How to Help?

Music units differ significantly from most university departments in that students and faculty share a common passion that often begins at an early age. They regularly engage in similar activities (practicing, attending recitals, rehearsals, and so on), and they spend significant time under the same roof, day and evening. Consequently, for better or worse, music units often function as an unusually large family. According to B. Janet Hibbs, "When a child . . . is hopeless or verging on [hopelessness], *families are incredibly, vitally important in maintaining hope*" (emphasis mine). She urges families to convey warmth, offer unconditional support, and reserve judgement.[16] Although not officially family, as faculty we can help our students by providing an accepting, supportive attitude and directing them to professional help. If we are not able to do so ourselves, we must find someone who can.

Recognizing the crisis among college students, and music students in particular, some faculty and administrators are taking steps to provide their students with professional guidance. Emily, a music major at the Jacobs School of Music at Indiana University, came to college with a previous diagnosis of depression and post-traumatic stress disorder. She tells her story in the *Indiana Daily Student* in an issue that focuses on the increase of anxiety and depression among University students. Emily writes, "When you're a music major, you're under a lot of pressure. . . . The professors aren't going to be nice to you just to save your feelings. . . . I don't know if it would be possible to have a nice music program."[17] Fortunately for Emily and her fellow music students, the Jacobs School of Music (in partnership with the university's counseling services) is one of a handful of music schools in the country with on-site mental health counseling. Students can drop in or make appointments with a counselor whose office is in the music building. Counselors also conduct educational seminars, outreach programs, and workshops for music students. They are available for consultations with faculty and staff, and same-day appointments are offered for students needing immediate care.[18]

The University of Michigan's School of Music, Theater, and Dance and the Cleveland Institute of Music provide similar on-site counseling services. Students at the Eastman School of Music have access to counselors at the school's Student Living Center. The Faculty of Music at the University of Toronto has gone further, incorporating courses on health, wellness, and performance anxiety as part of their curriculum; studio instructors are trained in recognizing mental health issues and a counselor is on-site once a week.[19]

For music units that do not have embedded counseling services, there are still ways to help. Making faculty aware of mental health issues among students, how to recognize distress, and what services are available on campus are important steps to an improved music community. Sponsor a "mental health day" and invite university and community mental health providers to exhibit informational materials and talk to the students. At the very least, ask faculty to post counseling services hours or contact information for mental health hotlines in their studios.

Faculty should be aware that students who talk about wanting to die, are feeling hopeless, are unusually withdrawn, or express being a burden to others should be taken seriously, as is any behavior that differs from the student's usual manner. These may be signs of suicidal ideation. Other indications are:

- acquiring a firearm or poison or stockpiling prescribed drugs
- increased use of alcohol/drugs
- preoccupation with death
- giving away personal items
- lack of or excessive sleep
- feelings of anger/revenge
- change in dress/hygiene
- risky behaviors

Missing lessons or a performance without notification can be a warning sign. As a faculty member, the first step is to see if the student has been missing other classes: isolation is a sign of distress.[20] If you believe a student is in a mental health crisis, reach out (or ask someone else to and follow through). Listen nonjudgmentally and offer emotional support and empathy. Most importantly, encourage the student to get help and provide information on how to do so. If possible, accompany the student to the counseling center.

If a student seems to be expressing suicidal thoughts, ask them directly: "Are you thinking of killing yourself?" and "Do you have a plan?" and "Have you taken any steps toward that plan?" (The more planning, the more the student is at risk.) Because these questions are difficult and may seem counterintuitive, or even dangerously suggestive, practice them with a partner. Asking the questions can "lance the boil" and students who are having thoughts of suicide may finally feel understood, relieved, and cared for. Talking (or asking) about suicide does not encourage the act or put the idea into someone's head.[21]

If a student indicates they are considering suicide, act immediately. *Do not leave the student alone*—take them to the counseling center or the emergency room, call 911, or follow campus policies, if available. Remain calm, comforting, and empathetic.[22]

Case Study
Part 4

Seven weeks after the Aspen incident, my friend was scheduled to transfer to the Eastman School of Music. Although she briefly attended counseling sessions, the time was too short. Depression set in shortly after arriving in Rochester; suicidal thoughts and overwhelming feelings of failure mingled with the pressures and fears of being a transfer student at an exceptional music school. What has, in retrospect, been identified as a major depressive episode lasted long into the second semester. By the grace of God, new friends, and supportive faculty, the depression finally lifted. The fear of its return, potentially triggered by another change in environment, is why this author has all three of her degrees from the Eastman School of Music.

The Pedagogy of Self-Disclosure

> "The stigma associated with mental illness is one of the most persistent problems individuals face. . . . It prevents treatment, and it impedes recovery. . . . Research on addressing discrimination and stigma has shown that individuals' attitudes improve when they have direct contact with persons with mental illnesses, when they can get to know people beyond labels and myths."[23]

Various degrees of depression have dogged me most of my life. Once I was finally diagnosed and medicated my life changed, but I continue to be monitored by a therapist and psychiatrist. I consider myself partially lucky and mostly blessed to have lived a productive and rewarding life in music—the life of my dreams.

During my thirty years as a faculty member, I've encountered many music students whose progress was hindered by mental health issues. I found myself listening to familiar stories. Per protocol, I distributed pamphlets from the counseling center and even drove students to walk-in hours when needed. As I listened to the students' stories of anguish, despondency, and often failure, my heart ached for them as I remembered my own experiences, when chronic depression nearly derailed my life. I wanted to tell these students that things could get better; there were people who could help and strategies to employ. I wanted them to know that these were not empty, *pro-forma* platitudes. I had been there.

Being well aware of appropriate lines of demarcation between students and faculty, as well as the risk of engaging in amateur therapy, I consulted with the staff of my university's counseling center and also began to investigate the literature on the pedagogy of self-disclosure, which provides a framework from which to consider motivations, efficacy, and best practices in sharing personal narratives with students.

The "self-disclosure theory" was first defined in the 1970s by psychologist Sidney M. Jourard as a therapeutic technique between therapist and client, though it can be applied to any trusting relationship that seeks mutual self-knowledge. It is also used as an educational tool that increases student engagement and motivation.[24] The pedagogical use gained currency in feminist scholarship in the early 1980s, primarily in writing and women's studies courses with the goal of breaking down hierarchies, opening new ways of learning, and empowering students.[25] Lad Tobin, who writes on self-disclosure in the writing classroom, notes: "To its critics, [self-disclosure] has been dismissed (and caricatured) as nonscholarly, intrusive, coercive, and philosophically naïve. To its advocates, it has been lauded as a path to empowerment, enlightenment, authenticity, and self-actualization."[26]

The early application of the pedagogy of self-disclosure has roots in Paulo Freire's call to eliminate the "culture of silence," giving voice to the disenfranchised,[27] and also bell hooks's belief that education is the practice of freedom and empowerment, which she maintains comes easiest to those who define teaching as less a practice of imparting information and more a means of sharing "in the intellectual and spiritual growth of our students." She writes that part of teaching is respecting and caring for our students' souls, which she maintains is essential if we desire meaningful learning.[28] Since the 1980s, feminist scholars have affirmed that "most women (and perhaps men, too) learn through a pedagogy that emphasizes connectedness between learner and educator."[29]

Focusing on the self-disclosure of identity, Janet M. Wright maintains that when teachers are forthcoming about their own struggles, students can "discover connections with themselves and penetrate barriers to understanding."[30] My own experiences with self-disclosure prove this to be true. I have never had a student, even if initially hesitant, refuse to go to the counseling center after I have self-disclosed. As Wright emphasizes, students need role models in order to "break the sense of isolation, hopelessness, and fear [regarding sexual identity]." The same issues of isolation, hopelessness, and fear affect students with mental health issues. When students know they are not alone they are comforted and affirmed.

Those who experience depression, anxiety, and other mental health issues, especially for the first time, find themselves in a body and mind that are not their own. Their psyche has betrayed them, and they are living in strange and unknown territory, bordered by shame and stigma. Many feel alone and hesitant to ask for help; they may also believe that nothing *can* help. Destigmatizing depression, anxiety, and other conditions through self-disclosure, through telling one's story, can alleviate feelings of shame, assure students they are not alone, provide hope, and penetrate barriers to seeking professional help. Thus, self-disclosure can provide a much-needed conduit between despair/failure and health/success for students suffering with mental health disorders.

The most persuasive argument for self-disclosure of mental health issues comes from a 2008 report published by SAMHSA (Substance Abuse and Mental Health Services Administration).[31] Although not focused specifically on teacher/student relationships, the document reveals that self-disclosure conclusively destigmatizes mental health issues, provides hope, and leads others to seek professional help. Although the report maintains that self-disclosure can be difficult, contributors to the study found that it also benefitted their own recoveries and helped them gain confidence.[32]

Jeffrey Berman, who uses the pedagogy of self-disclosure in his university-level writing classes, cautions that there are risks in self-disclosing: shame, rejection, misunderstanding, and ridicule and that "the more one discloses, the greater the threat of shame."[33] Therefore, those who self-disclose need to be emotionally stable and able to withstand potential consequences. It is important that the person self-disclosing is emotionally healthy in order to discern the appropriate level of self-disclosure and to gauge the effect it is having on the student. Self-disclosure is to help the student and should not be ego driven. Mental health self-disclosure should serve students by facilitating their personal and academic success and encouraging them to obtain help. It should be selective and strategic, cultivate responsibility, avoid personal glorification or self-pity (on either side of the equation), and steer clear of the "contagion effect"—when emotions or moods are spread by suggestion or influence.

Before disclosing, some questions to consider are:

1. Will self-disclosure help this student feel accepted and give them hope?
2. Will it help their quality of life and/or their academic/musical performance?
3. Will it help to remove the stigma of mental health problems and help them seek professional help?
4. Are there risks to myself or the student?

Finally, self-disclosure should not lead to amateur therapy. We are not our students' therapists, even if we have had therapy ourselves or training in counseling. Self-disclosure is not a time to focus on our own problems or impose our own solutions on our students. Although there is nothing wrong with encouraging students to get enough sleep, exercise, or eat well, we need to avoid discussions and/or advice that is best left in the client/therapist relationship. Recognizing these boundaries also protects faculty from those who might criticize the idea of self-disclosure, despite its proven efficacy.

No one is obligated to self-disclose. Age, gender, rank, or comfort level and stability within one's own mental health journey all factor in the decision to do so—or not. If a person is not comfortable with self-disclosing, perhaps there is someone else able to do so, or another way to help the student. For faculty who do self-disclose, it is important to have a support system in place and also to remember that the student's identity and situation should be kept confidential.

My own experiences self-disclosing began after I had tenure, which corresponded with my diagnosis, therapy, and medication, which helped me finally feel "normal." I rarely self-disclose in class (only if the topic arises and it is pedagogically called for). Most of the time my self-disclosure occurs during office appointments with students who are not doing well and who either reveal mental health issues to me or seem to be manifesting them. Self-disclosure is a particularly effective way to encourage students to seek help: "I've been there, I know it helps. You deserve to feel better." Now that I am "out," students who are not in my classes make appointments as well. I have also been called to the ER by music students who feared for a friend who was later diagnosed with schizophrenia. My job there was to calm and assure the student bystanders, comfort the student in distress, and encourage treatment. Experience and age can mitigate the fear, stress, and anxiety of disturbing events, and knowing that a person has lived through their own periods of darkness provides hope. My experiences with self-disclosure have been met with positive reception and outcomes.

The act of self-disclosure comes with long-term responsibilities and accountability. Once one has self-disclosed, it can't be taken back. People will want your support and input. Those who self-disclose, however, must guard their own health and time and be vigilant about their role—again, we are not therapists. Unrealistic expectations can be dealt with through kindness and referrals to professionals.

The main job of a person who self-discloses is to listen, to be supportive, to alleviate shame or feelings of alienation, to motivate students to seek help, and to facilitate academic and/or personal success. Although we may want students to remain in our music division, we need to reassure them that taking time off is OK; that they can still love music and participate in making music without being a music major (if that is in play); and that life does not unfold in a straight line. What we planned might not be how things turn out, and yet what turns out might be even better. We need to be authentic and genuine. We need to care for our students as we care for ourselves.

My own journey, which included a deep passion for music that began at a very early age, coupled with difficult, confusing, and nearly debilitating mental health issues, has given me the courage and desire to reach out to others. I believe that "to whom much is given, much is expected,"[34] and I have been given much.

Finally, self-disclosure is not the only way to help our students. Regardless of our own experiences, we can educate ourselves and help to destigmatize mental health issues, we can be sensitive to students showing signs of distress, and we can steer them toward professional help. We can encourage our administrators to promote mental health awareness and invite speakers and/or establish on-site counselors in our music units. We need to listen to our students, to believe their pain, and to realize that their world is very different from the one most of us grew up in—and ours was hard enough.

Resources

Suicide and Crisis Lifeline: 988
QPR Institute (suicide prevention training): https://qprinstitute.com
Metal Health First Aid: https://www.mentalhealthfirstaid.org
The Steve Fund (supports mental health for young people of color): https://www.stevefund.org

Notes

To Ellen K., who self-disclosed; Walling Mariea, who is wise and who listens; Ralph Locke, my friend and mentor; and Chris Watson, my beloved bard. For reading a draft of this essay and making helpful comments, my thanks to Garrett Gilmer, former director of the counseling center at Bowling Green State University, and my nephew, Samuel Theesfeld, a kindred soul.

Epigraph: Brian Rosenberg, "How We Can Help Students Survive in an Age of Anxiety," *Chronicle of Higher Education*, April 26, 2018, https://www.chronicle.com/.

1. "The Association for University and College Counseling Center Directors Annual Survey: 2019," https://www.aucccd.org/public.

2. Faculty also experience mental health issues; see Samantha Bassler, "'But You Don't Look Sick': A Survey of Scholars with Chronic Invisible Illnesses and Their Advice on How to Live and Work in Academia," *Music Theory Online* 15, no. 3–4 (August 2009), https://www.mtosmt.org/issues/issues.php.

3. Susanna Schrobsdorff, "Teen Depression and Anxiety: Why the Kids Are Not Alright," *Time*, October 27, 2016, https://time.com/, and Raychelle Casada Lohmann, "What's Driving the Rise in Teen Depression?," *U.S. News & World Report*, April 22, 2019, https://www.usnews.com/.

4. Annelle Primm, "College Students of Color: Overcoming Mental Health Challenges," *NAMI Blog*, July 16, 2018, https://www.nami.org/Blogs/NAMI-Blog/.

5. Substance Abuse and Mental Health Services Administration, *Behavioral Health Barometer: United States* 5 (2019), https://www.samhsa.gov/data/.

6. Janet Hibbs and Anthony Rostain, *The Stressed Years of Their Lives* (New York: St. Martin's Press, 2019), discussed on "College Students (And Their Parents) Face a Campus Mental Health 'Epidemic,'" *Fresh Air*, May 28, 2019; see transcription at https://www.npr.org/transcripts/727509438.

7. Primm, "College Students of Color"; H. L. Cheng, K. L. Kwan, and T. Sevig, "Racial and Ethnic Minority College Students' Stigma Associated with Seeking Psychological Help: Examining Psychocultural Correlates," *Journal of Counseling Psychology* 66, no. 1 (2013): 98–111.

8. Shannon McClain, Samuel T. Beasley, Bianca Jones, Olufunke Awosogba, Stacey Jackson, and Kevin Cokley, "An Examination of the Impact of Racial and Ethnic Identity, Imposter Feelings, and Minority Status Stress on the Mental Health of Black College Students," *Journal of Multicultural Counseling and Development* 44, no. 2 (April 2016): 104.

9. Greta Anderson, "The Emotional Toll of Racism," *Inside Higher Ed*, October 23, 2020, https://www.insidehighered.com/; Primm, "College Students of Color."

10. W. E. B. Du Bois, *The Souls of Black Folk*, ed. Brent Hayes Edwards (London: Oxford University Press, 2009).

11. See Brenda Wristen, "Depression and Anxiety in University Music Students," *Update: Applications of Research in Music Education* 31, no. 2 (2013): 20–27; Lisa Huisman Koops and Christa Kuebel, "Self-Reported Mental Health and Mental Illness among University Music Students in the United States," *Research Studies in Music Education* (November 2019): 1–15, https://doi.org/10.1177/1321103X19863265; L. S. Araújo, David Wasley, Emma Redding, et al., "Fit to Perform: An Investigation of Higher Education Music Students' Perceptions, Attitudes, and Behaviors toward Health," *Frontiers in Psychology* 8 (2017): 1558; Sally Anne Gross and George Musgrave, "Can Music Make You Sick? A Study into the Incidence of Musicians' Mental Health, Part 1," University of Westminster MusicTank, November 2016, https://westminsterresearch.westminster.ac.uk/.

12. David Sternbach, "Stress in the Lives of Music Students," *Music Educators Journal* 94, no. 3 (January 2008): 42–48.

13. Cynthia Cordes and Thomas Dougherty, "A Review and an Integration of Research on Job Burnout," *Academy of Management Review* 18, no. 4 (1993): 625, as cited in Helen Jane Orzal, "Undergraduate Music Student Stress and Burnout" (master's thesis, San Jose University, 2010), 1. See also Christian Bernhard, "A Survey of Burnout among College Music Majors," *College Student Journal* 41, no. 2 (2007): 392–401; Marilee

L. Teasley and Erin M. Buchanan, "When Music Goes Up in Flames: The Impact on Advising on Music Major Burnout," *NACADA Journal* 36, no. 1 (2016): 43–53.

14. Christian Bernhard, "A Comparison of Burnout between Undergraduate Music and Non-Music Majors," *Visions of Research in Music Education* 9–10, no. 1 (2007), http://www-usr.rider.edu/~vrme/.

15. Sherrie Bourg Carter, "Where Do You Fall on the Burnout Continuum?," *Psychology Today*, May 6, 2012, https://www.psychologytoday.com/us/.

16. Hibbs and Rostain, *Stressed Years of Their Lives.*

17. Emily Ernsberger, "State of Mind: Depression and Anxiety Diagnoses for College Students Are Up Nationally. IU Is No Exception," *Indiana Daily Student*, accessed March 4, 2021, https://idsnews.indiana.edu/news/mental-health/index.html.

18. Jacobs School of Music, "CAPS Counselor-in Residence Program," Indiana University Bloomington, accessed March 4, 2021, https://music.indiana.edu/about/student-life/health-and-safety.html.

19. Other music schools may provide on-site counseling services; those mentioned are a few examples.

20. The General Anxiety Disorder-7 (GAD-7), the Patient Health Questionnaire-9 (PHQ-9), and the Major Depression Indicator (MDI) are questionnaires that assess various mental health issues and are easily available online. Faculty may want to be aware of these documents but, as always, diagnosis should be left to mental health professionals.

21. Kristen Fuller, "Five Common Myths about Suicide Debunked," *NAMI Blog*, September 30, 2020, https://www.nami.org/Blogs/NAMI-Blog/.

22. These procedures are from *Mental Health First Aid USA: For Adults Assisting Young People* (Washington, DC: National Council for Behavioral Health, 2016).

23. Iris Hyman, *Self-Disclosure and Its Impact on Individuals Who Receive Mental Health Services* (Rockville, MD: Center for Mental Health Services, Substance Abuse and Mental Health Services Administration, 2008), https://store.samhsa.gov/.

24. See Jacob Cayan, Matthew Martin, and Alan Goodbye, "The Relation between Teacher Self-Disclosure and Student Motives to Communicate," *Communication Research Reports* 26, no. 2 (2009): 105–13; Jennifer Waldeck, "Teacher Self-Disclosure," *International Encyclopedia of Communication* (Washington, DC: International Communication Association/Blackwell, 2011); Gary Goldstein and Victor Benassi, "The Relation between Teacher Self-Disclosure and Student Classroom Participation," *Teaching of Psychology* 21, no. 4 (1994): 212–17.

25. Evelyn Torton Beck, "Self-Disclosure and the Commitment to Social Change," *Women's Studies International Forum* 6, no. 2 (1983): 161.

26. Lad Tobin, "Self-Disclosure as a Strategic Teaching Tool: What I Do—and Don't—Tell My Students," *College English* 73, no. 2 (2010): 199.

27. Paulo Freire, *Pedagogy of the Oppressed* (New York: Herder and Herder, 1972).

28. bell hooks, *Teaching to Transgress: Education in the Practice of Freedom* (New York: Routledge, 1994), 6.

29. Janet Wright, "Lesbian Instructor Comes Out: The Personal Is Pedagogy," *Feminist Teacher* 7 (1993), 29.

30. Carol Witherell, "The Self in Narrative: A Journey into Paradox," in *Stories Lives Tell: Narrative and Dialogue in Education*, ed. Carol Witherell and Nel Noddings (New York: Teachers College Press, 1991), as cited in Wright, "Lesbian Instructor Comes Out," 28.

31. Hyman, *Self-Disclosure and Its Impact.*

32. Hyman.

33. Jeffrey Berman, *Risky Writing: Self-Disclosure and Self-Transformation in the Classroom* (Amherst: University of Massachusetts Press, 2001), 22.

34. A paraphrase of Luke 12:48 (Holy Bible). My own journey to mental health has been facilitated by a faith in a higher power. However, as a faculty member in a public university, I do not discuss the spiritual aspect of my recovery unless the student brings up the topic. Even then, I proceed with caution as one cannot know what potentially damaging experiences a student may have had with organized religion. Offering unconditional love and a supportive, caring environment, giving hope, alleviating stigma, and facilitating professional help is what I believe "is expected."

CHAPTER 16

Modeling *Cura Personalis*

Caring for Our Students and Ourselves

TRUDI WRIGHT

As is documented throughout *Sound Pedagogy: Radical Care in Music*, recent pedagogy scholarship makes strong connections between well-being, enhanced intellectual growth, and student success. The content of this chapter was motivated by my personal witness to the ever-rising rates of declining mental health among college students and university faculty members.[1] As a music professor, I want to share my intentional search for better ways to care for my academic community.

In May 2017, I completed my first year on the tenure track at Regis University, which is one of twenty-eight Jesuit universities in the United States. In that first year, two Regis students took their own lives. Based on their educational behaviors, nobody suspected that they were at danger of death by completing suicide. These young people were highly motivated, smart, seemingly "put-together" twenty-one-year-olds. They were just like the students described in Julie Scelfo's 2015 *New York Times* article, "Suicide on Campus and the Pressure of Perfection." Scelfo reports that suicide rates among people ages fifteen to twenty-four have increased modestly but steadily since 2007: from 9.6 deaths per 100,000 people to 11.1 deaths in 2013. More frightening, however, is the 2014 Annual Report from the Center for Collegiate Mental Health (CCMH), which found that more than half the clients of college counseling centers "have severe psychological problems, an increase of thirteen percent in just two years. Anxiety and depression, in that order, are now the most common mental health diagnoses among college students."[2]

Consistent with the data of the CCMH, college music students are not immune to mental health struggles. In fact, music educator Brenda G. Wristen hypothesizes that music students may be more prone to perfectionism and thus mental health problems, due to the way they are trained and the competition they experience in their field, which is why she studied 287 music majors and minors at a large state institution in the Midwestern region of the United States.[3] Although her hypothesis was not completely proven by her limited study, the results are still striking. She states, "The rates of anxiety and depression are roughly equivalent to, or even perhaps slightly below those documented in other studies in general university populations." Pulling from various studies on college-student anxiety and depression, Wristen reports high rates for both and an unsettling rate of unreported and untreated anxiety on college campuses that can range from 50% to 80% of the student population.[4] This means that on a college campus like mine with around 2,000 undergraduates, 1,000 to 1,600 students may be suffering from anxiety, let alone depression or other common mental health concerns.

Mental health problems on college campuses are widespread and touch the lives of all types of students but are especially prominent for students of color, particularly those who are first-generation college students and those from low-income families, according to panelists at the 2019 Mental Health and Wellness for Students of Color Forum at the Harvard T.H. Chan School of Public Health. "While college is a time of transition for all students . . . [students of color] are not only dealing with everyday stresses unfamiliar to more privileged classmates (the poverty, increased violence, and lack of home that can plague poor neighborhoods), they are, on arrival, surrounded by trappings and traditions foreign to them, those of institutions founded by the nation's elite, usually wealthy and white, for the education of their children." Because many college campuses are ripe with incidents of repeated racism, discrimination, and microaggressions, students of color have an increased chance of experiencing anxiety, depression, and hopelessness.[5]

On campuses across our country seemingly happy and mentally well individuals, who are actually anxious and/or depressed to a potentially life-threatening degree, have been *labeled* by mental health professionals because the struggle is seen so frequently. At Penn State the condition of hiding one's anxiety under a "brave face" is called "Penn Face" and at Stanford, "Duck Syndrome," because a duck appears to glide calmly across the water, while beneath the surface it frantically paddles.[6] Reeling after the deaths of the Regis students, and knowing I was not able to help in the same sense that a trained counseling professional could, I found myself on a desperate search for answers and understanding. I was grateful to find that one possibility came in the form of a Jesuit value, *cura personalis*. *Cura* has become a guiding principle, which I am mindfully infusing into my class planning, preparation, student interaction, and community-building both inside the music history classroom and with my colleagues.[7] It is important to note that, although the Jesuits held and still hold humanism as an ideal, they, like many religious orders, were involved in violent settler colonialism, the Catholic Church's sexual abuse scandal, a position against birth control, and, of course, not allowing women to join their order. Most recently, news broke about the Jesuits running what is now Georgetown University selling 272 slaves to keep its doors open in 1838 and how they are now seeking reparation among the slave's descendants.[8] These difficult truths about the Jesuits and their institutions make the study of *cura personalis* complicated. Practitioners of this care-full teaching philosophy must wrestle with the complications of accepting its benefits while condemning other dreadful practices of the order from which it comes. These tensions continue to be grappled with at Regis University and the wider Jesuit education community.[9]

Cura personalis, a term most typically associated with Jesuit higher education, is a philosophy that pertains to all those concerned about "caring for the whole person." Although rooted in the educational practices of St. Ignatius of Loyola (the Order's founder) and the early members of the Jesuits, modern-day Jesuit educational identity is defined by the values celebrated and taught on all Jesuit campuses: contemplatives in action; finding God in all things; people for and with others; the *magis*; the unity of minds and hearts; and, of course, *cura personalis*.[10] *Cura* is typically thought about in three ways. First, it asks professors of today to act as the early educator-Jesuits: to attend to the intellectual, spiritual, and moral needs of their students, which is especially important when guiding them through the challenges of "adulting."[11] This definition is rooted in humanist thought, which was prominent when the Jesuits opened their first schools. According to Jesuit scholar Barton Geger, "The goal [of the early Jesuits] was [the] formation of a certain kind of person; a good citizen who is virtuous, articulate, magnanimous, and civic-minded"—a lofty goal, to be sure.[12]

The importance of cultivating civic-minded humans to create strong and just communities has been revisited many times since then, by Jesuit-led and humanist-minded groups and individuals. One prominent example comes from the work of sociologist Robert Putnam.[13] In his book *Bowling Alone*, Putnam reveals current Americans' reluctance to join social organizations (as opposed to Americans of the 1960s and 1970s), pointing to the erosion of the nation's social capital, which places value on social networks. Putnam explains that social capital is like civic virtue. He states, "the difference is that 'social capital' calls attention to the fact that civic virtue is most powerful when embedded in a dense network of reciprocal social relations. A society of many virtuous but isolated individuals is not necessarily rich in social capital."[14] To me, the attention we pay to our students as whole people is essential to their well-being, which then translates to their academic success in our classrooms and the community-creating adults they become. This care for community can be lacking in schools of music due to the competitive nature of performance degrees. Students are asked to compete against each other for chairs of the orchestra, first prize in the concerto competition, or roles in an opera production, which can cause unhealthy competition. Schools of music, however, can also be bastions of community when professors are modeling and promoting the ideals of *cura personalis*.

Other Jesuit scholars have examined this most widely understood definition of *cura personalis* and its function in the classroom. According to Dirk Dunfee and his colleagues, "the ideal educational experience would be tailored to the student's personality, goals, and learning style, all with the objective of empowering the student to take charge of his or her education. The more the educator knows about the student, the more likely this empowerment is to happen."[15] Although it is difficult to deeply "know" each student in the span of a semester, there are projects educators can plan to help with this process. One I use in my undergraduate music classroom is the Music and Identity Project. The main components of student inquiry include understanding music's role in their human identity, fieldwork assignments for students to connect with their family's music through interviews and live-event attendance, and an iSearch paper and presentation describing their research journey and findings.[16] This project allows students to better understand themselves—for some, it is the first time they have spent time thinking about their race, class, gender, sexuality, socioeconomic standing, ethnicity, and so forth, and how these identities position them in the world. In addition, because of the ways in which we share our findings throughout the semester, it allows the students and me to learn about one another on a deeper level than if the project were based on another research interest. This brings us to the second definition of *cura personalis*.

Cura also calls on faculty to "meet students where they are," both academically and personally, which manifests in ever-changing and ever-improving classroom exchanges.[17] In order for educators to give attention to the uniqueness of individual students and/or the cultures to which they belong, *cura personalis* asks educators to be "attentive to the particularities of students" and be willing and able to adapt to their needs and concerns. Geger suggests that our attention to this definition of *cura personalis* is an especially important one given our "rapidly-changing twenty-first century, when each generation of students can be so different from the last."[18] This, of course, includes the integration of racially and ethnically diverse ways of experiencing, teaching, and knowing, which is thoughtfully taking place in musicology classrooms across the country.[19] On a practical level, the early Jesuits learned about what their students enjoyed outside of the classroom and tried to bring those pastimes inside it. In the Renaissance and early Baroque eras, for example, the Jesuits' students loved theater, and so it was used as a teaching tool in the classroom. I feel that college educators all over the country are attending to this definition, including pedagogues in musicology. Louis Epstein and Sara Haefeli, for example, conduct a blogging project with their students in order for them to reflect on music's connection to and portrayal of race in American music and *avant-garde* expressionism, respectively.[20] These pedagogues are attentive to their students' digital literacy and have created projects that support and enhance student experience.

Recent musicological scholarship is also introducing new methods for analyzing music to push the discipline beyond its narrow gaze at strictly Western art music. Educator Jason Chu, for example, promotes his "4 'A's Model" for listeners who are contemplating cultural appropriation in music. He introduces and explains the categories of "appropriation, appreciation, apprenticeship, and authenticity," so the listener can make informed decisions about the ethical appropriateness of borrowing and transforming elements from a culture different from the dominant white European one traditionally found in the music history canon.[21]

Although the early Jesuits and current scholars were and are reacting to the pedagogical needs of students, we must also continue conversations around how to best attend to the particularities of the current generation of students' mental and physical well-being. This attention occurs on many college campuses and is currently being publicly considered by musicologists including William Cheng, in his book *Just Vibrations*,[22] and John Spilker, in a paper delivered at the 2017 Teaching Music History Conference, which has been expanded and included as Chapter 4 in this monograph. We, as musicologists, are adding our voices to the national discussion on the significance of cultivating personal relationships with our students. One example from the national conversation comes from administrator Jennifer Varney, who is a proponent of "proactive advising," which "involves intentional institutional contact with students such that personnel and students develop a caring relationship that leads to increased academic motivation and persistence."[23] As all of this scholarship suggests, professors need not be mental health professionals in order to intentionally engage with students' well-being. Attending to *cura personalis* can be as simple as checking in with their self-care habits. Here is an easy example from my classroom:

At the end of each of my classes students fill out an exit ticket on an index card.[24] Usually, I ask them to report on the perceived theme of the class or solicit questions about any confusing parts of the lesson. However, I also dedicate time throughout the semester to check in on their well-being. Here are some sample questions for class exit tickets:

1. When and where are you successfully taking care of yourself throughout the week?
2. Where do you show room for growth in your self-care habits?
3. What are a few specific ways you can care for yourself this week?

I then collect the tickets at the door as the students leave, review them, and begin our next class with a short discussion or presentation focused on the trends in their answers.[25] Simple activities like the self-care exit ticket are ways I am trying to be more intentionally engaged with the internal lives of my students and live out *cura personalis* with them.

As the first two definitions suggest, *cura personalis* rightly puts students' needs in the forefront of university life, but it is *cura*'s third manifestation that really has me thinking. Sometimes the Jesuits juxtapose *cura personalis* with another Latin phrase, *cura apostolica*, meaning "care of the work" or "care of the institution."[26] They are considered together because a community can experience a tension between these two goods. If, for example, a teacher wants to be effective, they must take time for rest and recreation, which will require them to say no, at times, to requests made by students or superiors. Just as students must attend to their inner lives, so too must faculty members. In order for faculty to demonstrate *cura personalis* toward their students, they must also be cared for. Although many of us are well-trained in caring for the needs of our students, are we modeling self- and colleague-care to ALL those with whom we work? Can this care extend beyond the walls of our own institutions and into the entire discipline of musicology? Can this care be extended to all faculty within a university community, not just to those who have the benefits and security associated with full-time or tenured status, and administrative support of a campus climate conducive to this ideology?

William Cheng thinks so. In his monograph *Just Vibrations* he asks, "Is musicology about the safety of a female music student? No it isn't, if we define musicology starkly as the study of music. But *yes, it is*, if we envision musicology as all the activities, care, and caregiving of people who identify as members of the musicology community."[27] I really appreciate Cheng's use of the word "community" because I believe that humans are built to be with each other. The strength of any community, however, lies in the health of each individual. The Jesuits knew this well.

When Ignatius of Loyola conceived of the Jesuit order, they were "to be dedicated to work in 'the world,' moving freely and rapidly to wherever the needs of the church were greatest."[28] Unlike most other monastic orders of the sixteenth century, they were not called to one place as their permanent residence, nor did they interrupt their day to return home for community prayer. This new emphasis on "work in the world" instead of a contemplative life of prayer presented challenges to the order. One was the real danger of exhaustion and burnout. As Geger reports, in Ignatius's time, "the idea that one might collapse from exhaustion in the service of God was widely perceived as a romantic ideal."[29] Although music students of the twenty-first century are not likely to collapse from exhaustion in the service of God, they are quite familiar with the long hours of work expected of them in their university studies—especially practicing their craft. In many music schools the number of hours you spend in a practice room is worn as a badge of honor, even if that results in mental and physical suffering.

Another challenge to the Jesuits' dedication to "work in the world" was that medieval Christians were by no means as self-confident about their salvation as Christians often seem today. They tended to emphasize God's justice over God's mercy, and according to Geger, "for this reason, those who wished to 'ensure' their salvation generally took one of two tacks: they worked themselves too hard, since their priority was not really the long-term good of the work, but instead, their own heroic sanctity. Or the opposite: they were wary of charitable works, since these meant less time for prayer and more ways to be distracted."[30] Ignatius broke with these traditional attitudes, creating a new priority for the Jesuits, which was to do their work, do it well, and to do as much of it as was *reasonably* possible over the course of a lifetime. Consequently, Jesuits were and are expected to be mindful of their health and energy levels. They believe that "moderation has staying power and what puts excessive strain on the body cannot last."[31]

Like the early Jesuits, I feel that my colleagues in musicology and, honestly, professors across all academic disciplines are in real danger of burning out, especially those experiencing systematic oppression, those with tenuous teaching appointments, and those who taught through the COVID-19 pandemic. In a 2007 national survey on occupational stress by the Canadian Association of University Teachers (CAUT), researchers questioned 1,470 faculty members from fifty-six universities across Canada. As reported, "a relatively large number of faculty members experienced a substantial number of physical and psychological health symptoms, and used stress-related medication over the past year."[32] The CAUT, thankfully, offers data, which backs up the ever-growing anecdotal accounts of the necessity for "work-life balance" or "self-care" within university culture.

Maggie Berg and Barbara K. Seeber, authors of *The Slow Professor*, add their voices to the discussion of faculty health by urging professors to adopt the principles of the "slow movement," which they believe are effective ways to "alleviate work stress, preserve humanistic education, and resist the corporate university." In the corporate university model, "power is transferred from faculty to managers, economic justifications dominate, and the familiar 'bottom line' eclipses pedagogical and intellectual concerns."[33] Slow professors, on the other hand, challenge the "frantic pace and standardization of contemporary culture," leaving more room for inquiry, reflection, and well-being.[34]

To radically shift an academic culture to one of "slow care" will take time, and it certainly cannot happen for everyone unless those in positions of power (those with tenure, department heads, administrators) ethically lead us into a new university model where we put the needs of all people above profit. The time to make change, no matter how large or small, is now. Historian and pedagogue Kevin Gannon agrees. He writes,

> I want to be clear, though, that this process will look different depending on who you are and your particular context. It may not be feasible to run the red flag up the pole and vociferously challenge departmental culture if you are a term-to-term adjunct faculty member. Being the only or one of the few women in an overwhelmingly male department brings with it challenges that might prevent an explicit avowal of what could be interpreted as nonscholarly, or "unprofessional" practices. I'm fully aware that challenging dominant narratives brings no small amount of risk, and I believe it's an obligation for those of us with secure platforms and positions to absorb that risk and deflect it from others. However it might look—avowedly public or quietly implicit within one's own practices—that ethical stance is a necessary one for us, though.[35]

Gannon suggests that challenging the current narrative of "productivity at all costs" will be hard and involve risk, but that together in community, professors can (and must) each do our part to care for one another, depending on our positions of power and privilege.

Musicologists are beginning to engage in self-care discussion in order to make a difference within the discipline. At the 2014 annual meeting of the Society for American Music, the Forum for Early Career Professionals (FECP) hosted a panel, "Balancing Personal and Professional Ambitions," which featured time for all participants to discuss their desires for and attempts at work-life balance. The FECP continued the well-being discussion in their 2016 inaugural column in the *Bulletin of the Society for American Music*. Musicologist Mark Katz wrote the short but moving article, "Work-Life Balance: How's One out of Three?"[36] He begins by recounting a "spectacular failure in [his] years-long project of achieving a happy work-life balance," which included a family work-trip that ended in a violent attack on two of the hip-hop artists he worked with for Next Level, a music diplomacy program Katz directs for the U.S. Department of State.[37] Although Katz kept/keeps a gruelingly hectic schedule, and never suggests he has the solution for those of us with unbalanced/unhealthy lifestyles, he does offer ways to guide personal and professional decision-making: "Think about what you want out of your career and more importantly out of your life in general."[38] Once you know what these things are, take them into consideration when making any personal or professional decision. "Have some non-negotiables in your life. There must be a limit to what you will sacrifice for the sake of your career."[39]

For me, Katz's second suggestion is most closely tied to the third definition of *cura personalis*. The Jesuits knew they needed to get away from their "work in the world" in order to recharge. This is exactly what Katz is suggesting. One of his nonnegotiables is walking. He walks about five miles per day and knows the walks "clear [his] head, help [him] to stay in shape and allow [him] to think through problems and opportunities."[40] However, it is Katz's conclusion to the article that gets our discipline closer to actual change within our current academic culture. It is a powerful suggestion to the university music community and beyond. Katz states,

> Finally, I have a few words for my peers and senior colleagues and anyone who has power over or an impact on those in various states of precarity. We have to stop celebrating workaholicism as a praiseworthy way of life. Although it's useful to share our struggles, we do real harm when we send the message that suffering and personal sacrifice are necessary for a successful career. We should avoid creating commitments and scheduling events that require colleagues (junior or otherwise) to neglect their families or other valuable parts of their lives. We must be more explicit about the ways in which we judge their success, and stop promoting the "just in case" mentality that leads them to take on ever more commitments just in case it might help them get ahead. We need to advise them when it's time to slow down and give them cover so they can say no to some of the endless requests that come their way. And we can at least try to get our own lives in order, in the hope of modeling good behavior.[41]

Modeling, a behavior Katz points out in his final sentence, is the main way in which classical musicians are trained. When many music pedagogues began our musical studies, the teacher/apprentice style of teaching and learning started with a studio teacher. As apprentices, we mimicked our teachers as they demonstrated or "modeled" musicality, technique, precision, practice habits, professionalism, and on and on in our weekly lessons. Now many of us find ourselves in the role of teacher or guide. Although we want to offer/mimic all of the valuable lessons we learned from our instructors, may we also examine the ways of being from our studies that we want to rethink for our students and our colleagues. Many of us, for example, were taught different forms of workaholism or the concept that feelings of worth only come from external awards/rewards/praise. These are lessons that the college music-teaching community can reconsider and revise with the health of our students, colleagues, and selves in mind.

One way I am bringing this awareness into my music-major senior seminar is through a class discussion based on the *New Music Box* article "The Cycle of Get."[42] Written from the perspective of composer Paul Mathews, the article appropriately identifies the complicated feelings of pain and low self-worth associated with the many rejections involved in a musician's life, including chair positions in an orchestra; grant applications; composition prizes; graduate schools; and landing academic jobs, making it a meaningful read for any student contemplating a life in music. The content of the article is also an important reminder for music faculty members to celebrate the worthiness of the creation process (the thing most of us fell in love with) as opposed to the accolades associated with "winning." How else can we help each other rewrite the script of what a successful music academic looks like so, in turn, our students have a healthier grasp on what they can aspire to be when they leave our programs?

We now have the opportunity to change what being a musicologist means for our academic communities. Our colleagues, and especially our students, are looking to us, as Katz puts it, to "model good behavior" or, as I have suggested, to "model *cura personalis*." It seems to me that we, as music pedagogues, because of our lifetimes spent modeling what we learned from our teachers, are the best-trained individuals for the job. Teachers do not have to be perfect people with all the power and all the answers to be good models. Instead, we can be fallible human examples walking alongside our students as we learn together. The modeling of *cura personalis* will be our act of radical care.

Notes

1. Centers for Disease Control and Prevention, "CDC Director's Media Statement on U.S. Life Expectancy," November 29, 2018, https://www.cdc.gov/media/releases/2018/; Julie Scelfo, "Suicide on Campus and the Pressure of Perfection," *New York Times*, July 27, 2015, http://www.nytimes.com/; Maggie Berg and Barbara Seeber, *The Slow Professor: Challenging the Culture of Speed in the Academy* (Toronto: University of Toronto Press, 2016); Brenda Wristen, "Depression and Anxiety in University Music Students," *Update: Applications of Research in Music Education* 31, no. 2 (May 2013): 20–27, https://doi.org/10.1177/8755123312473613.

2. Reported in Scelfo, "Suicide on Campus." See Center for Collegiate Mental Health (CCMH), "2014 Annual Report," Penn State University, January 2015, 22–27, https://ccmh.psu.edu/annual-reports.

3. Wristen, "Depression and Anxiety."

4. See Carlos Blanco, Mayumi Okuda, Crystal Wright, et al., "Mental Health of College Students and Their Non-College-Attending Peers," *Archives of General Psychiatry* 65 (2008): 1429–37; Johanna Soet and Todd Sevig, "Mental Health Issues Facing a Diverse Sample of College Students: Results from the College Student Mental Health Survey," *NASPA Journal* 43 (2006): 410–31; Daniel Eisenberg, Sarah E. Gollust, Ezra

Golberstein, and Jennifer L Hefner, "Prevalence and Correlates of Depression, Anxiety, and Suicidality among University Students," *American Journal of Orthopsychiatry* 77 (2007): 534–42. Wristen, "Depression and Anxiety."

5. Alvin Powell, "Trust, Belonging, Keys to Mental Health of Students of Color," *The Harvard Gazette*, https://news.harvard.edu/gazette/.

6. Scelfo, "Suicide on Campus."

7. I am certainly not the first Jesuit educator to consider the importance of *cura personalis* in my classroom. Other examples include: Monica Ella Harendita, Titik Kristiyani, Margaretha Madha Melissa, and Hongki Julie, "The Implementation of Ignatian Pedagogy in a Jesuit University in Indonesia: Students' Perspectives," *Jesuit Higher Education: A Journal* 8, no. 2 (2019): 59–67; Matthew Kostek, "Spiritan Pedagogy and *Cura Personalis* in a Large Lecture Hall," *Spiritan Horizons* 11, no. 11 (2016): 136–45; Dalibor Renic, "Intergenerational Dialogue in Religious Life: The Importance of *Cura Personalis*," *Doctrine and Life: Incorporating Religious Life Review* 67, no. 2 (2017): 33–43; Eileen Poiana, "*Cura Personalis*," *Planning for Higher Education* 8, no. 3 (1980): 23–26.

8. Rachel Swarns, "272 Slaves Were Sold to Save Georgetown. What Does It Owe Their Descendants?," *New York Times*, April 16, 2016, https://www.nytimes.com/.

9. To read about the painful history of Jesuits and settler colonialism see, for example: Micah True, *Masters and Students: Jesuit Mission Ethnography in Seventeenth-Century New France* (Montreal: McGill University Press, 2015), and Bronwen McShea, *Apostles of Empire: The Jesuits and New France* (Lincoln: University of Nebraska Press, 2019).

10. Dirk Dunfee, Sue Scherer, Ken Sagendorf, James D. Nash, and Cheryl Schwartz, "Revisiting the Promise and Foundations of a Jesuit Education," *Jesuit Higher Education: A Journal* 6, no. 1 (2017): 61.

11. Barton Geger, *Cura Personalis* brochure, Regis University, date unknown.

12. Geger.

13. Robert Putnam, *Bowling Alone: The Collapse and Revival of American Community* (New York: Simon and Schuster, 2000).

14. Putnam, 19.

15. Dunfee et al., "Revisiting the Promise," 59–65.

16. Our readings for Music and Identity begin with Kay Kaufman Shelemay, *Soundscapes: Exploring Music in a Changing World*, 3rd ed. (New York: Norton, 2015), 385–421. My students write introductory music identity essays based on the questions posed by Shelemay in the "Further Fieldwork" section on page 420. For more information on the iSearch paper, see Linda Bergmann, *Academic Research and Writing: Inquiry and Argument in College* (New York: Pearson, 2009).

17. Barton Geger, S.J., "Cura Personalis: Some Ignatian Inspirations," *Jesuit Higher Education: A Journal* 3, no. 2 (2014): 14–15.

18. Geger, 15.

19. For evidence of this see the program for the Teaching Music History Conference, 2021, https://docs.google.com/document/d/1CjZVP2co_yiROeRABYEp70gnlx1dWgxB8zPrwEYJsJQ/edit, and the work of the Pedagogy Study Group of the American Musicological Society, https://www.teachingmusichistory.com.

20. Epstein's student-led research blog project on Harry T. Burleigh can be found at

https://musicalgeography.org/mapping-h-t-burleigh-new/, accessed June 28, 2020. To read more about Haefeli's blog project ideas see "Using Blogs for Better Student Writing Outcomes," *Journal of Music History Pedagogy* 4, no. 1 (fall 2013): 39–70.

21. Amy Hartsough and Eric Hung, "Opening Difficult Conversations in the Music History Classroom through Asian American Songs," *Teaching Music History Conference Online*, June 15, 2020.

22. William Cheng, *Just Vibrations: The Purpose of Sounding Good* (Ann Arbor: University of Michigan Press, 2016).

23. Jennifer Varney, "Proactive Advising," in *Academic Advising Approaches: Strategies That Teach Students to Make the Most of College* (San Francisco: Jossey-Bass, 2013), 137.

24. During COVID online teaching I replaced the paper index card with a zoom comment sent to only me at the end of a session. The students identify themselves on the exit ticket, but the information on the card is only read by me. The exit tickets are never graded and are therefore low stakes.

25. When I share answers in class, either in summary or reading from a specific card, the students' identities are always kept anonymous. This policy is made clear from the first day.

26. Geger, "Cura Personalis: Inspirations," 14.

27. Cheng, *Just Vibrations*, 6–7.

28. Geger, "Cura Personalis: Inspirations," 9.

29. Geger, 9.

30. Geger, 9–10.

31. Geger, 10.

32. Vic Catano, Lori Francis, Ted Haines, et al., *Occupational Stress among Canadian University Academic Staff* (Canadian Association of University Teachers, 2007).

33. Berg and Seeber, *Slow Professor*, x.

34. Berg and Seeber, x.

35. Kevin Gannon, *Radical Hope: A Teaching Manifesto* (Morgantown: West Virginia University Press, 2020), 21.

36. Mark Katz, "Work-Life Balance: How's One out of Three?," *Bulletin of the Society for American Music* 42, no. 1 (2016): 9–11.

37. Katz, 9.

38. Katz, 10.

39. Katz, 11.

40. Katz, 11.

41. Katz, 11.

42. Paul Mathews, "The Cycle of Get," *New Music Box*, February 15, 2012, https://nmbx.newmusicusa.org/the-cycle-of-get/. Many thanks to my colleague Loretta Notareschi, for introducing me to this article and for team-leading the class discussion with our music seminar students.

Epilogue

Care for Now

(written 2021 in Canada and the United States)

COLLEEN RENIHAN, JOHN SPILKER, AND TRUDI WRIGHT

> We will not go back to normal. Normal never was. . . . We are being given the opportunity to stitch a new garment. One that fits all of humanity and nature.
>
> —Sonya Renee Taylor

> If we want a world that works for more people, we have to get into the practice of coming up with ideas together, and letting others as close as possible into the intimate space where ideas are born. In the sharing, an idea becomes more complex, more interesting, more likely to work for more people. . . . When you are tempted to say 'no,' try asking 'how?' instead. 'No' often expresses fear or worry that something can't work. 'How?' is a collaborative question, inviting the creation process to keep going, to come up with a way for the idea to grow to the next stage.
>
> —adrienne maree brown

Care pedagogy is timely. It seemed particularly so during the pandemic years when we began working on this collection. Forms of inequity made freshly and painfully visible and felt by the COVID-19 pandemic only magnify the relevance and urgency of care and kindness in our pedagogy. Everyone has been impacted by this devastating health crisis. Many have suddenly been required to take on eldercare or the education and care of children, not to mention massive financial, employment, and mental health hardships. Strikingly, research draws attention to the disproportionate impact of the COVID-19 pandemic on communities of color in the United States.[1] In March 2020, most faculty and administrators suddenly centered care in their teaching practices, focusing on personal needs, considering individual circumstances in accessing and delivering content or using unfamiliar online tools. Our hope is that this level of attention to student care continues and that the ever-present scarcity model of neoliberal university culture does not force care back to the periphery. Given the dominance of a consumer model of higher education, the care of faculty and staff, in particular, has been lacking, and the burden of "toxic positivity," a capitalist manipulation of kindness, has been leveraged by many institutions to promote productivity.[2] The interdependency of the personal and the professional constitutes one of the ways we understand radical care as social justice in education.

We stand at a turning point. While COVID-19 highlighted the immediacy for music faculty to learn about and integrate social justice and humanizing modes into our teaching and learning practices, in this volume we argue that care should receive more sustained attention and recognition as crucial work in contexts that extend beyond the temporal or geographic confines of the pandemic.

We are currently teaching a generation who will leave our institutions to immediately shoulder uncertainty and a series of crises, many of which exploded to the forefront in 2020: systematic racial inequality, racially motivated police violence, catastrophic fires due to global warming, and more. Each crisis demands care-full pedagogical responses with an insistence that we could never have predicted when we began *Sound Pedagogy* in 2018. We must help our students and colleagues create art, scholarship, careers, and lives that make a difference. We must teach them how to see and celebrate all their perfect imperfections. Multimedia musician Samora Pinderhughes's performance and panel discussion at the 2021 Society for American Music conference highlighted the power of using our art to engage with the deeply personal aspects of the political moments we find ourselves in. Pinderhughes's expressions and theorizing of depression and anxiety, for example, are understood as a vital part of his art—not to be hidden, ignored, or sidelined, but to be embraced and written into his story and his work.[3]

The charge Karl Paulnack offered the incoming freshmen at Boston Conservatory in 2003 remains as fresh today as it was then. He said:

> If we were a medical school, and you were here as a med student practicing appendectomies, you'd take your work very seriously because you would imagine that some night at two AM someone is going to waltz into your emergency room and you're going to have to save their life. Well, my friends, someday at 8 PM someone is going to walk into your concert hall and bring you a mind that is confused, a heart that is overwhelmed, a soul that is weary. Whether they go out whole again will depend partly on how well you do your craft.

> You're not here to become an entertainer, and you don't have to sell yourself. The truth is you don't have anything to sell; being a musician isn't about dispensing a product, like selling used Chevies. I'm not an entertainer; I'm a lot closer to a paramedic, a firefighter, a rescue worker. You're here to become a sort of therapist for the human soul, a spiritual version of a chiropractor, physical therapist, someone who works with our insides to see if they get things to line up, to see if we can come into harmony with ourselves and be healthy and happy and well.
>
> Frankly, ladies and gentlemen, I expect you not only to master music; I expect you to save the planet. If there is a future wave of wellness on this planet, of harmony, of peace, of an end to war, of mutual understanding, of equality, of fairness, I don't expect it will come from a government, a military force or a corporation. I no longer even expect it to come from the religions of the world, which together seem to have brought us as much war as they have peace. If there is a future of peace for humankind, if there is to be an understanding of how these invisible, internal things should fit together, I expect it will come from the artists, because that's what we do.[4]

Our challenge to readers and ourselves remains to create classrooms that allow our students to understand how the "internal things should fit together" through sound, care-full approaches to their complicated interactions with the world and with others through music. We teach orientations to the world, in addition to other discipline-specific content. But of course, there is much to be learned about living and caring *through* music—as we and our contributors have shown, a care-oriented approach to music in higher education should model and reflect a productive orientation, dare we say critically conscious *attunement*, to our communities and the world more broadly.

Dylan Robinson's 2020 book *Hungry Listening: Resonant Theory for Indigenous Sound Studies* provokes an example of this. He urges readers to reposition themselves in radical ways, to be care-full in their approaches to sound and traditional musical practices, so as to understand engagement with music much more intentionally. As Robinson explains, "part of what *Hungry Listening* seeks to expand in musical scholarship is this action of marking the normative discourses of listening positionality (primarily though not exclusively in relation to Western art music) as white, heterosexual, able-bodied, and middle class, through writing that explicitly illustrates and materializes other listening values in/and/from musical subjectivities."[5] This requires an act of radical care to upend and re-form the way we approach music as a phenomenon. Robinson's concern with settler and Indigenous modes of listening—in addition to other, more complex combinations of positionalities—constitutes ultimately a rooted, or radical, turn toward care. Considered as a disciplinary priority in addition to an orientation, care has the potential to inform the way we approach our work in higher-education music spaces. As we and our contributors have explored throughout *Sound Pedagogy*, this is not an easy ask. The execution of care in the classroom is filled with tensions that each instructor must consider as they create and ultimately re-create their learning community. It involves a radical, both drastic and rooted, rethinking of our discipline's ethics and practices: but it will be transformative.

Stitching, Improvising, and Listening a New Garment

All forms of resistance to the practices of individualism, shame, humiliation, competition, and control through kindness in our learning environments are effectively political moves. They involve the negotiation of power in spaces. Care can help us mobilize different ways of being with, relating to, and practicing learning with music. Care can empower us to interrogate and rethink our teaching and learning methods, the performance practices in which we enculturate our students, and the values we promote through the curricular choices we make.

Opposition to care and kindness—perhaps born from anxiety and a perceived or felt lack of control—has been expressed by some music instructors through the desire to more stringently police students' working habits through remote learning (by forcing them to keep their cameras on, for example), and through conversations about challenges vis-a-vis academic integrity in online exams (for listening-example identification, for instance). Indeed, as we taught remotely during the past years, we hopefully gained insight into how our students lived and learned as complex people. From their dorm rooms, in their kitchens, on breaks at work, with family and housemates in the backgrounds, they tuned in for synchronous class meetings and hoped they were learning something valuable, something that could sustain and transform their present and future selves. We learned about the benefits, frustrations, and limits of seeing into the personal through the Zoom frame, but also the difficulty inherent in making the personal public. Sometimes the surprise children or cats on the screen were a welcome reminder of the full lives we were all balancing on the other side of the screen. But at other times, the very real situations that were laid bare for the entire class betrayed reminders that some were struggling in previously unrecognized, tangible, material ways with impossible living conditions, poor internet connections, strained relationships, and so forth. And what about all the profound struggle that occurred off-screen, the things we can't even begin to know through e-mail? The focus on care that emerged from the COVID-19 pandemic will ideally carry forward in the period that follows, which is sure to be as turbulent, unpredictable, and stressful. Not to mention that trauma emerges well after something has occurred. Despite our Western tendency to rush and push forward, we urge our readers to pause, radically slow down, and hold space for care to emerge in our teaching. Now is our time; the present moment always contains urgent opportunities to notice and adapt.

The responsibility of educating with care during this pandemic has weighed heavily on us as editors. Some care-inspired practices that we have embraced over the past year include:

- An Examen self-reflection practice that moved online with remarkable ease (see Trudi Wright's forthcoming essay "Less Is More: Using the Jesuit Examen to Turn Music Classroom Reflection into Social Action");
- A slowed-down teaching practice, with a "less is more" mantra. This also included valuing things that were not traditionally regarded as "content," such as community care, self-care, or meditation;
- Beginning each class with a breathing exercise to center ourselves and acknowledge this need during a year-long crisis;
- A crowd-sourced document of ideas to promote community care;
- A flexible, student-centered approach to deadlines and schedules, led by the inherent assumption that everyone is doing their best.

As author and poet Sonya Renee Taylor has suggested, there remains an opportunity in light of all we have experienced—indeed, endured—in 2020, an opportunity to stitch a new garment that fits all experiences; this requires listening, relinquishing control, and imagining new possibilities. Coupled with this, adrienne maree brown posits, "we are touching the future, reaching out across boundaries and post-apocalyptic conditions to touch each other, to call each other out as family, as beloveds. 'All that you touch, you change. All that you change, changes you.' We are making ourselves vulnerable enough to be changed."[6] The shift to remote teaching and learning has meant a reimagining of pedagogical priorities, methods, and tools. Although troubled with unimagined difficulties, there remains great opportunity moving forward to reimagine what our pedagogical spaces in music could and should look like. Through our teaching practices, in our classrooms, we *produce*—indeed, *compose*—the social world. We stitch it anew every time we teach. As musicians, many of us learned through modeling, and our students are receptive to this mode of learning. During the pandemic academic year, we all learned that we need care to live and thrive. Thus, there is unmistakable value in explicitly naming care in our classrooms. We can be brave enough to name care for our students so they can learn it and claim it for themselves and our communities in music. As Chapman and Withers write, "By fundamentally changing social relations and the systems that real people have put in place to maintain oppression and domination, we can build a better, socially just world."[7] Just as Freire advocated for a classroom and teaching practice that emulated a better world, we advocate for modes of care in music-learning spaces that unsettle and upend oppressive disciplinary structures, thus rehearsing a more equitable world. Though care remains complicated, messy, and fraught, our academic music communities need care and kindness *now*.

Notes

Epigraphs: Sonya Renee Taylor, *Instagram*, April 2, 2020, https://www.instagram.com/p/B-fc3ejAlvd/, quoted in Jazmin Vega, description for the workshop "The Breathing Room: Envisioning a More Just Post-Pandemic World," April 17, 2020, https://today.uic.edu/events/the-breathing-room-envisioning-a-more-just-post-pandemic-world. adrienne maree brown, *Emergent Strategy: Shaping Change, Changing Worlds* (Chico, CA: AK Press, 2017), 264.

1. Sherita Hill Golden, "Coronavirus in African Americans and Other People of Color," *Johns Hopkins Medicine*, April 20, 2020, https://www.hopkinsmedicine.org/; Centers for Disease Control and Prevention, "Health Equity Considerations and Racial and Ethnic Minority Groups," April 19, 2021, https://www.cdc.gov/coronavirus/2019-ncov/community/health-equity/race-ethnicity.html.

2. Simone Scully, "'Toxic Positivity' Is Real—and It's a Big Problem during the Pandemic," *Healthline*, July 22, 2020, https://www.healthline.com/.

3. See https://www.samorapinderhughes.com, accessed July 1, 2021.

4. Paulnack's entire speech can be found at https://www.bc.edu/content/dam/files/centers/boisi/pdf/s091/Welcome_address_to_freshman_at_Boston_Conservatory.pdf.

5. Dylan Robinson, *Hungry Listening: Resonant Theory for Indigenous Sound Studies* (Minneapolis, MN: University of Minnesota Press, 2020), 81.

6. brown, *Emergent Strategy*, 162–63. brown quotes Octavia Butler, *Parable of the Sower*.

7. Chris Chapman and A. J. Withers, *A Violent History of Benevolence: Interlocking Oppression in the Moral Economics of Social Working* (Toronto: University of Toronto Press, 2019), 11.

Contributors

MOLLY M. BRECKLING is visiting assistant professor of musicology at Rollins College. Her research interests include the songs of Gustav Mahler and music history pedagogy. She holds a PhD from the University of North Carolina and master's degrees from UNC, the University of Wisconsin, and Austin Peay State University.

WILLIAM CHENG is professor of music at Dartmouth College and author of *Sound Play: Video Games and the Musical Imagination*, *Just Vibrations: The Purpose of Sounding Good*, and *Loving Music till It Hurts*. He is coeditor of *Queering the Field: Sounding Out Ethnomusicology*, *A Cultural History of Western Music in the Modern Age* (forthcoming), and the University of Michigan Press's Music and Social Justice series.

WILLIAM A. EVERETT is Curators' Distinguished Professor of Musicology Emeritus at the University of Missouri-Kansas City Conservatory. His books include biographies of operetta composers *Sigmund Romberg* and *Rudolf Friml* and *Music for the People: A History of the Kansas City Philharmonic Orchestra, 1933–82*. He is contributing coeditor of *The Cambridge Companion to the Musical* and *The Palgrave Handbook of Musical Theatre Producers*.

KATE GALLOWAY, assistant professor in ethnomusicology and games at Rensselaer Polytechnic Institute, specializes in sonic responses to environmentalism, sound studies, digital culture, and interactive media. Her monograph *Remix, Reuse, Recycle: Music, Media Technologies, and Remediating the Environment* examines how and why contemporary artists remix and recycle sounds, music, and texts encoded with environmental knowledge.

SARA HAEFELI is an associate professor at Ithaca College who has revolutionized the study of music history using a case-study approach. Sara is author of *Teaching Music History with Cases: A Teacher's Guide*, coauthor of *Writing in Music: A Brief Guide*, and editor-in-chief of the *Journal of Music History Pedagogy*. She also studies American experimentalism.

ERIC HUNG (he or they) is executive director of the Music of Asian America Research Center, curator of the Asian American + Native Hawaiian/Pacific Islander Learning Pathway for Smithsonian Folkways, and adjunct lecturer at the University of Maryland's College of Information Studies. He is an active pianist, Balinese gamelan musician, and dumbek player.

STEPHANIE JENSEN-MOULTON is associate professor of musicology and American studies at Brooklyn College, CUNY, and director of the Conservatory of Music. She published an edition of Miriam Gideon's 1958 opera *Fortunato*, and she is coeditor for the *Oxford Handbook of Music and Disability*. She has published numerous articles on American music topics.

MARK KATZ is John P. Barker Distinguished Professor of Music at the University of North Carolina at Chapel Hill. His books include *Capturing Sound: How Technology Has Changed Music*, *Build: The Power of Hip Hop Diplomacy in a Divided World*, and *Music and Technology: A Very Short Introduction*.

NATHAN A. LANGFITT is a licensed therapist and student-affairs professional. He is currently the director of career services for the College of Fine Arts at the University of Texas at Austin and a doctoral student at Indiana University Bloomington. He has served as an on-campus therapist who specializes in musicians.

MATTEO MAGAROTTO is lecturer in musicology at the University of Miami Frost School of Music, where he teaches Western music history and analysis. He has published in *Music Research Forum* and the *A-R Online Music Anthology* and has presented at the Teaching Music History Conference and in public contexts.

MARY NATVIG teaches music history/musicology at the College of Musical Arts at Bowling Green State University, where she has also served as the college's assistant dean of undergraduate studies. Her research areas include music in the Progressive Era and Renaissance music. Her collected edition, *Music History Pedagogy* (Routledge), helped to establish the field of music history pedagogy.

FREDERICK A. PETERBARK is dean of enrollment and aid for the Cleveland Institute of Music. He has copresented at the National Association of College Admissions Counselors' National Conference, the National Association of Schools of Music, and the Music Admission Roundtable Conference.

LAURA MOORE PRUETT is associate professor of music at Merrimack College. In-progress projects include an edited volume on *Teaching and Learning Difficult Topics in the Music Classroom* as well as a new edition of Louis Moreau Gottschalk's symphonies for the series *Music of the United States of America.*

COLLEEN RENIHAN is associate professor and Queen's National Scholar at Queen's University in Kingston, Canada. She has published articles in *The Journal of the Society for American Music, twentieth century music, Music, Sound and the Moving Image, The Journal of Singing, University of Toronto Quarterly*, and others. She is the author of *The Operatic Archive: American Opera as History* (2020).

AMANDA CHRISTINA SOTO is associate professor and coordinator of music education at Texas State University. She is coinstructor for the Smithsonian Folkways Certificate Course in World Music Pedagogy. Her ongoing research on social justice issues, mariachi and world music pedagogy, children's musical and cultural identity, and Mexican and Mexican American music and culture has been published in both music education and ethnomusicology journals.

JOHN SPILKER is associate professor of music and affiliate faculty in gender studies at Nebraska Wesleyan University. He has transformed the study of music history through a transdisciplinary case-study approach that prizes care pedagogy and intersectional equity. His research on dissonant counterpoint and Henry Cowell has been published in *American Music* and the *Journal of the Society for American Music.*

REBA A. WISSNER is assistant professor of musicology at Columbus State University. She is the author of *A Dimension of Sound: Music in The Twilight Zone, We Will Control All That You Hear: The Outer Limits and the Aural Imagination*, and *Music and the Atomic Bomb in American Television, 1950–1969.*

TRUDI WRIGHT is associate professor and director of the music program at Regis University (Denver, Colorado), where she investigates and analyzes music history with her students. Her scholarly work and publications focus on teaching and learning techniques, community singing, and the relationship between American labor and musical theater.

Index

The University of Illinois Press
is a founding member of the
Association of University Presses.

University of Illinois Press
1325 South Oak Street
Champaign, IL 61820-6903
www.press.uillinois.edu